Month-By-Month

GARDENING IN THE PRAIRIE LANDS

Iowa • Kansas • Nebraska • North Dakota • South Dakota

Barash, Cathy Wilkinson, 1949-
    Month by month gardening in the prairie lands / Cathy Wilkinson Barash and Melinda Myers.
        p. cm.
    Includes bibliographical references and index.
     ISBN 1-59186-092-X (alk. paper)
     1. Gardening--West (U.S.) I. Myers, Melinda. II. Title.
SB453.2.W4B37 2004
635'.0978--dc22

                         2004023900

Published by Cool Springs Press, a Division of Thomas Nelson, Inc.,
P.O. Box 141000, Nashville, Tennessee 37214

First printing 2004

Printed in the United States of America
10 9 8 7 6 5 4 3 2 1

Managing Editor: Bryan Norman
Horticultural Editor: Ruth Clausen
Production Design: S. E. Anderson
Illustrator: Bill Kersey, Kersey Graphics
Cover Design: James Duncan, James Duncan Creative

On the cover: *Rudbeckia*, photo by Cathy Wilkinson Barash

Cool Springs Press books may be purchased in bulk for educational, business, fundraising, or sales promotional use. For information, please email **SpecialMarkets@ThomasNelson.com.**

Visit the Thomas Nelson website at **www.ThomasNelson.com** and the Cool Springs Press website at **www.coolspringspress.net**

Month-By-Month

GARDENING
IN THE PRAIRIE LANDS

Iowa • Kansas • Nebraska • North Dakota • South Dakota

CATHY WILKINSON BARASH

MELINDA MYERS

COOL SPRINGS PRESS
A Division of Thomas Nelson Publishers
Since 1798

Dedication and Acknowledgements

CATHY:

I dedicate this book to Catherine Evans and Melinda Myers—whose support and help made this book possible.

A huge bouquet of Prairie Lands flowers to everyone at Cool Springs Press who were so accommodating, working long and hard with me on this book: Hank McBride, who asked me to write the book and had the insight to suggest sharing the work with friend—and now coauthor—Melinda Myers; Ramona Wilkes, my ever-cheerful and patient editor who got me started and ramped up on the book; Bryan Norman, who had his trial by fire, starting his first day as a new editor with this project, diligently seeing the book through completion; Cindy Games, the publicist for Cool Springs Press, who wanted to "get me on the road" publicizing Prairie Lands Gardener's Guide, and was uncomplaining while I worked on this book.

As always, my deepest gratitude to the Garden Writers Association for all the friendships, contacts, and knowledge the members unflaggingly have and continue to share. I am honored and proud to serve as president.

For allowing me to have my Prairie Lands edible landscape in the front yard, gratitude to Sarah Smith and Jim Keys.

Ton Stam and David Clem for their wonderful Dutch chocolate (made in Des Moines—Chocolaterie Stam, which never fails to get me through my deadlines), and David's ever-changing garden inspiration.

Bogart and Tiarella, my feline companions, who try to help by stepping on the keyboard. Their well-timed antics that always make me laugh when I am the most stressed; they'll deserve their own pot of catnip for the winter.

MELINDA:

This book is dedicated to my friends—you know who you are—who are always there to share laughter and tears on our often bumpy road filled with unexpected curves and beautiful vistas.

Thanks to my daughter Nevada who keeps me smiling. I appreciate your patience with the piles of paper and projects that bring insects, dead plants and interesting things into our home. You are a gem and the sunshine of my life.

I am grateful for the opportunity to work with Cathy on this book. Laughter and great chocolate enriched the partnership and helped with the tight deadlines. I look forward to working together in the future. Thanks also to Ramona Wilkes, Bryan Norman, and Hank McBride for the help in making this partnership and book happen. Thanks to Lola Honeybone and Cindy Games who help me get out and meet wonderful gardeners and Cool Spring press readers. I look forward to meeting many more Prairie Land Gardeners.

I want to thank Trish who helped me put the pieces of my jigsaw puzzle together into an exciting new adventure. To Michael and Cathy who are keeping my knees flexible and my energy and spirit in balance.

Thanks to Terry, Jim, Anna, Dan, Katie and my advisory board (Arlene, Dennis, Dave, Heather and Tisa). I appreciate your guidance and continued support as I grow my business and grow as a business woman.

A SPECIAL THANKS to all the gardeners, horticulturists, and professionals in related fields who have so willingly shared their enthusiasm, knowledge, experience, and insight to help make this book what it is. My past twenty five years in horticulture have been an incredible experience thanks to all of you, and I look forward to working with you for many years to come. Thanks also to my friends and mentors in the media and garden writers. You have helped me be a better communicator.

For the opportunity to write this and other Cool Spring's books, I extend my thanks to all the folks at Cool Springs Press.

Contents

Contents

Introduction

Benefits of a Gardening Schedule

As you thumb through *Month-by-Month Gardening in the Prairie Lands*, you will notice surprisingly short to-do lists from November to February for most of the plants. Yet, in the houseplants chapter, you will find that winter plants require plenty of attention. In the other chapters, things perk up during March and April (depending on the weather outside), and there are plenty of tasks on the to-do list. This is the reality of Prairie Lands gardening in black and white; the outdoor growing season is compressed into five months—if you're lucky. So, although it may slack off outdoors from mid-fall to early spring, that's the time to recoup your energy, get organized, and plan for the next growing season. This book is your key to doing just that— and more.

Mid to late spring is the busiest time of year for gardeners: repairing winter damage, waking up the garden, amending soil, digging new beds, planting, mulching, pruning...the tasks go on. It is so easy to get caught up with one activity that another one inadvertently falls by the wayside.

For eighteen years Cathy managed the grounds of a 14-acre property in Long Island, New York. Fortunately, woods and a 1,200 foot beach composed much of the land. Still, to say the least, there was enough to keep her busy. Surveying the property after the first two years, She realized her timing for various activities had been off—not to mention the chores she forgot to do. "The first year I had an excuse: I was new, just getting the feel for the grounds and what needed to be done and the best time to do it. The second year proved as difficult. I remembered some of the overlooked chores from the previous year but forgot others. I decided to jot down to do lists and tasks forgotten, but it was a bundle of scrap paper.

"I had to get organized or the gardens would reflect my shortcomings. So, I spent the second winter getting my act together. I got a large, blank month-by-month calendar and started entering the things I needed to do—week by week. Some were not date dependent, but relied on the weather for timing. I entered those in the approximate time

—in a different color ink. Other jobs repeated and some went through the entire growing season; they too were marked in yet another color. I went through each scrap of paper, entering the chore on the calendar. When I was done, my desk was a lot neater, I had charted a comprehensive care plan, and didn't have to worry about the cat playing in the memo scraps, losing some vital chore.

"Throughout the gardening season, I tweaked some of the dates, adding and deleting various tasks. By the third winter, I compiled enough experience to make what at the time was my "ultimate updated garden calendar." When I moved from Long Island, New York, to Des Moines, Iowa, my personal garden calendar was in the carry-on luggage.

"Since I had moved from a Zone 7 Location to one in Zone 5, acid to alkaline soil, and rich loam to rich clay, a lot of the information in my calendar didn't apply. Yet, I found that moving everything listed on the calendar ahead by one month achieved the target dates for central Iowa."

Introduction

When asked to write this book, Cathy jumped at the chance. How she wished she had a book like this twenty years ago! It would have saved her an immense amount of time and bypassed two years worth of aggravation. The estate garden would have been in tip-top shape from the get go.

This month-by-month book is so superior to my ultimate gardening calendar. Rather than having to look at small handwriting on a wall calendar and decipher the color codes, it's so quick and easy to turn to the relevant chapter and look up the month to see what should be done.

Giving a task a range of a month allows for the flexibility needed to deal with whatever Mother Nature has in store that year. Trying to nail a task to a single date leaves you with unanswered questions: What if the ground is still frozen? What if weather conditions aren't ideal? Conversely, if the ground is workable in the first week of the month, it's easy to see an overview of the month's tasks, and make your decision based upon the specific circumstances.

Though some months have an intimidating to-do list, you may actually be doing less garden work, because similar tasks have been grouped together. In addition to saving time, this organizational method makes journaling much less complicated.

Tracking what has been completed and what still demands attention is straightforward. I'll be making a small check mark next to each task as I finished it. By using a different color ink each year, it's easy to chart accomplishments for several years. (I still like the look of different colors of ink.)

Please, don't let talk of chores and tasks overwhelm you. No one says you must do *everything* on the lists. Unfortunately, too many people take gardening too seriously. Gardening should be fun; enjoy it. Remember that the garden reflects you—your style and taste.

WEATHER CONDITIONS

Before she was transplanted to Iowa eight years ago, she had been warned about the winters—a month or more with no sun, and endless days when the mercury drops down to the minus *twenties*. Cathy was determined to meet winter head-on. However, not a single soul mentioned that the summers are often unbearably hot and humid yet can be dry with meager rain. Nor was there a single whisper about the wind. Yet you must deal with these basic elements to create any garden in the Prairie Lands. As challenging as it may be, when it all comes together, the reward seems even sweeter. Take a long drive through the country and

you'll see the splendid and varied gardens that people have successfully created. Those charming front yard gardens on farms are not molly-coddled.

One of the first gardening tenets she learned as a child was not to bemoan a dead plant. Unless it is diseased, any garden casualty goes *on* the compost pile where it will break down over time, transforming into rich compost—gardener's gold. Amending the soil with compost adds nutrients and generally improves the quality of the soil, helping new plants to flourish. It's all part of the circle of life. Since moving to Iowa, she's made a lot of compost, which in turn makes my clayey soil much richer, more aerated, and with better drainage.

The Prairie Lands is a region of extremes. As people say, "If you don't like the weather, wait, and it will change within the hour." Fall can bring the first snow in October before the trees shed their leaves. Winter will blast the landscape with ice storms, blizzards, and temperatures in the minus 30s. Or it could be so balmy that you're cutting roses to grace the Christmas table, or so dry and windy that plants desiccate.

Spring is a tease—a few warm days so the buds on early blooming trees and shrubs swell. Suddenly, it seems that everything bursts into bloom at once—lilacs and daffodils, redbuds

Introduction

and tulips, forsythia and violets—a veritable phantasmagoria of flowers. The edibles burst forth—asparagus and lettuce, arugula and morels. Then there could be a 60 degree drop in temperature. This can be a season of drought or floods; if the winter was dry and spring rains are heavy, water doesn't have a chance to seep into the ground.

Severe weather marks the transition of spring into summer, bringing formidable thunderstorms that may include lightning, hail, torrential rains, and even tornados. It can also be a time of flooding. Summer, too, is capricious—filled with days of scorching temperatures and sultry or temperatures in the 70s, low humidity, and gorgeous blue skies.

Fall can be teasingly short or delightfully long. Some years, summer segues right into winter. In other years, the first frost may be early, yet followed by a delightfully long Indian summer. Relish each day, as the respite ends too soon, and the bleakness of winter descends.

It's amazing that plants can acclimate themselves to such a barrage of diverse weather, yet many do. In our ever-changeable climate, it pays to be tough: Either it grows or it doesn't.

SOIL CONDITIONS

Although some people use the words "soil" and "dirt" interchangeably, to my way of thinking, soil is the medium that nourishes our plants. Soil is living matter; a variety of biological, chemical, and physical forces are constantly at work. You may be surprised to know that soil has five major components: air; living organisms (such as microscopic bacteria, fungi, bacteria, earthworms, and insects); humus (organic material in varying states of decay); water; and inorganic particles of minerals and rocks.

Dirt is a different matter altogether—it is the result of a day in the garden. It's smeared on your face and lodged under your nails; it's in every crinkle and corrugation of your sneakers, leaving muddy tracks on the carpet. It leaves its mark on the back of your pants, where you habitually wipe your hands, or on the sides of your waist, denoting a pose of great concentration. Whatever you want to call it—soil or dirt— you want to know its particular qualities.

Determining your soil type can be high tech and expensive or low tech and dirt cheap. A simple test done right in the garden will get you off to a good start. Gently squeeze a small amount of soil in your hand, and then rub it between your fingers. Sandy soil is comprised of the largest particles, does not stay together when squeezed, and feels gritty to the touch. Sandy soil is easy to work. It also drains very well—almost too well. Water moves quickly and easily through sandy soil, draining off most of the nutrients. Clay (sometimes called heavy soil) absorbs and holds a tremendous amount of moisture. Its particles are so fine that it holds its shape when compressed. However, the fine texture of clay soil does not let air or moisture move through it. Silt is midway in size between sand and clay, with a smooth texture. Silt can be squeezed together but does not remain compacted, even when dry.

The ideal garden soil is loam—a mixture of sandy soil, clay, and silt. Rub it between your fingers and it breaks up into smaller particles. Loam holds moisture well and encourages the biological activity necessary for healthy, living soil.

No discussion of soil is complete without mentioning pH, which is the measurement of soil alkalinity and acidity, ranging from 0 (most acid) to 14 (most alkaline), with 7.0 as neutral. If the soil pH is not right for a particular plant, it cannot get the nutrients it needs from the soil. There are simple kits for home pH testing. Your local Cooperative Extension office often offers pH testing for a small fee, as do some nurseries and garden

Introduction

centers. Knowing the pH of the soil and the requirement of the plants leads to the next step—changing the soil pH. To make the soil more acid, add elemental sulfur (apply according to package directions), or to make the soil more alkaline (sweet), add granular limestone.

In many regions within the Prairie Lands, the soil is rich and dark, perhaps the remaining traces of a great inland sea millions of years ago. The soil is generally on the alkaline side, with a pH of about 7.5 varying from rich loam to clay, with some rocky and even sandy areas. In general, the soil is rich.

HARDINESS ZONES

The USDA Hardiness Zone Map, a publication of the United States Department of Agriculture, was first introduced more than 40 years ago. After studying the records of winter temperatures collected from agricultural colleges and Cooperative Extension Service reports, the map was compiled. It consists of 10 hardiness zones, each based on the lowest winter temperature; the difference between one zone and the next is ten degrees. The lower the zone number, the chillier the winter lows. The map was a remarkable tool for farmers and gardeners alike. For example, with a

quick glance at the map, Cathy could see that she was on the cusp of Zones 4 and 5, which would have an average minimum temperature between minus 30 and minus 20 degrees Fahrenheit. Zone 3 was 10 degrees chillier—between minus 30 to minus 40, while Zone 5 seemed almost balmy at minus 10 to minus 20.

Plant growers caught on, as did books about plants and gardening; suddenly there was much less trial and error involved in growing plants. In the 1990s, the map was revised. In general, the demarcations were the same, with the northern half of both Iowa and Nebraska a Zone 4, with the southern sections Zone 5. However, researchers divided each Zone in half, calling them A and B, so the increments between each of these was only 5 degrees.

The map also showed how many days there are in the growing season of each zone. Who doesn't have plant envy when Zone 10 can plant 365 days a year? Zone 9 has a growing season of 330 days; Zone 8, 270 days; Zone 7, 255 days; and Zone 6, 225 days. The reality of most of our region is a growing season of 210 days in Zone 5; Zone 4, 195 days; Zone 3, 165 days; Zone 2, 150 days; and Zone 1, 100 days. Arctic Zone 1 does not occur in the United States; most of it is beyond the Arctic Circle. Subarctic Zone 2 occurs only in

only the portions of North Dakota and Minnesota that border Canada; parts of Alaska qualify as Zone 2.

A revision of the Hardiness Zone Map is in the works. The new map expands to 15 Zones (adding warmer ones, which may affect those of you who are snowbirds, gardening in the South in winter) and removing the A and B zone subdivisions. In the new map, Iowa and Nebraska are solid Zone 5, with only small patches of Zone 4 dotted in the northern regions. In the present map, they divide, almost in half, between Zones 4 and 5. In addition, this map reflects the changes of a little more than a decade.

MICROCLIMATES

Knowing what will grow well for you is just a matter of looking up your Hardiness Zone, right? Wrong. Though knowing the Hardiness Zone is crucially helpful, it isn't the sole factor in determining what will grow well in your garden. No doubt, you've noticed that some areas of your yard and garden are warmer than others—against or near a south-facing wall, or protected by the hardscape or large stones. There are also cooler spots—the north-facing side of the house, exposed and open areas, as well as low-lying spaces. These are microclimates.

Introduction

Employ microclimates to your advantage. For example, if a plant is questionably hardy in your Zone, site it in one of the warmer places. Conversely, if you live in Kansas, and the plant you want to grow prefers cooler temperatures, place it where it will be kept cooler by shade and breezes. When considering the microclimate, take into account the soil type and drainage before you plant. It is one thing to have a plant merely survive; you want your plants to thrive!

PLANNING YOUR PRAIRIE LANDS GARDEN

After determining the soil's characteristics, it's time to make a major decision—one that will direct your garden's development. The choices: live with the soil you have and grow only the plants that thrive in that environment, or amend the soil to meet the particular needs of a broader selection of plants. Or, do a little of each, varying your landscape to sustain a boggy area where it is clayey, allowing drier portions for succulents and cacti, and building loam for the rest of the garden.

Adding research to the planning process brings confidence and calmness to your gardening. To learn what will grow well for you, visit friends and neighbors—see what's growing in their yards. If you see something that catches your eye, ask about the plant. You should take notes to remember what they suggest. (And they'll be impressed!)

Ask specific questions about plants that pique your interest. At least get the basics: name (both common and botanical, if possible), type of plant (annual, perennial, bulb, shrub, etc.), hardiness (how well it survives the winter, any special protection it needs), how long the person has had the plant (gives you idea of its long-term performance), and pest and disease problems (ideally you want plants that are free of these). Gardeners are the friendliest people, usually willing to share their knowledge. How can anyone resist when you walk up to them in their garden and complement its beauty and health?

When seeking advice and ideas, visit your nearest botanical garden or arboretum. Plan to make a day of it. Bring along a digital or Polaroid camera to take some snaps to refresh your memory later. And by all means, go with someone else—to share the beauty, and to have another set of eyes to see things you may overlook. Go on garden tours in your area to get some inspiration and fresh ideas.

Your local county Cooperative Extension Service is *the* local authority on what grows successfully in your Hardiness Zone. It may also offer soil testing and a lab where you can bring in samples of plant problems. It runs Master Gardener classes, which teaches where a broad base of plant knowledge in exchange for community service. Keep in mind that no Master Gardener is all-knowing. Even someone who has gardened all his or her life with formal training is constantly learning. So, have fun with it and get growing!

GENERAL HORTICULTURAL PRACTICES

Undoubtedly, digging in the garden requires more time than any other task. You dig to create a new bed, amend the soil, plant everything, transplant, divide, propagate, and even get rid of weeds. It's important to know that the soil is ready to be dug—especially as we get caught up in spring fever.

Before you start digging, test the soil moisture. As you did in the "fist test" for soil type, squeeze a handful of soil. If the ball of soil holds together for a short time after you open your hand and then crumbles, it's a perfect time for digging. The soil is too wet if it stays in a lump; let the ground dry for a few days and recheck. It's too dry if it falls apart as you pick it up; water it gently, slowly, and thoroughly so the moisture can seep deep into the ground; retest in several days.

Introduction

SOIL PREPARATION

Soil holds the major sources of food and water for any plant. Take the time to choose the proper location, and know what your plant requires. The highest quality, most expensive plant, if grown in the wrong soil conditions, will die. Conversely, a so-so plant put in ideal growing conditions will thrive with some TLC. For many plants, conditions such as good drainage, plenty of humus, and an abundance of nutrients cause the plant to flourish.

Most soils benefit from the addition of organic matter. Turn the soil with a pitchfork or spade, and break up any large clods. Add at least 10 to 15 lbs. of compost or well-rotted manure and 2 lb. of rock phosphate (ground up rocks) per 100 square feet. It may be easier, especially if you are putting in a few plants, to simply amend each hole with a couple of handfuls of compost and a half cup of rock phosphate as you go.

COMPOSTING

Cathy and Melinda are strong believers in composting. It saves hauling heavy garbage bags and reduces impact to the landfills. Amend soil with compost before planting. Mix compost into the soil, improving its clayey composition.

Good compost crawls with all those wonderful microorganisms that help get the nutrients—vitamins, minerals, and organic matter—from the soil to the plant through the plant's rootlets. Some gardeners call compost "black gold."

Composting can be as simple or as complex as you wish: You don't have to follow complicated recipes or spend a lot of money on a fancy tumbling composter. Organic matter rots—all on its own. When you compost, you're just arranging the material in such a way to make decomposition more efficient.

To compost, use two bins (it's simple and more aesthetic looking than large piles of garden and kitchen litter). Plain or fancy, a 3-foot-wide cube is the ideal size for optimal heat, which helps break down plant matter. Shape turkey wire or fencing into a box, 36 in. x 36 in. (round if you prefer). For a slightly more formal look, wire wood palettes together. Leave them in their natural state or paint them. Put the compost bin in a sunny spot and add several inches of soil (use the good stuff with lots of worms and microorganisms to get the pile "started"). Here is a list of some compost items (along with some trouble-shooting tips).

- small weeds (if in flower or seed, throw in the trash to avoid growing more weeds from the compost)

- healthy garden cuttings (less than 1/2 in. diameter—larger items take too long to break down. Make a brush pile for larger things or place them at the bottom of the pile for aeration.)

- shredded leaves (run the lawnmower through the leaves to get them to a compostable size; otherwise they tend to form an impenetrable mat)

- grass clippings (less than 1 in. at a time or they can compact and become slimy, preventing water and air from permeating the pile)

- all of the non-animal kitchen garbage: vegetable peels, leftover cooked vegetables, coffee grounds, egg shells (the exception to the animal rule), moldy fruit left in the crisper—you get the idea.

- shredded newsprint (black and white only)

When you first get the pile going, water it lightly. After that, rain should supply ample moisture. If the pile dries out, the process will slow down. Once you have the compost going, you'll feel less guilt about throwing food out when it's eventually going to enrich your soil. With two bins, you can start the second when the first pile is filled. By the time the second bin is filled, the material in the first will have broken down

Introduction

into black gold. No turning, no muss, no fuss.

SOIL AMENDMENTS

Most soil is not perfect, rich, dark, loam. They can benefit from the addition of various materials—organic or inorganic. If you had your soil tested by a lab, you can get a breakdown of the nutrients, often with suggestions to correct any deficiencies or excess. Various amendments affect clay and sandy soils differently. This list shows what to use for each situation. Be sure to mix the amendments thoroughly into the soil.

CLAY SOIL

- To loosen it, add compost, well-rotted manure, or leaf mold

- To improve aeration add humus, Canadian sphagnum peat moss, or a large amount of builder's sand (use in combination with one of the organic materials)

- To feed the soil, add leaf mold

SANDY SOIL

- For additional texture and volume, add compost, well-rotted manure, leaf mold, ground bark, or sawdust

- To increase water retention, add Canadian sphagnum peat moss, humus, or water-retentive polymer crystals

- To feed the soil, add compost, humus, well-rotted manure, leaf mold

If it is necessary to amend the soil further, what are the choices? Nitrogen is readily available in blood meal, cottonseed meal, fish meal, and fish emulsion. Activated sewage sludge is also a good source of nitrogen, but it may be high in heavy metals, so avoid it for edibles. Phosphorus is contained in bone meal and rock phosphate. The best sources for potassium are granite dust and ash from hardwoods.

SELECTING PLANTS

If you want only one or two plants of a particular variety, you are best off buying plants locally. They are available in a range of sizes—based on the container. A 4- or 6-cell pack is the smallest. Each cell is about 1-inch square. You can find individual young plants in 3-, 4-, or 6-inch pots or larger. Full-sized plants in a variety of containers, especially hanging baskets, are also available. The larger the container, the higher the price. If you want instant gratification and need to fill in a hole in the garden, by all means go for the larger pot.

Choose the best plant. When selecting plants, look at the bottom of the container for roots growing through the holes. Avoid these, as they are probably rootbound and likely to be stressed. Although it is tempting to buy a plant in full bloom, choose plants with buds and lots of leaves. While purchasing the plants, get a container of transplant/starting solution—invaluable when planting or transplanting. It consists mainly of vitamins in solution that stimulate root growth. Cathy uses it whenever she is planting or transplanting, and has found that it can bring new life to half-dead plants that find their way to the sale bin at the end of the season. Refrain from using this product on trees and shrubs until a year after planting.

PLANTING

It's helpful to have an overview of what should be planted and when. Nurseries and mail-order catalogs help gardeners keep their planting calendars straight by offering plants and bulbs at the proper times. Whether you're a novice or experienced gardener, It is helpful to see an overview of the gardening year. Of course, there are exceptions, but these are general guidelines:

Plant or transplant on a cloudy day or late in the afternoon when bright sunlight won't stress the plant. When you are ready to plant, dig a hole the size

Introduction

JANUARY · FEBRUARY · MARCH · APRIL · MAY · JUNE · JULY · AUGUST · SEPTEMBER · OCTOBER · NOVEMBER · DECEMBER

Helpful Hints

When to Plant

Annuals (seeds and seedlings)	After last spring frost to summer (some in fall to winter)
Vegetables	After last spring frost, midsummer for fall harvest
Bare-root vegetables and fruits	Spring, as soon as the ground can be worked
Bulbs	
Spring flowering	Late summer to fall (before freeze); plant small bulbs earliest
Summer flowering	Mid-spring to early summer.
Fall flowering	Summer to early fall
Shrubs and Trees	
Bare root shrubs and trees	Early spring
Balled and burlapped trees and shrubs	Early spring, early fall
Container-grown shrubs	Mid-spring, summer, and early fall trees and perennials

and depth of the container. Remove any flowers and buds from the plant. At this time, you want to stimulate root growth; flowers will take away energy from the roots. Mix up a batch of transplant solution in a container deep enough to set the plant in it to soak up the solution. The amount of solution to make depends on how many plants you are putting in the ground. Allow at least 1½ cups per small plant, 3 cups for 6-inch pots and larger. Dip the container in the transplant solution for about 1 minute. Gently remove the plant from its pot. If it is rootbound (lit-tle visible soil, roots wrapped around each other or coming out of the bottom of the pot) take these steps to loosen the roots so they can grow.

Planting rootbound plants (cell-pack size up to a 3-inch pot)

1 Rip (or cut) the bottom ½ inch of roots and soil off.

2 With both hands on the bottom of the plant, gently pull outwards to make a small separation in the middle of the root system.

3 If there are roots that wind around the bottom, gently tease them loose.

4 Cut off any overly long roots.

5 Set the plant in the hole so that the soil level from the pot is even with the soil level of the surrounding soil. You may need to add or take out soil.

6 Gently firm the plant and surrounding soil with your hands.

7 Water the soil with 1 cup of transplant solution.

Planting rootbound plants (from pots larger than 3 inches)

1 Skip steps 1 and 2 from above.

2 Work your fingers around the plant to loosen roots. If a large plant is very potbound (no loose soil comes off the plant when moved), use a knife to make four ½-inch-deep slashes down the side of the root mass.

3 Proceed to Step 3 above and follow the steps to the end.

Despite all good intentions, you may find that the plant becomes distressed after planting or is happier moved to a drier, moister, richer, or poorer site. Do not be too quick to give up on a plant. The mere act of putting it in the ground is a shock. Be patient and move it from one environment to another as a last resort.

14

Introduction

MULCHING

Mulch is almost as valuable as compost. It keeps the soil temperature more constant, helps retain water, and best of all keeps weeds out. Good mulching (at least 3 inches thick) solves the weed problem almost completely. A few noxious weeds may grow up through the mulch, but not many. Plan a tight garden or lay plenty of mulch to avoid large bare spots between plants; this way weed seeds won't have the space or light to germinate. Mulch at least an inch away from the stem of the plant so as not to introduce any pests or diseases to the stem or base of the plant.

Organic mulch is beneficial in several ways. In addition, mulch conserves water by cutting down on moisture lost from the soil through evaporation. Mulch moderates the soil temperature, keeping it more constant. Winter mulch applied after the ground freezes prevents the freeze and thaw cycle from heaving plants out of the ground; the soil remains evenly frozen. Eventually, organic mulch will break down, adding humus to the soil, improving soil structure, and providing nutrients. As the lower layer of mulch becomes part of the soil, add a new layer, usually once a year. Mulch in spring, before weeds get a chance to establish themselves.

The choices of mulch aren't just limited to pine bark nuggets. Whatever material you use is a personal, aesthetic choice. Some mulches have a more formal look while others are more natural. Some are free, while others are pricey—especially when mulching a large area. Your options include: grass clippings, straw, cocoa hulls, peanut hulls, buckwheat hulls, pine needles, wood chips, wood shavings, sawdust, shredded bark, pine bark nuggets, chopped oak or other leaves, well-rotted manure, and ground corn cobs. Now, you can even find some of the bark mulches in a variety of colors—black, green, red, and yellow-orange. As with most flowers, blue is elusive.

There are times when another type of mulch is preferred. Many herbs of Mediterranean origin, such as thyme, rosemary, and oregano don't tolerate wet soil. This applies to most silver- or gray-leafed plants. They all benefit from a mulch that lets water pass through quickly—such as sand, turkey grit, gravel, bluestone, pebbles, or river rock. The deciding factors are the size of the plant and your personal taste. The most unusual mulch Cathy has seen was potshards—bits of broken terracotta pots surrounding a large shrub. Not only was it unusual to look at, it kept critters away—and people as well.

In spring, add a layer of compost around your plants, which will feed the soil. Cover the compost with an organic mulch, such as wood chips, shredded bark, grass clippings (no more than $3/4$ inch at a time), or shredded leaves. Each spring renew the mulch, much of which will have broken down into compost itself. If you continue this simple process, you will have healthy soil, which then grows healthy plants, which in turn are less susceptible to pests and diseases.

LIGHT

Knowing how much light a plant requires is essential for successful gardening. Plant labels indicate the amount of light a plant needs, so it's important to define the terms. Full sun is more than 6 hours a day (including midday); part sun is 4 to 6 (including midday), part shade is 3 to 5 hours of indirect sun—morning or afternoon. Shade is less than 3 hours of sun. However, you cannot grow plants in complete darkness.

Look at the plant for a clue that you may be doing something wrong. A plant that is leaning toward the sun needs to be moved to where it gets more light. Sun lovers display more vivid colors in brighter light. Conversely, some shade-lovers wilt in the heat of the day, and colors fade.

Introduction

WATERING

All living things need water to survive. If you live in an area with drought and prohibitions against watering, this is not the time to start planting anything new (with the possible exception of cacti and succulents). Right after planting, a plant requires extensive nurturing; make sure you can give it the attention and water it needs to develop properly. Once established, a plant with well-developed roots fends for itself better than a newly planted one.

Drip irrigation is the most efficient way to water since the moisture is released at ground level, right where the roots are. It minimizes water loss through evaporation. And, by keeping the leaves dry, many fungal diseases can be avoided. You can purchase a kit and make your own custom system, complete with emitters, supply lines and timers. Systems, whether complicated or simple, are worth the trouble for areas where the soil is not frequently turned and replanted. As an alternative to drip irrigation systems, use "leaky pipe" hoses made of material that allows water to slowly seep into the soil. Once again, they deliver water right at ground level, near the root zone.

FEEDING/FERTILIZING

Packaged fertilizer labels have three numbers on the labels such as 5-10-5 or 20-20-20. This is the N-P-K ratio, which represent the percentage of available nitrogen, phosphorus and potassium in the fertilizer. These are the basic elements that plants need. Nitrogen promotes leaf growth. Phosphorus promotes strong roots, speeds up maturity, and is essential for seed and fruit development. Potassium, also called potash, is necessary for cell division in roots and buds.

After planting perennials, trees, or shrubs, do not fertilize until the next spring. If you amended the soil to suit the plant, it will get ample nutrition. Some annuals and vegetables are heavy feeders. Remember that they need enough energy to grow, flower, fruit, and set seed—all in one growing season.

There are three different ways to feed a plant. The first is to feed the soil. As mentioned earlier, if there's plenty of organic matter in the soil many plants don't require supplemental feeding. For those that need more than the soil has to give, you can provide nourishment from two different points of entry: the roots or the leaves. Traditional fertilizing entails spreading powder or granules on the soil, lightly

working it in to then top layer, and watering well to carry the nutrients down into the soil where the roots draw in the needed nutrients. It is possible to add too much fertilizer—especially around a shallow-rooted plant—and burn the roots.

Some traditional fertilizers skip right to the chase; mix the plant food with water and pour the liquid into the soil around the plant. Easy as can be, but make sure the dilutions you make are appropriate for the plant you're feeding. And don't use a lawn fertilizer on your roses, cabbage, or mums—and vice versa. Avoid the fertilizers that come in a container that screws onto your hose. The dilutions that come out of the sprayers are not consistent, varying with water pressure and the amount of fertilizer in the container. If there is some left over, what do you do with it?

My preferred method is to foliar feed. It is now known that plants can absorb nutrients through their leaves. Fish and kelp emulsions are the most widely used foliar feeds, although compost and manure teas are gaining in popularity. If you follow the directions on the package of fish or kelp emulsion, you know that you're getting the right amount of food for the plant. Note that the dilutions may change for different plants. With compost or manure tea,

Introduction

your guess is as good as mine as to how much of what nutrient the plant is or is not getting. Spray foliar food on the leaves of the plant—top and bottom—up and down the stems. Feed early to midday, or you risk a wet plant after the sun goes down—a personal invitation for fungus and disease. Never spray if the temperature is above 80 degrees. You'll find more specifics, such as how often to feed, in each of the chapters.

However you decide to fertilize, follow the package instructions carefully. In this case, more is not better. Note whether the fertilizer is recommended for the plant you are feeding. Some aren't recommended for use on edibles; they'd be banned completely from my garden. Make sure whatever you use is just fertilizer, with no additives. You'll see some fertilizers advertised, especially for roses and lawn. They may also contain an insecticide, herbicide, and/or pesticide. These are systemics; the plant absorbs chemicals through its roots and the entire plant becomes poisonous to its enemies.

PRUNING

Plants benefit from pruning. Indeed, some must be pruned to perform well in the cultivated garden. There are three major reasons for pruning: removing dead, diseased, or broken branches; shaping the plant; and stimulating new growth. When you prune, try to keep the natural shape of the plant; no lollipop trees or meatball shrubs, please. Dip pruners in alcohol after every cut to sterilize and avoid spreading disease.

The fear of cutting off too much and killing the plant makes pruning the scariest task in the garden for many uninformed gardeners. They approach a plant with trepidation, often with the wrong tool at the wrong time of year. Proper pruning, which adds health and beauty to the plant, requires proper tools and timing. Using the wrong tool or pruning at the wrong time harms a plant more than excessive cutting.

Consider these results of a consumer survey done by the Garden Writers Association. The statistics showed that 72% of people select tools neither by price (which was the assumed choice), nor by brand. They go for the best-made, longest-lasting tools, regardless of price. Indeed, if you compare prices, in the long run you save money by buying a single high-quality tool that can outlast five or six cheaper ones.

The basic tools include secateurs (a.k.a. hand pruners or pruning shears), loppers, and a pruning saw. Secateurs are best for hand pruning and work on stems up to $1/2$ inch in diameter. They are perfect for pruning back perennials, most of the pruning that needs to be done on roses, and other shrubs.

Your hand strength will help you decide which pruners suits you. Bypass pruners make the cleanest cuts with their scissorlike action. Anvil pruners cut with a single blade that closes against a flat anvil. Rose growers often choose this type of pruner. If you don't have strong hands, ratchet pruners will do the job. They are modified anvil pruners; the ratchet mechanism allows the cut to be made in stages, rather than cutting right through with a single squeeze. The ratchet action can remove branches up to $3/4$ inch in diameter. Some high-end brands of pruners come in different sizes. So if you are a petit woman, you don't have to use two hands to get a grip on the handles. Similarly, if your hands are large, you can find comfortable pruners that don't make you feel like Gulliver with the Lilliputians.

For larger stems and branches, up to $1 1/2$ inches, loppers make the cut. Basically, loppers are two-handed, long-handled pruners. Use them on smaller stems and branches. In fact, many gardeners prefer to use these on roses, especially when working near the center of the bush; the long handles protect hands from thorns. Loppers also come in bypass, anvil, and ratchet versions. The ratchet

Introduction

loppers can take on a branch up to 2 inches in diameter.

Once you cross the 2-inch mark, a pruning saw gets the job done. Also called a Japanese saw, its sharp, toothed, curved blade enables you to cut from a better angle on the curved surface of a branch. Many pruning saws are foldable and safely portable as some come with a cloth case.

With overhead pruning use pole loppers or a pole saw. If you have little experience, and are not familiar with these tools, they may feel awkward to use. It is worth it to call in a professional arborist. If you decide to do it yourself, remember to wear safety goggles.

A simple rule of thumb for pruning: When in doubt, prune flowering trees and shrubs right after they finish blooming. This works for plants that set their flowers for next year soon after they bloom—you won't be cutting off next year's flowers.

PEST MANAGEMENT

Despite your best efforts, pests sometimes invade your garden. They come in all shapes and sizes, from the smallest insects to shrub-crunching pests like deer. It's worth a weekly 30 minute garden inspection in order to prevent a minor pest problem from growing into a full-fledged infestation. Stroll around the garden with a cup of tea (iced if it's a very warm day) and look closely at each plant—tops and bottoms of leaves, stems, flowers, and fruit. It's a productive way to relax in the garden! Hand-pick pests and drop them into a zippered plastic bag, or drowned them with a strong stream of water from the hose.

Keep larger four-legged pests out of the garden with a barrier or fence. A 2-foot high fence is sufficient to keep hungry rabbits from nibbling the spring lettuce, but dogs, cats, raccoons, and deer will be undeterred by that. An electric fence, or a six-foot fence will deter most deer and other large wildlife. Some deer can even jump that! If yours are Olympic jumpers, an eight-foot fence, or two six-foot fences spaced about two to three feet apart should do the trick. You can set the height of the wires on an electric fence to best deal with the particular animal you are trying to discourage. Obviously a three-foot high wire would not keep dogs, cats, or raccoons out; they could happily saunter under the wire.

Birds, which eat many of the insects that you don't want, can become pests themselves when they eat the fruit you covet. The simplest way to deter them is with bird netting; just throw it over the tree or shrub you want to protect. With time and effort, you can build elaborate walk-in cages for your prized fruit that birds and animals cannot enter; but beware of smart raccoons who can turn knobs and open doors with apparent ease.

The only garden that is pest-proof is painted concrete. In the real world, planting a diversity of plants usually results in fewer problems than a monoculture (only one type of plant). Including one or two plants that persist through winter (a small tree or shrub, or a dwarf evergreen), offers praying mantids a safe haven for depositing their egg cases. Praying mantids are "good bugs" that eat a prodigious number of aphids, whiteflies, and garden pests.

Attract toads and frogs into the garden; they are also good guys in the war against insect pests. Make a tempting hideaway for them by turning a clay pot on its side in a shady part of the garden; it may attract a toad or frog.

If you have or suspect a pest or disease problem, it is vital to identify the pest—accurately. Call your local Cooperative Extension Service; it is likely to have a telephone hotline or a place to bring plants and pests for identification.

Handpick larger insect pests early in the morning when they are slow to react. If only a small section of a plant is diseased, cut it out and get rid of that portion. (Remember, no diseased material should be allowed on the compost pile.)

Introduction

JANUARY · FEBRUARY · MARCH · APRIL · MAY · JUNE · JULY · AUGUST · September · October · November · December

Helpful Hints

Types of Pest Controls

- Physical
- Hand picking
- Water spray
- Pinching/pruning
- Traps/lures
- Biological predators—birds, ladybugs, green lacewings, predatory mites, soldier bugs, spiders, ants, bats
- Pathogens—*Bacillus thuringiensis* (Bt), milky spore disease, fungi
- Parasitoids—Tiny wasps, predatory nematodes
- Genetic alteration—Built-in Bt, nitrogen-fixing bacteria, resistance to Roundup®
- Chemical
- Mineral—Fungicides: sulfur, copper, baking soda, diatomaceous earth (DE)
- Soaps—Fatty acids
- Oils—Heavy oil; (dormant, Volck) Light oil (superior, horticultural)
- Botanical poisons—Sabadilla, garlic, hot pepper, Neem

Common Insect Pests and Controls

Insect	Damage Done	Control
Aphids	Suck plant juices, weaken leaves	Predators: lady beetle larvae, small wasps, syrphid fly larvae, lacewings. Spray water, use insecticidal soap, horticultural oil. Remove and destroy infested part of plant.
Caterpillars (Many types)	Eat leaves, may defoliate plant	Handpick and destroy Spray with Bt *(Bacillus thuringiensis)* when less than 1 in. long; remove and destroy newly laid egg masses. Spray trees and shrubs with dormant oil in early spring to smother any overwintering insects or eggs.
Grubs	Beetle larvae may live 1 to 3 years underground eating roots of grass and other plants	Use milky spore disease in lawn and garden. Cultivate soil well and let birds feast on fat white grubs

Introduction

When possible, avoid using any chemicals in the garden. Even the "organic" ones, unless pest-specific, impact all the creatures living in your garden—both good and bad. Being in harmony with your garden and nature is the ideal. Although complete harmony may be a challenge to achieve, the close you come to it, the better you, your garden, and, in the big picture, the earth will be. That is what it is all about.

Winter Care

Prairie Lands winters are a challenge, really testing the hardiness of plants.

They face a greater challenge to survival here than they would growing in upper New York state. Because of the whipping winds, blowing snow and ice, reflections from snow, and wildly fluctuating temperatures, even hardy plants need some protection.

To keep perennials from heaving out of the ground because of fluctuating temperatures thawing and freezing the soil, add a 3-inch layer of mulch over the plants once the ground has frozen. Premature mulching beforehand will keep the soil warm, possibly encouraging new growth. Remove the mulch in spring to allow the plants to get up and growing.

Don't prune trees or shrubs after the middle of August or you risk new growth that won't be tough enough to make it through winter and which will die back.

Broadleaved evergreens can get sunburned from reflected snow and are susceptible to windburn. Wrap burlap around them to prevent winter injuries.

Is it dead? The label may have read, "hardy to zone 4", but it looks like the plant died and you live in Zone 5. Never remove entire plants in winter. What may appear dead may be dormant, or the stems may have died back to the ground but the roots are still alive. Give the plant the benefit of the doubt through spring. If it's still lifeless, chuck it on the compost pile.

Overwintering Tender Plants

Some of the garden plants that we call annuals are, in fact, tender perennials. In a warm climate, where temperatures rarely, if ever, dip below freezing, they would keep growing. These plants include coleus, fuchsia, impatiens, and begonias to name a few.

If you have a tender perennial that you cherish:

1 In late August or early September, cut off all flowers and trim the foliage back by one third. Wait a day or two and then dig up the plant.

2 To prevent any pests from coming inside with the plant, gently shake the soil off the roots.

3 Fill a sink with water that feels slightly cool; cold water shocks the plant too much. Add a couple of drops of Ivory™ liquid dish detergent.

4 Gently swish the entire plant in the water.

5 Pot it up in soilless potting mix. Water in with transplant solution.

6 Place it in a spot where it will get the light it needs.

What if you don't have enough room to keep full-grown plants? Take cuttings.

1 Cut off a 3- to 6-inch length of a growing stem. Cut just above a set of leaves.

2 Remove all but the top two sets of leaves.

3 Dip the cut end into rooting hormone (be sure to use the appropriate hormone).

4 Fill a 3- to 6-inch pot with soilless potting mix. Make a planting hole with a pencil.

5 Put the cutting in the hole and gently firm the soil. Water well.

6 Loosely cover the pot with plastic wrap; place a rubberband around the rim of the pot to form a cap. Set it in

Introduction

a warm, bright place. Avoid full sun or you'll risk steaming the cutting.

• Keep the soil lightly moist. After three to six weeks, the stem should be rooted. Try to wiggle it and if it remains firm, it has good roots.

Some plants, such as coleus, root easily in water.

• Take cuttings as described above.

• Put the cuttings in a glass of tepid water, with the two sets of leaves above water. Place it in a warm, bright place.

• If the water starts to turn green or gets cloudy, rinse the glass and add fresh water.

• Once the roots reach 1/2- to 1-inch long or more, pot up the cuttings.

GENERAL OVERVIEW FROM THE COAUTHORS

As a gardener, cherish and protect all the plants you invite into your garden. To do this, you need to choose the right plants for the right places in the landscape. Take into account each of these factors: the right amount and type of light, ample water, and suitable soil for each plant. In addition, it is your duty to fend off predators, whether they are insects, dogs, deer, or raccoons.

It is reassuring to realize that all green, growing things—whether trees, shrubs, vines, flowers, or vegetables—want to live. None of them comes into your garden with the intention of expiring at the earliest possible opportunity. Nor do they wish to succumb to diseases, infestations of pests, lack of water, excess of heat or cold, or the depredations of voles, rabbits, or deer. They would rather not be dug up by the cat or trampled and broken by the dog. They propose, indeed prefer, to establish, thrive, flourish, and fruit. With knowledge and care, you can make this happen.

Throughout Month-by-Month Gardening in the Prairie Lands, Cathy and Melinda give you time-tested information. Cathy Wilkinson Barash contributed "Bulbs," "Herbs and Vegetables," "Roses," the introduction and all appendices. Melinda Myers contributed "Annuals & Biennials," "Houseplants," "Lawns," "Perennials and Ornamental Grasses," "Shrubs," "Trees," and "Vines and Ground-covers." Most often, they provide the simple facts. Sometimes, they tell stories of their own gardening experiences. In both cases, Cathy and Melinda recede into the background and let the tips and information take front and center to make your garden all it can be. Happy Gardening!

USDA Cold Hardiness Zones

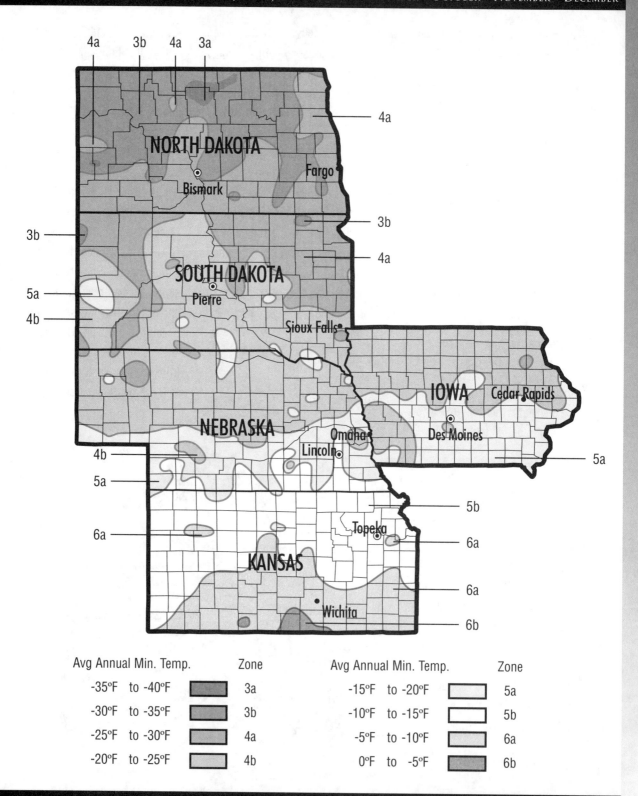

4a · 3b · 4a · 3a

NORTH DAKOTA

4a

Fargo

Bismark

3b

SOUTH DAKOTA

3b

4a

Pierre

5a

4b

Sioux Falls

IOWA · Cedar Rapids

NEBRASKA

Omaha · Des Moines

Lincoln

4b

5a

5a

5b

6a

Topeka

6a

KANSAS

6a

Wichita

6b

Avg Annual Min. Temp.	Zone
-35ºF to -40ºF	3a
-30ºF to -35ºF	3b
-25ºF to -30ºF	4a
-20ºF to -25ºF	4b

Avg Annual Min. Temp.	Zone
-15ºF to -20ºF	5a
-10ºF to -15ºF	5b
-5ºF to -10ºF	6a
0ºF to -5ºF	6b

CHAPTER ONE

Annuals & Biennials

The first plants that most people grow are annuals. They grow and flower quickly and can be purchased in full bloom. Also, they keep flowering all season until they go to seed or a frost kills them off.

Annuals and biennials—interspersed among perennials and shrubs, or just planted on their own—provide the long-lasting color you want in the garden throughout summer. They may be changed seasonally and yearly for added interest. Annuals have traditionally been used in both front and backyard gardens. They can be found in pots or growing in the soil. Often restricted to small gardens just outside the door, they create a colorful and friendly entrance for family and friends

In the Prairie Lands, annuals are exactly what their name implies—plants that live one year. Plant annuals in spring (timing depends on the plant). They bloom, set seed and die in autumn, usually with the first killing frost. For those of you who are snowbirds and travel to warm climates for winter, you'll see a number of plants down South that we in the Prairie Lands call annuals that keep growing year-round, with or with or without a period of dormancy. They are really perennials—in their ideal or native climate.

There are some annuals that self-sow; that is, their seeds drop to the ground and germinate the following year. They give the impression of being perennial, when in fact, if they were deadheaded and not allowed to set seed, they would not return.

By definition, biennials grown from seed produce leaves the first year, and often die back in fall. However, the roots do not die, and often the leaves remain, looking rather tattered by spring. It is not until their second year that they flower. Once the flowers set seed (reproduction is what a plant's entire life cycle is all about), the plant dies.

Biennials can be a bit confusing—sometimes mistaken for annuals and sometimes for perennials. Generally, when you purchase a biennial plant—a **hollyhock** or **foxglove**, for example—at a nursery, garden center, or home store, it is already in its second year and is either in bloom or about to bloom. It will bloom in the garden, go to seed, and die.

Here is where the magic of Mother Nature steps in, especially with these two biennials.

Let the seedheads remain on the plant. Some of the seeds will fall on the ground near the original plant and germinate that season. Therefore, next year, they will be in their second year and bloom. Don't remove the seedheads immediately. Since the new plants are in the same general location as the original plant, an erroneous assumption may be made that the plant is perennial, when in truth it is a biennial.

Self-sowers or self-seeders, as they may be called, are my favorites among both annuals and biennials. Once you plant them, you will continue to have long-lasting bloom for years to come with virtually no effort. With some plants, such as **perilla**, **datura**, **four-o'clocks**, and **amaranths**, this can almost be too good to be true as they are very prolific and can easily overrun a garden within a few years. However, if you are like me and love these plants, you will quickly learn to recognize the seedlings and pull unwanted ones out when they are young.

Annuals & Biennals

If the plants are cultivated hybrids and they self-sow, it is quite possible that the resulting plants will not be the same as the original ones. Melinda enjoys letting these plants go to seed and watch the variations that pop up the following year. Only space limits me as to the many beautiful and colorful annuals and biennials for Prairie Lands gardens. To really explore the tremendous range of these plants, visit friends' and family's gardens, go to a local botanic garden, and, of course, take a trip to nurseries, garden centers, and home stores. You will be amazed at the diversity and variety of plants that can enliven your garden all summer long.

Consider expanding your use of annuals throughout the landscape, using some of the following suggestions:

• Mix annuals with perennials. Use them to provide continuous bloom and to fill in empty spaces reserved for expanding perennials. Select informal and subtler annuals that have the look and feel of perennials.

• Add annuals to bulb plantings. A groundcover of **pansies** makes a nice backdrop of color for spring-flowering bulbs. Or use **impatiens** to mask the declining foliage of late-blooming **daffodils.** Plant annuals in between spring-flowering bulbs. They will help cover the fading bulb foliage.

Helpful Hints

Self-Sowing Annuals and Biennials

Common Name	Botanical Name	Type
Bachelor's Buttons	Centaurea cyanus	Annual
Black-eyed Susan	Rudbeckia hirta	Annual
Calendula	Calendula officinalis	Annual
Cleome	Cleome hassleriana	Annual
Cosmos	Cosmos bipinnatus	Annual
Flowering Tobacco	Nicotiana alata & N. sylvestris	Annual
Foxglove	Digitalis species	Biennial
Golden Coreopsis (Tickseed)	Coreopsis tinctoria	Annual
Golden Marguerite	Anthemis species	Biennial
Hollyhock	Alcea rosea	Biennial
Johnny Jump-Up	Viola tricolor	Annual
Money Plant	Lunaria annua	Biennial
Rose Moss	Portulaca grandiflora	Annual
Sweet William	Dianthus barbatus	Biennial

• Use annuals in containers to brighten areas that lack planting space. Combine upright and trailing annuals to balance and complement the container. Select a mixture of plants with similar growing requirements and foliage and flowers that combine well.

• Tuck a few annuals in tree and shrub planting beds. Never add soil or do extensive digging around the base of trees and shrubs. Instead, dig several holes throughout the planting bed. Sink 8- to 12-inch nursery pots in these holes. Plant a few annuals in slightly smaller containers. Set the potted annuals inside the sunken pots. It will look as if they were always there. This technique saves time and allows you to replace plants at any time.

Annuals & Biennials

PLANNING THE ANNUAL AND BIENNIAL FLOWER GARDEN

A good design starts with a good plan.

Place the garden in an area where it can be viewed without creating a maintenance nightmare. Avoid building flowerbeds in areas that are hard to reach, require hand trimming of the surrounding grass, or are beyond the reach of the garden hose.

Start small and build on your gardening success. Create a garden that can be managed in the time and with the effort you want to expend. We all get excited at planting time, but interest and energy may wane once mid-July and the weeds arrive.

Make the garden wide enough for visual impact. A 3-foot by 6-foot garden will have greater impact than a 1-foot-wide planting that encircles the yard. Try making the garden width two-thirds the height of the background. For example, if planting your garden next to a 6-foot fence, then the garden should be at least 4 feet wide.

Add pathways or stepping-stones to any gardens over 6 feet wide. You will then be able to reach all the plants in the garden for easy care and maintenance.

Add warm colors of orange, red, and yellow to attract attention, warm the location, and make large spaces appear smaller. It takes only a few warm-colored annuals to steal the show.

Consider using cool colors of green, blue, and violet to make a small area appear larger or to make hot spots feel cooler. A basket of blue **pansies** or a planter filled with green foliage plants can make a small, south-facing patio feel cool and roomy.

Use contrasting colors—warm with cool—for an attractive, eye-catching blend. Yellow and blue or red and green are just two of the many attractive combinations.

Use color echoing—repetition of a color from one plant to another—to provide a sense of unity in your flower gardens. Repeat the color from one flower to the next plant's flower, flower part, or foliage. Using this type of repetition is subtle, but it is as effective as repeating the same plant throughout the design.

Consider the plant's texture in your design. Use fine-textured plants—those with spiky flowers and grasslike leaves—as filler and background. Add bold-textured plants—those with large, round flowers and wide leaves—for focal points and accents.

Select plants suitable for your growing conditions and gardening style as well as for their design features.

For healthier plants that need much less care from you, match plants to the available sunlight and soil type. Plants that are poorly matched to the available sunlight and soil type not only look bad, but they are more susceptible to insects and disease.

Avoid annuals and biennials that require deadheading, pinching, and staking if you do not like to fuss over your garden. Look for varieties of low maintenance plants that may be more free-flowering or dwarf.

Seek out some of the more unusual and hard-to-find annuals and biennials. You may need to start these annuals from seed indoors. Look at it as an early start to the growing season or as a fun activity for your whole family to enjoy. See January and February "Planting" for tips on starting annuals from seeds.

Invest some time in soil preparation before planting. Your effort will pay off with less work during the remainder of the season. Start the preceding fall or in spring as soon as the soil can be worked.

1 Outline the border of the new garden. Use a garden hose or rope to help visualize and mark the boundaries. Once you have the desired size and shape, use flour or lime to outline the bed once. Then you can remove the hose or rope and get to work!

2 Edge the bed with a sharp edger or spade.

3 Remove the grass with a sod cutter, or use a total vegetation killer such as Roundup or Finale to kill the existing grass. This also works on existing beds filled with quackgrass, ground ivy, and other perennial weeds. Wait the required time listed on the label, usually 7 to 14 days, to start preparing the soil. If you have the time, kill the grass and any weeds by covering the area with black or clear plastic. Cover the area in fall and by spring, you'll be ready to plant.

4 Take a soil test to find out what type of fertilizers and amendments should be added. Contact your local Cooperative Extension Service for directions on how to take a soil test. Work in a 2- to 3-inch layer of compost, shredded leaves, or other organic matter into the top 6 to 12 inches of the soil. The organic matter improves the drainage of heavy clay soils and increases the water-holding capacity of sandy soils.

5 Add the type and amount of fertilizer recommended by the soil test report provided by your local Cooperative Extension Service. If soil test recommendations are not available, add 1 to 3 pounds per 100 square feet of a low nitrogen fertilizer. Use the higher amount of a slow-release formulation if you plan on fertilizing just once during the growing season. Check the label for specific recommendations.

6 Wait until the soil is slightly moist before spading or tilling in the fertilizer and amendments. Test the moisture content by grabbing a handful of soil. Gently squeeze the soil into a ball, and then tap it. If it stays in a ball, it is too wet and you need to wait a few days. If it breaks into smaller pieces, it is ready to work.

7 Work the fertilizers and amendments into the top 6 to 12 inches of soil. Sprinkle the garden with water long enough to moisten the top 2 to 3 inches of soil or wait a few days for the soil to settle.

PLANTING

Do not be too anxious to start planting. The air may be warm, but the soil stays cool for a long time. Harden off plants by gradually preparing them for their move outdoors. Stop fertilizing, reduce watering, and gradually expose them to the cool temperatures and direct sunlight. After two weeks, they will be ready for their outdoor location. Seeds need warm soil to germinate as well. Check package directions for planting times.

Plant hardened-off, frost-tolerant plants, such as **snapdragons** and **pansies**, in late April to early May. Young plants will need protection from hard frosts.

Wait until after the danger of frost has passed (late May to early June) to plant partially frost tolerant annuals such as **ageratum**, **cleome**, and **lobelia**. Plant **impatiens**, **coleus**, and other frost-sensitive (tender) plants once air and soil have warmed. Check planting tags for more specific information on timing, spacing, and care.

Make sure the roots of transplants are lightly moist when planting outdoors. Carefully remove the transplants from their containers. Squeeze the planting pack and slide out the transplant. Gently massage the roots of potbound plants. This encourages the roots to grow beyond the rootball and into the surrounding soil.

Annuals & Biennials

Water deeply, moistening the top 6 inches of soil. Check new plantings every few days. Water when the top few inches of soil just start to dry. As the roots expand, water thoroughly but less frequently.

Remove the flowers and pinch back leggy transplants. This encourages root development and branching for fuller plants. Remove the flowers on every other plant or every other row if you cannot sacrifice all the blooms at one time. Remove the remaining flowers as the others start to form new blooms.

CARE

Established annual and biennial gardens need some regular care. The amount of care depends on individual plant needs and the weather, but the following are some general care tips:

- Provide established annuals and biennials with about 1 inch of water each week. Water established plants growing in clay soils in one application each week and those growing in sandy soils in two applications of $1/2$ to $3/4$ inches each week. Let soil moisture, not the calendar, be your guide. See the "Watering" sections for more tips.

- Spread a thin layer of mulch, such as shredded leaves, herbicide-free grass clippings, or compost over the soil surface. These mulches will help conserve moisture, reduce weeds, and improve the soil.

- Fertilize annual and biennial gardens based on soil test results. Make one application of a slow-release, low-nitrogen fertilizer at planting. Use 3 pounds per 100 square feet to take care of your fertilizer needs for the season. Or use 1 pound (2 cups) per 100 square feet, or 4 tablespoons per 10 square feet, of a low-nitrogen fertilizer once a month for the first three months of the growing season. Or, foliar feed the plants every three weeks.

- Avoid fertilizers high in phosphorus and potassium unless recommended by soil test results. Most garden soils have high to excessive levels of both these nutrients. Adding more can interfere with the uptake of other nutrients.

- Remove faded flowers to encourage continual bloom. Some flowers, such as **impatiens** and the **wave petunia**, need little if any deadheading. Don't deadhead all the flowers of the biennials or you will have none to ripen, set seed, drop seed, and start their first year of growth, so that you will have flowers again next year. Deadheading biennials completely defeats the main purpose of growing them to begin with.

PESTS

You cannot control the environment, but you can work with nature to keep pest problems under control. Keep plants healthy to minimize the damage caused by insects and disease.

Check plants frequently for signs of pests. Pick off infected leaves and insects as soon as they appear.

Remove weeds whenever they appear. It is much easier to pull and cultivate young weeds after a rain or watering. Be careful not to damage desirable plants when removing the weeds. Melinda has accidentally weeded out a few of my flowers in an overzealous attempt to control the weeds!

Annuals & Biennals

Common Name (*Botanical Name*)	Frost Tolerance	Light	Size	*Space Between Plants	When to Start Seeds Indoors**
Ageratum (*Ageratum houstonianum*)	PFT	Full to part sun	6 to 24 inches by 6 to 12 inches	6 to 9 inches	6 to 8
Alyssum (*Lobularia maritima*)	FT, DS	Full to part sun	4 to 8 inches by 10 to 15 inches	6 to 8 inches	4 to 6
Begonia, Wax (*Begonia semperflorens-cultorum*)	FS	Sun to shade	6 to 12 inches tall and wide	6 to 12 inches	12
Cleome (*Cleome hassleriana*)	PFT	Full to part sun	36 to 48 inches by 18 to 24 inches	24 inches	6 to 8
Cockscomb (*Celosia argentea*)	PFT	Full sun	6 to 36 inches by 8 to 20 inches	6 to 15 inches	4 to 6
Coleus (*Solenostemon scutellarioides*)	FS	Full to part shade	6 to 24 inches by 12 inches	10 to 12 inches	8
Cosmos (*Cosmos* spp.)	PFT, DS	Full sun	12 to 72 inches by 12 to 24 inches	12 inches	6 to 8
Dusty Miller (*Senecio cineraria*)	FT	Full sun	6 to 15 inches by 8 to 12 inches	8 to 12 inches	8 to 10
Flowering Tobacco (*Nicotiana alata*)	PFT, DS	Full to part sun	8 to 60 inches by 6 to 24 inches	8 to 12 inches	6 to 8
Four o'clocks (*Mirabilis jalapa*)	FS, DS	Full sun to part shade	8 to 18 inches by 24 to 36 inches	12 to 18 inches	12+
Geranium (*Pelargonium* x *hortorum*)	FS	Full sun	12 to 20 inches by 12 inches	8 to 12 inches	12
Hollyhock (*Alcea rosea*)	FT, DS	Full sun	1 to 2 feet by 3 to 8 feet	6 to 10 inches	12 to 18 4 to 6
Impatiens (*Impatiens walleriana*)	FS	Full to part shade	6 to 18 inches by 12 to 24 inches	8 to 12 inches	12 to 14
Lobelia (*Lobelia erinus*)	PFT	Full to part sun	4 to 8 inches by 6 to 16 inches	6 to 8 inches	10 to 12
Marigold (*Tagetes* spp.)	FS	Full sun	6 to 36 inches by 6 to 15 inches	6 to 15 inches	4 to 6

Annuals & Biennials

Common Name (Botanical Name)	Frost Tolerance	Light	Size	Space Between Plants	When to Start Seeds Indoors**
Nasturium (Tropaeolum majus)	PFT, DS	Full sun	8 to 12 inches by 12 to 14 inches	8 to 12 inches	6 to 8
Pansy (Viola x wittrockiana)	FT, DS	Full to part sun	4 to 8 inches by 9 to 12 inches	6 inches	10 to 12
Petunia (Petunia x hybrida)	PFT	Full to part sun	6 to 18 inches by 6 to 36 inches	6 to 24 inches	10 to 12
Salvia (Salvia splendens)	FS	Full sun	8 to 30 inches by 8 to 12 inches	8 to 12 inches	6 to 8
Snapdragon (Antirrhinum majus)	FT	Full to part sun	6 to 48 inches by 6 to 12 inches	6, 8, or 12 inches	6 to 8
Sunflower (Helianthus annuus)	PFT, DS	Full sun	24 to 120+ inches by 12 to 24 inches	24 inches	3 to 4
Verbena (Verbena species)	PFT	Full sun	6 to 15 inches by 8 to 24 inches	6 to 12 inches	12 to 14
Vinca (Catharanthus roseus)	FS	Full to part sun	8 to 18 inches by 8 to 12 inches	8 to 12 inches	12
Zinnia (Zinnia elegans)	PFT, DS	Full sun	3 to 36 inches by 15 to 24 inches	6 to 15 inches	4

*KEY: OUTDOOR PLANTING TIME

DS—Direct sow seeds, a week or two before the frost-tolerance time for planting

FT—Frost tolerant; plant early. when soil is workable; withstands frost

PFT—Partial frost tolerant; plant when all danger of frost has passed; protect from heavy frost

FS—Frost sensitive; plant when all danger of frost has passed and the soil temperature is at least 60 degrees Fahrenheit plant at same time as tomatoes); frost kills the plant

** Weeks Ahead of Outdoor Planting Time

JANUARY

PLANNING

Catalogs are pouring in and the wish list keeps growing. Develop a plan for this season's garden and choose other spaces you'll want to add annuals before placing your order.

List the flower seeds you have and want to use this season. Then compare it to the list of seeds you plan to order.

Review your garden journal and pictures of last year's landscape. Plan to expand or reduce planting space based on last year's experience.

Consider increasing space by expanding existing gardens or adding new planting areas. Remember that more planting space can mean an increase in maintenance.

Cut down on care by selecting low-maintenance annuals, mulching, sharing the workload, or by decreasing the planting space. Reduce the size of the garden or convert it to a perennial, shrub, groundcover, herb, edible, or mixed plant area.

Sketch the proposed changes. Put it aside for a few days to consider the impact on the appearance and maintenance of the landscape.

Develop a plant list. Make sure the plants are best suited to the growing conditions and will give you the desired look.

Order any seeds that you plan on starting indoors. It will soon be time to start planting them.

PLANTING

Although it is too early to plant outside, it is never too early to prepare for the season ahead. Now is the time to prepare your light setup for starting annuals indoors.

1 Select an out-of-the-way area that will not be forgotten. You will need a nearby power source and enough room for all the seedlings you plan to start.

2 You can purchase a seed starting system from a garden supply catalog or build your own. All you need are cool, fluorescent lights, a light fixture to hold them, and a system for keeping the lights 6 inches above the tops of the seedlings.

3 Build your own system by mounting the light fixtures on shelves, creating tabletop supports for the lights, or designing a stand-alone system. Note that the pulley system allows the

lights to be lowered and raised over the growing seedlings.

4 Paint the shelving white or use reflective surfaces under and around the unit to increase the light reaching the young seedlings.

Once the light system is in place, you are ready to start planting seeds. For the best chance of success, give seeds warm temperatures to germinate and light as soon as sprouting occurs. Many gardeners germinate seeds in a warm location and then move the seedlings under lights after sprouting. Others use bottom heat or a warm location along with the lights to germinate seeds and grow seedlings. (See February "Planting" for tips on starting seeds and their care.)

Start **pansies** at the end of the month to have large transplants ready for your early spring garden.

CARE

Check on **geraniums** overwintering in the basement or other cool, dark locations. Pot up any that have started growing. Move them to a warm, sunny location and treat them as you would your other houseplants.

Develop a plant list. Make sure the plants are best suited to the growing conditions and will give you the desired look.

WATERING

Adjust your watering schedule to match the needs of **coleus**, **geraniums**, **fuchsias**, and other annuals overwintered as houseplants. The shorter days, less intense sunlight, and low humidity of winter changes the plants' needs. Water the soil thoroughly and wait until the soil is slightly dry before watering again.

Water seedlings often enough to keep the soil lightly moist but not wet. Overwatering can cause root rot and seedling failure. Allowing the soil to dry stresses seedlings, resulting in poor growth, or even seedling death.

FERTILIZING

Do not be overanxious to fertilize **impatiens, geraniums**, and other annuals you are growing as houseplants for winter. The poor growing conditions of indoors during winter results in slow plant growth that requires very little if any fertilizer. Only fertilize plants that have stunted growth, yellow leaves, or other signs of nutrient deficiencies.

Fertilize seedlings once they have sprouted and are actively growing. Use a diluted solution of foliar plant food according to label directions.

Helpful Hints

Some insects can become pests in the garden. Proper identification and early intervention are the best way to control these pests and minimize the negative impact on the environment.

Check the upper and lower leaf surfaces and stems for aphids, mites, and plantbugs. These pests suck out plant juices, causing leaves to yellow and brown. Spray plants with a strong blast of water to dislodge these insects. Use insecticidal soap to treat damaging populations. This is a soap formulated to kill soft-bodied insects, but it will not harm the plant or environment.

Ignore frothy masses (they look like spit) that appear on the stems of various plants. This is the hideout for spittlebug—not the work of neighborhood children. These insects feed on plants but rarely cause damage. Use insecticidal soap to control high populations if they at are damaging the plants.

Watch for holes in the leaves. See the hole but not the pest? The culprits are probably earwigs or slugs. Both pests prefer cool, dark, and damp conditions. They feed at night, leaving holes in leaves and flowers.

PRUNING

Keep pinching back leggy **geraniums**, **coleus**, **impatiens,** and other annuals that are overwintering as houseplants. Remove the growing tips or pinch stems back to just above a set of healthy leaves to encourage branching and stouter stems.

PROBLEMS

Monitor plants for fungus gnats, mites, aphids, scale, and whiteflies.

Fungus gnats do not hurt the plants, but they are a nuisance. Often mistaken for fruit flies, they can be found flitting throughout the house. These insects feed on the organic matter in the soil, such as dead plant roots and peat moss. Keep the soil slightly drier than normal to reduce the populations.

Aphids, mites, and whiteflies suck out plant juices, causing leaves to yellow and brown. Look for poor growth and a clear sticky substance called honeydew on the leaves. See November "Pests" for details on managing these insects.

FEBRUARY

 ## PLANNING

Make your final wish list and order your seeds as soon as possible, especially those you need to start indoors. Gather your planting materials while waiting for your seed order to arrive.

Finish assembling your light setup and seed starting area. See January "Planting" for ideas on creating your own system.

Purchase a sterile seed starting mix. These mixes increase your success by retaining moisture, providing good drainage, and allowing you to start disease-free.

Gather and clean your planting containers. Use flats and pots purchased at the garden center or recycled from last year's garden. Disinfect used pots in a solution of one part bleach to nine parts water. Or gather emptied yogurt containers or used paper coffee cups for seed starting. Rinse these containers and punch holes in the bottom.

Buy or make plant labels. Use them to label flats and pots with the name of the seeds you are growing. Try adapting Popsicle sticks, discarded plastic spoons, or similar items into labels. Be sure to use a permanent marker.

Create a seeding chart for recording plant names, starting dates, and other important information. Use your garden journal or other notebook to record and save this valuable information for next year. Consider investing in a journal if you do not already own one. For some, a loose-leaf notebook works well, as you can take a sheet out when you need to or add another.

 ## PLANTING

Seeds can be started in one of two ways. Sow them in a flat and then transplant young seedlings into individual containers. Or sow one to two seeds directly into the individual pots. To start seeds:

1 Fill flats or containers with a sterile starter mix. Moisten the mixture prior to seeding. Sprinkle fine seeds on the soil surface and water them in. Larger seeds need to be planted a little deeper. Use a chopstick, pencil, or similar item to dig a shallow furrow or punch a planting hole into the mix. Plant seeds at a depth that is about twice their diameter.

2 Sprinkle seeds in the furrow or drop one or two in each hole. Cover with soil, and water lightly with a fine mist. Avoid a strong stream of water that can dislodge the seeds.

3 Keep the soil warm and moist to ensure germination. Use commercially available heating cables or place the flats in a warm location. Melinda has seen flats on top of refrigerators, heating ducts, or other warm places to keep the starting mix warm. Cover the containers with a sheet of plastic to help conserve moisture. Check daily and water often enough to keep the soil surface moist, but not wet.

4 Remove the plastic and move the container to a sunny window as soon as the seedlings appear. Place lights 6 inches above the plants and keep them on for 16 hours a day. Lighting them longer will not help the plants, but will needlessly increase your electric bill.

5 Transplant seedlings growing in flats as soon as they form two sets of leaves (seed and true). The seed leaves are nondescript, while the true leaves look like the particular plant's leaves.

Check the planting dates on the seed packets and in catalogs. Sow seeds according to the label directions. February is the time to start many of the spring-blooming and long-season annuals.

Start **impatiens, petunias, pansies, Wax begonias,** and **coleus** in early to mid-February. Mix small seeds with sand and shake them out using a salt shaker. This helps you spread the seeds more evenly over the soil surface.

Sow **ageratum, lobelia**, and **love-in-a-mist** seeds in mid- to late-February.

CARE

Continue monitoring annuals that you're storing in the basement. Pot up any that start to grow and move them to a sunny window. Water the soil thoroughly whenever the top inch starts to dry.

Check annuals that are growing indoors as houseplants. Pinch back the stems that grow and stretch for the light. Root these cuttings and use them to start new plants for this year's garden.

WATERING

Check seeded flats and seedlings every day. Keep the soil moist until the seeds germinate. Once germinated, continue to check seedlings every day. Water often enough to keep the soil lightly moist but not wet.

Continue watering annuals that you are growing as houseplants. Water thoroughly until the excess runs out the bottom. Allow the top inch of soil to dry before watering again.

FERTILIZING

Fertilize seedlings once they begin to grow. Use a diluted solution of a complete water-soluble fertilizer every other week. Follow mixing directions on the label.

PRUNING

Pinch back indoor plantings to keep them compact. Remove the stem tip or a portion of the stem just above a healthy leaf.

Start new plants from stem and leaf pieces that are 4 to 6 inches long. Here's how:

1 Remove the lowest set of leaves and dip the stem in a rooting compound. This material contains a fungicide to prevent rot and hormones to encourage rooting.

2 Place cuttings in moist vermiculite, perlite, or a well-drained potting mix. Roots should form in one to two weeks.

3 Transplant rooted cuttings into a small container of potting mix. Water frequently enough to keep the soil slightly moist, but not wet.

PROBLEMS

Check seedlings for sudden wilting and rotted stems caused by damping off. This fungus disease causes young seedlings to collapse. Remove infected plants as soon as they are discovered. Prevent this disease by using a sterile starter mix and clean containers. Ignore fungus gnats. These pests do not harm the plants. Decrease populations by keeping potting mix slightly drier than normal.

Look under the leaves and along the stem of annual plants for signs of mites, aphids, and whiteflies. Get out the hand lens and check for speckling, a clear sticky substance, and the insects themselves. See November "Pests" for specific suggestions.

MARCH
Annuals & Biennials

PLANNING

Continue to monitor and record seed starting results in your journal. This information will make next season even more successful.

Take advantage of any sunny, snow-free days. Measure the length and width of flowerbeds. Multiply these two dimensions to calculate the square footage of the bed. Use this information to calculate the number of plants you will need.

This is also a good time to locate areas for new planting beds. Mark beds and begin preparation as soon as the soil can be worked.

PLANTING

Continue seeding annuals. Plant seeds in flats or individual containers filled with moist sterile starting mix.

Plant **coleus**, **dusty miller**, **flowering tobacco**, **pinks**, **melampodium**, **snap-dragons,** and **verbenas** in early to mid-March.

Sow **alyssum**, **moss rose** (**portulaca**), and **salvia** in mid- to late March.

Keep the soil warm and lightly moist until the seeds germinate. Move them under lights as soon as they sprout.

Transplant seedlings from flats into individual containers as soon as the first set of true leaves appear. The first leaves to appear are seed leaves. The next to appear are true leaves, and it is then time to transplant.

Plant or repot **geraniums** that were stored in a cool, dark location for winter. Use a well-drained potting mix and a clean container with a drainage hole. Cut plants back to 4 to 6 inches above the container. Water the soil thoroughly, allowing the excess to run out the bottom of the pot.

CARE

Move **pansies** started indoors in January to your cold frame to harden off. The cold frame will protect them from frost but will allow them to adjust to the cooler, harsher outdoor conditions. Reduce watering and stop fertilizing until they are planted in their permanent location.

Vent your cold frame on sunny days to prevent heat damage. Automatic venting systems are available from some garden centers and through many garden catalogs. Unless you are home 24/7 to monitor the temperature in the cold frame, an automatic vent will keep your plants alive.

WATERING

Check seedlings every day. Water whenever the soil surface begins to dry. Apply enough water to thoroughly moisten the soil. Avoid overwatering, which can lead to root rot and damping-off disease.

Water potted annuals whenever the top few inches of soil start to dry. Apply enough water so that some runs out the drainage holes. Pour off any excess water that collects in the saucer. Leaving water in the saucer can lead to root rot.

Take a walk out to the cold frame. Check soil moisture and water as needed. Plants growing in the cold frame will need less frequent watering during this hardening off process.

FERTILIZING

Start fertilizing recently potted annuals when new growth appears. Use a dilute solution of any flowering houseplant fertilizer on these and other annual plants.

Fertilize or foliar feed seedlings every other week with a dilute solution of any complete water-soluble fertilizer. Check the label for mixing rates.

PRUNING

Pinch out the growing tips of leggy annuals to encourage branching. Pinched plants will develop stouter stems and more branches.

Take 4- to 6-inch cuttings from annuals you want to propagate. Root cuttings in moist vermiculite, perlite, or well-drained potting mix. Transplant rooted cuttings (usually ready in one to two weeks) into small containers filled with moist, well-drained potting mix.

PROBLEMS

Continue monitoring for whiteflies, fungus gnats, aphids, scale, and mites.

Use yellow sticky traps to capture the whiteflies. High populations causing plant damage can be controlled with insecticides. Use a product labeled for controlling whiteflies on indoor plants. Make three applications, every five days, in a well-ventilated location. Start the process over if you miss one application.

Control aphids and mites with insecticidal soap. Spray the upper and lower surface of the leaves and stems. Repeated applications may be needed to control large populations.

Monitor seedlings for damping-off. See February "Problems" for more information.

Helpful Hints

Spring never seems to arrive early enough for gardeners. Get a jump on the growing season by using cold frames and row covers. These systems allow you to move plants outdoors earlier in spring. Use them to harden off indoor grown seedlings or to start annuals from seed.

Purchase or make your own cold frame from plywood and old window sashes or plastic. Most cold frames are 3 to 6 feet or made to fit the size of the window sashes or other material used for the cover. To build your own cold frame:

1 Make the back wall 18 to 30 inches tall and the front slightly lower, about 12 to 24 inches.

2 Cut side walls 3 feet long and with a slanted top to match the height of the front and back walls. The cold frame cover can be a wood frame covered with plastic or discarded windows.

3 Use 2-by-2s for the corners. Make the posts longer than the sides if you want to use them to anchor the frame in place.

4 Face the front of the cold frame toward the south for maximum light and heat. Position the back of the cold frame north or against a building. Placing the cold frame next to the house will provide screening from the wind and a little additional heat due to the foundation.

Row covers of polypropylene fabrics can also be used to extend the season. The row cover fabrics help trap heat around the plants while allowing air, water, and light through to the plants. Loosely drape fabric over the plants. Anchor on the sides, leaving enough slack in the fabric to allow for plant growth.

PLANNING

Visit local garden centers and greenhouse growers for new ideas. Find a vacant space in your garden or add a few planters to accommodate these late additions to your plan.

Make sure your journal is current. Record weather conditions, seed starting dates, and other helpful garden information. Compare the current season with last year's garden records. Make needed adjustments in planting times based on current weather and past experience.

The changeable weather is hard on gardens and anxious gardeners. Make sure both the air and soil are warm before planting. Only the seeds of frost-tolerant plants can withstand the cold soils of April—if it is thawed.

PLANTING

Prepare annual and biennial gardens for planting.

1 Check the soil moisture: Grab a handful of soil and gently squeeze it into a ball. Open your hand and lightly tap the soil ball. If it breaks up, the soil is ready to work. If it stays in a wet ball, wait a few days and try again.

2 Once the soil is dry enough, work 2 inches of aged manure, compost, or peat moss into the top 6 to 12 inches of garden soil. The organic matter will improve the drainage of heavy clay soils and increase the water-holding capacity of sandy soils.

3 Rake the garden smooth, sloping the soil away from building or center of island beds. Lightly sprinkle with water or wait a week to allow the soil to settle.

Plant seeds of **cleome**, **cosmos**, **four-o'clocks**, **globe amaranth**, **gloriosa daisies**, **morning glories**, **moss rose**, and **snapdragons**.

Plant hardened-off frost-tolerant annuals, such as **pansies**, **dusty miller**, and **snapdragons**, outdoors in late April. Let the weather and soil temperature be your guides. Keep mulch or row covers handy to protect transplants from unexpected drops in temperature.

Start **zinnias**, **marigolds**, **calendula**, **celosia** (**cockscomb**), and **gaillardias** (**blanket flowers**) indoors in mid-April.

Transplant seedlings as needed. Move seedlings from flats to individual containers as soon as the first set of true leaves appear. Label everything.

CARE

Adjust lights over seedlings. The lights should be about 6 inches above the tops of the young plants. Lower the lights if seedlings are long and leggy. Raise the lights as seedlings grow.

Check seedlings and transplants growing in cold frames. Open the lid on sunny days to prevent heat buildup. Lower the lid in late afternoon to protect cold-sensitive plants from cold nights.

Harden off indoor-grown transplants before moving them into the garden.

Move transplants to a cold frame or protected location two weeks prior to planting.

Cut back on indoor watering and stop fertilizing the first transplants.

Gradually introduce plants to full sun conditions. Start by placing them in a partially shaded location. Give them direct sun for a few hours. Increase the amount of sun the plants receive each day.

Cover the transplants or move them into the garage when there is a danger of frost. By the end of two weeks, the plants are ready to plant in the garden.

WATERING

Do not stop now. Keep potted annuals, seedlings, and transplants growing and thriving with proper watering. Check seedlings and young transplants daily. Water potted annuals thoroughly every time the top inch of soil starts to dry.

Check plants growing outdoors in the cold frame and garden. Water only when the soil is slightly dry. Overwatering can lead to root rot.

FERTILIZING

Incorporate fertilizer into the soil prior to planting. Follow soil test recommendations. If these are not available, apply 3 pounds (2 cups equals 1 pound) of a slow-release, low-nitrogen fertilizer per 100 square feet or 1 pound of a quick-release formulation.

Continue fertilizing indoor plants and transplants every two weeks. Use a diluted solution of any complete water-soluble fertilizer or foliar feed.

Helpful Hints

Ever return from the garden center with too few or too many annuals? Do your homework before visiting the garden center. Calculating the number of plants you need ahead of time will save you money and frustration caused by running short of transplants.

PRUNING

Prune back leggy annuals as needed. Use the cuttings to start additional plants for this summer's garden.

PROBLEMS

Continue monitoring and controlling mites, aphids, and whiteflies. Spray the upper and lower surface of leaves and stems with insecticidal soap to control high populations of aphids and mites. Repeat as needed. Try trapping whiteflies with commercial or homemade yellow sticky traps. See December "Problems" for additional details.

Avoid damping-off with proper germination, watering, and care of seedlings. Remove weeds as soon as they appear. Pull or lightly hoe annual weeds. Pull and destroy ground ivy, quackgrass, and bindweed to prevent rerooting. Consider treating badly infested gardens with a total vegetation killer prior to planting. Begin preparing the soil for your annuals 4 to 14 days after treatment. Be sure to read and follow all label directions carefully.

MAY
Annuals & Biennials

PLANNING

Hopefully you made a plan before you started planting and plant shopping. Or maybe you had a plan but the labels and pictures of other plants were too tempting to resist. Join the club! Now is the time to take inventory and reevaluate planting space and garden locations.

PLANTING

Continue planting frost-tolerant annuals. Plant partial-frost-tolerant annuals in the garden after the danger of a hard frost has passed—mid- to late-May. Wait until both the air and the soil are warm to plant frost-sensitive annuals. This is usually not until early June.

Proper soil preparation is critical in planting success. Add organic matter and fertilizer to the top 6 to 12 inches of garden soil. Rake smooth and allow the soil to settle.

Harden off indoor-grown transplants prior to placing them in the garden.

Transplanting into the Garden:

1 Start two weeks prior to planting. Cut back on water and stop fertilizing. Move transplants outdoors to a protected location. Give plants several hours of direct sun. Increase the amount each day. Cover or move transplants into the garage in case of frost.

2 Carefully remove the transplant from its containers. Squeeze the container and slide the plant out of the container. Do not pull it out by the stem. Plant one at a time so you don't risk the plant drying out as it lays on the soil with roots exposed,

3 Gently and ever so slightly loosen the roots of root-bound transplants. Place annuals in the soil at the same depth they were growing in the pot. Cover with soil and gently tamp to remove air pockets.

4 Space plants according to the "Planting Chart" in the chapter introduction or the directions on the plant tag. The spacing may look too wide, yet before you know it, those transplants will fill right in.

Overplanting reduces air circulation, increasing the risk of pests and diseases. Use extra plants for container gardens, herb gardens, shrub beds, or to fill bare spots in perennial gardens. Or share them with a friend or neighbor. Melinda has a wonderful neighbor who also gardens; we swap our extras with each other—we both have more variety without more work!

Remove flowers and cut back leggy annuals when transplanting. This encourages root development, branching, and better looking, healthier plants in the long run. Can't stand to remove those beautiful flowers? How about a compromise? Remove the flowers on every other plant or every other row at planting. Remove the remaining flowers the following week. Then it will not seem so long before the new flowers appear.

CARE

Thin or transplant annuals directly seeded into the garden. Leave the healthiest seedlings properly spaced in their permanent garden location. Move extra transplants to other areas with bare space.

Place stakes next to tall annuals and biennials, such as **foxgloves**, **larkspur**, and **hollyhocks** that need staking. Early stake placement prevents root and plant damage caused by staking established annuals that are already flopping over.

Remove flowers and cut back leggy annuals when transplanting. This encourages root development, branching, and better looking, healthier plants in the long run.

WATERING

Water transplants and potted annuals growing indoors as needed. Keep the soil lightly moist but not wet. Cut back on watering as you prepare the plants to move outdoors. See February "Planting" for more details on hardening off transplants.

Check new transplants every few days. Water deeply enough to moisten the rootball and surrounding soil. Apply water when the top inch of soil starts to dry. Cut back on watering frequency as the transplants become established.

FERTILIZING

Stop fertilizing indoor- and greenhouse-grown transplants two weeks prior to planting outdoors. Use a transplant solution at the time of planting. Check the label for mixing directions.

Mix organic matter into the soil prior to planting. Follow soil test recommendations or use 3 pounds of a slow-release, low-nitrogen fertilizer per 100 square feet.

Incorporate a slow-release granular fertilizer into the potting mix for container gardens. A small amount of the fertilizer will be released each time you water throughout the next several months. This constant feeding is good for both the plants and the gardener, as it saves you some work.

PROBLEMS

Protect new plantings from cutworm damage. These insects chew through the stems of young transplants. They are most common in planting beds recently converted from lawn. Use cutworm collars made of metal or plastic. Recycle cat foot and tuna fish cans, plastic margarine tubs, or yogurt containers. Remove the bottom of the metal and plastic containers. Use them as collars around the new transplants. Sink them at least an inch deep or close to the rim down into the soil.

Keep an eye out for aphids, mites, spittlebugs, slugs, and earwig damage. See June "Problems" for details on these insects. Pull or dig out weeds as soon as they appear. Be careful not to damage the frost-sensitive roots of transplants while weeding.

Watch for signs of deer, rabbits, and woodchucks. These animals appreciate a few fresh greens—your new transplants—in their diets. Repellents applied before they start feeding may give you control. Fencing small garden areas may help keep out deer, as they do not seem to like to feed in small, fenced-in areas. A 2-foot high fence anchored in the ground will help keep rabbits out. Fencing may not be the most attractive remedy, but it beats having no flowers at all.

Protect hanging baskets from birds and chipmunks. Cover baskets with bird netting. Secure the netting above and below the container. Do this at the first signs of a problem. Quick action discourages the birds and animals so they will find a better place to go. Remove netting once wildlife is no longer a threat.

PRUNING

Remove flowers at planting time to encourage root development. Pinch back spindly transplants above a set of healthy leaves. Pruning encourages branching and will ultimately result in more flowers.

Annuals & Biennials

PLANNING

Take a walk around the yard. Look for bare or drab areas that would benefit from a boost of annual color. Use annuals to hide spring bulbs as their leaves start to turn yellow and brown, as well as early blooming perennials. Consider adding a pot of annuals to the patio, deck, or entranceway. You will be amazed at the difference a few plants can make.

PLANTING

Get busy planting. Early June is peak planting time for Prairie Lands gardeners. The air and soil have finally warmed. Transplants quickly adjust to these warmer outdoor conditions.

Finish planting frost-sensitive annuals early in the month for the best and longest possible flower display. Check out your local garden center for larger transplants. Use these for a quicker show or for later plantings.

Reduce transplant shock by planting in early morning or late afternoon. Always water in with transplant solution. Proper planting and post-planting care will help the transplants adjust to their new loca-

tion. See May "Planting" for tips on hardening off, planting, and care.

CARE

Now is the time to mulch. Use compost, well-rotted manure, fine wood chips, pine needles, shredded leaves, and other organic material as mulch. A 1- to 2-inch layer of mulch helps conserve moisture, moderates soil temperature, and reduces weeds.

Finish staking tall annuals that need a little added support. Stake early in the season to reduce the risk of damaging taller, more established plants.

WATERING

Check new plantings several times per week. Water whenever the top inch or so of soil begins to dry.

Water established annuals thoroughly, but only when needed. Adjust the watering schedule to fit the plant's needs and growing conditions. Water when the top few inches of soil start to dry. In general, apply 1 inch of water once a week.

Apply water in early morning to reduce disease caused by wet foliage at night, leaf burn due to wet leaves in midday, and moisture loss due to evaporation.

Consider using a watering wand or drip irrigation system to water the soil without wetting the foliage. This puts the water where it is needed and helps reduce the risk of disease.

Do not be fooled by wilting plants. Drooping leaves can indicate drought stress. It is also one way that some plants conserve moisture. Wait until the temperature cools and see if the plants recover. Always check the soil moisture before reaching for the hose.

FERTILIZING

Use a transplant solution at planting. This diluted solution will help get the transplants off to a good start, encouraging strong root growth. Check the label for mixing directions.

Incorporate a slow-release, complete fertilizer in the potting mix for your containers. Every time you water, you will be fertilizing. Or foliar feed every two weeks. Mix the fish emulsion or liquid kelp with water according to the package directions.

PROBLEMS

Remove spotted, blotchy, and discolored leaves as soon as they are discovered. Several fungal diseases can damage annuals. Sanitation is the best way to control and reduce the spread of disease.

Monitor the garden for insects. Minimize your use of pesticides. The fewer pesticides used, the greater number of beneficial insects you will find. Look for ladybugs, lacewings, praying mantises, and other insects that eat aphids and other troublesome pests. Also watch for bees, butterflies, and hummingbirds that come to visit your garden. Protect and encourage these visitors by minimizing your use of pesticides. See July "Problems" for ideas on controlling unwelcome insect pests.

Continue pulling weeds as they appear. It is much easier to keep up with a few weeds than it is to reclaim an entire garden gone bad. Pull and destroy quackgrass, creeping charlie, crabgrass, and other perennial weeds that invade the annual garden.

Watch for signs of deer, rabbits, and woodchucks. Spray plantings with repellents or use scare tactics to keep the animals away. Reapply repellents after

Helpful Hints

Earwigs are slender insects with pinchers at their rear. They do not crawl into your brains, but they are known to give many gardeners the willies! Trap them with a bamboo tube or crumpled paper under an overturned pot. European gardeners move their earwigs to the orchard. These insects eat codling moths, larvae and other harmful pests. If this is not your choice, drop them into a bucket of soapy water to destroy them. As a last resort, use an insecticide labeled for controlling earwigs on annuals.

Slugs are snails without shells. Use beer traps to control these pests. Place a shallow tin filled with beer in the soil. The slugs crawl in and drown. Or empty half a bottle of beer and lay it on its side. The bottle acts as shelter, keeping rain from diluting the beer. The slugs crawl in the hole and drown in the beer. Tuck bottles under the plants for a neater appearance.

bad weather and vary the scare tactics to increase success.

Protect containers and new plantings from birds and chipmunks. Cover new plantings and containers with bird netting to discourage the animals. Hopefully they will find another place to nest or dig. Remove netting once plants are established and the threat of wildlife is passed.

PRUNING

Remove flowers—deadhead—as they fade. Pinch or cut the flowering stem back to the first set of leaves or flower buds. Use a knife or garden shears to make a clean cut. This improves the plant's appearance and encourages continual bloom.

ageratum, cleome, gomphrena, New Guinea impatiens, narrow-leaf zinnias, Impatiens, wax begonias, and **pentas** are self-cleaning. These drop their dead blooms and do not need deadheading.

Remove **begonia** and **ageratum** flowers during wet weather to reduce disease problems.

Remove flower stalks on **coleus** as soon as they appear to keep the plants full and compact.

Pinch back leggy **petunias** to encourage branching all along the stem. Cut stems back above a set of leaves.

Annuals & Biennials

 ## PLANNING

This is a great time to get newly inspired. Everyone's gardens are looking good, so it is a ideal time to get some fresh and innovative ideas from other gardeners.

Visit botanical gardens, participate in community garden tours, and take a walk through the neighborhood. Be sure to bring your garden journal, camera, or sketchpad to record planting schemes and combinations that you want to try.

Evaluate your own landscape. Make notes on what is working and what needs to be redesigned for next year. Jot down a few possible solutions based on your recent tour of gardens.

 ## PLANTING

There is still time to plant. Stop by your favorite garden center. Many offer late-season transplants as replacements or late additions. You might even find a bargain or two worth adding to the garden.

 ## CARE

Continue staking tall plants that tend to flop. Loosely tie plant stems to the stake. Use twine or cushioned twist ties to secure the plants to the stake.

Mulch the soil in your annual garden. Shredded leaves, compost, well-rotted manure, and pine needles make attractive mulches. Apply a thin layer to help conserve moisture, moderate soil temperature, and reduce weeds.

Harvest flowers for fresh indoor enjoyment. Cut the flowers early in the morning for the best quality. Use a sharp knife or garden shears to cut the stem above a set of healthy leaves. Indoors, recut the stems just prior to placing the flowers in the vase. Harvest a few extras to share with friends and neighbors.

Wait until midday to harvest flowers for drying. Pick flowers at their peak. Remove the leaves and gather a few stems into a bundle. Secure with a rubber band. Then use a spring-type clothespin to hang the bundle from a line, rack, or other structure in a dry, dark location.

 ## WATERING

Water established plantings when the top few inches of soil are slightly dry. See June "Watering" for more information.

 ## FERTILIZING

Do not fertilize annuals where you used a slow-release fertilizer. That fertilizer is still providing your annuals with the nutrients they need.

Apply a low-nitrogen, quick-release fertilizer if this is your method of choice. Apply these fertilizers once each month (per label directions) throughout the growing season.

Be careful not to overfertilize **cosmos** and **nasturtiums**; too much nitrogen can prevent bloom and encourage floppy growth.

 ## PRUNING

Deadhead flowers for continual bloom and beauty. Pinch back leggy plants to encourage branching and more flowers.

Cut back **lobelia** and heat-stressed **alyssum**. Cut plants back halfway, continue to water, and wait for the weather to cool.

Stagger pinching and pruning within each flowerbed. This will keep you in flowers all season long.

Compost trimmings to get a second benefit from the plants. As these stems break down, they turn into compost that can be used to feed the soil.

Mid-July through mid-August are usually the hottest times during the growing season. Extreme heat can cause annuals to stop blooming, decline, and even die. Reduce the stress to your plant with a little preventative care.

Mulch soil with shredded leaves, compost, well-rotted manure, pine needles, or other organic mulch. A thin layer of mulch helps keep the soil and plant roots cool and moist.

Water plants slowly and deeply, but less often. This encourages deep roots that are more drought tolerant.

Stop fertilizing during extremely hot, dry weather. This can damage already stressed plants.

Use heat and drought-tolerant plants, such as **zinnias**, **moss rose**, **gazanias**, **dusty miller**, **sunflowers**, and **cleome**, for the hotspots in your landscape.

 # PROBLEMS

Continue monitoring for pests.

Japanese beetles have crossed the Mississippi River and are starting to appear in the Prairie Lands. These small, shiny beetles eat holes in plant leaves. Lacy leaves are often the first clue that the beetles are present. Remove and destroy the beetles. Insecticides can be used, but they are harmful to other beneficial insects. Do not use commercially available traps. These tend to bring more Japanese beetles into your garden. Japanese beetles are not early risers, so you can shake the insects off the flower or leaf into a zippered plastic bag.

Check plantings for signs of leafhoppers. These wedge-shaped insects hop off the plant when disturbed. Their feeding can cause stunting and tip burn on the leaves. These insects also carry the aster yellows disease that causes a sudden wilting, yellowing, and death of suscepti-

ble plants. Prevent the spread of this disease by controlling the leafhoppers. Treat problem leafhoppers with insecticidal soap. Several applications may be needed for control.

Sanitation is usually sufficient to keep flower diseases under control. Pick off spotted leaves as soon as they appear. Deadhead flowers during rainy periods to reduce the risk of botrytis blight. Thin out plantings infected with powdery mildew. This increases air circulation and light penetration to help slow the spread of the disease.

Continue pulling and cultivating weeds. Mulched gardens need much less attention.

Keep applying repellents to discourage troublesome deer, rabbits, and woodchucks. Make sure fencing is secure and still doing its job.

AUGUST
Annuals & Biennials

PLANNING

Keep visiting botanical and public gardens. Participate in their educational events and garden tours. This is a great way to find out if those annuals do as well in our area as the catalogs claim.

PLANTING

Replace weatherworn annuals with fall bedding plants. Purchase **pansies, flowering kale**, and other cool-weather annuals to spruce up the garden for fall. You may have to wait until late August when transplants are more available.

CARE

The heat usually continues and often peaks this month. Protect your plants and yourself from heat stress.

Mulch annuals to keep the roots cool and moist. Place a thin layer of shredded leaves, compost, well-rotted manure, or other organic material on exposed soil around the plants.

Watch for heat stall in the garden. **purple alyssum**, **snapdragons**, **garden pinks**, **lobelia**, and **French marigolds** are a few annuals that stop flowering during extremely hot weather. Wait for the weather to cool for these plants to start flowering. If this is a yearly problem, find a cooler location for these plants. Next year, replace them with **zinnias**, **moss rose**, small **sunflowers**, and other more heat-tolerant plants.

Look around the base of biennials, such as **hollyhocks** and **foxgloves** to see if any seeds have sprouted. You might want to mark off the area so that tiny plants aren't accidentally trod upon. When they get several sets of leaves, you can thin them, and pot up the thinnings for friends and neighbors. Volunteer to plant them for a church, school, hospital, or care facility. They should love these easy growers that can give the feel of a cottage garden when they are growing together.

Wear a hat and long sleeves to protect eyes and skin from the sun's rays. Try gardening in early morning or evening to avoid the extreme heat. Just watch out for the mosquitoes!

WATERING

Let the weather and your plants determine your watering schedule. Water annuals and biennials whenever the top few inches of soil start to dry. Mulched and shaded gardens need less frequent watering. Check plantings several times a week during extremely hot, dry weather.

FERTILIZING

Do not fertilize gardens that received a slow-release (season-long) fertilizer treatment in spring.

Make your monthly application as the weather conditions allow. Don't foliar feed when the temperature is above 80 degrees. Adding fertilizer to the soil when water is limited can damage plant roots.

Continue to feed container gardens.

PRUNING

Continue to deadhead faded flowers. Cut back to the first set of leaves or flowering offshoots. Pinch back leggy plants for a fresher look. Use a sharp knife or hand pruners to prune the plant one-fourth to halfway back. Cut just above a bud or set of healthy leaves. The remaining plant looks better and recovers faster.

Take cuttings now to start new plants for overwintering annuals. See "Helpful Hints" on the following page for details.

Wear a hat and long sleeves to protect eyes and skin from the sun's rays. Try gardening in early morning or evening to avoid the extreme heat.

Enjoy the flowers of your labor.

Harvest flowers in the morning when the plants are full of moisture. Take a bucket of water out to the garden to keep the cut flowers fresh. Once inside, recut the stems and place in clean water.

Wait until midday, when flowers have less moisture, to harvest them for drying. Pick flowers when they have just reached maturity. Harvest **strawflowers** when the blossoms are only half open. Remove foliage, tie in a bundle, and hang the flowers upside down to dry.

PROBLEMS

Continue monitoring plants for insects and disease. Mites and aphids are big problems during hot, dry weather. Watch for slugs and earwigs in shaded locations and during cool, wet weather. See

Japanese beetles are just finishing their aboveground feed. They will soon enter the soil and lay their eggs. Their young larvae, grubs, will begin feeding on grass roots. Treat the adults now to reduce future problems.

Helpful Hints

It is never too soon to start preparing for winter. Start taking cuttings from annuals you want to overwinter indoors. Your garden plants are healthier and will root faster now than they will later in the season.

1 **Coleus**, **geraniums**, **wax begonias**, **browallia**, **impatiens**, **fuchsias**, **annual vinca**, and **herbs** are commonly saved this way.

2 Take a 4- to 6-inch cutting from the tip of a healthy stem. Remove any flowers and the lowest set of leaves.

3 Dip the cut end in a rooting hormone to encourage rooting and discourage rot. Place the cutting in moist vermiculite, perlite, or a well-drained potting mix.

4 Place in a bright location away from direct sun. Keep the rooting mix lightly moist.

5 Plant rooted cuttings—usually ready in two weeks—in small containers filled with a well-drained potting mix. Move to a sunny window and care for them as you would your other houseplants.

Check **zinnias**, **begonias**, and other annuals for powdery mildew. This fungal disease looks as if someone has sprinkled baby powder on the leaves. Make a note in your journal to use mildew-resistant plants and to correct growing conditions next year. Proper spacing for improved air circulation and ample sunlight help reduce the risk of this disease.

Remove leaves with spots and discolored flowers. Sanitation is often the most effective treatment for fungal diseases in the garden. Discard infected plant parts to reduce the spread of disease.

Continue pulling weeds before they set seed. One plant can leave behind hundreds of seeds for next season. Spend a little time pulling weeds now and save yourself a lot of time next year.

Watch for signs of deer, rabbits, and woodchucks. Apply repellents, vary scare tactics, and consider fencing in plantings that have been constantly plagued by these animals.

45

SEPTEMBER

 PLANNING

Your garden has filled in and reached its peak. It always seems to happen just before the first killing frost. So get out the camera and start taking pictures. This visual record of your garden will make it easier to plan future gardens. Plus, it may help you through those long, dark winter months.

Continue to record successes, challenges, and new ideas in your journal. These notes and your pictures will help make winter planning easier. Or join other gardeners who use their video or digital cameras for this task. Walk around your yard filming and critiquing your landscape. Use this "home movie" when planning landscape and garden improvements.

 PLANTING

Garden centers are filling with **pansies, ornamental kale, chrysanthemums,** and other fall annuals. These plants tolerate the cool fall temperatures and extend your garden enjoyment even after frost.

Try planting **second season pansies** and other cold-hardy **pansies.** Plant them now for two seasons of enjoyment.

These will bloom in fall, survive the winter, and provide another floral display in spring. Plant them in bulb gardens as groundcover around **tulips, daffodils,** and **hyacinths.** Their colorful flowers make a nice addition to blooming bulbs and help mask the declining foliage.

 CARE

Get out the floating row covers, blankets, and other frost protection. Late September frosts are common, especially when the sky is clear and the jet stream dips. Protect the plants from the first frosty days of fall, and then you often have an additional week or two or more of warm weather. Those few extra days of flowers mean a lot when the snow begins to fall.

Apply frost protection in late afternoon when the danger of frost is forecast. Cover plants with floating row covers (season extending fabrics) or blankets.

Remove blankets in the morning once the temperature is warm. Recover plants each night there is a danger of frost. Row covers can remain on the plants day and night during threatening weather. These products let air, light, and water through while trapping heat near the plants.

Move containers into the house, porch, or garage when there is a danger of frost. Move them back outdoors during the day or when warmer weather returns.

Move **hibiscus** and other tropical plants to their indoor locations. These plants need bright light for the winter. Place them in a south-facing window or under artificial light for best results.

 WATERING

Keep watering container gardens. Check them daily and water as needed.

Check soil moisture before watering flower gardens. Only water when the top few inches of soil begin to dry. Continue to water thoroughly, but you will probably need to water less frequently. Cooler fall temperatures and rain showers usually take care of this job for you.

 FERTILIZING

Keep foliar feeding container plants as needed. Follow label directions on the container. Most gardens do not need to be fertilized this late in the season.

Late September frosts are common, especially when the sky is clear and the jet stream dips. Protect the plants from the first frosty days of fall, and then you often have an additional week or two or more of warm weather.

 PRUNING

Take cuttings of **browallia**, **coleus**, **fuchsias**, **geraniums**, **impatiens**, **wax begonias**, **annual vinca**, and **herbs** you plan to overwinter indoors. See August "Helpful Hints" for details.

Continue to harvest flowers for fresh arrangements and drying. Collect extra flowers to dry and use later for holiday decorations and gifts. See August "Pruning" for harvesting and drying tips.

 PROBLEMS

The season is winding down and so are some of the pest problems. Remove all diseased and insect-infested plant material during fall cleanup. This reduces the potential for problems next season.

Powdery mildew often peaks in fall. Make a note to replace susceptible plants or use slightly shorter plants in front to mask the discolored foliage.

Remove weeds as they appear and before they have a chance to set seed.

Watch for squirrels digging in the garden. They love to store their nuts in gardens where the digging is easy. Tolerate the disturbance or discourage them with scare tactics and repellents.

Helpful Hints

The cooler weather reminds us that winter is on its way. Many gardeners like to bring their annuals indoors and keep them for next year's garden. Melinda generally want to save more plants than she has room for indoors, so let Jack Frost have his way with some of them. Yet, there are those choice annuals you can't bear to part with. Here are a few ways to keep plants for the winter. Choose the method that works best for the type of plant and the time and space you have available.

Take cuttings from your favorite plants. This method, described in August "Helpful Hints," takes up less space and minimizes the risk of bringing insects and diseases inside.

Transplant flowers from the garden into a container. Or bring outdoor planters inside. Isolate these plants for several weeks before introducing them to your indoor plant collection. Unwanted insects often move inside with the plants. Place plants under lights or in a sunny window. Water and care for them as you would your other houseplants. Do not be alarmed if the leaves begin to yellow. These leaves often drop and are replaced by new, more shade-tolerant leaves. Some gardeners cut back the plants; Melinda prefers to leave them intact. The more leaves on the plant, the more energy will be produced to help it through the transition.

Dig up your **geraniums** and store them in the basement in a cool, dark area. This method worked for most of our parents and grandparents. Unfortunately, we do not always have the cool basements and root cellars they possessed. It is very difficult to keep these plants from growing or drying out while in storage. This is the least successful method. If it is your only option, it is worth a try. You know that they will die if left outside.

OCTOBER

Annuals & Biennials

 PLANNING

Take one last look at the garden. Make your final evaluations, being sure to include both successes and failures. Write down all those new plants and great ideas you want to try next season.

All America Selection® winners have been tested and judged at trial gardens across the United States. They are selected for their superior performance in garden situations. There have been over 300 AAS® winning annuals since the program started in 1933. See *www.all-americaselections.org* for a list of current and past winners.

Proven Winners® are selected by an international group of growers and propagators. They develop and test new hybrids for growers and home gardeners. Proven Winners® are more colorful, vigorous, and versatile than existing varieties. For more information see *www.provenwinners.com.*

Note which plants are frost tolerant. **Pansies, snapdragons, ornamental cabbage** and **kale**, and **pinks** are a few annuals that tolerate frost. Plan to include these in future fall gardens.

Record the locations and flowers that are first to freeze. **Coleus**, **impatiens,** and **begonias** are killed by the first frost and often leave a big hole in the garden. Plant them where their early—and ugly—demise will not be a problem. Or plant them under trees, near the south side of the house, or in other warm microclimates.

 PLANTING

Nature is busy planting your garden for next year. **Flowering tobacco**, **cosmos**, **hollyhock , cleome**, and **snapdragons** are a few of the annuals and biennials that may reseed in the garden (see the Introduction on page 24 for a complete list). Most are lost to fall cleanup and soil preparation. Count on these volunteers to fill in empty spaces in the (annual, perennial, and shrub) garden. Pull out dead plants, but do not cultivate the soil. Sprinkle any remaining seeds over the soil surface. Next spring, wait for the surprise. You may want to turn only a few small spaces over to nature and save the rest for spring planting.

 CARE

Hopefully the weather has been mild and the gardens are in their glory. Here are some tips for getting your garden ready for winter:

Keep frost protection nearby. Cover plants in late afternoon when there is a danger of frost. Remove the coverings when temperatures warm. Recover as needed.

Move containers into the garage, porch, or house when there is a danger of frost. Move them back outdoors when warm weather returns.

But wait, you're not done yet! Shred fallen leaves with your mower and work them into the top 6 to 12 inches of garden soil. The leaf pieces decompose over winter, improving the drainage of heavy clay soils and the water-holding capacity of sandy soils.

Do not till areas where you are trying to let annuals reseed.

Call it quits when you are tired of gardening or the meteorologist says cold weather is here to stay.

 WATERING

Keep watering container gardens. It is almost time to pack away the garden hose and water wand.

Water annuals moved indoors whenever the top few inches of soil start to dry. Water thoroughly. Empty any excess water that collects in the saucer.

Shred fallen leaves with your mower and work them into the top 6 to 12 inches of garden soil. The leaf pieces decompose over winter, improving the drainage of heavy clay soils and the water-holding capacity of sandy soils.

FERTILIZING

Take a soil test if you have not already. See the introduction to this chapter or contact your local Cooperative Extension Service for soil test information. Send the sample in now so that you will have the results back in time for winter planning and spring soil preparation.

PRUNING

Remove faded flowers as well as dried up leaves and stems on plants moved inside for winter. Allow them to adjust to their new location before cutting back severely.

PROBLEMS

The killing frost signals the end of the growing season and the start of fall cleanup. Remove all insect- and disease-infested plants. Discard—do *not* compost—these plants. Also, don't leave them for the town leaf collection; you don't want to infect the municipality's compost. Fall cleanup is the best way to reduce the risk of insects and disease in next year's garden.

Helpful Hints

Hibiscus, bougainvillea, oleander, and other tropical shrubs need to be moved indoors for winter.

1 Start by bringing them into the garage, screened-in porch, or indoor room away from your houseplants. Keep them isolated for several weeks. Check for insects. Use insecticidal soap to treat any mites and aphids you discover. Handpick and destroy larger caterpillars, slugs, earwigs, and beetles.

2 Move the plants indoors to a warm, sunny location. A south-facing window, Florida room, or atrium would work fine. Or add an artificial light to improve the light conditions found in most of our homes.

3 Continue to water thoroughly whenever the top few inches of soil start to dry. Do not fertilize until the plant adjusts to its new location and shows signs of growth.

4 Prune only enough to fit the plant into its winter location. Do not worry about the falling leaves. The plant will replace the fallen leaves as soon as it adjusts to its new location.

5 Continue to watch for pests and water as needed. Enjoy the added greenery and occasional flowers.

6 Prune overgrown plants in late February.

Record pest problems, control methods used, and successes and failures. These records will help you anticipate and reduce future pest problems through proper planning and plant selection.

NOVEMBER
Annuals & Biennials

PLANNING

It is never too soon to start planning for next season. Take inventory of all your tools, seeds, and gardening equipment as you pack them away for winter storage. Start a list of replacement tools and supplies that you will need for next year. Do not forget to include those items you have always wanted but keep forgetting to buy. Remember, the gift-giving season is not too far away.

PLANTING

Finish soil preparation as the last few leaves drop and before the ground freezes. Take a soil test now if you did not get around to it last month. Test soil every three to five years, or whenever soil conditions change or plant problems develop.

Store leftover seeds in their original packets. These contain all the plant and planting information you need. Store these in an airtight jar in the refrigerator. The consistent storage conditions help preserve the seeds' viability.

CARE

Clean garden tools before storing them for winter. See this month's "Helpful Hints" for details.

Move all fertilizers and pesticides to a secure location. Liquid materials should be stored out of direct light in a frost-free location. Granules must be kept dry. All pesticides should be kept in a locked location away from children and pets.

Check on **geraniums** and other annuals in dormant storage. Move plants to a cooler, darker location if they begin to grow. If growth continues, pot them up and move them to a sunny window or under artificial lights.

WATERING

Water annuals overwintering indoors. Apply enough water so that the excess runs out the drainage hole. Pour off any water that collects in the saucer. Repeat whenever the top inch or so starts to dry.

FERTILIZING

Indoor plants, including annuals grown indoors, need very little fertilizer. Use a dilute solution if plants are actively growing and showing signs of nutrient deficiency. Otherwise, wait until plants adjust to their new location and begin to grow.

PRUNING

Prune and shape as needed. Most of the plants are spending their energy adjusting to their new location. They are trying to survive and very little new growth appears. Things will improve as the days lengthen and light intensity increases.

PROBLEMS

Watch for whiteflies, aphids, mites, and any other insects that may have moved indoors on the plants. These pests suck out plant juices, causing the leaves to yellow and eventually brown.

It is never too soon to start planning for next season. Take inventory of all your tools, seeds, and gardening equipment as you pack them away for winter storage.

High populations of aphids and mites can be controlled using insecticidal soap. Check the label before mixing and applying this or any other chemical.

Whiteflies can also stress and stunt plants. These insects multiply quickly and are much harder to control. Try trapping whiteflies with commercial or homemade yellow sticky traps. Check your local garden center to purchase ready-to-use traps. Or make your own using yellow cardboard and Tanglefoot, a sticky pine resin—even cooking oil or car oil will work. The whiteflies are attracted by the yellow color, stick there, and die. Although this won't get rid of all the whiteflies, it reduces the populations enough to minimize stress to plants. Whiteflies are difficult to control with pesticides. It's safer for you, your children, and pets not to use chemical pesticides indoors.

Fungus gnats are small insects that are often found flitting across the room. They do not hurt the plants; they just annoy us. These insects feed on the organic matter in the soil, such as dead plant roots and peat moss. Keep the soil slightly drier than normal to reduce their populations.

Helpful Hints

Clean hand tools, shovels, rakes, and hoes before putting them in storage for winter. It is easier to do the job now than to wait until spring when the rust and hardened soil are harder to remove.

1 Wash or wipe off excess soil. Use a narrow putty knife to remove hardened soil. Or soak soil-encrusted tools in water and scrub with a wire brush.

2 Remove rust with a coarse grade of steel wool or medium-grit sanding paper or cloth. Add a few drops of oil to each side of the tool surface. Use a small cloth to spread it over the metal. This will help protect the surface against rust.

3 Sharpen the soil-cutting edges of shovels, hoes, and trowels to make digging easier. Use an 8- or 10-inch mill file to sharpen or restore the cutting angle. Visit your local hardware store for all the necessary equipment.

Press down and forward when filing. The file only cuts on the forward stroke. Lift the file, replace it to the original spot and push down and forward on the file again. Repeat until the desired edge is formed. File into or away from the cutting edge. It is safer to file away from the cutting edge. The edge will not be as sharp, but there is less risk of hurting yourself.

4 Check the tool handles for splinters and rough spots. Use 80-grit sandpaper on rough, wooden-handled tools. Coat with linseed oil.

5 Make sure the handles are tightly fastened to the shovel, hoe, or rake. You may need to replace or reinstall missing pins, screws, and nails. It is cheaper to replace a problem tool than to pay the doctor bills when the shovel flies off the handle!

DECEMBER

 ## PLANNING

Garden planning often gets lost in the chaos of the holiday preparations. Take advantage of the coming holidays to extend your garden season and share it with others. Frame your best garden and flower photos and give them as gifts to friends and relatives. Use dried flowers from your garden to decorate gift packages and cards. A bouquet of dried flowers makes a great gift for any house-bound person—gardener or not.

Score points with the family and start cleaning out the basement. (They don't need to know that you are making room for a new or expanded seed starting setup!) See January "Planting" for more details.

 ## PLANTING

Make a wish list of materials needed for your new seed starting endeavor. Be sure to include seeds, flats, containers, and other supplies that you will need. Your family will now be on to you and your recent cleaning frenzy—but you can solve their gift buying dilemmas. Consider giving the same type of gift or gardening gift certificate to your favorite gardening friends.

 ## CARE

Check on plants stored in the basement. The stems should be firm but dormant. Move them to a cooler, darker location if they start to grow. If growth continues, pot them up and move them to a sunny window or under artificial lights.

Continue to care for annuals and tropicals (**hibiscus** and such) that are growing indoors for the winter. Keep them out of drafts and in the brightest possible location.

 ## WATERING

Water indoor plants whenever the top few inches of soil start to dry. Apply enough water so that the excess runs out the bottom. Pour off any water that collects in the saucer.

 ## FERTILIZING

Plants are still struggling to adjust to their indoor location. The poor light and low humidity result in poor growth. Wait until plants start to grow before feeding. Foliar feed—following package instructions—any plants that are actively growing and showing signs of nutrient deficiencies.

 ## PRUNING

Pinch and clip as needed. Keep pruning to a minimum; remove only dead leaves and dead stems.

 ## PROBLEMS

Continue to check plants for signs of whiteflies, mites, and aphids.

Try trapping whiteflies with commercial or homemade yellow sticky traps. Coat a piece of yellow cardboard with Tanglefoot. Place treated cardboard in and near the infested plants. This will not kill all the whiteflies, but it is often enough to reduce the damage to a tolerable level. Use insecticides as your last resort. Select one labeled for controlling whiteflies on indoor plants. Spray three times, five days apart in a well-ventilated location. If you miss an application, you must start over.

Control mites and aphids with a strong blast of water followed by a treatment of insecticidal soap. This product is a soap that is effective at killing insects, but it is safe for people and the environment. Repeated applications may be necessary.

CHAPTER TWO

Bulbs, Corms, Rhizomes, & Tubers

There are no other types of plants that offer more beauty, or a wider range of variety, color, and bloom times than flowering bulbs.

Bulbs will produce flowers of incredible colors from one end of the growing season to the other. Nothing else in the garden rewards you with so much pleasure for so little effort.

The word "bulb" includes corms, tubers, rhizomes, tuber-corms, and true bulbs. These types of plants have an underground food-storage organ and go into dormancy once the foliage ripens after blooming. It's helpful to know the differences among them.

A corm is a swollen, vertical, solid stem with the bud (for leaves and flowers) at the top. Buds on the sides (lateral buds) form offsets called cormels. Even though a corm is an annual, which uses its stored food to grow leaves and flowers, it develops a new replacement corm from each lateral bud. **Gladiolus, winter aconite,** and **crocus** are corms.

Rhizome is another form with a modified stem. Think of it as a horizontal corm, or planted just below soil level. The apex (the upper portion of the rhizome) gives rise to leaves, stems, and flowers. The lower portion produces roots. **Cannas** and some **irises** are categorized as rhizomes.

In a tuber (or tuberous root), a swollen root that grows just beneath the soil surface stores food. Buds develop around the base of the old stem and become new plants. New fibrous roots form, which feed the plant during the growing season in this area.

The tuber-corm is disk- or top-shaped, having one or more buds on the upper portion and annual roots on the bottom. This category includes **tuberous begonias** and **cyclamen.** Like a tuber, tuber-corms are perennial, growing in size each year.

The true bulb is a modified, enlarged bud with a shortened stem sprouting leaves tightly along the stem, forming a dense, somewhat spherical mass. If you look under the skin of true bulbs (easily seen on **lilies**), you'll see the somewhat scaly leaves that have swelled with stored food. Cut a **daffodil** or **tulip** in half and the structure is evident.

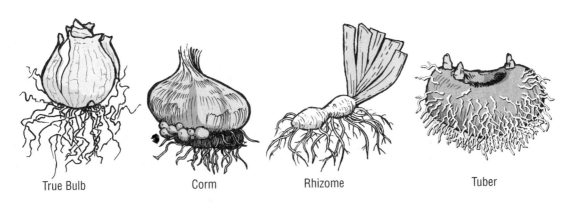

True Bulb   Corm   Rhizome   Tuber

Bulbs, Corms, Rhizomes, & Tubers

HARDY OR NOT?

Bulbs can be classified either as hardy or tender. Most spring-blooming bulbs (**crocus, daffodils, tulips, glory-of-the-snow, snowdrops,** etc.) are hardy. They require a cold period to induce bloom. Once spring-blooming bulbs are planted, they remain in the ground for years. Summer-blooming bulbs (**dahlias, cannas, calla lilies, peacock orchids,** and **gladiolas**) distinguish themselves because they cannot survive when the temperatures dip below the freezing level. These tender bulbs enhance your garden year after year—provided they are dug up in fall and stored inside for the winter.

PLANNING

Color and time of bloom are two of the most important elements to consider when planning bulbs in the scheme of your entire garden. It is helpful to make a sketch of your garden before planting. Don't panic, nobody is grading you on your drawing ability. This sketch is for your eyes only. Consider where to plant bulbs based on height, sunlight requirement, color and blooming time. Remember, most of the bulbs you plant in fall are hardy enough to stand our winters; once planted, they can remain undisturbed for years. On the other hand, most of bulbs you plant in spring are tender and must be dug up and stored before the first frost.

Spring-blooming bulbs put on such a great show, brilliantly contrasting winter drabness. When you are planning to add bulbs to an existing garden or cre-ating a new garden, think big. Bulbs have the most impact in natural-looking clusters or swaths. For large bulbs, such as **hyacinths** or **tulips,** plant groups of five, seven, or more. Planting in odd numbers is one of the tenets of gardening. Small bulbs, such as **cro-**

Did You Know?

Bulb Dos and Don'ts

Do plant bulbs in soil that has good drainage. Planting bulbs in well-drained soil is vital.

Don't use any strong commercial fertilizer or fresh manure to amend the soil before planting bulbs; it could burn the bulbs.

Do cut as little foliage as possible when cutting flowers to enjoy indoors. The leaves are essential; they play a fundamental role in the bulb's food storing process so the plant has the energy for next year's blooming.

Don't let flowers go to seed.

Do cut flowers as they fade and remove any seedpods that form.

Don't trim back healthy green foliage or the bulb will not perform well next year.

Do let the leaves die back on their own before trimming them back or digging them up.

Don't dry bulbs in the sun; always dry them in the shade in a well-ventilated area.

Do store bulbs in a dry, well-ventilated area to prevent mold or mildew.

Don't store bulbs in an airtight or plastic container.

Do label the bulbs as you plant them. Use labels that are big enough so that 2 to 3 inches of the label is below soil level. Smaller labels can heave out of the soil during spells of winter freezing and thawing. Labeling reminds you where the dormant bulbs are, keeping you from accidentally digging them up.

Don't rely on your memory alone; labeling is much safer.

cus, snowdrops, glory-of-the-snow, and Siberian squill, are outstanding in groups of 15, 25, or more.

PLANTING

Good soil preparation is the first step to successful bulb gardening. Well-drained, loose, porous soil is a must; otherwise bulbs will rot.

Work plenty of organic matter (compost, well-rotted manure, or leaf mold) or peat moss to a depth of a foot for large bulbs (hyacinths, daffodils, lilies, giant allium, tulips) and 8 inches for small bulbs (crocus, snow-drops, glory-of-the-snow, tuberose).

To ensure good root development, mix in a bulb nutrient, such as Bulb Booster into the soil.

Interplant spring-blooming bulbs with each other to cause a riot of spring color and continuous bloom. In addition to the color, subsequent flowers and leaves hide the ripening foliage of the earlier sprouts. Cathy often includes several daylilies—even though they are perennials and not bulbs—because they hide the foliage of later bulbs through their bloom season. Although you can plant them individually, the trick to a breathtaking display of bulbs is planting one large area in layers.

1 Dig a large hole to the planting depth of the largest bulb. Don't make a circular or rectangular hole; give it a naturalistic shape.

2 Place the large bulbs first; feel free to put those of the same size in clusters at the same level within the hole (hyacinths, lilies, and large daffodils). Don't plant bulbs in soldierly rows.

3 Place plant markers in with the bulbs that to reach well above soil level.

4 Cover the bulbs with an inch or two of soil.

5 Plant another layer with the next largest bulbs, such as tulips and species daffodils, with markers.

6 Add more soil and plant smaller bulbs (crocus, snowdrops, etc.) so that each bulb is at its proper depth.

7 After planting, cover bulbs with soil, water well, and mulch with shredded leaves.

If you start out with large lilies, you may have four layers of bulbs. Try not to put one layer right on top of the layer below.

Plant summer-blooming bulbs in late spring, after all danger of frost has passed. Since these tender bulbs start to grow as soon as they are planted, no

pest deterrents are necessary. Include summer-blooming bulbs in perennial beds, mixed borders, and other plantings. They are more easily incorporated into existing plantings than spring bloomers. Since they cannot tolerate the cold, dig up these tender bulbs after the first frost and store them indoors for the winter. Although drying times and storage media vary from plant to plant, all summer bloomers must be kept in a place where the temperature is between 40 and 50 degrees Fahrenheit.

The rule of thumb for spacing is not carved in stone. The amount of space you allot for each plant depends on the effect you are trying to achieve. If you want bulbs to naturalize, leave plenty of room for them to fill in as time passes. If you are looking for an "instant garden" next spring, plant them closer following the rule of thumb.

Bulbs are most effective planted in clumps or swaths—not one by one or in single rows. Space bulbs according to color with the softer colors in the front and the more vibrant in the background. The bold colors pull your eyes into the garden, giving it a greater sense of depth. Group bulbs according to height and in sequential bloom pattern for a long-lasting show of color.

Bulbs, Corms, Rhizomes & Tubers

Did You Know?

Force Hyacinths for Easter

The perfume of **hyacinths** evoke the memories of past Easters—hunting for eggs, digging out the best-flavored jellybeans—in a somewhat warmer climate. Although hyacinths won't be in bloom outdoors, you can enjoy the aroma indoors while munching on a chocolate bunny.

Hyacinth glasses have a narrow "neck" and flare out at the top. Choose a good-sized, firm bulb. Place it in the top portion of the glass. Fill the bottom of the glass to within 1/4 inch of the bottom of the bulb. If the hyacinth is prechilled, place the glass in a dark space for several weeks for roots to develop. If the hyacinth is not prechilled, put the glass in the refrigerator for four to six weeks or until the lower portion of the glass is filled with roots. Check the glass weekly and refill if necessary. Once there is 1 to 2 inches of top growth, bring the glass out into the light. Set it in a bright place—not in direct sun. Keep the water at the same level. If the water starts to turn green, carefully pour it out and add fresh tepid—not cold—water. Avoid having to do this by covering the lower part of the glass with aluminum foil.

Within a few weeks the **hyacinth** will burst into bloom. Once the flower fades, put bulbs in the compost pile.

CARE

Bulbs are low-maintenance plants. The key to success is letting the leaves die back on their own. Although it may be tempting, don't cut down the foliage of long-leafed, spring-blooming bulbs, such as **daffodils** and **tulips.** You may have seen or read about some gardeners braiding the leaves or tying them back with rubber bands to disguise their maturation as the foliage turns yellow or brown. If you revisited those gardens next spring, the bloom would be much less showy than it was the previous spring. Leaves play an important role in a bulb's life cycle. Through photosynthesis, they replenish the bulb's food stores. Remove the leaves too early and the odds of the bulb returning the following year are not good.

Most summer-flowering bulbs are tender and cannot withstand temperatures below freezing, much less a Prairie Lands winter. Bulbs must be dried before storing or they will rot. Exceptions are noted and described in the the following chapter. In general, follow these directions for storing tender bulbs.

Dig the bulbs when the foliage has turned brown due to a light frost.

Set bulbs on a screen (raised up from the table or floor so air can circulate all around the bulbs). Air dry in a dry, well-ventilated area for a week.

Remove all soil from the bulbs. If you have had a problem with rotting in past years, consider dusting the bulbs with sulfur before putting them to bed for winter.

Put the bulbs in dry peat moss or wood shavings in a brown paper bag, open crate, netted bag or even old pantyhose. Store at 50 to 55 degrees Fahrenheit in a dry location until it is time to replant.

MULTIPLYING

Tiger lilies, which are bulbs, produce bulbils, which look like black jellybeans along the stem just above each leaf. Bulbils store food, drop to the ground, and germinate like seeds. It takes several years for a bulbil to produce a flowering plant.

WATERING

Water the bulbs well after planting. For fall-planted bulbs, keep the soil lightly moist until the ground freezes. In spring, if there is no rain, water deeply until they begin to flower. Once it fin-

Bulbs, Corms, Rhizomes & Tubers

ishes blooming, reduce watering to allow the bulbs to dry out.

FERTILIZING

In spring when the first shoots appear, sprinkle again with bulb food (Bulb Booster) or a slow release fertilizer low in nitrogen if this wasn't done at planting. This will encourage the flowering and also help rebuild the bulb for the next year. If the weather is dry, water the bulbs during their growing period. When the flowers begin to fade and before a seedpod forms, cut the flower. Leave the foliage to die back naturally. Spring-flowering bulbs do not have to be dug and stored in most Hardiness Zones.

PESTS AND DISEASES

In late summer and autumn, squirrels, mice, and other critters look upon newly planted bulbs as haute cuisine. To deter these freeloaders, lay chicken wire over the new planting and pin it down. There's even an added bonus: Cats don't like the feel of chicken wire on their tender foot pads; they will steer clear of the area. Remember to remove the wire in late winter before you anticipate any early bulbs sticking their heads up through the snow. This technique doesn't work for summer-blooming bulbs since the bulbs start growing right after planting.

Planting Chart

Common Name (*Botanical Name*)	Type	Bloom Time	Planting Time	Depth	Spacing	Hardiness
Allium *Allium* spp.	Bulb	MS - ES (depend on species)	LS – EF	3-6 in.	2-6 in.	Hardy
Amaryllis *Hippeastrum* spp.	Bulb	Force indoors	F – W	1/3 above soil in pot	1–3 in.	Tender
Autumn Crocus *Colchicum autumnale*	Corm	LSU–F	MSU–LSU	4–6 in.	2–4 in.	Hardy
Autumn Daffodil *Crocus speciosus*	Bulb	LSU–F	MSU–LSU	3–5 in.	2–4 in.	Hardy
Caladium *Caladium bicolor*	Tuber	foliage plant	MSP–ESU start indoors	3–4 in.	3–6 in.	Tender
Calla Lily *Zantedeschia* spp.	Tuberous rhizome	SU	LSP–ESU start indoors	2–4 in.	18–24 in.	Tender
Canna *Canna x generalis*	Fleshy rhizome	SU	LSP–ESU start indoors	3–4 in.	6–8 in.	Tender
Crocus *Crocus* spp.	Corm	SP	LSU–EF	3–4 in.	3–4 in.	Hardy
Crown Imperial *Frittilaria imperialis*	Bulb	LSP–ESU	LSU–EF	5–6 in.	8 in.	Hardy
Daffodil *Narcissus* spp.	Bulb	SP	LSU–EF	4–6 in.	3–6 in.	Hardy
Dahlia *Dahlia* spp.	Tuberous root	MSU–F	MSP–LSP	4–6 in.	4–6 in.	Tender

Bulbs, Corms, Rhizomes & Tubers

Planting Chart

Common Name (*Botanical Name*)	Type	Bloom Time	Planting Time	Depth	Spacing	Hardiness
Gladiola *Gladiolus* cvs.	Corm	MSU–LSU	LSP–ESU	3–4 in.	4–6 in.	Tender
Glory-of-the-Snow *Chionodoxa* spp.	Bulb	ESP–MSP	LSU–EF	3–4 in.	3–4 in.	Hardy
Grape Hyacinth *Muscari* spp.	Bulb	ESP–MSP	LSU–EF	3–4 in.	3–4 in.	Hardy
Hardy Cyclamen *Cyclamen persicum* (*C. coum*)	Corm	LF–EW	LSU–EF	Just below soil	3-4 in.	Hardy
Hyacinth *Hyacinthus orientalis*	Bulb	MSP–LSP	LSU–EF	6–8 in.	3–5 in.	Hardy
Italian Arum *Arum iltalicum* 'Pictum'	Tuber	LSP Berries SU	LSP–EF	3–5 in.	3–5 in.	Hardy
Lily *Lilium* spp. and cvs.	Bulb	SU MS	LSU–EF	6–8 in.	8–15 in.	Hardy
Magic Lily *Lycoris squamigera*	Bulb	LSU	LSU–EF	4–6 in.	4–6 in.	Hardy
Netted Iris *Iris reticulata*	Bulb	ESP–MSP	LSU–EF	3–5 in.	3–5 in.	Hardy
Peacock Orchid *Gladiolus callianthus*	Corm	MSU	LSP–ESU	4–6 in.	3–5 in.	Tender
Siberian Squill *Scilla siberica*	Bulb	MSP	LSU–EF	3–5 in.	3–5 in.	Hardy
Snowdrop *Galanthus nivalis*	Bulb	ESP–MSP	LSU–EF	3–5 in.	3–5 in.	Hardy
Spring Snowflake *Leucojum aestivum*	Bulb	MSP–LSP	LSU–EF	4–5 in.	4–6 in.	Hardy
Tuberose *Polianthus tuberosa*	Rhizome	LSU	LSP	2–3 in.	3–4 in.	Tender
Tuberous Begonia *Begonia* x *tuberhybrida*	Tuber	SU–F	LSP start indoors early	4–6 in.	1–2 in.	Tender
Tulip *Tulipa* spp. and cvs.	Bulb	ESP–LS	LSU-EF	6–10 in.	3–6 in.	Hardy

*Timing on this chart is for Zone 5, for colder areas bloom time can be two to three weeks later; for warmer areas, bloom time can be up to two weeks earlier

Key: E – early, M – mid, L – late, SP – spring SU – summer, F – Fall, W – Winter, BFR – Before first frost, AFR – After last frost

JANUARY
Bulbs, Corms, Rhizomes, & Tubers

 PLANNING

Now that the holidays are past, gather up the catalogs that have been filling the mailbox and start browsing through them for the summer-blooming bulbs you may want to add to your garden. Remember to order some to pot up in containers.

Check the Internet for companies that sell bulbs; you may find some bargains or markdowns. It's likely that you'll fall in love with some bulb new to you. Treat yourself and order them—you deserve it.

Take a trip to your local nursery, garden center, home store, or grocery store with an eye out for after-Christmas sales of **amaryllis** and **paper-white narcissus.** Feel the bulbs to make sure they are firm, not mushy or shriveled and dried out. You may also find some prechilled **hyacinths** that are perfect for forcing in a hyacinth glass.

 PLANTING

Place the bulbs in a pot slightly larger than the bulb; point the smaller end of the bulb with its tip above soil. Move to a bright indoor location and water so that the soil is moist, not wet.

Harden off the plant and move it outdoors after the danger of frost has passed. Bring it back indoors before the first fall frost.

Did You Know?

Grape Hyacinth—An Outstanding Minor Bulb

Grape hyacinth is aptly named. Growing only 6 to 8 inches high, it resembles a miniature **hyacinth** or a tiny bunch of grapes, depending on your point of view. The flowers have a delightful, light grapey aroma and naturalize well.

 CARE

It amazes me that every year when January thaw arrives—even if it is February—people panic at the sight of bare soil and flowers or leaves emerging in the garden. They run around like Chicken Little convinced that the sky is falling. Not to worry; the earliest of the spring bulbs grow low to the ground, even generating heat that melts snow around them. They were designed to be tough; if they weren't, they would have died out years ago. Snow or cold weather won't bother the early risers.

 WATERING

If the ground is dry during a January thaw, water the garden.

Keep the bulbs you are forcing lightly moist. Do not overwater; in the cold of the refrigerator or garage there is a good likelihood of mildew.

 FERTILIZING

Forced bulbs do not need to be fed unless you want to save them to plant in the garden in spring. In that case, use a liquid fertilizer at half strength every few weeks. If the bulbs are tight in their pot, it is worth the effort to pot them up into a 2-inch-larger container. Bulbs forced in water have spent all their energy blooming, they have nothing left; put them on the compost pile.

 PRUNING

Cut off any foliage that is yellow or brown.

If you forced any double-nose bulbs (large bulb, usually a **daffodil,** with two small bulbs on the side), the baby bulbs will likely bloom after the mother bulb. Be patient and give them time.

 PROBLEMS

Check on the bulbs that are chilling. Keep an eye out for dryness, mold, or mildew on the soil.

FEBUARY
Bulbs, Corms, Rhizomes, & Tubers

PLANNING

A greater variety of bulbs is available through mail-order sources than at most local nurseries or garden centers. Plan your garden and order your bulbs as soon as you get your catalogs. Remember to add extra bulbs so there are enough in bloom that you can cut some to enjoy indoors without leaving the garden bare. Don't worry about having to store them, the bulbs will be shipped at the appropriate time for planting.

PLANTING

Start **tuberous begonias** indoors, both new tubers and ones saved from last year. The ideal time to start **begonias** for the outdoor garden is six weeks before the last frost. Weary of winter foliage and eager for the look of something tropical, Cathy starts them early to enjoy the magnificent leaves indoors.

If you are short on space, use a flat to plant the **begonias** en masse, otherwise use individual 4- to 6-inch pots. If the **begonia(s)** is going to be in a container outdoors, start it in the container to avoid the stress of transplanting and the probability of breaking off a stem or two.

Fill the pots to within 2 inches of the rim with a soilless potting mix.

Plant the tuber round side down. Cover with 1 inch of soil. Tamp gently.

Water well and then keep the soil moist, but not soggy.

Keep the pots in a warm, semi shady area at about 70 degrees Fahrenheit. Bottom heat helps the tubers root; Try using household appliances for bottom heat; set it on top of your drier if it's in the right light.

When all danger of frost has passed, transplant outdoors being careful not to disturb the roots.

CARE

Be sure that the storage temperature is within the proper range.

WATERING

Monitor bulbs that are still in the cold stage of forcing. The soil should be just lightly moist.

Water **amaryllis, paper-whites,** and any other bulbs growing in the house. Maintain the water level in hyacinth glasses and soilless **paper-white** plantings.

FERTILIZING

When the growing bud or leaf emerges from the **amaryllis** bulb, start feeding it with half-strength liquid fertilizer weekly. Stop feeding when you move it outside in late spring or early summer.

PRUNING

Remove any spent flowers from forced bulbs that are in bloom.

PROBLEMS

Check the summer bulbs in storage carefully for signs of rot, mildew, or soft spots. If you find any, discard the bulbs.

MARCH
Bulbs, Corms, Rhizomes, & Tubers

 PLANNING

Consider planting **alliums** in the garden next year. They come in a wide assortment of sizes, shapes, and colors. As members of the onion family, some have a somewhat pungent scent, yet that makes them a good pest deterrent. Pick out some interesting varieties and order them right away. The bulbs will be delivered in time for late-summer planting.

Lilies are unique among summer-blooming bulbs, as you can plant them in spring or in fall. There are so many species and hybrids to choose from—**Easter lilies** to **tiger lilies**, fragrant **Oriental lilies** to **Turk's cap lilies.** So, if you didn't plant lilies last fall, you can always plant them after the soil warms this spring. Although it is probably too late to order lilies (but check on the Internet anyway), start making your wish list for fall.

 PLANTING

Start caladiums indoors six to eight weeks before the last frost date. Caladiums are magnificent in hanging baskets. In moss-lined baskets, plant one on the top, and poke several tubers into the soil on the sides and bottom of the basket. As the leaves grow, the outside of the basket will be aglow with the showy, variegated leaves.

Before planting the tubers, check each one carefully for rot (soft, squishy spots or discoloration). When in doubt, throw it out.

Fill 6-inch pots (use a flat for mass plantings) to within 3 inches of the rim with damp milled sphagnum moss or vermiculite. If you plan to grow the caladiums in a container outdoors, start them in that pot.

Place the caladium tuber on the soil round side up; allow 1 inch between tubers.

Cover the tubers with 1 inch of soil. Water well.

Keep the pots between 80 to 85 degrees Fahrenheit (try a heating mat) and moist.

Transplant outdoors when all danger of frost has passed and the soil has warmed.

Outdoors, transplant so the tubers are 1 inch deep and about 10 inches apart. Grow in full to partial shade. Water frequently and fertilize once a month.

Pot up canna rhizomes

Check the rhizomes for any signs of rot (soft spots, discoloration) or evidence of mold or mildew.

Cut the canna so there are one or two buds per piece.

Plant the rhizomes 2 inches deep in 6-inch pots (see caladium above).

Water well; set on a sunny windowsill until planting time.

 CARE

Although the minor bulbs (**snowdrops, glory-of-the-snow, Siberian squill,** etc.) are not usually thought of as cut flowers a group of eight to 12 flowers is charming in a small container like an antique inkwell.

 WATERING

Keep **crocus, snowdrops, Siberian squill,** and **glory-of-the-snow** lightly moist during their growing season.

 FERTILIZING

As bulbs emerge, sprinkle bulb food around the planting area, following package instructions. Water it in well. Be sure to wash any fertilizer from the leaves or flowers. Feed **crocus** weekly with compost tea.

 PRUNING

Cut off any brown or yellow leaves from forced bulbs.

 PROBLEMS

Check the forced bulbs you are saving to plant for any sign of rot or mildew. If you find any, throw away the entire pot.

APRIL
Bulbs, Corms, Rhizomes, & Tubers

 PLANNING

Don't be disappointed if **glory-of-the-snow's** first year bloom is not as spectacular as you had hoped. Leave the bulbs in place. They self-seed freely; within a couple of years, you'll have a starry carpet to dazzle friends and neighbors.

 PLANTING

When forced **hyacinths** finish blooming, keep the plants watered until the soil is workable. Plant them outdoors and they will bloom the following spring.

Start **tuberous begonias** indoors for earlier blooms outdoors. If it is to be a container plant, start it in the decorative container. Otherwise use a 4- to 6-inch plastic pot. See "February" for complete planting instructions.

Grow **hardy cyclamen** beneath shrubs, around trees in rock gardens or mixed borders. It thrives in well-drained, moist, slightly alkaline soil in light shade. Plant tubers concave side up (round side down), $1/2$ inch deep and 6 to 8 inches apart. Protect from harsh, heavy rains, but do not let tubers dry out. Once established, do not disturb and they will slowly multiply.

Give **dahlias** a head start by planting them in pots indoors four to six weeks before last frost. Separate the tubers from the stalk.

Did You Know?

Crocus in the Lawn—Wait to Mow

Growing **crocus** in the lawn gives a naturalist look. To keep that look for years to come:

Grow your lawn 3 inches high (the current recommended height).

Fertilize the lawn **only** in fall and you'll have no problem.

Do not fertilize the lawn in spring, as this increases leaf growth at the expense of root growth. Otherwise, your lawn may be 6 inches high before the **crocus** ripen.

Crocus naturalize readily; the **crocus** lawn will look better with each passing year.

Leave 1 inch of stalk attached to each tuber; be sure the tuber has an eye or bud, which is essential for bloom. Pot **dahlias** in a damp mix of equal parts peat moss and vermiculite with the tuberous root about 1 inch below soil level. Plant them in individual pots to make transplanting easier.

Plant **tuberoses** when the weather is relatively warm—60 degrees or more at night. Space bulbs 8 inches apart and 1 to 2 inches deep. Feed after the foliage appears. **Tuberoses** are very fragrant; avoid planting them near other sweet-scented flowers, as two different perfumed aromas can clash.

CARE

Remove forced bulbs from storage. Use some for indoor enjoyment. Move a few of the potted bulbs from cold storage directly outdoors to planters and window boxes. This is a great way to brighten up drab areas and create a surprise in the spring landscape.

Remove winter mulch as the bulbs begin to grow and the weather consistently hovers near or above freezing. Northern gardeners may want to keep some mulch handy in case of sudden and extreme drops in temperature.

Replant or firm frost-heaved bulbs back into place. Frost heaving occurs in unmulched gardens or those with inconsistent snow cover. The fluctuating temperatures in the exposed soil cause the soil to shift, pushing bulbs and other plants right out of the soil.

 WATERING

Keep **crocus, snowdrops, Siberian**

Give dahlias a head start by planting them in pots indoors four to six weeks before the last frost.

squill, and glory-of-the-snow lightly moist during their growing season.

Water hyacinths throughout their growing season. Water crown imperial deeply in spring.

FERTILIZING

Feed crocus weekly with compost tea.

PRUNING

Deadhead daffodils or cut down the flower stems when the bloom fades. This enables the plant's energy to go to the bulb.

After flowering, remove the head of tulips; allow the stem and foliage to die back naturally.

PROBLEMS

Good Deer Repellent. If deer are a problem in your garden, you know that there is a limited menu that deer will turn their noses up at. What they refrained from eating last year, they may chomp away at this season, especially if the winter is harsh. One of the lesser known stalwarts in the ongoing territorial battle between humans and deer is the crown imperial, also known as tears of Mary for the large drops of nectar in the flowers. With the

Did You Know?

Allium

Alliums thrive in a sunny spot with rich, well-drained soil. Plant the smaller varieties of *Allium* 4 inches deep, the larger varieties 7 to 8 inches deep. They multiply rapidly, so give them some elbowroom when planting.

Botanical Name	Height	Flower Color	Bloom Time
Allium aflatunense	24–60 in.	Purple	LSP
Allium albopilosum (*A. christophii*)	24 in.	Pale red-violet	LSP–ESU
Allium caeruleum	10–24 in.	Blue	LSP–ESU
Allium gigantium	36–72 in.	Purple	LSP–ESU
Allium 'Gladiator'	48–60 in.	Purple	MSP–LSP
Allium karataviense	7–10 in.	Palest pink	ESP–MSP
Allium moly	10–15 in.	Yellow	LSP–ESU
Allium multibulbosum (*A. nigrum*)	24–36 in.	White	MSP
Allium neopolitanum	12–18 in.	White	ESP–MSP
Allium ostrowskianum	4–6 in.	Violet	LSP–ESU
Allium roseum	18–24 in.	Rose-pink	LSU
Allium siculum	30–40 in.	Cream, green, pink	MSP–ESU
Allium sphaerocephalum	24–36 in.	Magenta	MSP–ESU

skunky aroma of the leaves and bulbs (never use crown imperial as a cut flower, no matter how beautiful it is—not even in an outdoor flower arrangement), this underutilized bulb is a great deterrent. Cathy can't help smiling when she sees the plants. As they emerge from the ground and grow upward, the single stems look very much like lilies, but the smell is a dead giveaway. The stem rises 3 to 4 feet tall and produces a cluster of

orange (it also comes in red and yellow, but they are more temperamental and costly) 1- to 2-inch, bell-like florets that ring the stem. Mother Nature must have a sense of humor; a topknot of green leaves bursts above the flowers. You, too, will smile when you see this unique beauty—if not for its looks, for the knowledge that it will keep the deer away from the garden when planted at the perimeter.

MAY
Bulbs, Corms, Rhizomes, & Tubers

PLANNING

Check out the catalogs for hardy spring-blooming bulbs. Take notes of new bulbs you want to grow for next spring. Refer to your journal or garden notes to see what performed well this year, and what didn't.

Lilies make superb container plants, especially the dwarf varieties. Although like all plants, the choices of **lilies** are much more varied when you shop at a mail-order or Internet nursery, local nurseries; garden centers, and even home stores offer a dozen or more different **lilies.** See the following chart for types of lilies.

PLANTING

Once the danger of frost has passed, plant **lily** bulbs in groups of three or more as soon as you get them. Be careful not to break off any stalks or growth that may be on the bulb. Choose a sunny spot with well drained porous, sandy soil enriched with compost is the best. The ideal site is one where the plants get full sun at the tops and are shaded at the soil level to keep the ground moist.

Did You Know?

Lilies

Type	Height	Bloom Time
Asiatic hybrids	30–60 in.	ESU–MSU
Dwarf Oriental hybrids	16–18 in.	MSU
Henryi	60 in.	MSU
Oriental hybrids	30–48 in.	MSU
Rubrum	60 in.	MSU
Tiger	24–48 in.	MSU–LS

*Refer to the chapter introduction for "Bloom Time" abbreviation chart.

CARE

If you've ruled out hungry animals and early frost and if **tulips** or **daffodils** don't bloom despite their healthy leaves, it's time to divide them.

1 Dig up the clump of bulbs.

2 Gently tease the bulbs and roots apart.

3 Replant the bulbs at their original depth. Space them two to three times the width of the bulb (center to center) apart.

4 Water well with transplant solution.

Some **hyacinths** are magnificent the first year and maybe more, but subsequently have fewer florets. If this happens, move them to a less prominent area. It's wonderful to come along them at a woodland's edge.

WATERING

Keep **crocus, snowdrops, Siberian squill,** and **glory-of-the-snow** lightly moist during their growing season.

Stop watering **crocus** as soon as the leaves begin to yellow.

Water **caladiums** frequently.

Water **crown imperials** and **hyacinths** deeply.

Keep **tuberoses** lightly moist.

FERTILIZING

Foliar feed **autumn crocus** leaves when they emerge. They will only be there for a month or so. Be sure to mark the spot so you don't accidentally plant anything in the same space. Follow these recommendations using organic products:

- Foliar feed **caladiums** once with a solution of kelp or fish emulsion (following package instructions).

- Fertilize **lilies** monthly until the plants finish blooming.

- Feed **tuberoses** after the foliage appears.

 PRUNING

Remove the dead flower heads from your **crown imperials** before they go to seed. Cut off individual spent florets to keep the topknot intact or cut the stem just below the flowers.

After flowering, remove the head of **tulips** but allow the stem and foliage to die back naturally.

Did You Know?

Crocus for Fall

Crocus are one of the heralds of spring; yet some species are heralds of autumn. Most do not have common named, their names can be tongue twisters.

Crocus gouilimyi is a gem; each corm gives rise to one to three delightfully scented, lilac-colored flowers and narrow green leaves at the same time.

Each *Crocus speciosus* sends up a diminutive (1/2 to 1 1/2 inch tall) single blue flower with deeper blue veins and vibrant orange stigmas. Plant in drifts of 25 or more for the look of a miniature sea of blue. *C. speciosus* 'Alba' has white flowers.

Crocus pulchellus bears honey-scented, lilac flowers with deep yellow throats and white anthers.

Saffron crocus (*Crocus sativus*) has orange-red stigmas—each is a thread of culinary saffron—within rich lilac flowers, a gorgeous contrast. Saffron crocus bloom in mid- to late fall. To collect the saffron, pick the stigmas as soon as the flowers open. Air dry the stigmas as quickly as possible; store in a closed container away from light or heat. Now you can understand why saffron is so precious and expensive. It is hardy to Zone 5.

Crocus medius, the last **fall crocus** to bloom, has 1- to 2-inch-tall, deep lavender-purple flowers with prominent scarlet-red stigmas. The leaves appear about a week after the flowers open.

JUNE

Bulbs, Corms, Rhizomes, & Tubers

 PLANNING

If you haven't already ordered fall- and spring-blooming bulbs, do it now. Most mail-order companies have web sites where you can browse through the catalog and order whatever you want. As convenient as the Web is, for me nothing beats slowly going through the catalogs, using Post-its™ to denote the plants that pique my interest. Cathy goes through a process of elimination, whittling the list down until it is affordable and can fit in the garden. The bulbs are shipped at the proper planting time, so you don't have to worry about summer storage.

 PLANTING

Transplant **caladiums** outdoors once the soil is at least 60 degrees Fahrenheit. Allow 8 to 10 inches between plants. Water well with transplant solution.

Transplant **cannas** outdoors at the same time as **caladiums. Cannas** can take very moist soil; grow them at the edge of your pond and in the garden. Site colorful-leafed **cannas** such as 'Tropicanna' so the early-morning or late-afternoon sun can shine through the leaves, making them look like stained glass. Plant **cannas** at the same time as **tomatoes,** space plants 18 inches apart. Water well with transplant solution.

If your **daffodils** had lots of leaves but fewer flowers than in previous years, they are too crowded. Dig and divide the bulbs after the foliage has turned brown. Replant at once.

Begin planting **gladiolus.** To extend the period of bloom, plant some corms every two weeks until 90 days before the first fall frost. Start mid-May in warmer regions.

Dig a 6- to 8-inch-deep trench or large round or oval hole, depending on the way you want to group (nine or more bulbs) the **glads.**

Add 1 inch of organic material (compost, well-rotted manure, leaf mold) and 1 cup of bonemeal per 10 feet.

Top with 1 inch of builder's sand to ensure good drainage.

Firmly place the corms in the hole, pointed end up, spacing them 6 inches apart.

Fill in with soil, press the soil firmly with your palms—do not compact soil.

Water well.

Top with 2 inches of mulch to keep the roots cool and conserve moisture.

Start planting **peacock orchids.** They are a type of **gladiolus** and bloom from the lower part of the stem up. They are especially fragrant at night. White, with deep burgundy at the throat, they are an excellent addition to an evening garden; in moonlight they appear to be fluttering moths. Plant the corms in clusters of five or seven (or any larger odd number) 4 to 6 inches deep and 3 to 5 inches apart. Stagger the planting to extend the season; plant several clusters every two weeks for 6 to 8 weeks. Water well. Plant **caladiums** in the proper location.

 CARE

Spray leaves frequently during hot, dry weather if necessary.

Move potted **amaryllis** outside after all danger of frost is passed. Place them in semi-shade such as under a shrub.

To extend the period of bloom, plant some corms every two weeks until 90 days before the first fall frost.

WATERING

Keep **caladiums, cannas, calla lilies, tuberoses,** and **peacock orchids** lightly moist. Don't let them dry out.

Water **crown imperials** and **hyacinths** deeply.

FERTILIZING

Foliar feed **caladiums, calla lilies,** and **cannas** monthly with a solution of kelp or fish emulsion (following package instructions).

Fertilize **lilies** monthly until the plants finish blooming.

PRUNING

Pinch **dahlias** back, especially dwarf or compact varieties, so they will retain their low compact size.

If you want later-blooming, larger **dahlia** blooms (like the dinner plate ones you see at flower shows) pinch and disbud the plants, leaving only one or two flower buds for each stem.

Remove the dead flower heads of **crown imperial** before they go to seed.

Did You Know?

Invest in the Future

Most **cannas** are available as potted plants. Even though they are more costly than rhizomes, buy a couple of plants. Think of them as an investment in the future. They will be beautiful this summer and next spring you can make a surprising number of cuttings from each rhizome.

Dahlias

Name	Height	Bloom Time
Anemone Dahlias	18–24 in.	July–frost
Cactus Dahlias	12–45 in.	August–frost
Decorative Dahlias	30–40 in.	August–frost
Dinner Plate Dahlias	36–48 in.	August–frost
Dwarf Dahlias	12 in.	August–frost
Giant Dahlias	16–40 in.	August–frost
Magic Carpet Dahlias	10–12 in.	July–frost
Pompon Dahlias	36–48 in.	July–frost
Royal Dahliettas	7–8 in.	July–frost

PROBLEMS

Thrips can be serious pests for **gladiolus.** To avoid problems, soak the bulbs in a solution of 1¼ tablespoons of Lysol mixed in 1 gallon of water for two to three hours just before planting them.

JULY
Bulbs, Corms, Rhizomes, & Tubers

PLANNING

Most minor bulbs (the small, early bloomers) need full sun. Think full sun for when the bulbs are up and blooming, not planting time. While it may be shady under a deciduous tree or shrub in late summer or fall, it will be sunny when the early bulbs blossom because the tree will not have leafed out. Look on page 69 to see some bulb combinations that will help extend the blooming season in your garden.

Grape Hyacinths. Whether you purchase **grape hyacinths** at a nursery, garden center, home store, or through a mail-order nursery, get them early (by mid-August) and plant them within the next two weeks. They need time to develop a strong root system and send up their leaves before the weather turns cold.

PLANTING

Continue planting **gladiolus** every two weeks until 90 days before the first frost date.

Before planting, do a perk test:

1 Dig a 10-inch hole, fill it with water, and wait.

2 If there is water standing in the hole after an hour, dig 6 inches deeper,

amend the soil with builder's sand and organic matter (compost, well-rotted manure, or leaf mold).

3 Add 6 inches of the amended soil back into the hole. Refill the hole with water.

4 If the hole still holds water, you may want to install drains if there is a place to send the water. However, that can be time-consuming and costly.

5 A raised bed is the easiest solution. If it's not as easy as it used to be for you to bend, dig down, and work at soil level, consider making a 2-feet-tall (or higher) raised bed with a broad edge so you can sit and garden. The bed can be as long as you like; make it narrow enough so you can reach into the middle of the bed from both sides. In the Prairie Lands states, a raised bed has an advantage besides good drainage—the soil warms up earlier in the spring so you can start enjoying your flowers before your neighbors.

CARE

Spray **caladium** leaves frequently during hot, dry weather.

Remove spent **lily** flowers as they finish blooming. Enjoy the green foliage for another month or more.

Gladiolus is a superb cut flower, lasting at least a week, when you treat it right:

• Pull out faded blossoms

• Cut ½ inch off the stem

• Change the water daily

• If grape hyacinths become congested:

• Dig them up in summer or fall when the plants are dormant.

• Gently tease the bulbs and roots apart.

• Replant at the original depth and spacing.

• Use the extra bulbs to start a new area, or share with friends.

After lilies finish flowering, remove only the blooms, **not** the stems or leaves. Allow the foliage to die back naturally.

WATERING

Keep **caladiums, cannas, calla lilies, tuberoses,** and **peacock orchids** lightly moist. Don't let them dry out.

Refrain from watering **crown imperial** until bulb planting time.

Keep watering **hyacinths** until their foliage dries out and yellows or browns.

In the Prairie Lands states, a raised bed has an advantage besides good drainage—the soil warms up earlier in the spring so you can start enjoying your flowers before your neighbors.

FERTILIZING

Foliar feed **caladiums, calla lilies,** and **cannas** once with a solution of kelp or fish emulsion (following package instructions).

When **gladiolus** flower spikes reach one-third of their height, apply a high potash fertilizer (following package instructions) every 10 days until they finish flowering.

Fertilize **lilies** monthly until the plants finish blooming.

PRUNING

If you are cutting **lily** flowers for an arrangement, you may want to cut off the anthers, as the pollen can drop off and stain. Cut off the entire anther, or for a more natural look, just cut off the ends with the pollen.

Cut off faded **caladium** leaves.

Deadhead **cannas** to prolong bloom.

Pinch **dahlias** back—especially dwarf or compact varieties—so they will retain their low compact size. Stop pinching by the the middle of July.

If you want later-blooming, larger **dahlia** blooms (like the dinner plate ones you see at flower shows) pinch and disbud the plants, leaving only one or two buds. Do not pinch or disbud after the 15th of the month.

PROBLEMS

Check **cannas** for any sign of fungal leaf spot. Cut off and destroy any suspect leaves.

AUGUST

PLANNING

The "August Doldrums" is a period of 10 days to two weeks when the weather is so hot that you take a vacation from outdoor gardening (since you've been paying enough attention to the plants you've invited). You just ignore the garden, except in a drought (you may want to consider an automatic water system for next year). This is the dirty little secret that most gardeners guiltily hide. It's okay; we all feel the same way. All of our inner clocks may not be in sync, but you know when that feeling comes over you. That is a perfect time to take a mental inventory of all the tender bulbs in your garden. Mull it over for a few days, picturing each in your mind's eye, and then decide whether you want to make the effort to dig them all up in fall and store them for winter. As you go through this process, you may want to write out a list of everything and then cross out plants as you consider the following and make the decisions:

Is it hardy? If you are lucky enough to live in Zone 6 and have a nice warm microclimate, you could possibly get away with leaving some in the ground and covering the soil with a 3- to 6-inch layer of mulch as the ground freezes. Try it with a few different bulbs and see what works. **Amaryllis, caladium, tuberose,**

and **tuberous begonia** definitely will **not** survive outside in winter.

Do you have ample space to store all the bulbs indoors?

Do you like the plant? If not, offer it to a friend. Dig it early and pot it up or let him/her dig it up at the right time. This is the first cut; it may take a lot of bulbs out of the running or you may like them all. Continue to weed out the bulbs as you go down this list.

How much time and energy do you realistically think you'll have when it's time to dig up the bulbs? Going through this survey when you are exhausted allows you to see your capabilities in their true light.

Was the bulb expensive? **Peacock orchids,** for example, are very inexpensive, so it is easier to treat them as annuals than a special exotic **lily.**

How many bulbs do you have of that particular plant? If it is a lot, consider digging up some to overwinter and leave the rest in the ground.

Do you have avid gardener friends who might want to share the work and the bulbs?

PLANTING

As soon as you get **autumn crocus** bulbs, plant them in rich, deep, well-drained soil with the top 4 inches below the soil surface. Cluster seven or more bulbs 2 to 3 inches apart for an impressive show. Water well and they will bloom within a few weeks. To prove their magical quality, place one or two on a sunny windowsill. Watch them send up their goblet-shaped, 2- to 3-inch, lavender-pink flowers.

Plant **crocus** corms soon after you get them; otherwise they could dry out.

CARE

Cathy sprays **caladium** leaves with water frequently during hot, dry weather.

After **lilies** finish flowering, remove only the blooms, **not** the stems or leaves. Allow the foliage to die back naturally. Carefully cut back the stalks when the foliage has died back completely.

One way to save **amaryllis** is to put it into dormancy.

Give the potted **amaryllis** a strong spray of water on the way into the house to dislodge any critters that might have made it their new home.

Put the pot on a sunny windowsill for a few days to dry it out.

Move the pot to a cool, dry, dark location. Lay it on its side in to encourage dormancy. Don't be surprised if it stays green; that's fine.

After a rest of at least six weeks, start forcing it again and top-dress with rich compost.

If you need to repot **amaryllis,** remember that it likes to fit tightly in a pot, with no more than an inch between the bulb and the side of the container. Wait to repot **amaryllis** until after it has gone through its dormant stage.

Did You Know?

The Magic Bulb

The best known and showiest of the fall-blooming bulbs is often advertised as a "magic bulb" that will bloom right on the windowsill, without a pot or water—and it will. Plant it as soon as you get the bulb, as it could bloom in the boxes if you wait. Plant 4 inches deep and 6 inches apart.

Autumn crocus (*Colchicum autumnale*) is a misnomer; it's not a **crocus** at all, though it resembles one. It's a member of the **lily** family. In late summer, each bulb produces two to six showy, goblet-shaped, leafless blossoms. The flowers can last for several weeks with ample water and cool temperatures. A grouping of bulbs will give an impressive show. The leaves come up in the spring, big and bold, deep green, and growing up to 6 inches high. After about six weeks, the leaves disappear and the plant goes dormant, disappearing from sight until it blooms. **Autumn crocus** is also known as **meadow saffron** and **magic lily**.

WATERING

Keep **caladiums, cannas, calla lilies, tuberoses,** and **peacock orchids** lightly moist. Don't let them dry out.

Refrain from watering **crown imperial.**

Keep **crocus** and other newly planted bulbs lightly moist until the ground freezes.

 # FERTILIZING

Cathy recommends that you foliar feed **caladiums, calla lilies,** and **cannas** monthly with a solution of kelp or fish emulsion (following package instructions).

When **gladiolus** flower spikes reach one-third of their height, apply a high potash fertilizer (following package instructions) every 10 days until they finish flowering.

Fertilize **lilies** monthly until the plants finish blooming.

PRUNING

Cut off faded **caladium** leaves.

Deadhead **cannas** to encourage new blooms.

PROBLEMS

Check **cannas** for any sign of fungal leaf spot. Cut off and destroy any suspect leaves.

SEPTEMBER
Bulbs, Corms, Rhizomes, & Tubers

 PLANNING

Sometimes planning does not involve what you're putting in the garden but rather what you're taking out of it and giving to friends and neighbors. What could be nicer than a pretty pot full of bulbs in bloom as a holiday gift? Cathy thought it would be easy. She got the bulbs and counted up the number of weeks they had to be kept cold. She figured on 10 weeks as a minimum, added on another three weeks for them to come into flower and came up with 13 weeks before hoping to see a flower. It was early October, but couldn't rely on **crocus** blooms before New Year's. **Paper-whites** weren't the answer: Cathy planted them the day before Thanksgiving, and by Christmas they had all finished blooming.

The solution: Give the bulbs **before** they bloom.

The recipient enjoys the anticipation and the crocus flowers.

Present **amaryllis** after foliage growth or flower stalk is about 3 inches high.

Give **paper-whites** a week or two after they are planted.

With every bulb gift, include a pretty card with instructions for its care.

Forced bulbs make relatively inexpensive gifts that give the impression of costing much more. Often the recipient will return the pot with a request to "Fill it up" again next year. Cathy could not ask for a nicer compliment for her gift.

 PLANTING

You will know when the **crown imperial** bulbs arrive by their scent, alternatively described as skunky or fox-like. That should be enough impetus to get them in the ground quickly. Plant the bulbs 5 to 6 inches deep and 8 inches apart in well-drained, alkaline, deep, sandy loam enriched with organic matter in a lightly shaded, sheltered area. The leaves have the same aroma as the bulbs, so you might not want to put crown imperial next to the bedroom window or adjacent to an outdoor dining area. Crown imperial does not take well to being moved, so take some time to choose their location before you plant them. Water them deeply after planting; keep the soil lightly moist until the ground freezes.

For **hyacinths,** choose a nice spot in full sun to light shade that has fast-draining, rich soil. Plant clusters of three to five bulbs 4 to 6 inches deep and 4 to 8 inches apart. Water deeply.

Summer snowflake shows off best when planted in drifts of 11 or more. Interplant it with its smaller, earlier-blooming relative: snowdrops.

Plant **tulips** in humus-rich, sandy, well-drained soil in an area where they will get at least five or six hours a day; full sun is preferable. Dig the soil to a depth of 10 to 12 inches and work in Bulb Booster or other bulb food. If your soil is very clayey, dig an inch deeper and add an inch of builder's sand. Set the bulbs 10 to 12 inches deep and 4 to 8 inches apart, depending on size and variety. After flowering, remove the head of the tulip but allow the stem and foliage to die back naturally. Tulips perform best their first year; many gardeners treat them as annuals, discarding the plants after they finish blooming. Planting tulips this deep gives them a much better chance of coming back and blooming for several years at least. Early-flowering species tulips come back year after year planted at a depth of 6 to 8 inches.

Plant **Siberian squill, glory-of-the-snow, crocus,** and **snowdrops** once you get the bulbs. They grow happily in rich, well-drained, sandy soil in full sun or partial shade. Space bulbs 3 to 4 inches apart and 3 inches deep in clumps of seven to 11. Leave the bulbs undisturbed and they will soon naturalize.

Sometimes planning does not involve what you're putting in the garden but rather what you're taking out of it and giving to friends and neighbors.

 # WATERING

Keep **caladiums, cannas,** and **peacock orchids** lightly moist. Don't let them dry out.

Spray **caladium** leaves frequently during hot, dry weather.

Keep newly planted **crocus** lightly moist until the ground freezes.

 # FERTILIZING

If weather is moderate, foliar feed **caladiums** and **cannas** once with a solution of kelp or fish emulsion (following package instructions).

Did You Know?

Overwintering Gladiolus

Since **gladiolus** isn't hardy, you have the choice of treating it as an annual and throwing it out after it blooms or saving it for next year.

When the leaves start to wither, lift the corms.

Cut the stem close to the corm.

Roll the corm in sulfur.

Place the corms on a screen in a well-ventilated area for several weeks to dry.

Separate the new corms from the old, discarding the old ones and any that show signs of rot.

Nest the corms in sawdust or shredded paper if you want, or hang them in a netted onion or potato bag or in pantyhose. Store in a cool, dry area.

This also works for **peacock orchids**.

 # PRUNING

Cut off faded **caladium** leaves.

Carefully cut back **lily** stalks when the foliage has died back completely.

After frost blackens **canna** leaves, cut off the stems and leaves, and dig up the rhizomes. Store in barely moist peat moss in a cool (above freezing) place for the winter.

 # PROBLEMS

Inspect **daffodil, tulip,** and **hyacinth** bulbs for fungal infections—soft, greenish-blue, or black areas. Throw out any suspicious bulbs.

 PLANNING

Review the chart to the right to prepare for bulb forcing.

PLANTING

The following instructions are general guide to forcing spring-blooming bulbs. Bulbs that need special attention are described in other listings.

Fill a pot 3/4 full with potting soil.

Place the bulbs 1/2 inch apart with pointed ends up.

Gently press the bulbs into the soil so that the tips of the bulbs are level with the rim of the pot.

Once the bulbs are positioned, fill the pots with soil to within 1/4 to 1/2 inch of the rim, leaving the tips of the bulbs exposed.

Water gently until soil is evenly moist.

Put the bulbs in a cool, dark place to grow roots for a minimum of eight weeks, averaging 12 to 15 weeks (see the chart above). The best places for the big chill are the refrigerator (not the crisper drawer) or outdoors. Heat interferes with the forcing process, so any outdoor storage space has to stay between 35 and 50 degrees Fahrenheit.

Did You Know?

Chilling Bulbs for Forcing

Name	Weeks of Cold	Weeks to Bloom	No. Bulbs in 6 In. Pot
Amaryllis	None	6 – 8	1
Crocus	15	2	8 – 12
Daffodil	15 – 17	2 – 3	3 – 5
Danford Iris	15	2 – 3	5 – 8
Glory-of-the-Snow	15	2 – 3	6 – 10
Grape Hyacinth	13 – 15	2 – 3	5 – 8
Hyacinth	(Pre-cooled)	10 – 12	3
Hyacinth	11 – 14	2 – 3	3
Netted Iris	15	2 – 3	5 – 8
Paper-white Narcissus	None	3 – 5	5 – 7
Puschkinia	15	2 – 3	8 – 10
Siberian Squill	12 – 15	2 – 3	8 – 10
Snowdrop	15	2	6 – 10
Tulip	14 – 20	2 – 3	5

Dig a 2-foot trench and line it with 6 inches of mulch or hay. Set the pots in the trench and cover them with 6 to 8 inches of chopped leaves, mulch, or hay. Top it with 3 to 4 inches of soil. Don't let the pots dry out.

Check the pots after eight weeks. If the bulbs stay in place when you try to wiggle them and shoots have begun to emerge from the bulb, gradually move the pots into the warmth and light. Start with a cool room and indirect sunlight. After a week, move the pots into full sun at 60 to 65 degrees Fahrenheit. Keep the soil lightly moist; within a month you'll be enjoying flowers.

Once the bulbs are in full bud, you can slow down or speed up the process by controlling the temperature: warmer temperatures make the flowers open faster, cooler temperature will make them last longer.

 # CARE

Mulch **lilies** and **hyacinths** with 3 inches of organic matter (leaf mold, chopped leaves, compost, well-rotted manure) as soon as the ground freezes.

After the first frost, carefully dig **caladium** tubers. Place them on a screen in a warm, dry, airy place for about a week to dry. Store them on a shallow tray in a warm, dry place.

After the ground freezes, mulch **tulips** with straw or hay.

In warmer areas of the Prairie Lands, when the leaves of potted **caladium** begin to droop, take the pots inside. Water sparingly until the leaves fall off. Store the pots in a warm place (about 55 or 65 degrees Fahrenheit).

Did You Know?

Paper-white Narcissus

Paper-white narcissus is native to Israel and the surrounding regions, where they grow outdoors, lightly perfuming the air with their scent. In our cold climate, we can only grow them indoors, forcing them into bloom.

Overwintering Dahlias. After frost kills **dahlia** foliage, carefully dig the tubers. Cut the stalk approximately 6 inches above the tuber. Allow tubers to dry thoroughly. Pack them carefully in dry sand, peat moss, or sawdust. Store in a cool (40 to 45 degrees Fahrenheit), dry place.

 # WATERING

Keep **crocus** and other newly planted bulbs lightly moist until the ground freezes.

 # FERTILIZING

No feeding necessary this month.

 # PRUNING

To overwinter **cannas:**

Wait until frost blackens the leaves.

Cut off the stems and leaves.

Dig up the rhizomes.

Store in barely moist peat moss in a cool (above freezing) place for winter.

PROBLEMS

If mold or rot has been a problem in the past, roll bulbs in sulfur before storing them for winter. Pack the bulbs so that they don't touch each other.

November

Bulbs, Corms, Rhizomes, & Tubers

 ## PLANNING

Make a list of the people to whom you want to give forced bulbs during the holiday season. If you haven't started enough pots of bulbs, there's still time to plant more.

 ## PLANTING

For an instant bulb gift or a beautiful blooming decoration for your house you can buy pre-planted, pre-cooled **crocus**. Make sure that the **crocus** are larger than the holes around the sides of the pot. Often the side holes of a crocus pot are planted, yet the top is not. Plant five to seven **crocus** in that space for an even more spectacular display. The pre-potted, pre-cooled **crocus** bulbs will open within two to three weeks. Simply water the bulbs three times a week. When the flowers start to open, keep the **crocus** pot in the coolest part of the room away from radiators or direct sun. You can prolong the bloom by moving the pot into a cool room at night. When the flowers fade, water bulbs only once every two weeks. When the weather warms in spring, remove the bulbs from the pot and plant outside. They will lie dormant during summer and winter, and then bloom again in the garden for your enjoyment the following spring.

 ## CARE

Put a 2- to 4-inch layer of mulch over fall-planted bulbs after the ground starts to freeze. The mulch helps maintain a consistent soil temperature and keeps bulbs from being heaved out of the ground during winter's alternate spells of freezing and thawing.

 ## WATERING

Keep **crocus** and other fall-planted bulbs lightly moist until the ground freezes. Check moisture and water level on all the bulbs that are being forced.

 ## FERTILIZING

When the **amaryllis** starts to bloom, feed them with half-strength liquid fertilizer.

 ## PRUNING

Remove any faded flowers from forced plants.

 ## PROBLEMS

Check stored bulbs for any sign of rot or disease. Discard any that have rot or disease.

Put a 2- to 4-inch layer of mulch over fall-planted bulbs after the ground starts to freeze.

Did You Know?

Amaryllis

Amaryllis is the showiest of all bulbs that can keep growing for many years. Four flowers, 6 inches or more across, open atop a tall, hollow stem. I have grown **amaryllis** with stems nearly 4 feet tall—exceptional plants. Flower stems average about 2 feet and need support. The larger the bulb, the more flower stems it will put out.

Choose a pot no more than 2 inches larger in diameter than the bulb. Do not use a shallow bulb pan, **amaryllis** need depth for their roots.

Amaryllis tend to be top-heavy. If the bulb is large, put a stone or an inch or so of gravel at the bottom of the pot to keep it from tipping.

Fill the pot two-thirds full with a good potting soil.

Place the bulb on top of the soil; add soil to fill the pot. Half of the bulb should be above the soil level.

Place one stake on either side of the bulb. Make sure the stake goes down to the bottom of the pot. As it grows, use the stakes to stabilize the stem and keep it straight.

Water lightly.

To encourage root growth before flower emergence, give the plant bottom heat. Place the pot on a wet/dry heating pad set to low. Once the leaves emerge, remove the heating pad.

Water the **amaryllis** sparingly until growth begins, then increase water.

Apply a liquid fertilizer at half strength when the plant begins to flower.

After the flowers fade, cut back the flower stalk, taking care not to cut the leaves. Multiple stalks may appear simultaneously or may follow one another.

After the last frost, move the **amaryllis** out into the garden. Plant the entire pot in a sheltered spot with dappled sun.

DECEMBER

PLANNING

Dahlias should be a mainstay for every garden. Once planted, they are easy to grow, especially if you're content with a nice bushy plant and are not trying to grow giant, exhibition-size **dahlias.**

Since **dahlias** come in an array of colors, forms, and sizes, it's easy to find at least one for every garden. They range in size from small mum-like flowers to the 12-inch dinner plate varieties in almost every color of the rainbow (except for the ever-elusive blue) including exquisite bi- and tricolors. With several different kinds of **dahlias,** you can, depending on the weather, have blooms from July right up to the first frost.

PLANTING

Although Cathy always start growing **paper-whites** in water and gravel in October, those plantings end up as gifts. They are perfect last-minute hostess and holiday presents that give the impression that they were planned for the recipients. To overcome the post-holiday letdown, plant some **paper-whites** in soil for yourself. It is curious that **paper-whites** planted late in the season—even if purchased in December—come into flower in a much shorter time than **paper-whites** started in October. It's almost as

if they have an inner clock set for a specific time.

Plant the **paper-whites** in any kind of well-moistened potting soil with just the tip of the bulb showing above the soil surface.

Water well and keep the evenly moist.

Place the pot in a sunny window. Flowers will appear within four to six weeks.

When Cathy first started growing **paper-white**s as a child, the directions were to put the planted **paper-whites** in a dark place for six weeks. For her, out of sight is out of mind, so there were too many **paper-whites** that were desiccated by the time she remembered them. When she was diligent, the foliage was 6 or more inches high and almost white when she brought them into the light. The foliage was always weak and lanky. So, she tried growing **paper-whites** in the open; the results were much more rewarding. She's been growing them that way ever since.

It seems that people either love or hate **paper-whites.** Their fragrance is intense, especially indoors. 'Ziva' emits the mildest scent. I never keep **paper-whites** in the kitchen or dining room, as their perfume can overwhelm the great cooking smells.

CARE

Tie a colorful ribbon around the stems or foliage of all gift plants. It gives them a professional appearance and supports the foliage.

WATERING

Check all the bulbs you are forcing and water when necessary.

FERTILIZING

No feeding is necessary. Enjoy all the holiday goodies.

PRUNING

Clean up any plants you are giving away. If there is very loose skin on the **paper-whites,** remove it.

PROBLEMS

Check summer-blooming bulbs in storage for any sign of rot. If you do find rot in bulbs stored in sawdust or other material, examine all the bulbs carefully and feel for any soft spots. Discard the storage medium and replace it with fresh material.

CHAPTER THREE

Fruits

You don't need to have an orchard or even large yard to raise fruit for your household. It's as easy as planting fruit trees in place of ornamental trees, raspberries and currants in place of hedges, strawberries in place of ground cover, and grapes instead of ornamental vines on your arbor. Soon you will find yourself living in an attractive and edible landscape.

PLANNING

All good landscapes, even the edible ones, start with a plan. Sit down with your family, friends, and whomever will be sharing the work and harvest. Make a list of the fruits that they like to eat. Check on the space and growing conditions required by each one. Most fruits need full sun and moist, well-drained soil for best growth and productivity. Now look at your landscape plan. How much suitable growing space do you have available, and for what type of fruits? Consider using dwarf varieties for small locations. Espalier (pruning so they are flat) a fruit tree or two against a sunny wall. It can add interest to a bare wall, while producing fruit in a very small area. Or train **apples** or **pears** into Belgian fences. The pruning and training of the trees is not as difficult as it may appear; the result is a living and edible fence that also provides screening.

Check your list against your local Cooperative Extension Service's recommendations. This is the most up-to-date source of information on fruit varieties suited to your climate. Eliminate fruit that is not hardy or may be problematic to your area. Select the most pest- and disease-resistant varieties available.

Make note of any plants that need pollinators. This means you will need two different plants to ensure fruit production. Some fruits are particular and only accept pollen from certain varieties, while others are less particular. Make sure the two varieties bloom at the same time so they can lend each other a helping hand. Some plants are dioecious, which means they have male flowers on one tree and female flowers on another. Make sure you get one of each sex; otherwise you'll have lovely flowers but no fruit.

Once you have your list, start looking for sources for the plants. Very few nurseries, garden centers, or home stores carry a wide selection of fruit plants. Check out garden catalogs that carry or specialize in fruit plants. They offer the biggest selection and give you the best chance of finding the desired varieties. A time-saving tip: Google the plant name (including the specific variety, if there is one) on the Internet. You can readily find out who is selling it—and get the best price.

SOIL PREPARATION

A good harvest starts with proper soil preparation.

Small fruits, such as **raspberries** and **strawberries**, grow in small beds or planting areas.

1 Edge the bed with a shovel or edger.

2 Remove the existing grass and weeds with a shovel or sod cutter. You may choose to kill the grass with a total vegetation killer such as Roundup or Finale. In Melinda's

Fruits

experience, "In the long run, it's easier and safer for me to just dig the space." Wait four to seven days for the grass to die. Remove the dead sod. Check the label for replanting information. Or use one of these non-chemical methods to eliminate existing grass.

Cover the area with black plastic in fall to kill the weeds and grass. The soil will be ready to work in spring.

Cut the grass very short. Cover with several layers of newspaper and woodchips. Plant the **raspberries** and **strawberries** right through the mulch and buried turf.

Create a raised planting bed. Cover the short grass with several pieces of wet cardboard and one half inch of newspaper. Water, and then top it off with 6 to 8 inches of topsoil. You are ready to plant. The newspaper and grass eventually decompose.

3 Take a soil test to find out what if any sulfur, organic matter, or fertilizer you need to add. Most fruits prefer a soil pH of 6 to 6.5. Do not lime your soil unless the soil test recommends it. Much of the Prairie Lands has alkaline soil and you do not need to add lime. If anything, you may need to add sulfur to acidify the soil.

4 Follow soil test recommendations for fertilization.

5 Almost all soils benefit from additional organic matter. A 2- to 4-inch layer of organic matter worked into the top 12 inches of soil improves drainage in clay soils and allows sandy soils to retain moisture.

Plant tree fruits, such as **apples**, **pears**, **plums**, and **cherries,** in full sun and well-drained soil. Place trees on a southeast-facing slope if at all possible. Avoid hilltop locations where the winds can be damaging and fireblight, a deadly bacterial disease, is more likely to invade. Do not plant in low spots; they tend to be frost pockets in the spring and fall. A late spring frost can kill the flowers (needed for fruit to form) and an early fall frost can damage the harvest.

It is no longer recommended to amend the soil before planting any kind of tree or shrub. Plant them in the existing, native soil and let them adapt to their permanent growing conditions right away.

PLANTING

Plant fruit trees in spring for best results. Purchase trees as bare-root or container-grown plants. Most catalogs and a few nurseries carry bare-root plants. These trees cost less, but require more care and have a greater risk of failure. Container-grown fruits can be planted throughout the early part of the growing season.

If you are planting in fall, plant early so the roots are established before cold winter temperatures set in.

Check bare-root plants as soon as they arrive at your home. Unwrap the roots and make sure they are moist. Wet the roots and cover with moist peat moss or sawdust. Store in a cool, frost-free, partially shaded location.

Store container-grown plants in a protected location out of the wind. Keep the soil moist, but not soggy. Water thoroughly so that the excess water runs out of the drainage holes. Water again when the top 3 to 4 inches begin to dry.

Begin planting when the soil is workable and plants are available.

Fruits

Planting bare-root fruit trees:

1 Dig a hole at least two to three times wider than, but not deeper than, the container. Use your shovel to scrape and roughen the sides of the planting hole.

2 Soak the roots of bare-root trees for 1 to 2 hours in transplant solution (following label instructions). If their roots dried in transport or storage, soak for 2 to 4 hours.

3 Place the bare-root tree in the planting hole so that the graft is 2 to 3 inches above the soil line. Bury the graft union if non-hardy rootstocks are used. Check the plant label for specific guidelines.

4 Position the tree so that the roots spread away from the trunk. Cut off any broken or extremely long roots.

5 Fill the hole with the original soil removed from the planting hole. Water in with the transplant solution in which the roots soaked to help settle the soil and remove air pockets.

6 Prune thin, unbranched stems (whips) back to 30 to 45 inches tall. Remove only broken and damaged limbs on branched trees. Leave four or five evenly spaced branches on the stem. See February "Did You Know?" for more on pruning tree fruits.

7 Stake trees on dwarfing rootstocks at time of planting. Place a stake next to the tree trunk on the windward side. This way the wind will usually blow the tree away from, not into, the stake. Use fabric strips to secure the tree to the stake in a figure eight.

8 Mulch with a 2- to 3-inch layer of woodchips, compost, coffee grounds, or shredded bark. Keep the mulch away from the trunk. Cover at least the planting area with the mulch.

Planting container-grown fruit trees:

1 Dig a planting hole the same depth as the container and at least two to three times wider in diameter. Use your shovel to scrape and chop the sides. Roughening the inside of the hole encourages the roots to grow beyond the planting hole.

2 Cut the bottom off the pot. Set it in the hole so that the tree will be planted at the same depth it was growing in the pot. Plant deeper if the graft union is located above the pot and the rootstock is not reliably hardy. Check the label for specific planting directions.

3 Slice through the side of the container and peel away the pot. Use this technique to avoid damaging young plants that have not yet formed a tight rootball.

4 Slice through roots that encircle the pot. This helps potbound plants develop roots that will grow into the surrounding soil. Place the tree in the hole.

5 Fill the planting hole with the soil removed for planting. Water with transplant solution to help remove air pockets and settle the soil.

6 Apply a 2- to 3-inch layer of woodchips, compost, coffee grounds, or shredded bark over the planting hole. Pull the mulch an inch or more away from the tree trunk and extend it just beyond the edge of the planting area.

Planting Currants, Gooseberries, and Elderberry:

Plant these fruits in cool, moist locations. Grow them in full sun or partial shade with good air circulation. Avoid hot, dry, and poorly drained locations. You may have to hunt a bit to find a source for these plants. Surfing the internet speeds that up. Purchase one-year-old plants if possible.

Fruits

1 Plant dormant plants in the garden as soon as they arrive. Remove any broken stems and roots. Soak the roots of bare-root plants for 2 to 4 hours in transplant solution before planting.

2 Dig a planting hole slightly deeper and two to three times wider than the rootball. Set the plant in the hole so that the roots point outward and the lowest branch is even with the soil line.

3 Fill the hole with the soil removed from the planting hole. Water with the transplant solution in which the roots soaked to remove air pockets and settle the soil. Mulch the soil with woodchips, compost, coffee grounds, or shredded bark to keep roots cool and moist.

4 Space **currants** and **gooseberries** 3 to 4 feet apart within rows 6 to 8 feet apart.

5 Plant **elderberries** 7 to 8 feet apart within rows 10 to 12 feet apart.

Blueberries:

1 Grow hardy **blueberries** in full sun and moist, acidic soils. Avoid low areas or other frost pockets in the landscape. Grow **blueberries** in an area where you can easily cover the plants to protect the buds from late spring frosts.

2 Have your soil tested before amending the soil. Lower the pH of alkaline soils (found in much of the Prairie Lands) by adding sulfur or aluminum sulfate. Follow soil test recommendations before attempting to lower soil pH. See May "Planting" for details on amending the soil and planting **blueberries**.

Grapes:

1 Buy dormant, bare-root plants from quality garden catalogs or their sites on the Internet. Or check your local nurseries, garden centers, and home stores for two-year-old bare-root or container-grown plants.

2 Start your own **grapes** from hardwood cuttings taken in late winter. Or try layering a one-year-old cane. See May Vines and Groundcovers "Helpful Hints" for details on propagating **Grapes** and other small fruit by this method.

Handling Bare-root Grapes:

1 Store bare-root plants in a cool (non freezing), shaded location until they can be planted. Cover them with moist sawdust or peat moss to prevent the plants from drying.

2 Soak roots in transplant solution (following label instructions) for several hours (no longer) before planting.

3 Dig a hole larger than the roots. Roughen the sides of the planting hole. Cut any broken or extremely long roots. Spread the roots so that they extend away from the trunk. Plant at the same depth it was growing in the nursery. Fill with the soil removed from the planting hole. Water in with the transplant solution used to soak the roots to help the soil settle and eliminate air pockets.

Handling container-grown grape plants:

1 Dig the planting hole the same depth as, but two to three times wider than, the container. Use your shovel to roughen the sides of the planting hole.

2 Remove the bottom of the container and set the pot in the planting hole.

3 Slice the side of the pot and peel it away from the rootball. Use a knife to cut through any girdling roots.

Fruits

JANUARY · FEBRUARY · MARCH · APRIL · MAY · JUNE · JULY · AUGUST · SEPTEMBER · OCTOBER · NOVEMBER · DECEMBER

4 Backfill with existing soil. Water with transplant solution (following label instructions) to help settle the soil, remove air pockets, and stimulate root growth.

Strawberries:

1 Plant **strawberries** in early spring when the plants are available and the soil can be worked.

2 Store plants that arrive early in a cool, moist location. Either heel them in outdoors or store in a refrigerator until they can be planted in the garden.

3 Remove dried leaves and dead runner stems prior to planting. Dig a hole deep enough for the roots to hang straight down without hitting the bottom. Spread out the roots and fill the hole with soil.

4 Make sure the roots and the base of the crown (the point where stems join the roots) are covered with soil. Firm the soil around the planting and water in with transplant solution, following label instructions.

5 Space **strawberries** based on the training method you choose:

Remove the wrapping from plants to be heeled in. Dig a trench 6 to 8 inches deep in a cool, shaded location. Place plants 2 inches apart in the trench with the roots down. Fill the trench with soil. Water lightly. Plant the **strawberries** within several weeks.

Keep plants in the plastic shipping material if they are to be refrigerated. Do not moisten the plants prior to storage. Excess moisture causes disease and rot. Wrap dry roots with a moist paper towel if necessary. Store in the refrigerator for as long as six weeks. Keep **apples** and

pears out of the refrigerator as they give off ethylene gas which reduces storage life and plant quality.

Use the Matted Row System for lower maintenance. Plant **strawberries** 14 to 24 inches apart in rows 36 inches apart. Allow runners to develop and fill in, creating rows 12 to 15 inches wide.

Use the Hill System to maximize the harvest in small spaces. Plant **strawberries** in beds made of three rows. Space plants 12 inches apart within the bed. Leave 30 to 36 inches between each bed. Remove the runners as soon as they appear.

Raspberries:

1 Purchase disease-free plants from a reputable nursery or mail-order catalog. Store plants in a cool, moist location until planting. Check to make sure roots and the surrounding packing material stays moist.

2 Plant in spring as soon as the soil is workable and plants are available. Control weeds and prepare the soil by working several inches of organic matter into the top 6 to 12 inches of soil prior to planting.

3 Place the **raspberry** plants slightly deeper in the planting furrow or hole than they were growing in the nursery. This will prevent root exposure as the ground settles. Gently firm the soil, and water in with transplant solution, following label instructions.

4 Select a planting and training method that best suits you and your gardening location:

Consider using the Narrow Hedgerow Planting System. Plant **red raspberry** plants 2 to 3 feet apart in rows that are at least 6 feet apart. Space **black** and **purple raspberries** 4 feet apart in rows that are at least 8 feet apart. Confine new growth to 12- to 15-inch wide rows.

Fruits

Grow **raspberries** in clusters instead of rows when using the Hill System. Space individual plants 4 to 5 feet apart. Allow new shoots to develop within 1 foot of the original planting.

PRUNING

Many backyard fruits require special pruning and training systems to ensure a good harvest. Match the training system with the available space, landscape style, and your gardening goals.

Prune fruit trees every year to maintain the health and productivity of your trees. Maintain a strong, open framework that allows light to penetrate the canopy for flower and fruit production. Train young fruit trees to establish a strong framework. Prune so that the top of the tree is narrower than the bottom. This allows light to reach all parts of the tree. The more light, the greater the productivity.

Consider using a Central Leader Pruning System. It is good for the plant's health and productivity and is easy for you. See February "Did You Know?" for details.

Training Grapes:

Grow **grapes** on a fence, arbor, or a trellis constructed just for them. Select a support system strong enough to hold the weight of the plant and easy enough for you to prune and train the **grapes.**

Pruning and training **grapes** is not for the faint of heart. You must be aggressive with the pruners and remove a large amount of growth each spring. Insufficient pruning will result in excessive, but less productive growth. See March "Did You Know?" for details on training and pruning **grapes**.

Blueberries:

Prune **blueberries**, like all the other fruit, in spring—before growth begins. In the first two years, prune out only broken and dead branches. Once the plants are established—by the third spring—you will need to do a little more aggressive pruning.

Start by removing any damaged or broken branches. Remove some of the smaller, bushy growth and a few young shoots. Leave the most productive shoots. These are thick, hard, and 3 inches or longer. The more pruning you do, the smaller the crop will be, but the bigger the fruit.

Change your pruning strategy after the fifth year. Remove the weakest and oldest canes to ground level. Leave five or six of the healthiest, heavily budded stems intact. Prune back extremely tall canes to the height of the other branches.

Currants and Gooseberries:

Train **currants** and **gooseberries** the same way. Prune when the plants are dormant in late winter or early spring. You can remove winter damage and train the plant at the same time.

At Planting: Prune right after planting. Remove any broken or damaged stems. Prune remaining stems back to 8 to 10 inches.

2nd year: Remove all but six to eight of the healthiest canes. Always remove any canes lying on the ground or shading out the center of the plant.

3rd year: Leave three or four of last year's stems in place. Keep four or five of the new stems. Remove everything else.

4th year and beyond: Keep three or four each of the two- and three-year-old canes. Repeat this each spring.

Fruits

Elderberries:

Elderberries are easy to prune and train. Remove any broken or damaged stems at the time of planting. Prune the remaining stems back to 8 to 10 inches. The following year, in late winter or early spring, remove any weak or broken branches. Prune out any shoots rubbing other stems or growing toward the center of the plant. Leave six to eight healthy canes for the coming season. Repeat this each year in late winter or early spring.

Raspberries:

Train **raspberries** to keep the plants healthy and productive while making it easier for you to harvest. Proper timing is critical for fruit production.

The Hill System: Place a wooden or metal stake at the center of each hill. Allow canes to develop within 1 foot of the stake. Loosely tie the canes to the stake after pruning.

The Narrow Hedgerow System: Use a trellis made of sturdy posts and wire to keep the **raspberries** within bounds. Place posts every 20 to 30 feet for adequate support. Prune old and new growth to maintain narrow rows that are 12 to 15 inches wide.

summer-bearing red raspberries produce their fruit on second-year growth (floricanes). **fall-bearing raspberries** produce the fall crop on new growth (primocanes) and a summer crop on these same canes the following summer.

Consider planting both **summer**- and **fall-bearing raspberries**. Sacrifice the summer crop on the **fall-bearing** plants to reduce maintenance and increase fall production. You will still get two crops (summer and fall) of **raspberries**—just from separate plantings.

See February and July "Pruning" for more specifics on pruning **raspberries**.

WATERING

Young trees need regular watering to establish a healthy root system. Give new plants 1 to 2 inches of water (3 to 5 gallons per tree) each week. Water whenever the top 4 to 6 inches of soil start to dry. Water the planting hole and surrounding soil. This will encourage a larger, more drought-tolerant root system.

Give established plants the same amount of water, just less frequently. Their larger root system is able to seek out and find more available water. Apply 1 inch of water to the root zone.

Water more frequently in hot weather and less often in cooler periods. Check sandy soils twice a week and clay soils every seven to ten days. Water when the top 6 inches begin to dry.

Make sure small fruits receive sufficient moisture throughout the season. Water is necessary for flower bud development, fruit set, and fruit development on **raspberries**, **strawberries**, and other small fruits. Continue watering fruit during dry spells, even after the harvest. This will ensure a healthier, hardier, more productive plant for next season.

Small fruits generally need 1 inch of water each week. Adjust watering based on rainfall. Water plants growing in clay soils once a week. Provide the needed water in two applications to plants growing in sandy soils.

Fruits

Mulch the soil to conserve moisture, reduce weeds, and moderate soil temperature. Use some type of organic mulch that will also help improve the soil as it decomposes.

Use woodchips, shredded bark, or shredded leaves for tree fruits, **raspberries**, and other shrub-type fruits. Use shredded leaves for **strawberries**. These create fewer problems when renovating the plantings.

When using shredded leaves and other fine mulches, you only need to put down a thin layer (1 to 2 inches) of mulch. Use a thicker layer (3 to 4 inches) of woodchips and other coarse mulches.

FERTILIZATION

Use your soil test as a guide. Provide fruit plants with needed fertilizer to improve health and increase fruit production. Overfertilization can lead to little or no fruit and increase the risk of fireblight disease. Follow these guidelines if soil test information is not available.

SMALL FRUIT FERTILIZATION

Blueberries: Sprinkle fertilizer on the ground in a 12- to 18-inch circle around each plant.

Planting year: 2 tablespoons of ammonium sulfate (21-0-0) applied two to four weeks after planting.

2nd year: $1/4$ cup of ammonium sulfate (21-0-0) per plant as growth begins or blooms appear.

3rd and 4th years: $3/8$ cup of ammonium sulfate per plant as growth begins.

5th year and beyond: $1/2$ cup of ammonium sulfate per plant as growth begins.

currants, **gooseberries**, **elderberries**, and other bush fruits, such as **viburnums** and **juneberries**: Sprinkle fertilizer on the ground in an 18-inch circle around each plant.

Planting year: 2 tablespoons of ammonium nitrate (33-0-0) per plant, applied three to four weeks after planting.

2nd year: $1/4$ cup ammonium nitrate per plant in the spring before new growth appears.

3rd year: $3/8$ cup of ammonium nitrate in spring before new growth begins.

4th year: $1/2$ cup ammonium nitrate in spring before new growth begins.

5th year and beyond: $2/3$ cup ammonium nitrate per plant in spring before new growth begins.

Or use organic matter—well-rotted manure, compost, or leaf mold—instead of the fertilizer. Spread 10 pounds of the organic matter around each plant. Keep it 1 foot away from the plant.

Grapes: Sprinkle fertilizer on the ground in an 18-inch circle around each plant.

Planting year: Apply 2 tablespoons ammonium nitrate two to three weeks after planting, or use 20 pounds of aged manure applied between 1 and 4 feet from the trunk.

2nd year: $1/4$ cup ammonium nitrate per plant before the buds swell.

3rd year: $1/4$ to $2/3$ cup ammonium nitrate plus 1 tablespoon of a high potassium fertilizer (0-0-60) or (0-0-50) per plant before the buds break.

Reduce the amount of nitrogen fertilizer applied if you get excessive vine growth. Apply half the recommended rate before growth begins and the remainder in mid-June if the leaves sprout early and experience frost damage.

Raspberries: Apply fertilizer alongside all the plants in the row or sprinkled in an 18-inch circle around individual plants grown in the Hill System.

Fruits

Planting year: Apply 1 to 1 1/2 pounds (2 to 3 cups) of ammonium nitrate (33-0-0) per 100 feet, or 1/4 cup per plant in the Hill System, after the plants are established (mid- to late-June).

Bearing years: Apply 3/4 pound (1 cup) of ammonium nitrate (33-0-0) per 100 feet or 1/4 cup per plant before growth begins and again in late May or early June.

Or use 150 pounds of well-rotted cow manure or compost per 100 feet before growth begins in spring. Spread the manure along the row, keeping it 1 foot away from the plants.

June-bearing Strawberries:

Planting year: 3/4 to 1 1/2 pounds (1/2 to 1 cup) ammonium nitrate (33-0-0) per 100 feet of row, or 1 teaspoon of ammonium nitrate per plant, when runners begin to form (mid-June). Apply the same amount of fertilizer in early August.

Bearing years: 3/4 pound or 1 cup of 33-0-0 per 100 feet of row, after harvest and again in early August.

Everbearing Strawberries:

Planting year: 1 teaspoon of ammonium nitrate per plant about 3 weeks after planting and again in mid-July.

Bearing years: Fertilize every month they flower and fruit.

TREE FRUIT FERTILIZATION

Apples, **pears**, **peaches**, **plums**, and **cherries** need a minimal amount of fertilizer to stay healthy and productive. Use the plant's yearly growth as your guide. Young fruit trees typically grow 10 to 20 inches each year. Bearing trees grow 8 to 12 inches. Do not fertilize in spring if the previous season's growth is longer than normal. Fertilize in spring before growth begins, only if growth is at or less than the normal rate.

Apply 1 ounce of actual nitrogen per each year of tree age. This is equal to 3 ounces (6 tablespoons) of ammonium nitrate (34-0-0) or 10 ounces (about 1 cup) of a 10 percent commercial fertilizer. Multiply the age of the tree (years in the ground at this location) times the amount of fertilizer per year to get the total amount needed. Never exceed 1 pound of actual nitrogen per tree per year, no matter how old. Sprinkle the needed fertilizer over the soil under the tree canopy.

Cut this rate in half for **pear** and other fruit trees at high risk for fireblight disease. Spring fertilization encourages lush growth that is more susceptible to this disease.

PESTS

Animals are by far the biggest pest problem. Birds, squirrels, deer, rabbits, and voles all want to share in the harvest, or at least nibble on the plant. Barriers, repellents, and fencing can help give you an edge over the wildlife. Start controls before you have to chase the animals out of their fine dining location—your backyard! Vary tactics to keep them guessing and leery of moving in. See August and October "Did You Know?" for more details on keeping animals at bay.

Fruits

Apples: (Zones 3 to 5; needs pollinator; Use **'Malling M26'**, **'M7'**, or **'M7A'** dwarf rootstock for shorter trees. **'Cortland'** has good quality, tender flesh and ripens in late August. **'Empire'** is a high-quality **'McIntosh'** with firm flesh that ripens in early October. **'McIntosh'** is the one of the most popular apples; it ripens in mid-September. Try disease-resistant types, such as **'Macfree'** and **'Novamac'**. **'NovaEasygro'** is a new disease-resistant fall apple with good quality; it ripens in late September. **'Spartan'** has good quality fruit on a medium-sized tree; it ripens late September to October.

Apricot: (Zones 4 to 7; winter hardy—the fruit is often lost to spring frost; needs pollinator) The **'Harcot'** has sweet, firm flesh and is self-fruitful; it ripens in mid-July. **'Moongold'** has a tough skin; it is good for processing or desserts. It ripens in mid-July. **'Sungold'** has tender skin and a sweet, mild flavor. It ripens in mid- to late July.

Blueberries: (Zones 3 to 7; self-fruitful cultivars need pollinator) **'Northcountry'** (self-fruitful) has sky-blue fruit on a small plant.

'St. Cloud' (self-fruitful) is a Minnesota introduction; it is the least hardy but has superior fruit. **'Northbluedark'** blue fruit has a good fall color, is self-fruitful, and ripens in July. **'North Sky'** is a small, 10- to 20-inch plant with medium sky-blue fruit, a good fall color, and better winter hardiness. It is self-fruitful. **'Friendship'** has sky-blue fruit that ripens in July to August; it is self-fruitful.

Cherries, Sour: (Zones 3 to 7; self-fruitful) **'Montmorency'** is the standard tart cherry; it is moderate quality and ripens in mid-July. **'North Star'** is the hardiest with good quality fruit and leaf spot resistance; it ripens in mid-July. **'Meteor'** is very hardy, has large red fruit with yellow flesh, and resists leaf spot; harvest in late July.

Currants: (Zones 3 to 7; self-fruitful) **'Wilder'** is vigorous with red fruit; harvest begins in early July. **'Red Lake'** is hardy and vigorous, producing large red fruit with mild flavor.

Elderberry: (Zones 3 to 8; self-fruitful) **'Adams'** has large fruit and vigorous growth; it ripens in early August. **'York'** is more productive than **'Adams'** and has large, sweet fruit and an attractive plant; it ripens in mid to late August.

Gooseberries: (Zones 3 to 7; self-fruitful) **'Downing'** is hardy and productive with good quality, pale green fruit. **'Poorman'** is hardy, less thorny, and produces red fruit. **'Pixwell'** is hardy and moderately productive with pink, mild-flavored fruit.

Grapes: (Zones 3 to 7; self-fruitful) **'Valiant'** is a medium-sized, tart blue grape; it is hardy and ripens in mid-August. **'Beta'** has small, blue, tart fruit; it also ripens in mid-August. **'Fredonia'** is a good quality **Grape** for fresh use or for preserves; it is hardy and productive and ripens in early September. **'Edelweiss'** is a **'White Swenson'** with good flavor for fresh use; it is ready in early September. **'Red Swenson'** produces red, high-quality fruit; it ripens in mid- to late September.

Fruits

Peaches: (Zones 4 to 8; self-fruitful) Peach crops are often lost to the spring frost, and the trees are short-lived, but nothing beats the sweet flavor of a sun-warmed peach picked right off the tree. Plant every three years to ensure a replacement for dying plants. **'Reliance'** is one of the hardiest.

Pears: (Zones 3 to 7; needs pollinator) **'Parker'** is a good quality, but poor keeper; it ripens in mid-August. **'Gourmet'** is a very hardy dessert pear with crisp, juicy fruit; it ripens in mid-September. **'Luscious'** is sweeter than **'Bartlett'** and hardy; it ripens in late September.

Plums: (Zones 3 to 8; some self-fruitful) **'Amount Royal'** is a good quality, blue plum for Zones 4 and 5; it is self-fruitful and ripens in early September. **'Stanley'** is a late-blooming, heavy producer that is sweet and moderately hardy. It is self-fruitful; plant with **'Amount Royal'** for a better yield. **'Underwood'** is a good quality, red, round plum; it is hardy, needs a pollinator, and ripens in mid-August. **'Pipestone'** is very large, red plum; it is very hardy, needs a pollinator, and ripens mid-August. **'Alderman'** is a new introduction from the University of Minnesota. It has burgundy-red fruit of excellent quality, needs a pollinator, and ripens in late August. **'Superior'** is an excellent quality red plum; it is moderately hardy, needs a pollinator, and ripens in late August. **'Ocala'** and **'Atoka'** are red plum pollinators.

Red Raspberries, Summer-bearing: (Zones 3 to 7; self-fruitful) **'Boyne'** is vigorous and hardy with good quality fruit; it ripens in late June. **'Reveille'** has a very good flavor, tolerates fluctuating spring temperatures, and is very winter hardy. **'Nordic'** fruit is superior to **'Boyne'**, has fewer thorns, and greater disease resistance. It is a cold hardy cultivar from Minnesota. **'Latham'** is hardy and productive with a mild flavor.

Red Raspberries, Fall-bearing: (best in Zones 4 to 7; self-fruitful) **'Redwing'** is a newer variety from Minnesota; it ripens in mid-August. **'Fallgold'** is a yellow-fruited cultivar with good winter hardiness; it ripens in late August.

Strawberries, June-bearing: (Zones 3 to 8; self-fruitful) **'Earliglow'** is an early season berry with good flavor and some disease resistance. **'Honeoye'** is very productive and very hardy. **'Kent'** produces a lot of large fruit with a mild flavor. **'Sparkle'** is a high-quality, tasty berry and very hardy.

Strawberries, Everbearing: (Zones 3 to 8; self-fruitful) **'Ogallala'** produces large quantities of soft fruit on vigorous, hardy, and drought-tolerant plants. **'Ozark Beauty'** has good flavor, is winter hardy, and has some disease resistance.

Strawberries, Day-neutral: (produces crops midsummer and fall): (Zones 3 to 8; self-fruitful) **'Tribute'** has bright red, firm fruit and some disease resistance. **'Tristar'** has sweet, firm fruit and works well in hanging baskets.

JANUARY
Fruits

 PLANNING

The holidays are over, and tight clothes signal that it is time to start eating healthy. What better way to make this prospect appealing than to grow your own healthy fruit?

Break out the landscape plan and start looking for areas to add some fruit trees, a row of **raspberries**, or a patch of **strawberries**. You do not need a lot of space, just some sunlight and creative planning. If you have lost a tree or shrub, or there are ones that are not performing well, replace them with fruits.

Start gathering catalogs for planting ideas and potential plant sources. Check with your local botanical garden or county Cooperative Extension Service for addresses.

 PLANTING

The ground is frozen and most likely covered with snow. Get your planting tools ready for the season. Do not use shovel, trowels, and other tools. Make sure they are clean, oiled, and sharp.

Use a wire brush to knock off any soil. Follow this with steel wool or medium-grit sandpaper to remove any rust that may have collected.

Sharpen the edges with a metal file. Sharp shovels, hoes, and trowels make digging and planting easier and less tiring. Rub in a few drops of oil to help prevent rust.

 CARE

Check winter mulches on **strawberries**. Replace any that were dislodged in bad weather. Can't see the mulch for the snow? That's great. Snow is the best insulation available. No snow and no mulch? Get busy. Find some straw or evergreen branches. Cover plantings to protect the overwintering flower buds and prevent frost heaving.

 WATERING

Do not water. Check the landscape and fruit plantings for flooded areas and ice. Make a note of these problem areas in your journal and on your landscape plan. These areas are more likely to be damaged or die over winter. Evaluate landscape changes that can fix these

problems. It may be as easy as moving a downspout or sump pump discharge. Or you may need to move the plants or raise the planting beds if the water cannot be redirected.

 FERTILIZING

Check the yearly growth on tree fruits, such as **apples**, **pears**, **plums**, and **cherries**. Start at the tip of the branch and trace it back to the terminal bud scale scars. These ridges encircle the stem and mark one year's growth. Young fruit trees typically grow 10 to 20 inches each year. Bearing trees grow 8 to 12 inches. Stunted plants will benefit from a spring application of fertilizer. Make a note not to fertilize those that are growing more than normal. Overfertilization can stimulate stem and leaf growth, prevent fruiting, and increase the risk of disease.

 PRUNING

Remove hazardous or storm-damaged branches. Save major pruning for late winter when you can correct winter damage, adjust for animal feeding, and do structural pruning all at one time.

PROBLEMS

Check stems of **plums**, **cherries**, and other stone fruits for black knot cankers. The mature canker is a black, bumpy growth on the stem. The immature canker looks like an abnormal swelling of the branch. Prune out any mature and immature cankers you see. Discard—don't compost—the prunings. Prune 9 inches below the canker and disinfect your tools between cuts. Use rubbing alcohol or a solution of one part bleach to nine parts water.

Look for tent caterpillar, gypsy moth, and other egg masses throughout winter. Tent caterpillars eggs look like a glob of mud stuck on the branch. Prune out or smash the eggs. This will prevent feeding damage caused by these wormlike insects in May. Gypsy moth egg masses are yellow to beige. Scrape these egg masses off tree trunk, and destroy.

Look for signs of animal damage. Droppings, tracks, and feeding damage are clues you need to address the problem. Use repellents to keep deer and rabbits away. Reapply after bad weather or as recommended by the label directions.

Did You Know?

Consider some nontraditional fruit plants for the landscape. Many of the plants grown for their beauty also produce edible fruit.

Juneberry or **Serviceberry** (*Amelanchier* spp.) produces tasty blueberry-like fruit that birds and people enjoy. Their nutty blueberry flavor is good fresh from the tree or baked in a pie. Melinda will never forget climbing over her trash container to beat the birds to a handful of **Juneberries**. All **Juneberries** are edible, but some species and cultivars produce larger fruit. **Saskatoon Serviceberry** (*Amelanchier alnifolia*) and its cultivars, 'Honeywood', 'Smokey', 'Northline', 'Parkwood', 'Pembina', and 'Theissen' produce large, tasty fruit and are hardy in Zones 4 and 5. **Allegheny Serviceberry** (*Amelanchier laevis*), another North American native, produces large ($3/8$-inch), sweet fruit on trees hardy to Zones 4 and 5.

Cornelian Cherry Dogwood (*Cornus mas*), hardy in Zones 4 and 5, has bright red fruit in July. It is used for syrups, pies, and preserves. Both Melinda and Cathy have eaten a few right off the plant. We both concur that one or two were tasty, but to eat more than a few fruit, we needed a little sugar to improve the taste.

Hardy Kiwi (*Actinidia arguta*) became popular soon after the tropical Kiwi fruits were a hit at the grocery stores. These Asian introductions produce small grape-size fruit, but are hardier than the tropical types. The small fruits are sweet and high in vitamin C—and you don't need to peel them. You need a male and female plant, with a few exceptions, to produce a crop of fruit. Rated hardy for Zones 3 to 5, give them a little winter protection the first few years. Plant in a sheltered location and protect the trunks in Zones 4 and 5. The entire plant may need protection in Zone 3. Or try the more ornamental **Arctic Beauty Kiwi** (*Actinidia kolomikta* 'Arctic Beauty'). This plant produces beautiful green leaves with cream and pink blotches. The male is more colorful, but you will need a female as well to get fruit.

Make sure all animal fencing is still in place and working. Add an extra section of hardware cloth to areas buried in snow. The 4-foot rabbit fencing will do no good if half of it is buried in snow. An extra section will help reduce rabbit damage.

FEBRUARY

 PLANNING

So, you filled every possible planting location in your landscape? Consider growing **strawberries** and **dwarf apples** in containers.

 PLANTING

It is still too early to plant. Look through your potting supplies and locate suitable containers for planting **strawberries** and **dwarf apples**. These plants can be ornamental as well as fun to eat. You will need to find a place (an unheated garage or enclosed porch) to overwinter them.

 CARE

Check on any potted fruit plants you have stored for winter. Make sure the temperatures are cold enough to keep them dormant. Temperatures should be near freezing. Check on mulch or other insulation used to keep the roots from freezing. Adjust the location and winter protection as needed.

 WATERING

Water container plants overwintered in an unheated garage or porch. Water thoroughly anytime the soil thaws and the top 4 to 6 inches are dry. No need to water outdoor plants.

 FERTILIZING

Do not fertilize frozen soil. The plants cannot use the fertilizer and it washes off the soil, into the sewer, and pollutes our waterways.

 PRUNING

Start thinning and pruning **red raspberry** plantings when the snow begins to recede. Starting now until the time growth begins, you can prune any plantings that you ignored last summer. See the general information in this chapter's introduction and July's "Pruning."

Start with **summer** and **everbearing raspberry** crops. Remove all the older canes that bore fruit that summer. Cut these back to ground level. Thin the plantings to three to four canes per foot or six to eight canes per hill. Cut back long canes and side shots. Remove no more than one-fourth of the total height. The more you prune, the smaller the harvest.

Now prune your **fall-bearing red raspberries**. See November "Pruning" for details.

 PROBLEMS

Keep monitoring for animal damage. See August "Did You Know?"for more control suggestions.

Apply dormant oil, such as Volck, All Seasons, or lime sulfur, to control mites, scale, and other overwintering insects. Only apply dormant oils when the temperature will be above 40 degrees Fahrenheit when you spray as well as for the following 12 hours. The January thaw is a good time to make this application.

Watch for cankers (sunken, discolored areas) on stems. Prune 9 to 12 inches below the canker. Discard or destroy the infected branch. Disinfect tools between cuts to prevent spreading the disease to healthy tissue. Use rubbing alcohol or a solution of one part bleach to nine parts water as a disinfectant.

Continue checking for egg masses of tent caterpillar and gypsy moths. See January "Pests" for details.

Check on any potted fruit plants you have stored for winter. Make sure the temperatures are cold enough to keep them dormant.

Did You Know?

Training Your Fruit Tree

Take some time now and go over the training method for tree fruits. It is easier to read and study the information in a warm house than trying to remember when you are standing in front of the tree, cold wind blowing, and saw in hand.

Consider training your tree fruits in the Central Leader System. It is easy for you and good for the tree. Follow this step-by-step process:

At planting: Prune whips (thin, unbranched stems) back to 30 or 45 inches at planting. Do minimal pruning on branched trees. Remove only the damaged or broken branches at this time.

1st spring after planting: Prune in late winter or early spring before growth begins. Evaluate the tree and branching structure. Look for evenly spaced branches with wide crotch angles (angle between branch and trunk). Leave four to five of the strongest and most evenly spaced branches with the lowest being 24 to 36 inches above the ground. These branches should be evenly spaced around the trunk and located within 18 inches of the lowest branch. Prune the other branches back to the branch bark collar.

See the Trees chapter for more information on pruning.

2nd and 3rd years: Remove broken and damaged branches each spring before growth begins. Remove suckers (shoots that arise at the base of the tree) just below ground level. Prune off watersprouts (branches that grow straight up from scaffold branches) that interfere with growth and fruit development. Remove any drooping, crossing, rubbing, and parallel branches. Remove branches back to the point where they join another branch. Prune flush with the branch bark collar (the swollen area at the base of the branch).

3rd or 4th year: Select another set of scaffold branches 24 inches above the first. This will allow light to reach the first set of scaffold branches. Keep the upper tier of scaffolds shorter than the bottom set, allowing light to reach all parts of the tree. Spurs (the short fruiting stems) will begin to form along the branches.

5th year and beyond: Maintain the leader as the tallest branch. Prune back any side branches that are starting to reach the height of the leader. Cut the tip of the branch back to a side branch. Slow down tree growth once it reaches the desired height. Most gardeners like to keep dwarf trees 8 to 10 feet tall and semi-dwarf trees 12 to 16 feet tall. Prune the tip of the leader back to a weak side branch to slow upward growth. Repeat yearly as needed.

Yearly: Remove watersprouts, suckers, broken, and damaged branches. Watch for and prune out crossing and parallel branches that will eventually rub. Remove all inward- and downward-facing spurs and branches. Do the heaviest pruning just before the bearing season on alternate-bearing **apples** (those that fruit well every other year).

MARCH
Fruits

 ## PLANNING

Call or visit your local county Cooperative Extension Service. Ask to see a list of their fruit publications. They have many excellent publications that can provide more detail and pictures than we can in this chapter. Or seek out their Website. You can view many of the publications and print many useful tips on selection, planting, care, and harvest.

 ## PLANTING

Let the weather and plant availability be your guide. Some years, those of us in the southern regions of the Prairie Lands can begin planting dormant tree fruits and **raspberries** this month. Other years, we may still be waiting for the snow to melt. Prepare a storage area for any early arrivals that cannot be planted right away. Find a cool (not freezing) location. An unheated garage, enclosed porch, or root cellar would work. See the "Planting" section in the chapter introduction for specifics.

 ## CARE

Take a walk around the landscape. Clean up any debris that may have collected over winter. Check the base of trees for signs of vole and rabbit damage. This may influence your plant order. You are likely to need extra replacement plants after a bad winter.

 ## WATERING

Water overwintered container plants whenever the soil is thawed and the top 4 to 6 inches are dry. Water thoroughly so that the excess runs out the bottom.

Keep the roots moist of any bare-root plants you have in storage. Pack roots in moist sawdust or peat moss to help retain moisture.

 ## FERTILIZING

Start fertilizing at the end of this month or in early April— after the ground thaws and before growth begins. This is usually the best time to fertilize most fruit trees and berries. See the "Fertilization" sections in the chapter introduction for specific recommendations.

 ## PRUNING

Continue pruning. This will be one of the busiest times of the year for you and your pruning tools.

Finish pruning and thinning **red raspberries** if this hasn't already been done. See February "Pruning" for specifics.

Continue pruning and training young fruit trees. Remove broken, crossed, and damaged branches on older trees. Remove suckers and watersprouts on both young and old trees. See February "Did You Know?" for year-by-year pruning guidelines.

Don't forget your **currants**, **gooseberries**, **elderberries**, and **blueberries**. They benefit from yearly pruning. Remove the weakest and any damaged branches. See the "Pruning" section of the chapter introduction for specific guidelines.

Sharpen your tools and contact the crafty grapevine wreath makers in your area. It is time to prune the **grapes.** Be aggressive and you'll be rewarded with a large harvest.

Start fertilizing at the end of this month or in early April—
after the ground thaws and before growth begins.
This is usually the best time to fertilize most fruit trees and berries.

 PROBLEMS

Continue looking for egg masses of tent caterpillar and gypsy moth. Look for mudlike globs (tent caterpillars) on stems and branches. Prune out the egg mass and discard the stem or smash the eggs with your hand. Check the trunks and major branches for the yellow to beige, downy egg masses of gypsy moth. Remove and destroy these as well.

Prune out cankered (sunken, discolored areas) or oozing (bacterial gummosis) stems. Make your cut 9 to 12 inches below the damage. Disinfect tools between cuts with rubbing alcohol or a solution of one part bleach to nine parts water.

Check **plums**, **cherries**, and other stone fruits for black knot. This fungal disease causes stems to swell and develop black lumpy growths. Prune out the old black knots and the new swollen stems. Finish removing the knots by April 1st to prevent the release of spores and reduce future infections.

Did You Know?

Pruning Grapes

Late March is the time to start training and pruning **grapes**. Train your plants over an arbor, across a fence, or on a trellis constructed for this purpose.

Select a training system for your **grapes**. The Four-cane Kniffen System is one of the most popular, although some of the newer systems allow more sunlight to reach the plants.

At planting: Start training your **grapes** now. Cut the stem back leaving only two buds above the soil. These two buds will produce new stems and leaves the first summer. Secure the trunk to the trellis.

2nd year: Get out the pruning equipment in late March. Select one or two straight stems to be your permanent trunk. Remove other stems back to the main trunk.

3rd year: Select the four strongest and best placed side branches in late March. Attach these to the trellis. Cut these side branches back to 8 to 12 buds each. These will be the fruiting canes that produce this season's harvest. Select secondary sideshoots close to each of the first ones selected. Prune these back to two buds. These are the renewal spurs that will be next year's fruiting canes. Prune off all other growth.

4th year and beyond: Remove last year's fruiting canes. Replace them with the renewal spurs. Cut the new fruiting canes back to 8 to 12 buds. Select new renewal spurs close to the fruiting canes. Prune these back to two buds. Remove all other growth.

APRIL
Fruits

PLANNING

As the snow melts (hopefully) and the buds begin to break, check for winter damage and plant survival. Harsh winters provide the opportunity to add new plants to the landscape. As Oscar Wilde said, "For every gain there is a loss, and for every loss there is a gain."

PLANTING

Prepare the soil for planting. Follow soil test results and add the necessary organic matter and fertilizer.

Add 2 to 4 inches of organic matter to the top 12 inches of soil when planting **raspberries** and **strawberries**. **blueberries** require major steps to grow in most landscapes. See May "Planting" for details.

Either amend the whole planting bed or none of it when planting fruit trees and shrubs. Do not add lots of organic matter to the planting hole. This results in roots that fail to explore the soil beyond the planting hole, ultimately girdling the tree. It is important to plant these fruits in a well-drained area.

Plant bare-root trees, shrubs, **Raspberries**, and **Strawberries** that arrived in a dormant state. Prepare the soil and plant as directed in the "Soil Preparation" and "Planting" sections of the chapter introduction.

Purchase and plant container-grown trees and fruits as they become available. Those grown outdoors locally can be planted as soon as the soil can be worked. Imported or greenhouse-grown plants must be hardened off and protected from freezing temperatures.

Wait at least until the end of this month or early May to plant **blueberries**. This will prevent damage to the tender buds. Keep blankets or row covers handy to protect them from freezing temperatures. See May "Planting" for details.

CARE

Remove winter mulches on **strawberries** as the temperatures begin to hover above freezing or when the covered plants begin top growth. Rake the straw into the aisles between plantings. Leave it there to serve as a summer mulch, reducing weeds and conserving moisture. Or add the straw to the compost pile and let it decompose for future use in soil preparation.

WATERING

Water new plantings thoroughly so that the roots and surrounding soil are moist.

Check new plantings once or twice a week. Keep the soil around bare-root plantings moist. Give tree fruits 3 to 5 gallons of water each week. Water small fruits when the top 4 to 6 inches of soil begin to dry.

Check established plantings throughout the season. Make sure plants receive 1 inch of water each week. Nature usually provides this in the form of melting snow and spring showers. Provide the needed water in one weekly application for plants growing in clay soils and two applications (of $1/2$ to $3/4$ inch each) in sandy soils.

FERTILIZING

Fertilize fruits before growth begins. Err on the conservative side if soil test recommendations are not available. Follow recommendations in the "Fertilization" section in the chapter introduction.

Avoid complete fertilizers such as 10-10-10 or 12-12-12 unless recommended by your soil test. Most soils contain high to excessive levels of phosphorus and potassium (the last two numbers). Adding more can interfere with the uptake of other nutrients and reduce water quality.

Either amend the whole planting bed or none of it when planting fruit trees and shrubs. Do not add lots of organic matter to the planting hole.

 # PRUNING

Finish dormant season pruning before growth begins. Prune new plantings according to the transplant's size and the crop being grown. Prune established plantings to maximize light penetration and fruit production.

See February "Pruning" and "Did You Know?" and March "Did You Know?" for additional pruning information.

 # PROBLEMS

Continue monitoring for and protecting plants from animal damage. Tender spring growth makes good appetizers for rabbits and deer. Secure fencing materials and apply repellents as needed.

Spray stone fruits that have continually suffered from brown rot disease. Spray trees with a fungicide (labeled for disease control on stone fruit) at the early bloom stage and three to twenty-one days prior to harvest if the weather is wet.

Begin scab control on any **apples** and **pears** that have a history of this disease. Infected plants have spotted leaves and fruits that often drop prematurely. Start spraying susceptible plants as buds

begin to swell. Repeat every seven to fourteen days until dry weather returns.

Remove weeds as soon as they appear. Maintain a circle of mulch around fruit trees and shrubs to help reduce weeds.

Keep a constant watch on **strawberry** and **raspberry** plantings. If the weeds take over, it is time-consuming and no fun to try and reclaim the ground.

Did You Know?

Training Apple Trees

Prune overgrown **apple** trees to improve their productivity and simplify maintenance. Overgrown trees tend to be too tall, too densely branched, or both. Be patient; it will take several years to get these trees back in shape. Heavy pruning stimulates lots of leaf and stem growth while discouraging fruiting.

1 Start by reducing the height of tall trees. Take a close look at the tree's structure. Remove one or two of the tallest branches back to the trunk. Then remove any damaged or diseased branches. Wait a year to do additional pruning.

2 Open up the dense canopy. This can be done the first year on short trees or the second and third year on trees for which you have reduced the height.

3 Remove deadwood, suckers, watersprouts (stems that grow straight up from branches) and broken branches.

4 Next remove crossing, rubbing, or parallel branches that will eventually grow together.

5 Always make cuts back to the trunk or where one branch joins another branch. Make the final cut flush to the branch bark collar. This is the swollen area that occurs at the base of a stem.

6 Use the three-step system when pruning larger (3 inches in diameter or greater) branches.

7 Do not use pruning paints. Plants will naturally seal the wound and fight off pests—all on their own. In fact, the paints often do more harm than good.

MAY

PLANNING

Spring has arrived and you're busy doing instead of planning. Take a little time to record the work you are doing around your property. These records will help you continually improve your planting and maintenance practices. All this will result in a larger harvest.

Make a planting list. Record the name and variety of every fruit plant you add to the landscape. Record the planting date and place of purchase.

Note fertilizer practices. Later, you can compare the input of fertilizer to the output of healthy plants and produce. The recommended rates may need to be adjusted for your growing conditions.

Record pest control methods used—the type and amount of materials used, time of application, and weather conditions. These should all be considered when evaluating the need for and effectiveness of your pest management system.

PLANTING

Continue planting. Container and balled-and-burlapped trees are more readily available now. Keep the plants in a cool, shaded location until they can be planted. Cover the rootball with mulch and make sure the soil stays moist.

When the temperatures warm, it's time to plant **blueberries**. Select the hardiest half-high varieties you can find. Prepare the soil as described here to get the plants off to a good start.

Add several inches of organic matter, such as peat moss or compost, to the top 12 inches of soil. This improves drainage in heavy soils and the water-holding ability in sandy soils.

Some gardeners remove the existing soil and totally replace it with a more suitable planting medium. If you're ambitious, here's what to do: For each plant, remove the soil from an area 15 inches deep and 24 inches wide. Mix together two bushels of peat moss or compost, one bushel of loam soil, and one-half cup of sulfur. Use this mix to fill the planting hole.

Plant **blueberries** deep enough that the top roots are covered with 3 to 4 inches of soil. Firm the soil and water in with transplant solution (following label instructions) to remove any air pockets and stimulate root growth. Water often enough to keep the top 4 to 6 inches of soil constantly moist.

Mulch with shredded leaves, woodchips, or other organic mulch. This will help keep roots evenly moist throughout summer.

CARE

Replenish woodchip and bark mulch around fruit trees and **grape** vines. Add shredded leaves or similar material to **raspberry** and **strawberry** plantings.

Continue to remove weeds as soon as they appear. Keeping the plantings weed-free reduces pest problems and competition for water and nutrients. Mulch newly weeded gardens to reduce future weed growth.

WATERING

Check new plantings once or twice each week. Water these plants whenever the top 4 inches of soil begins to dry. Give newly planted fruit trees 3 to 5 gallons of water each week. Be sure to moisten the rootball and beyond.

Most established fruit prefer one inch of water each week. Supply this in one watering in clay soils and two waterings in sandy soils based on rainfall.

FERTILIZING

Make a second application of fertilizer for **raspberries** in late May or early June. Apply 1 cup of ammonium nitrate (33-0-0) per 100 feet of row or 1/4 cup per hill.

When the temperatures warm, it's time to plant blueberries.
Select the hardiest half-high varieties you can find.

Apply post-planting fertilization for the following crops:

Apply 2 tablespoons of ammonium nitrate fertilizer to **grapes** planted two to three weeks ago.

Give **currants** and other fruiting bushes 2 tablespoons of ammonium nitrate three to four weeks after planting.

Fertilize new **blueberries** two to four weeks after planting with 2 tablespoons of ammonium sulfate.

PRUNING

Remove flowers that form on new plantings of **june-bearing strawberries**. Remove all flowers that form on **day-neutral** and **everbearing strawberries** during the first six to eight weeks after planting. This allows the plant to expend energy on establishing a strong root system and strengthening the plant for winter survival and long-term production.

Pick any fruits that start to develop on young (first two years after planting) fruit trees. This directs the growth into root and branch development for longevity.

Did You Know?

Unwanted Fruit

After you fill your landscape with new pest-resistant trees, you may have a few old timers that are creating a mess in the yard and a garden. You hate to cut them down because they are a family heirloom, sentimental member of the family, or a good source for shade. Keep the tree and flowers but eliminate the fruit. Timing and proper application are the key to success. You may want to hire a professional arborist, who has the training and experience to do the job safely and effectively. To eliminate the fruit on old fruit trees:

Call your local nurseries and garden centers or check your favorite gardening catalog for Florel fruit eliminator. This product can be used to eliminate unwanted fruit on **apples**, **pears**, and several other ornamental trees.

Apply this growth regulator when trees are in full bloom. Make sure all flowers and buds are thoroughly covered. Early or late applications are not effective. Insufficient coverage and improper timing can result in fewer but larger fruits.

PROBLEMS

Continue spraying for apple scab. Use a fungicide labeled for scab control on fruit trees. Do not use home orchard sprays during bloom time. These contain insecticides that kill pollinating bees and prevent fruit formation.

Remove fireblight-infested branches. Look for hooked branches with brown or blackened leaves. Find the canker (sunken, discolored area) before removing the branch. Prune at least 9 inches below the canker. Disinfect tools with a solution of one part bleach to nine parts water between cuts.

Remove the webby nests of tent caterpillars. Prune out the tent or use a stick to knock it out. Destroy the insects. Or spray the nest and surrounding 2 feet with Bt (*Bacillus thuringiensis*). This bacteria kills true caterpillars, but does not harm other insects and wildlife. Do not spray insecticides on flowering plants. This includes home orchard sprays that contain both fungicides and insecticides. These products kill nature's pollinators (bees) and can prevent fruit set.

PLANNING

Continue writing in your journal. Your working records help you to plan what will stay and what will disappear from the landscape. You may decide it is more fun to visit the farmer's market and buy a bushel of **apples**, yet growing and harvesting your own **currants** is also exciting.

 ## PLANTING

Continue planting. See April and May "Planting" for details.

 ## CARE

Harvest **strawberries** every other day to ensure quality and reduce the number of overripe berries on the plants. Overripe berries attract insects and increase the risk of disease.

Harvest all large and small **strawberries** when they are fully colored. Hold the berry in your hand, pinch the stem with your finger, and twist as you pull.

Use quart- or pint-size containers to carry and store berries. These shallow containers prevent overstacking that can damage the tender fruit.

Get the berries into the refrigerator as soon as possible. Put cooled berries—containers and all—in vented plastic bags and store for up to four days.

Rake and compost all immature **apples** that fall from the tree. This is a common phenomena called June drop. It occurs when **apples** produce more fruit than the plant can support. The fruit drop is nature's way of thinning the crop to a more manageable size. Eliminate June drop by thinning young fruit.

Thin **apples** by removing all but one or two of the developing fruit in each cluster. Or thin to one fruit every 6 to 8 inches along the stem. Remove and compost unwanted fruit by mid-June to increase fruit size and improve flower set next season.

Mulch new plantings and replenish mulch on existing plantings. Straw and shredded leaves are suitable for **strawberries**. Shredded leaves and woodchips can be used around **raspberries**, **blueberries**, and other fruiting shrubs. Use woodchips or shredded bark for fruit trees and fruiting shrubs. Use a 1- to 2-inch layer of fine mulch materials, such as shredded leaves, and a 3- to 4-inch layer of coarser materials, such as woodchips.

 ## WATERING

Continue watering as recommended in July "Watering."

 ## FERTILIZING

Make the second application of fertilizer for established **raspberry** plantings if it was not done in late May. Apply 1 cup of (33-0-0) per 100 feet of row or 1/4 cup per hill.

Give new plantings of **june-bearing strawberries** 1 cup of ammonium nitrate (33-0-0) fertilizer per 100 feet of row, or 1 teaspoon per plant, when the runners begin to form. Fertilize established plantings with 1 cup of (33-0-0) after harvest.

Apply 2 cups of ammonium nitrate per 100 feet of row to **everbearing strawberries** after their first crop.

Apply the second part (1/3 cup of 33-0-0 per plant) of the two-part fertilization for **grapes** suffering from frost damage.

PRUNING

Continue to prune broken and damaged branches. Remove disease infested branches and canes as soon as they are found. Always disinfect tools between cuts with a solution of one part bleach to nine parts water or straight rubbing alcohol.

 # PROBLEMS

Pest management is a very personal decision. Some gardeners grow their own fruit to avoid pesticides. Planting disease-resistant varieties and sanitation will help reduce pest problems. It is impossible to grow perfect **apples** without pesticides. If perfection is not your goal, do minimal or no pesticide spraying; you'll have delicious, tasty, good-for-you fruit with some imperfections.

Insects. Place sticky traps in fruit trees to monitor insect populations. Some gardeners use trapping for limited pest control, while other strictly use the traps to monitor insects for spraying.

Evaluate past damage, monitor traps, and decide whether you want to control these fruit damaging insects: apple maggots, codling moths, and plum curculio.

Lumpy **apples** with brown streaks through the flesh are the results of apple maggots. The adults lay their eggs in the developing **apples**. The larvae feed through the fruit, causing the damage. Some people use these **apples** for cider, applesauce, and baking, while other insist on their control.

Codling moths are the "worms" in the **apples**. Reduce problems by raking and destroying fallen fruit. Preventative sprays will help eliminate this pest.

The plum curculio prefers **plums**, but will damage **apples** and **pears** as well. Female curculio lay their eggs on the fruit surface. This scar results in lumpy and misshapen fruit. The surviving offspring feed inside the fruit, causing it to fall prematurely.

Harvest **strawberries** as often as possible to keep overripe berries off the plants. Any overripe fruits attract picnic (also called sap) beetles that will feed on all the berries.

Minimize your pesticide use and still provide substantial control for these pests by following this program: Apply an insecticide labeled for insect control on fruit trees at petal fall, two weeks later, mid-July, and early August.

Diseases. Continue to prune out fireblight and black knot cankers. See March "Problems" for more specific information.

Check **raspberries** for signs of cane blight and anthracnose. Infected canes are discolored, have yellow leaves, and produce crumbly fruit. Remove and destroy infected canes as soon as they are discovered.

Renew **strawberry** plantings infected with leaf spot fungal disease. Regular renewal, sanitation, and proper spacing will usually keep this disease under control.

Animals. Cover **strawberries** and **raspberries** with netting to protect your harvest from the birds. Anchor the netting securely to prevent the birds from going in under the netting to reach the fruit. Apply the netting early to encourage them to go elsewhere for their snacks.

JULY
Fruits

PLANNING

Record harvest dates and time spent harvesting to help you plan for next year. You may want to recruit friends and neighbors to help in the harvest and share the bounty. Consider sharing surplus fruits and vegetables with a local food pantry or soup kitchen. The Second Harvest Food Bank can help you locate a food pantry in your community. This is a great way to share your love of gardening with people, especially children and seniors in need.

PLANTING

Finish renovating **strawberries**. Continue planting container-grown tree and shrub fruits. Make sure they are properly watered throughout the hot, dry part of summer.

CARE

Harvest the summer crop of **raspberries** when the fruits are fully colored and pull easily off the core. If this coincides with mosquito hatch, wear some mosquito-netting clothes to make picking more enjoyable and the mosquitoes more tolerable.

Try using a gallon milk jug to gather the **raspberries**. Cut away the top front of the container. Leave the bottom and handle intact. Tie the jug around your waist so you can keep both hands free for picking. Pile the **raspberries** in thin layers to prevent crushing the bottom layers of berries.

Chill the berries within 2 hours of picking. Wash just before use.

Harvest **cherries** when they have colored up, and are flavorful and juicy.

Hold the **cherry** between several fingers. Pull and twist to remove the fruit, but not the spurs and branches from the tree. Leave stems attached to **sweet cherries** for storing. Move to cool storage (32 to 40 degrees Fahrenheit) if you want to keep them for several weeks.

Check and harvest **currants** and **gooseberries** when they are sweet and juicy. Store these in shallow containers and refrigerate as soon as possible to increase storage life.

WATERING

Adjust watering rates to compensate for weekly rainfall. Apply needed water in one application to fruits growing in clay soils. Make two applications (of half the needed amount) in sandy soils. Refer to the chapter introduction for additional watering information.

FERTILIZING

Apply 1 teaspoon of ammonium nitrate per plant, or 1 cup of ammonium nitrate per 100 feet of row, to **day-neutral** and **everbearing strawberries** that are flowering and fruiting. Sprinkle fertilizer on the soil, brushing off any that lands on the foliage. Water it in.

PRUNING

Prune **summer-bearing** and **everbearing raspberry** plants right after harvest. Remove all the older canes that bore fruit this summer. Cut these back to ground level.

Thin **summer-bearing red raspberries** at this time. Summer thinning increases airflow and reduces disease problems. Remove all but three to four canes per foot, or six to eight canes per hill. Secure the remaining canes to the stake or within the trellis.

Remove only disease- and insect-infected canes on **fall-bearing red raspberries** that had been cut to the ground last winter. The remaining first-year canes will produce fruit this fall.

 # PROBLEMS

Diseases. Check **raspberry** canes for insects and disease. Cane blight and anthracnose cause purple and brown spots on stems. Leaves yellow and brown, and the fruits are dry and crumby. Prune out and destroy infected canes as soon as they are found.

Fireblight is a problem on **raspberries**, as well as **apples** and **pears**. Wilted tips that quickly turn black indicate this disease is present. Check the stems or branches for sunken, discolored areas called cankers. Prune infected **raspberry** canes down to ground level. Prune 9 to 12 inches below the canker on infected **apple** and **pear** branches. Disinfect tools between cuts to reduce the risk of spreading this disease. Use a solution of one part bleach and nine parts water.

Continue treating for **apple** and **pear** scab during wet periods. This fungal disease causes black spots on leaves and fruits. Use a fungicide labeled for controlling this disease on fruit trees, every ten to fourteen days. Make sure it is safe for edibles. Some fungicides recommend waiting weeks or days before it is safe to eat the fruit. Mark that date on your calendar.

Prune out black knot (black knobby growths) on **plums**, **cherries**, and **peaches**. This reduces future infection.

Spray stone fruits that have a history of brown rot if the weather is wet. Use a fungicide labeled for controlling this disease on stone fruits. Apply when the fruits begin to turn from green to ripe color.

Insects. Prune out and destroy cane borer- and cane maggot-infested stems. Both feed inside the stem, causing it to wilt. Prune canes to ground level.

Harvest **raspberries** as often as possible to keep overripe berries off the plants. The overripe fruits attract picnic (also called sap) beetles that feed on all the berries.

Treat tree fruits suffering from repeated insect infestations with an insecticide the middle of this month. Always start by using the least toxic pesticide; remember, unless you are using a insecticide that targets a specific insect, you are killing the good bugs a well. This schedule will give you substantial insect control with a reduced amount of pesticide applications. Check label for wait times between spraying and harvesting. See June "Problems" for details on insects.

Protect the harvest from birds, squirrels, and other uninvited guests. See "Did You Know?" for August.

AUGUST

PLANNING

The big harvest season is quickly approaching. Soon the cool places in your home will be filled with **apples** and **pears**. Start making plans now for handling all this produce. Many gardeners turn their harvest into sauces, pie fillings, and preserves that can be canned and stored for winter. Others find a cool corner of their basement, or a second refrigerator to store fruits. Stock up on perforated plastic bags to help extend the life of your produce. Make a plan now so that you will not be overwhelmed when you are faced with trees producing fruits in large quantities.

PLANTING

Garden centers, home stores, and nurseries often have container-grown fruit plants at their end-of-season sales so they do have to deal with overwintering. Buy what you need and get them in the ground as soon as possible. Be sure to water each one in with transplant solution to stimulate root growth so the plants have a chance to get established before winter sets in. Make sure new plantings are watered throughout the remainder of the season. Check on them more frequently during this hot, dry month than you do spring-planted fruits.

CARE

Follow these guidelines for harvesting:

Harvest **blueberries** when they are fully colored, sweet, and juicy. Like other berries, store them in shallow containers to prevent crushing the fruit.

Harvest **elderberries** throughout the month. Taste the fruit to check for ripeness. Pick when the berries are fully colored and juicy.

Start harvesting **apples** just before they are fully mature. Early season varieties will start ripening this month. Look for a color change in the indentation where the stem attaches to the fruit. The background color turns from a leafy green to a lighter green and eventually yellow in most **apples**. Pick the fruit when this is just starting to turn yellow.

Mature **apples** will also pull off the tree easily. Hold the fruit in the palm of your hand, twist, lift, and pull. The fruit should come off with minimal resistance. Do not pull down on the tree, as this can damage the fruiting spurs and branches.

Start harvesting **pears** before they turn yellow and fall to the ground. Pick them when the skin turns from a dark green to a lighter green or yellowish green. The dots on the skin, known as lenticels, will turn from white to brown. Ripe fruit separates easily from the stem when gently twisted. Use the same technique used to harvest **apples**.

Monitor **peaches** and **plums** for ripeness. **Peaches** are in full production, if you are lucky enough to get a crop, and **plums** are just starting to ripen. Harvest when the fruits are fully colored, sweet, and juicy. Harvesting at peak maturity maximizes flavor, but minimizes storage time. Store fruit immediately after harvest. They will only keep for several weeks in refrigeration, so be prepared to eat, preserve, and use the bountiful harvest.

With all the bounty you have, share some with the hungry. Join the Plant a Row (PAR) program. PAR can direct you and others to local food banks, soup kitchens, or other locations that are grateful and gladly accept donations of fresh-from-the garden produce and fruit. As part of the PAR program, started by the Garden Writers Association, donations are weighed. In 1993 alone, over 1.7 million pounds of produce were collected, which translates to 6.8 million meals. For information, go to www.gardenwriters.org.

WATERING

Continue watering throughout the growing season. Late season water is important for next year's harvest. Properly watered plants are more winter hardy, better able to resist pests, and

Harvesting at peak maturity maximizes flavor, but minimizes storage time. Store fruit immediately after harvest.

produce a larger crop the following year.

 # FERTILIZING

Fertilize **june-bearing strawberries** in early August. Apply 1 cup of 33-0-0 (ammonium nitrate) to 100 feet of row. This will aid in flower bud development for next June's crop. Apply 1 cup of ammonium nitrate fertilizer per 100 feet of row, or 1 teaspoon of fertilizer per plant, to **everbearing** and **day-neutral straw-berries** that are flowering and fruiting.

 # PRUNING

Remove watersprouts (the branches that grow straight up from trunk and other branches) in early August. Prune early in the month and only if the weather is dry. Avoid pruning during wet weather, which can spread fireblight disease.

Finish pruning bearing canes of **rasp-berries** and **blackberries** and destroy them. Summer pruning helps open up the plants and reduces pest problems.

 # PROBLEMS

Make the last of the insecticide applications for tree fruits suffering from repeat infestations. Apply insecticide early in

Did You Know?

Protecting Your Harvest

The sweet, juicy **cherries**, **raspberries**, and **strawberries** are too much for anyone, including the wildlife, to resist. Try these tips to protect your harvest from the birds and other unwanted guests.

Cover trees and bushes with bird netting. Secure the netting around tree trunks, the base of bushes, or the edges of your **strawberry** bed. This will keep them from going under the netting to reach the fruit.

Try scare tactics, such as whirligigs, clanging pans, rubber snakes, and blow-up owls. Vary scare tactics to keep the animals fearful. Make sure your scare tactics do not annoy the neighbors.

Check the label before purchasing and using repellents on fruit trees. Most repellents cannot be used on food crops. Hot Pepper Wax™ and Hinder™ are two that are safe to use on food crops.

Try making your own repellents. Some gardeners report good success with hanging strongly scented deodorant soaps from fruiting trees and bushes. Vary repellents to increase the chance of success.

the month. Check the label to make sure there is sufficient time between the last application and harvest. If not, skip this application. See June "Problems" for details on insect problems.

Make cleanup an ongoing part of your gardening routine. Remove fallen leaves and fruit to reduce future pest problems.

Prune disease- and insect-infested **rasp-berry** canes to ground level. Look for wilting, swellings, spots, or discoloration of the stems and leaves. Remove and destroy when found. Disinfect tools between cuts.

Continue spraying for apple scab. Treat susceptible plants every ten to fourteen days during wet weather. Do not spray if the disease has not been a problem or the weather is dry. Check the label for the waiting period between the last spray and harvest. Stop spraying so that the fruit can be harvested and enjoyed.

If the weather is wet, treat stone fruits that have suffered from brown rot in the past. Spray as the fruit begins to color. Stop spraying in time to allow for the waiting period between the last spray and harvest.

SEPTEMBER
Fruits

PLANNING

Keep recording information in your journal as you harvest, store, and manage your fruit gardens. Be sure to record harvest and storage information. This will help you better prepare for next season's bumper crop.

Take a few minutes to evaluate new plantings. How are they doing so far this season? Make needed adjustments in care; and be sure you build in time to give them proper care throughout the rest of the season. Give these plants the proper care they need so they are well-established by winter. The fruits of your labors are literally rewarded—tenfold at least. The care and attention you invest in them during their first year often determines their future successes—healthy plants yielding abundant harvests in years to come.

PLANTING

Fall is not the best time to plant fruit trees in our region, yet you may find that you cannot resist the temptation of the end-of-summer sales. Follow planting directions given in the chapter introduction. Mulch to insulate roots, conserve moisture, and reduce weed problems. Keep the soil around the plant roots moist, but not wet. Water thoroughly enough to wet the root zone (6 to 12 inches deep). Water again when the top 4 inches begin to dry. Do not fertilize fall-planted fruit trees.

CARE

Follow these guidelines for harvesting:

Continue harvesting **apples**, **pears**, and **plums**.

Pick **apples** when the stem end indentation turns from green to yellow. Ripe fruit easily twists off the branch without breaking the spur or branch.

Harvest **pears** before they start falling from the trees. Remove fruit when they turn from a dark green to a yellowish green and the lenticels (small pores on fruit) turn from white to brown.

Pick **plums** when they are fully colored, sweet, and juicy. You will get the best flavor by harvesting ripe **plums**.

Harvest **grapes** as they reach maturity. Use your taste buds as your guide. Pick a **grape** at the tip of a bunch that looks ripe. Harvest the bunch if the **grape** is sweet and tasty.

Harvest **early ripening fall raspberries** when they are fully colored and sweet. See July "Care" for harvesting tips.

Move the fruit into cold storage (the basement, root cellar, or spare refrigerator) as soon as possible after harvest. The cooler the temperature (near 35 degrees Fahrenheit), the longer the fruit will last in storage. Place fruit in perforated plastic bags to help retain moisture and reduce shrinkage. Do not store **apples** with **carrots** and other vegetables. **apples** give off ethylene gas which encourages ripening and shortens storage life of other fruits and vegetables stored with it.

Mulch the soil around fruit trees, fruiting shrubs, **raspberries**, and **blueberries** with woodchips or shredded bark. Use shredded leaves or straw for **strawberry** beds.

Move tropical fruit plants, such as **orange**, **lemon** and **pineapple guava** trees, indoors for winter. Isolate the plantings for several weeks to avoid bringing unwanted insects into your houseplant collection. Grow in a sunny location, and water when the top few inches of soil begin to dry.

WATERING

Continue watering whenever the top 4 to 6 inches of soil begin to dry. Give tree fruits 3 to 5 gallons of water and other fruit plantings 1 inch of water each week. Adjust the amount according to the rainfall received.

Do not store apples with carrots and other vegetables. Apples give off ethylene gas which encourages ripening and shortens storage life of other fruits and vegetables stored with it.

FERTILIZING

Do not fertilize. Late-season fertilization can lead to an unwanted spurt of growth that is subject to winterkill.

PRUNING

Wait until winter to do major pruning. Prune only what is absolutely necessary—repair and disease control. Remove broken, damaged, or diseased branches as soon as you find them. Prune back to a point where the branch joins another branch or next to the trunk.

Always cut flush with the branch bark collar, not the trunk of the tree. The branch bark collar is the swollen area that can be found at the base of branches. Do not treat with pruning paints. These compounds trap moisture and pests in, rather than keeping them away from the tree.

PROBLEMS

Continue monitoring and controlling pests as needed. Sanitation, cleanup, and disposal of fallen leaves and fruit greatly reduces future problems.

Did You Know?

Growing from Garbage

Can you start a tree from a **peach** pit? Or how about that **grapefruit** seed? Starting plants from kitchen scraps is fun if you have room to experiment. If your planting space is limited, stick to buying the most pest-resistant and productive variety available. But then again, part of the gardening appeal is trying to beat the odds, break the rules, and grow something from nothing. Children get a kick out of "growing from garbage." Try these:

Keep in mind that the seed you plant may not look exactly like the fruit it came from or the plant it grew on. Offspring of hybrids do not always come true (look and taste like their parents) from seed.

Take your clue from Nature. If you are trying to start a tropical plant, it probably does not need a cold treatment. These plants don't naturally go through a cold period in their native lands. Fruits from more temperate areas that mature in fall probably need a cold treatment (stratification; time in the refrigerator) to break dormancy and sprout. Place nuts in moist sand or peat moss in plastic bags during stratification.

Plants with hard seed coats like the **avocado** need a little help sprouting. Nick (scarify) or soak the seeds to absorb water and sprout.

Give seeds their needed treatments. Plant treated seeds in a moist, warm soil. Once the seeds sprout, move them to a bright, sunny window.

Grow as you would a houseplant until it is warm enough to move outside.

Avoid pesticide applications during harvest. Always check the label to make sure you allow the necessary time between spray and harvest and that the pesticide is safe for use on food plants.

Prune out the branches that are infected with fireblight. Fireblight bacterial disease attacks **apples**, **pears**, and **raspberries**. Remove infected **raspberry** canes to ground level. Prune 9 to 12 inches below the canker (sunken discolored area) on fireblight-infected **apple** and **pear** branches. Disinfect tools between cuts.

Remove and destroy black knot (black knobby growths) from **plums**, **cherries**, and other stone fruits. Prune 9 to 12 inches below the growth. Disinfect tools between cuts.

OCTOBER

PLANNING

Winter is fast approaching. Review last year's journal to see what winter preparation is necessary. Check winter and spring comments to make sure you protect susceptible plants from winter cold and animal feeding.

PLANTING

Give the squirrels a hand and plant a few nut trees for the future. It may be easier to start them indoors than to fight the squirrels for them later.

Collect nuts and remove the outer hull (fleshy covering). Wear gloves when cleaning **black walnuts**, otherwise your hands will match your walnut stained furniture. Pack the nuts in moist sand, peat moss, vermiculite, or sawdust. Store them in a plastic bag in the refrigerator for three to four months.

Plant stratified seeds in spring. Place them directly outside in their permanent location. Be sure to protect them from curious squirrels and rodents. Or plant the seeds in a deep container filled with well-drained potting mix. This allows you to get the plants off to a good start before you offer them up as an early bird special to your local marauding animals.

Or plant the seeds directly outside in fall. Cover the planted seeds with wire mesh to protect them from the squirrels and other rodents. Plant the seeds 2 inches deep in their permanent location or in deep pots for transplanting at a later date. Sink the pots in the ground for added insulation over the winter.

Do not plant **black walnuts** in small yards and gardens. The roots contain juglone, which is toxic to many other plants. So that's why many plants (except **hostas**) won't grow under your majestic **walnut.** Keep these large, long-lasting trees at least 50 feet, but preferably 200 feet, away from the garden.

CARE

Follow these harvesting guidelines, and refer to September "Care" for more information.

Check **fall raspberries** for ripeness. Harvest berries that are fully colored and pull easily off the core. Ripe fruit is sweet and juicy. Pick often to prevent overripe fruit from collecting on the bushes. This reduces the risk of picnic beetles moving in to share the bounty.

Harvest **grapes** when the fruit is sweet and juicy. Pick one **grape** from the tip of a bunch that looks ripe. Harvest the bunch if the sample **grape** is sweet and tasty.

Gather **hickory** and **black walnuts** as soon as they drop from the tree.

Remove the hulls (fleshy covering) as soon as possible. Wear rubber or latex gloves to prevent staining your hands in the process.

Spread the nuts in a thin layer in a dry, airy location. Allow them to cure for four to six weeks.

Now comes the fun part—cracking the hard shells to get to the nutmeat. Melinda has heard of gardeners spreading them on driveways, covering them with boards, and driving over them with their cars. Perhaps a bit drastic and very messy!

You may prefer Melinda's father's method. "He used to keep a supply of **black walnuts** in his workshop. He could be found at the end of a hard day at work, his hammer in hand and the nuts secured in his vise. We would end the winter with a good supply of **black walnuts** for baking."

Separate the shells from the nutmeat. Dry the nutmeat thoroughly and refrigerate in an airtight jar.

Collect nuts and remove the outer hull. Pack the nuts in moist sand, peat moss, vermiculite, or sawdust. Store them in a plastic bag in the refrigerator for three to four months.

Check stored fruit. Remove any rotten or shriveling fruit. One bad **apple** really does spoil the whole bunch, so get rid of the bad fruit before it ruins the rest of the fruit in storage.

 # WATERING

Keep watering fruits during dry spells in the fall. Fruits need about 1 inch of water each week. Provide whatever Nature does not. Water fruits growing in clay soils once a week. Apply the needed water in two applications, four to five days apart, in sandy soils.

Water aboveground planters anytime the soil thaws and the top 4 inches begin to dry. Water thoroughly so that the excess runs out the bottom.

 # FERTILIZING

Do not fertilize. Take a soil test now if you have not already done so. Use this as a guide to help you plan next year's fertilization program.

 # PRUNING

Remove any diseased, broken, or damaged branches. Save major pruning for late winter. This way you can see what

Did You Know?

Wintertime Care

Protect fruit trees and berries from hungry rabbits and deer.

Start by placing cylinders of hardware cloth around the trees. Sink this heavy wire mesh several inches below the soil surface. Make sure it extends at least 4 feet above the ground. This creates a physical barrier between the animals (voles and rabbits) and your trees. Monitor plantings for damage throughout the winter. Keep in mind that the rabbits' reach extends as the snow accumulates.

Try applying homemade or purchased repellents. Some gardeners swear by them while others swear at them. Try a variety of products, such as Ropel™, Hot Wax Pepper™, or Tree Guard™ to increase your chance of success. Use only those products labeled for food crops.

Hang highly scented deodorant soap or handfuls of human hair in old nylon stockings from the trees and bushes. Research shows that these can help deter animals. We agree that they are not as effective in urban areas where animals are used to these smells. Experiment with dog and cat fur, collecting the fur after pets have been combed or brushed. Once you have a handful or more of fur, put it in a stocking and hang outside.

Try clanging pans, whirly gigs, or other scare tactics to discourage the animals. Vary techniques to keep them leery of the area.

Fence small areas with 5-foot-tall snow or mesh fence to reduce the risk of deer damage. Even though they can jump the short fence, they seem to avoid going into these small areas.

the animals have destroyed (or left behind), eliminate winter damage, and take care of routine pruning all at the same time.

 PROBLEMS

Clean up and remove all fallen fruit and leaves. To reduce the risk of future infec-tion, discard or destroy pest-infested material. Get out the repellents and fencing. Put animal protection in place for the winter. Protect new and young fruit trees and plantings; they are favorite winter snacks for rabbits, deer, and voles. See the above "Did You Know?" for details.

NOVEMBER

 PLANNING

There's still some work left to do. Continue evaluating the health and productivity of new and established plantings. Note any plants that will need moving or replacing in spring. Although it is always sad to lose a plant, think of it as an opportunity to grow something new and different.

Note any crops that failed to produce. Did they receive the proper care? Or maybe you gave them a little too much kindness, in the form of water and fertilizer? Make a note to correct this next spring.

Make sure you have the needed pollinators in place. Many fruits, such as **apples**, some **plums**, and **pears**, need two plants for pollination and fruit production.

 PLANTING

Wait until spring to plant fruit trees, shrubs, and berries. Protect any late purchases that did not get planted.

Find a vacant garden location in a protected site. Sink the planting containers in the soil before the ground freezes.

Protect the area with hardware cloth to keep out the voles and rabbits. Make sure the material is buried several inches in the soil and is at least 4 feet high.

Mulch the soil with woodchips or shredded bark once the ground freezes.

 CARE

Mulch **strawberries** with a 4- to 6-inch layer of straw or marsh hay for the winter. Apply the mulch after the top 1/2 inch of soil is frozen. This is usually after the temperatures begin hovering around 25 degrees Fahrenheit in mid to late November. Do not use tree leaves, unless you double shred them. Otherwise they mat down when wet, trapping moisture and providing poor insulation.

Move aboveground containers into winter storage. An unheated garage makes a suitable location. Or move the planter to a protected outdoor location. Place bales of straw or hay around the planter to reduce the risk of root damage from cold winter temperatures. Use repellents, fencing, or other animal protection to protect these plants as well.

Keep checking and using stored fruit. Discard any damaged and rotting fruit, which can cause the other fruit to spoil.

Dry, can, or create edible holiday gifts using some of the surplus fruit. Nothing tastes better than a gift from the garden.

 WATERING

Keep watering until the ground freezes. Make sure new plants receive 1 inch of water a week either from rainfall or from your garden hose. Water established plants thoroughly before the ground freezes. Proper watering will improve winter survival and next year's harvest.

Water aboveground planters anytime the soil thaws and the top 4 inches are dry. Water thoroughly so that the excess runs out the drainage holes.

Check tropical plants moved indoors for winter. Water thoroughly so that the excess runs out the bottom. Pour off the excess water. Or better yet, place pebbles in the drainage saucer. Allow the pot to sit on the pebbles and not in the excess water. As the water evaporates, it increases the humidity around the plants.

Drain and store your garden hose, sprinkler, and other watering tools for winter. Make sure faucets are shut off or properly insulated for winter as needed.

 FERTILIZING

Do not fertilize. Store fertilizer products in a cool, dark area away from children and pets. Keep liquids away from the sunlight and in an area where they will not freeze. Keep granular fertilizers in a dry area.

Keep watering until the ground freezes. Make sure new plants receive 1 inch of water a week either from rainfall or from your garden hose.

PRUNING

Cut **fall-bearing raspberries** to the ground. Although this eliminates the summer crop, you'll have a larger and earlier fall crop next year. Use sharp pruning tools or a mower with a heavy duty, sharp blade. Sharp tools make your work easier and reduce the risk of injury to the plants.

Check **summer** and **everbearing raspberries** for pest-infested or old bearing canes. Look for spots, discoloration, and wilting. Cut these back to ground level. Destroy or discard canes to prevent the spread of insects and disease. Disinfect your tools between cuts with a solution of one part bleach to nine parts water.

PROBLEMS

Finish fall cleanup. Remove brush piles that make a good habitat for rabbits and codling moths. Remove and destroy any cankered (sunken, discolored area) stems. Disinfect tools between cuts with a solution of one part bleach to nine parts water. Place cylinders of hardware cloth around trees and shrubs. Sink the wire mesh several inches into the soil to keep out voles. Make sure it is at least 4 feet high to discourage rabbits.

Start applying repellents before the animals begin feeding. Reapply after severe weather or as directed by the product label.

Store pesticides (fungicides and insecticides) in a locked area away from heat, freezing temperatures, and sunlight. Make a quick inventory of these products. Write it in your journal or other location. This will prevent you from purchasing more product than you need next year.

Did You Know?

Grapefruit, **lemon** trees, **pineapple guava**, and **avocados** are all fun plants for the Prairie Lands. In summer, it is no problem finding growing space and keeping the plants healthy. Winter is a different story. Limited space, poor light, and low humidity add to the challenge of keeping these plants alive. Give your tropical fruit trees the best possible winter care.

Grow them in the sunniest location available. Supplement the natural light with artificial lights. Use spots or other fixtures to shine the light into large plants from the side. This will help ensure that light reaches all the leaves.

Avoid drafts of hot or cold air and heater vents. The plants can tolerate cooler temperatures, but not drafty locations.

Group with other plants or use gravel trays to increase the humidity. Place pebbles in the drainage saucer. Place the pot on the pebbles. Allow the excess water to collect in the saucer. As the water evaporates, it increases the humidity around the plants.

Water the soil anytime the top 2 to 3 inches begin to dry. Water thoroughly so that the excess drains out the bottom and collects in the gravel tray. Wait until the top few inches are slightly dry before watering again.

DECEMBER
Fruits

 PLANNING

Start your planting list now. Write down the plants you want to add and the spaces you have available for planting. Review your journal to see what plants need to be moved to open up additional space for new plants. Use this as you review catalogs and put together your plant order for next season. Consider using the layering technique to start new **grape**, **hardy kiwi**, or other vine crops next year.

 PLANTING

Happy Holidays! Enjoy the few months until planting time returns.

 CARE

Keep monitoring stored fruits and remove any that have rotted. Use the harvest for holiday dinners. What a nice way to share your garden with others!

Check on aboveground planters stored outdoors or in the garage. Make sure the roots are well insulated and plants are protected from animals.

 WATERING

Water aboveground planters whenever the soil thaws and the ground is dry. Water thoroughly so that the excess runs out the drainage holes. Water again when the top 4 to 6 inches begin to dry. Check these planters throughout winter.

Water indoor tropical fruit plants throughout winter. Water whenever the top 2 to 3 inches of soil begin to dry. Water thoroughly so that the excess runs out the bottom and collects in the gravel tray.

 FERTILIZING

No need to fertilize. The ground is frozen outdoors and the tropical plants are just trying to adjust to their new location. Fertilizing these plants could damage the tender roots.

 PRUNING

Finish pruning **fall-bearing red raspberries** if this has not yet been done. However, it may be too late to prune for northern gardeners. Prune all the canes to ground level. Use sharp pruners or a mower with a heavy duty, sharp blade to avoid damaging the plants. Use this method of pruning when you only want a fall crop. Removing all the stems eliminates the summer bearing canes, but results in a larger and earlier fall harvest.

Remove any storm-damaged or pest-infested stems and branches. Wait until late winter to do major pruning. That way you can remove winter damage, assess animal damage, and take care of routine pruning all at one time.

 **PROBLEMS**

Take a walk through the landscape and start looking for signs of pests. Check the twigs of **apples**, **plums**, and other fruit trees for eastern tent caterpillar eggs. These egg masses look like a shiny glob of mud on the stem. Smash or prune out the pest. This is the most environmentally friendly way to control this pest.

Check the trunks and major branches of trees and shrubs for gypsy moth eggs. The fuzzy yellow to beige masses contain hundreds of eggs. Remove and destroy these as soon as soon as they are found. Check nearby trees and shrubs whenever you discover these pests.

CHAPTER FOUR

Herbs & Vegetables

*Can there be anything better than the bite of your first sun-warmed tomato,
eaten right in the garden? Or the corn that is so young and sweet that you can eat it
without boiling? Sugar-snap peas that are so crispy and fresh straight from the garden?
The piney scent of fresh rosemary? Or the mild flavor of sage blossoms?*

By definition, an herb is a useful plant. Herbs and spices are often grouped together and considered interchangeable, as they are both seasonings. Nevertheless, there is a difference. Generally, an herb is the leafy portion of a temperate climate plant (herbaceous, soft-tissued, not woody), while a spice is derived from the seeds or bark of tropical plants (most often trees).

Over the years, herbs have been used for many purposes. Today, herbs are generally divided into three categories: culinary, medicinal, and dye plants. This will only address culinary herbs.

Many of the plants that are called vegetables are, in fact, fruits. A fruit forms when the flower is pollinated and the ovule swells, creating the fruit with seeds inside. **Tomatoes**, **eggplants**, **peppers**, **cucumbers**, **melons**, **squash**, and **pumpkins** are all fruits. For the purpose of this book, edible leaves, shoots, stems, roots, and fruits all fall under the umbrella of vegetables.

From my earliest days Cathy viewed herbs, vegetables, and other edible plants from a different perspective than most people. She admired their ornamental qualities, and planted them freely among annuals and perennials. One of her first garden memories is of planting **tomatoes** in the flower bed alongside the **marigolds**. Her outraged father pulled up the tomatoes and replanted them in the vegetable bed where he said they belonged. It was many years later that she discovered that she had been simply creating an edible landscape.

Economically and ecologically, growing vegetables and herbs among ornamentals makes a lot of sense. With the high cost of good, fresh produce, it makes sense to grow whatever you can. You can't beat the flavor and freshness of homegrown. Growing edibles close to the house is a real time and energy saver. On a rainy day, you might think twice about running down to the vegetable patch to pick fixings for dinner, but would be likely to reach out the kitchen door to pick or snip a delightfully ripe **tomato**, some **salad greens** or **beans.** With limitations on water use in many areas, by incorporating edibles into the landscape, you can optimize the use of this precious commodity.

Edible landscaping opens up new vistas in the garden. Look at the catalogs as they come each day, and visualize the fruits, vegetables, herbs, and nuts you can grow. Imagine an arbor covered with **grapes** and **hardy kiwi,** with **scarlet runner beans** twisting their way up the sides, a sunny hillside covered with the flowers of **Jerusalem artichokes**. See your garden edged with frilly summer **lettuce** that is slow to bolt and 'Spicy Globe' **basil** with its dwarf topiary look. The choices and combinations are nearly limitless. Whatever you do to make your garden a more edible landscape, you cannot help but reap the rewards of your labor.

Cathy steals furtive glances out into her garden. She's planning on taking a break and giving herself a treat. With pruners, garden-toting Bos bag, a paring knife, and a paper grocery sack, she heads out into the front yard where

Herbs & Vegetables

there is no grass. Instead, there is a bounteous garden comprised of perennials, herbs, vegetables, fruit, and annuals.

It is her edible landscape, the bounty enjoyed by neighbors and passersby. There are six different heirloom **tomato** plants that fondly called octopuses; with the cool, rainy summer, they have grown over and out of the cages, covering everything within a four-foot radius. That's why they are called indeterminate—they just keep growing and growing. She'll start with the yellow, thumbnail-sized 'Yellow River'. It's so sweet it is best before any other food, or at the end of the "meal." She'll meander—picking and munching individual leaves of the various **basils** to complement the **tomatoes**—green and yellow 'Mr. Stripey', slightly fuzzy 'Georgia Peach' (rub the fuzz off before eating), the many ribbed 'Genovese', and others.

The Prairie Lands growing season is short; plants have to be tough to withstand the heat of our summers as well as the winds. Yet we are undaunted and find ways to grow a wide range of herbs and vegetables. Some herbs that are perennials in warmer climes, we grow as annuals. Others, like **rosemary** and **lavender,** we can overwinter indoors.

When growing food for your family to eat, It is important to grow organically, and without pesticides. Although there have been a number of studies done, it is not clear yet how different pesticides interrelate, and how our children, who have smaller body weights, are affected.

Planning

When you are planning what herbs and vegetables you are want to grow, take into account what their preferred growing season is—cool or warm weather. This information is invaluable, especially if you plan to jump-start the season by sowing seeds indoors. It should be obvious that if you grow plants out of season, their performance may be remarkable for its poorness. Out of season, some plants will die.

Cool weather vegetables are relatively hardy in the Prairie Lands, tolerating temperatures down to 28 degrees Fahrenheit. Traditionally many think of these as spring crops; often their seeds are started indoors 6 to 8 weeks before outdoor planting. These tough plants also make excellent fall crops. Some, such as **Brussels sprouts** and **kale**, even taste better after a freeze. In the northern regions of the Prairie Lands (Zones 3 and 4), start seeds of fall-weather crops in July, in the more temperate regions (Zones 5 and 6), start seeds in August.

These dual season vegetables include **Asian greens, beets, broccoli, Brussels sprouts, cabbage, fava beans, garlic, kale, leeks, lettuce, onions, peas, potatoes, spinach**, and **turnips.**

Warm-weather vegetables, on the other hand, thrive when the night temperatures range from 60 to 65 degrees Fahrenheit and daytime temperatures are in the 75 to 85 degree range. These plants can be particular; the seeds will not even germinate if the soil temperature is below 50 degrees Fahrenheit; the ideal sprouting temperature is 60 degrees Fahrenheit. Plant seeds indoors four to six weeks before the last frost for a jump start or seed directly in the ground when the soil has warmed up. These herbs and vegetables include: all annual **herbs, beans, corn, cucumbers, eggplant, melons, okra, peppers, squash, sweet potatoes, tomatillos,** and **tomatoes.**

Most herbs and vegetables require at least six hours of sun a day to reach their potential. Fortunately, there are a few exceptions. **Sweet woodruff** wilts in full sun, yet is happy in part shade. Many of the cool-loving plants will grow where tree are deciduous; the plants are up an d growing well before the trees start to leaf out. **Lettuces** and **greens** do best in partial shade, especially as the weather warms in summer. They benefit from the shady coolness; it is 15 degrees cooler in the shade than in the sun.

Herbs & Vegetables

PLANTING

Get a jump-start on the season by starting seeds of plants that need a long growing season and warm-weather plants indoors. There is a wealth of helpful information—albeit in very small type—on the back of seed packets. Often there is a map of the U.S. with planting dates for various regions (these may not be the same as the USDA Hardiness Zones). Planting time, depth, spacing, transplant information, thinning, and more is on the seed packet. Often you will find good information in the seed catalogs, as well. Follow these directions for the ideal indoor and outdoor sowing times.

Read the instructions for planting times and then group seed packets together that get planted—inside or out—at the same time. Cathy secures them with a rubber band and write the planting time on a 3 by 5 index card that slip in front of the top pack of seeds. She uses an old file box to keep the seeds in chronological order. Note also when to sow for a fall crop if you think you will do a mid- to late-summer planting. Cathy finds that she never has room to do this as so many of her plants continue to produce; she doesn't harvest entire plants, rather she picks off what she needs for the next meal or the whole day. Cathy grows **leaf lettuces** because leaves grow at the center of the plant that emerge after she picks the outer leaves.

Grow varieties that are heat-tolerant and plant **lettuces** in semishade for a summer-long harvest.

When sowing seeds outside (direct seeding), sow twice as many seeds as called for, at half the recommended spacing. Once the seeds have germinated and there are two sets of true leaves, prick out the weaker seedlings and let the strong ones keep growing.

TO SEED OR NOT TO SEED

Even though this chapter talks about sowing seeds you don't have to grow everything from seed.

Today, you can find starts or seedlings of a number of common vegetables and herbs at nurseries, garden centers, home stores, many grocery stores, and even some hardware stores.

Caveat emptor (buyer beware). Often these small plants are put on display when the ground is still frozen—much too early to think of planting, or buying plants. The seedlings are in a fast-growing mode; unfortunately their containers are usually cell packs that have very little room for root growth. It doesn't take very long before the seedling is rootbound, which puts it in stress.

When you're buying plants in containers—especially cell packs—look a the bottom of the container or cell pack. If you see roots coming out of the drainage hole, put the plant back on the shelf. That plant is already too stressed; it may live, but it will not thrive.

Some venues have personnel who know plants and can care for them, including providing ample water and potting up plants before they become rootbound. Cathy gives these places her business.

CARE

Wait a week or so after planting to mulch transplants; wait until direct-seeded plants have at least two sets of leaves before mulching. Keep the mulch a half inch away from the stem. Use rich, organic mulch (compost, well-rotted manure, leaf mold) and spread a two-inch layer all around the plant. Top dress with a decorative mulch such as small bark, weed-free straw, finely chipped wood, and cocoa hulls. **Warning:** do not use cocoa mulch if you have dogs or dogs frequent your garden. Chocolate is toxic to dogs.

Most of the perennial and tender perennial herbs are native to the Mediterranean (**thyme, oregano, rosemary, sage**, etc.) and prefer well-drained soil. The same goes for their mulch. Do not use organic matter that will preserve soil moisture and eventually break down and feed the

Herbs & Vegetables

plant. Instead, choose sand (well-washed beach sand or builder's sand), gravel, pebbles, or even small terra cotta pot shards. Water can pass quickly through these materials.

Some companion plants help nourish adjacent plants, in addition to the role they play in the fight against insect pests. Any legumes, including **peas** and **beans,** fix nitrogen from the air and add nutrition to the soil. Plant them with root vegetables—**carrots**, **turnips**, **radishes**, **rutabagas**, and **beets**.

In contrast, some plants have a negative effect on one another. They may compete for the same sun, soil, and nutrients, attract pests or disease, or inhibit growth of the other. Have you noticed that some plants—not the proliferating weeds—don't grow well near a bird feeder. Sunflower hulls are the culprits. Black walnut trees have a substance in their roots that inhibits most other plant growth. Although **fennel** stunts neighboring plants, plant it by itself near the garden as it attracts beneficial parasitic wasps.

WATERING

The best time to water is early in the morning. Watering at ground level, using leaky pipe hoses or an irrigation system with emitters low to the ground, is the most efficient, least costly way to water. The moisture goes directly to the roots, where it is needed. No water splashes on the leaves or evaporates into the air as a traditional sprinkler would do.

Even if you have to water from above, aim as low as possible and keep the stream gentle. You don't want to wash away soil or tender seedlings. If the leaves do get wet during an early watering they have a chance to dry off before the cool of evening, thus cutting down on potential fungal diseases.

For seeds and young transplants, keep the soil lightly moist until they are established. Depending on the soil and weather, large vining plants may need watering daily to keep them in good health. However, you want to encourage deep roots, so check the soil with your finger; if the top inch is dry, water, if not it can go another day or so.

Once plants are established, many herbs and vegetables can thrive on an inch of water a week; the Mediterranean herbs are happy with less water. Interestingly, once fruit is set on **melons,** they can grow without much water; although the fruit will be smaller, it is sweeter. **Tomatoes, peppers**, **beans**, **winter squash**, and **corn** will have better flavor if stressed (once they have set fruit). Watering once every two to three weeks suffices.

Some plants, such as **basil**, **eggplant**, **summer squash**, **cucumbers,** and **lettuces** are guzzlers and need more water; keep their soil lightly moist.

Root vegetables, like **carrots**, **radishes**, and **beets**, will become pithy without ample moisture; yet an inch a week will keep them going.

Don't water by the calendar, saying that "Tuesday is watering day." Water in synchronization with the weather. This year Cathy watered once when planting and since then Mother Nature has provided more than enough moisture. If we get into a weather system with five or more sunny days with temperatures in the 90s, I'll check the soil and water if needed.

There's no need to water the entire garden; water those plants that need it. Although it is not very aesthetic (although some people have painted their pop bottles so they look like primitive yard art), 2-liter plastic soda pop bottles make excellent automatic watering systems. Cut the bottom off the bottle and insert the top third (or more if you want) in the ground near the plant you want watered. Take care not to damage roots. Water the plant well and then fill the bottle with water. Slowly, it will disburse water to the roots—no waste through evaporation. If you are going to be away, use pop bottles to water indoor plants, as well.

Herbs & Vegetables

FERTILIZING

If you have enriched your soil with plenty of organic matter before planting, you can hold off on fertilizing for at least a month.

Do not fertilize any of the perennial or Mediterranean herbs.

Foliar feed plants once every two weeks, spraying a dilution (follow package instructions) of fish emulsion or sea kelp. Spray all the leaves. Do this early in the day—wait until the dew has dried—and never spray if the temperature is going to be over 80 degrees Fahrenheit.

If you're going to be doing a lot of traveling during the growing season, it's enough to ask a friend to water if need be, but feeding the plants is above and beyond expectations. Make sure to mulch your plants well with compost after planting them. Cover the compost, after watering the plant, with another organic mulch, either leaf mold, straw, or finely ground bark. This way, each time the plants are watered, they get some compost tea to nourish them.

HARVESTING

The best time to pick vegetables or harvest herbs is early in the day—after the dew has dried. In general, it is the herb's leaf or stem that is picked. The flavor of some herbs, especially **basil,** becomes much stronger once flowering has begun.

The same holds true for many green leafy vegetables—the stalk may elongate or flowers appear. When **lettuce** leaves start to appear milky where you've cut them off the plant, they are too bitter to eat.

It isn't often that Cathy harvests an entire plant, with **cabbage** being the only exception. Even then, as with **broccoli,** cut off the head, but leave the plant in the ground. Often she's rewarded with side shoots that produce "baby" vegetables.

Pick vegetables at their peak of ripeness. Although some veggies like **tomatoes** continue to ripen after they are picked, others like **peppers** and **peas** remain at the state of maturity they were when harvested.

To avoid injuring the plant when harvesting, use a sharp knife or hand pruners to cut off vegetables and the stems or leaves of herbs.

PROBLEMS

Companion planting makes use of pairings of herbs and vegetables to create a well-balanced garden. The insects, good and bad, in your gardens are different from those in other people's gardens; each habitat is unique. Experiment with companion plants to see how they work for you.

Marigolds exude a substance from their roots that repels eelworms and root-sucking nematodes. Try a border of **marigolds** to keep these pests away from precious edibles. **Garlic** is a good all-purpose pest repellent, giving off sulfur compounds (hence its smell) that kill aphids and onion flies. **Borage** and **tomatoes** are great companions. **Borage** attracts bees that help pollinate **tomatoes,** increases the yield of **tomatoes,** deters tomato worms, strengthens the growth of the **tomato** plant, and improves the flavor of its fruit.

Herbs & Vegetables

Companion Planting for Vegetables

Some plants benefit by proximity to other plants. Plant allies generally help each other grow better; they make good neighbors in the garden. Plant enemies, conversely, hinder each other's growth, so keep them well away from each other in the garden.

Vegetable	Allies	Enemies—Effects
Beans	Beets (only bush beans) broccoli, cabbage, carrots, corn, cucumbers, peas, potatoes, radishes, Swiss chard	Onions - Stunt growth
Beets	Bush beans, broccoli, cabbage, lettuce, onions	Pole beans - Stunt growth
Broccoli	Beets, cucumber, lettuce, onions, potatoes, spinach, Swiss chard	None
Cabbage	Beets, cucumber, lettuce, onions, potatoes, spinach, Swiss chard	None
Carrots	Beans, lettuce, onions, Peas, peppers, radishes, tomatoes	Dill - Retards growth
Corn	Beans, cucumber, peas, potatoes, pumpkins, squash	Tomatoes - Attract worm that feeds on corn
Cucumber	Beans, broccoli, cabbage, corn, peas, radishes, tomatoes	Sage - Retards growth
Lettuce	Beets, broccoli, cabbage, carrots, onions, radishes	None
Peas	Beans, carrots, corn, cucumbers, radishes, turnips	Onions - Stunt growth
Peppers	Carrots, onion, tomatoes,	None
Potatoes	Beans, broccoli, cabbage corn, peas	Tomatoes - Attacked by same blights
Pumpkins	Corn, squash	Potatos - Inhibits growth
Radishes	Beans, carrots, cucumbers, lettuce, peas	Hyssop - Inhibits growth
Spinach	Broccoli, cabbage	None
Squash	Corn	Potatos - Inhibits growth
Swiss chard	Beans, cabbage, onions	None
Tomatoes	Carrots, cucumbers, onions, peppers	Corn - Attracts tomato worm Dill - Retards growth Potatos - Attacked by same blight
Turnips	Peas	Potatos - Inhibits growth

Herbs & Vegetables

Name	Grow From	Planting Time/ Start Indoors	Spacing Between Plants, Rows (inches)	Days to Harvest
Asparagus	crowns	ESP	18 to 24/ 36 to 48	3 years first planting
Beans, bush	seed	MSP, ALF, ESU	2 to 3/ 24	50 to 70
Beans, lima	seed	ALF	4 to 6/ 24	65 to 90
Beans, pole	seed	ALF	4 to 6/ 24	45 to 65
Beets	seed	ESP, SP, MSP, ALF	2 to 3/ 12 to 18	60 to 110
Broccoli	plants	ESP, ESU	18 to 24/ 24 to 30	60 to 80
Cabbage	plants	ESP, SP, ESU	18 to 24 20 to 28	60 to 100
Carrots	seeds	ESP, SP, ALF, ESU	2 to 3/ 12 to 18	60 to 100
Cauliflower	plants	ESP, ESU	18 to 24/ 24 to 30	60 to 80
Chinese cabbage	plants	MSU	12 to 18/ 20 to 24	80 to 100
Corn, sweet	seeds	MSP, ALF, ESU	8 to 12/ 30 to 36	65 to 110
Cucumbers	seeds	ALF, ESU	15 to 18 / 48 to 60	50 to 80
Eggplant	plants	ALF	18 / 24 to 30	75 to 85
Endive	seeds	ESP, MSU	2 to 4 / 6	65 to 85
Kale	seeds	ESP, MSU	4 / 12 to 18	60 to 70
Kohlrabi	seeds	ESP, SP, MSP	4 to 6 / 15 to 24	50 to 60
Lettuce (leaf)	seeds	ESP, SP, MSP	6 / 6 to 15	40 to 60
Melon	seeds	ALF	18 to 24 / 48 to 60	90 to 120
Mustard	seeds	ESP, SP, MSP, MSU	4 / 12 to 18	40 to 60
Onion	seeds	ESP, SP, MSP	2 to 3 / 12 to 15	100 to 140
Onion	sets	ESP, SP	2 to 3 / 12 to 15	90 to 100
Parsley	seeds	ESP, SP, MSP	4 / 12 to 18	80 to 100
Peas	seeds	ESP, SP	1 to 2 / 6 to 12	45 to 90
Peppers	plants	ALF	8 / 24 to 30	70 to 75
Potatoes	eyed pieces	ESP, SP, MSP	12 / 24 to 36	140 to 150
Pumpkins	seeds in hills	ALF	4 / 60 to 72	90 to 120
Radishes	seeds	ESP, SP, MSU	1 to 1 to 2 / 6 to 12	30 to 60
Rhubarb	crowns	ESP	36 to 72/ 36 to 60	1 year
Spinach	seeds	ESP, SP, MSU	3 / 12 to 18	50 to 70
Summer squash	seeds	ALF	4 / 24 to 30	60 to 75
Swiss chard	plants	ESP, SP	6 to 8 / 15 to 18	60 to 75
Tomatoes	plants	ALF	24 to 36 / 24 to 48	70 to 100
Turnips	seeds	ESU, MSU	18 to 24 / 18 to 24	60 to 90
Watermelons	seeds	ALF	60 to 84 / 60 to 84	90 to 130
Winter squash	seeds in hills	ALF	4 / 60 to 72	90 to 120

Key: Planting Date
ESP – Early spring or whenever you can work the ground and it is not too wet
SP – Ten to fourteen days after ESP
MSP – Twenty to twenty-four days after ESP
ALF – After the danger of frost has passed
ESU – Early summer (late June, early July) plantings of slow-growing autumn plants
MSU – Mid-summer (mid to late July) plantings of fast-growing autumn plants

PLANNING

Begin to look at the catalogs that you have received in the mail. Make a list of any herbs and vegetable you want to put in your garden this year. Be sure to consider both seeds and plants. Check out both herbs and vegetables on the Internet. Search the general topic as well as individual plant names. You are sure to discover new mail-order sources and exciting herbs and vegetables you haven't seen before—both new introductions and heirlooms.

Look beyond the common, green-leafed plants for color interest. Many herbs have variegated forms, most commonly with the green leaf edged or spotted with cream or white. There are tricolor froms too: **tricolor sage** has green, purple and cream variegation. **Pineapple mint** has lovely cream and green variegated leaves. **Bronze fennel** is prized for its graceful bronzy foliage, which look like pony tails when they start to come out in spring. Other interesting purple- and bronze-colored leaves are found on **basils**, **orach**, **perilla**, and **sage**.

Silver- or gray-leaved plants provide foliage contrast. They are generally drought tolerant and cannot tolerate too much moisture. **Lavender**, some **dianthus**, **cardoon**, and **rue** are all wonderful accents with their grey to blue-green leaves.

Edible flowers, fruit, and vegetables all add a dash of color to the mixed border, bed, or garden. Depending on your taste, position the plants in the garden by their flower colors. Group the yellow-flowered herbs and yellow vegetables together, then have oranges together, reds, pinks, etc. In an informal garden, you can plant seemingly randomly, but you may want to employ silver-leaved or white-flowered plants to separate colors that may clash. For a cool-colored garden; just choose blues, purples, and whites.

Have a hot garden with **peppers** in hues of red, orange, and yellow. **Tomatoes** in every shade of red, orange, and yellow; brilliant orange, red, or yellow **nasturtiums**; and some golden or orange **calendulas** finished off with brilliant red-flowered **pineapple sage**.

Some good edible yellows include: **mustard**, **calendula**, **dill**, **fennel**, **tomatoes**, and of course, **sunflowers**. **Bee balm**, **orach**, **safflower**, **daylilies**, **peppers** and **eggplants** take you into the reds and oranges.

For a cool-colored garden, choose herbs, fruits, and vegetables in hues of blue, purple, silver, and white. Foliage counts, too. **Borage**, **cardoon**, **artichoke**, **French tarragon**, **purple peppers**, **angelica**, **anise hyssop**, **pansies**, **borage**, **chicory**, **chives**, **eggplant**, **mint**, **rosemary**, **sage**, **thyme**, and **violets**.

The species of a plant may be one color, while the hybrids offer a greater color range. For shades of pink, look to **chives**, **eggplants**, **hyssop**, **oregano**, **pinks**, **rugosa rose**, **thyme**, and **tomatoes**.

PLANTING

It is too early to start seeds indoors for the spring and summer garden.

However, you can make a windowsill salad garden that you can begin to eat within three weeks.

Use a windowbox liner with drainage holes as the container. You will need a lipped try to set under it so you don't get the floor, windowsill, or table wet.

1 Lightly moisten some soilless seeding mixture and fill the windowbox to within 3/4 inch from the top.

2 Sow **lettuce**—leaf not heading type—seeds, mix in other greens (**arugula**, **mache**, **kale**, **mizuna**, and **cornsalad**) if you like. Sprinkle them over the soil so that the seeds are about half an inch apart.

3 Add a few baby **carrot** and **radish** seeds if you like.

4 Cover the seeds with a thin layer of moist seed mix. Cover the top of the container with plastic wrap, creating a greenhouse. Set it in a warm place—not in the sun.

5 Lift up the plastic and check on the seeds daily. It moisture has clung to the plastic wrap, gently tap it off onto the soil. If the top of the soil is dry, water by spraying with a mister. Recover the container.

6 Once you see green seedlings emerging, gradually over a few days, bring the container into bright light and into sun. Do not let the soil dry out.

7 As everything grows, it will become crowded in the windowbox. Thin the plants, cut the roots off the thinnings and use their leaves in a salad. You will probably have to repeat this.

8 Once the leaves are two to three inches high, begin the harvest. Take one or two leaves from each plant—or as many as you need—for salad. Because you are continually removing leaves from the outside of the greens, they will keep producing new leaves at the center.

 ## CARE

If your potted herbs are getting too small for the pot, repot them in fresh soil in a pot no more than 2 inches in diameter than the original pot.

 ## WATERING

Water any inside plants as needed.

If you have forced air heat, the humidity is lower than your plants like. Set the pots (all but the Mediterranean herbs) on a shallow tray filled with pebbles. Add water to the tray—not quite to the top of the pebbles. If the water level was higher, the plants would be sitting partially in water and couldn't drain properly.

If there is a January thaw, check any perennial or shrubby herbs and vegetables in the garden. If the soil is dry, water slowly but deeply.

 ## FERTILIZING

Wait one to two months to feed the plants.

 ## PRUNING

Cut herbs, taking only as much as you need each time.

 ## PROBLEMS

Keep an open eye for any signs of bugs on indoor herbs. Generally a good strong shower (cover the soil with aluminum foil) in water that feels slightly cool to the touch for several minutes can wash off the culprit. For good measure, repot the plant in a clean pot and new soil just in case any insects were in the soil.

FEBRUARY
Herbs & Vegetables

 PLANNING

Last call for ordering seeds. Pick out a second choice in case the variety you want is new and in such demand that it is sold out.

Potted dwarf citrus will grow in northern climates. Move it outside in summer, keep it in a cool, sunny location during winter, and you can pick homegrown citrus and enjoy its juicy sweetness.

Are you content eating one type of **tomato** all season when there are hundreds of varieties? Think about **sweet basil**. Wouldn't it be great to have variety (both for flavor and appearance in the garden) of growing purple leafed 'Opal' or 'Purple Ruffles", large leafed 'Genovese', **leaf lettuce** 'Crispum', cinnamon scented 'Fino Verde', **lemon basil** 'Citriodorum', and dwarf **basils** like 'Spicy Globe' and 'Dwarf Bush Basil'? The choices are greater when you grow from seed, yet each year, Cathy sees more and more different varieties at nurseries, garden centers, and home stores.

The Culinary Herbs. There is a wealth of plants that you probably have never tried. Most times, people are more enthusiastic about experimenting with new flavors and colors, when they have grown the plant themselves. Just look at the myriad herbs—far greater than the old standard **parsley, sage, rosemary,** and **thyme.**

 PLANTING

For a continuing harvest of salad greens, plant another windowbox like the one described in January "Planting", on page 120. Instead of **carrots** or **radishes**, plant a few **Johnny jump-up** seeds or **pansies**. Their edible flowers will add a subtle hint of minty flavor to salads or desserts.

 CARE

Renew mulches on potted plants.

Unless you are growing your plants directly under a fluorescent grow light, give each pot a quarter turn so the stems stay straight and the plant isn't reaching for the sun.

 WATERING

Continue the watering regime described in January "Watering."

 FERTILIZING

Give herbs (except for the Mediterranean ones), greens and any other culinary plants indoors a foliar feeding. As the emulsions smell a bit briny, you may want to do this in a room where the plants can remain overnight. Bring them back to their proper homes the next day.

 PRUNING

Enjoy your fresh herbs and salad greens—so much tastier and more nutritious than anything from the supermarket.

 PROBLEMS

If you notice little fruitflies flying around any plant—they seem to come free with bananas—swatting does no good. Instead, put about an inch of sugar water in a clear jar. Top it with a funnel. If you don't have a funnel, fashion one from a coffee filter. Cut a half-inch hole at the base and set the paper funnel on the jar (part of the funnel extends down into the jar. The insects are attracted by the sugar water and can easily fly down the funnel to drink. However, they won't be able to get back out. When the sugar water gets too full of bugs, pour it down the drain and make up a new batch.

MARCH

 PLANNING

Save any leftover seed from this month's or future month's plantings, Store them in a well-labeled, clean, dry envelope. Mark the date you opened the seed packet.

 PLANTING

Those of you who live in the warmer parts of our region—Kansas, southern Iowa and southern Nebraska—can start seeds of some of the cool-loving plants. Grow them indoors completely, or start them indoors and then put them in a cold frame when they have reached a good size.

Start the hardiest plants—those that can withstand a frost. This includes most of the mustard family (*Brassicas ssp.*): **broccoli**, **cauliflower**, **cabbage**, and **Brussels sprouts**.

Plant them in pots, peat pots, yogurt containers, seed flats, margarine tubs, or milk cartons cut to half their height. These are suggestions for seed-starting containers; you will undoubtedly come up with other good planters.

Follow the instructions for seed starting on page 120 (January "Planting"), being sure to know that the directions on the back of the seed packet supercedes anything—at least as far as planting goes.

I always sow two or three seeds in the individual containers. Sometimes one seed doesn't germinate, but the other one does. Once they are up and starting to put out true leaves, remove the weaker or smaller one and leave the other to grow on. . . Darwin's Law—survival of the fittest. Label the containers.

If you can't bear disposing of any living thing (although it contribute nourishment to its relatives if it's added to the compost pile), repot the seedling and keep it or give it to a fellow gardener.

 CARE

Once the *Brassica* seeds germinate, move the pots into a cool, bright place. If they are kept at regular house temperature, they will need a longer period to harden off before they can go in the garden.

If the weather permits, take a good look around the garden. Do a light cleanup and get rid of any debris. Check whether the ground has started to thaw. Check shrubs for any winter damage; make a clean cut on broken limbs.

 WATERING

Follow February's watering regimen.

If the ground has thawed and it has been a dry winter, water existing plants.

 FERTILIZING

No feeding is necessary this month.

 PRUNING

Enjoy your luscious salad greens. Try drizzling them with a little balsamic vinegar and the juice from an orange as a tasty, no-fat, easy-to-prepare dressing.

 PROBLEMS

Diversity is all-important. Incorporate some of these herbs in your plantings to attract beneficial insects: **caraway**, **catnip**, **daisy**, **dill**, **fennel**, **hyssop**, **lemon balm**, **lovage**, **mint**, **parsley**, **rosemary**, **thyme**, and **yarrow**.

APRIL
Herbs & Vegetables

 PLANNING

Even though we're talking about plants as food to be enjoyed through the sense of taste, don't ignore the sense of smell or sight. Imagine the sweet perfume of **lavender** in summer and the way **Rainbow chard** looks like stained glass when the sun shines through its colored leaves, stems, and veins.

Every garden needs some fragrant foliage; site the plants in a place that you may lightly brush as you pass. Many culinary herbs fit the bill. You will notice that some herbs have many varieties, such as **mint,** each with a unique scent. Other multi-aromatics include **basil, lavender, rosemary,** and **thyme, Scented geranium** are the most prolific of the group. In Victorian times, there were well over one hundred different varieties.

Consider some of these plants as well; each has a distinctive aroma: **anise hyssop, beebalm, borage, chamomile, chervil, chives, coriander, dill, fennel, lemon balm, lemon grass, lemon verbena, marjoram, oregano, parsley, sage, sweet woodruff,** and **tarragon**.

 PLANTING

Be aware of the mature heights of the herbs and vegetables you put in the garden. You don't want tall plants in the front or edge of the garden, dwarfing the small plants behind. As in any other garden, taller plants like **lovage, tomatoes, corn,** and **fennel** go in the back (or center in the case of a round bed) with decreasing height as you go towards the edge. **Thymes, parsley, lettuces,** additional salad greens, **strawberries** (even though they are fruit), **radishes, carrots,** and other low-growing sprawling herbs and vegetables are excellent along the edge of an informal bed, softening any hard edges.

Be creative and don't plant in soldierly rows. As soon as the soil is workable and not too wet, plant **peas**—all kinds: **sugar snap, Chinese podded peas,** and traditional **English peas**.

Harden off the *Brassica* you started inside and plant them. Direct seed **kohlrabi** in the garden as well as the other *Brassica species* if you did not jump start them inside. Sow seeds of lettuces and other salad greens outdoors. Plant them singly or all mixed together. Refer to January "Planting" on page 120 for a listing of greens. In addition,

include **arugula**, various **kales,** 'Rainbow' **Swiss chard, spinach**, and **Japanese red mustard**. Add a few **dill** and **Johnny jump-up** seeds to the mix.

Consider edging a path or bed with a salad mix. Put it where the neighbors can see it—but not their dogs. Show your friends how to harvest—outer leaves first—as you'll have more than enough to share. Don't worry about the varying heights of the plants; you will be harvesting them all when they are young.

Use the planting chart at the beginning of this chapter or follow the instructions on the seed packets for starting seeds of certain warm-weather plants indoors, including **tomatoes, eggplants, peppers, basil, cilantro,** and most annual herbs. Wait until the soil is about 60 degrees Fahrenheit before sowing the larger-seeded vegetables, or any root vegetables—they don't transplant well.

 CARE

If a light frost threatens, especially within a week of transplanting or as young seedlings are emerging from the ground, or a heavy frost at any time, cover the plants. Use bent hangers as hoops to keep the cover from squashing the tender seedlings. To conserve heat—

Wait until the soil is about 60 degrees Fahrenheit before sowing the larger-seeded vegetables, or any root vegetables—they don't transplant well.

Reemay or other floating row covers, sheets, blankets, large garbage bags; anything that will protect the plants.

In the morning, if frost is visible on the covering, remove the cover when the mercury is climbing above freezing. You don't want the frost to melt and drip through onto the plants or refreeze.

 WATERING

Make sure that new transplants are just lightly moist; if they are too wet, they are prone to fungal problems.

For indoor plants, continue the watering regimen described in February "Watering."

 FERTILIZING

You have a continued reprieve from feeding this month.

Did You Know?

Give **peas** and **beans** some support for their tendrils wend their way upward. A trellis can work, but the pieces may be too big for the pea tendrils to grasp. Put five-foot stakes in every 24 to 36 inches along the row of peas. Attach the support—chicken wire, turkey wire, or bird netting—to each of the stakes in progression. The simplest way is to fasten string or fishing line to screws or nails placed 4 inches apart to the maximum height of the plant and run it from one end stake to another.

 PRUNING

After a few more harvests from your salad windowboxes, move them outdoors into dappled shade. As long as the plants aren't pulled out or cut so short there are no leaves, the green will keep producing for a month or more depending on the weather

 PROBLEMS

When you think of animals in the garden, you imagine them creating problems, not as the solution to a problem. Yet these creatures—some of which you may rather not see—wield control over the true pests. So, next time you see a bat, snake, or spider, thank it for its efforts on your behalf.

The little brown bat eats moths, caddis flies, midges, beetles, and mosquitoes.

Spiders do a good job of insect control both outdoors and indoors. In their intricate webs, they catch a wide variety of insects and tie them up with their silk to eat later.

Snakes are more valuable than we care to admit. Garter snakes, green snakes, grass snakes, and brown snakes eat slugs, snails, and insects. Corn snakes and milk snakes dine on mice and rats.

It pays to keep a bird feeder and a birdbath going all year to attract these feathery friends. Flycatchers, swallows, warblers, nuthatches and others consume a huge number of insects.

PLANNING

For a sunny hillside, consider growing **winter squash** and **pumpkins**. They are perfect hillside groundcovers; the vigorous vines keep the soil from eroding, without bullying other plants. The dark green leaves are attractive and the variety of shapes and colors of the **squash** and **pumpkins** provide interest throughout autumn.

PLANTING

For some of you, this is a May activity; in colder areas, transplanting happens in June. After all danger of frost is past (get information on your last frost date from the local Cooperative Extension Service) and the soil temperature is consistently over 60 degrees Fahrenheit, harden off and transplant **tomatoes** and other warm-weather plants outside. Be sure to use transplant solution to water them in.

If you did not start them inside, sow **tomato**, **eggplant**, **peppers**, and **basil**, and other annual herb seeds directly in the garden, labeling as you go.

Sow **carrots** and **radishes** together. The **radishes** grow faster than the **carrots**, so they help loosen the surrounding soil.

Dig a twelve-inch-deep trench; put the soil along the sides. Mix in two inches of compost. Plant seed potatoes or potato eyes in the trench spacing them about two feet apart. If you are using cut potatoes with eyes, lightly dust them with sulfur before planting to discourage any soil-borne diseases, rot or mold. Cover with two inches of soil and water in with transplant solution. As the **potato** shoots begin to emerge in the trench, cover them with two inches of soil. Continue doing this every couple of weeks until all the amended soil is on the plants.

Direct sow the other warm-weather plant that grow too quickly to start inside, including **beans, corn, cucumber, squash,** and **malabar spinach.** Make successive sowings of **corn** and **beans** every two weeks to extend the harvest.

CARE

If you are short on space, but long on plants, consider growing up. Many of the vines can be trained skyward as long as the resulting fruit is not very heavy and can be supported with a pantyhose "sling" without pulling the support down: try **cucumbers**, **melons**, **pole beans**, **pumpkins**, **runner beans**, **squash**, and **zucchini**. With **squash**, **melons**, and **pumpkins**, choose the small-fruited varieties, often described as "mini" or "baby."

Thin direct-seeded seedlings to their ideal spacing (see the Planting Chart on page 119).

After all danger of frost has passed, start hardening off warm-weather herbs and vegetables. Gradually introduce them to the outdoor sun and temperatures, starting with an hour a day, and increasingly give them more outdoor time, slowly adding in nighttime outings as well. Within a week to ten days, they'll be ready to move to their outdoor home permanently.

If you are in a hurry to get the tender vegetable and herbs into the garden, create individual hothouses from plastic 1-gallon milk jugs. Cut off the bottom of the jug. Three to four weeks before normal planting time, set the bottomless jugs in places you plan to grow individual plants. Push them into the ground a bit so they don't fly off in a heavy wind. Screw the cap on and let it warm the soil for a few weeks. Remove the jug only long enough to get the plant into the ground and then replace it. During the day, if it is warm, remove the cap to let the jug vent. Be sure to recap the jug before nightfall.

Make sure everything is well mulched.

If you are short on space, but long on plants, consider growing up. Many of the vines can be trained skyward as long as the resulting fruit is not very heavy and can be supported with a pantyhose "sling" without pulling the support down.

WATERING

Most new transplants need at least an inch of water a week. Established plants can get by with less.

FERTILIZING

By the middle of the month, if the temperatures have been mild enough and the warm-season vegetables have been transplanted into the garden, begin foliar feeding vegetables and annual herbs every two weeks with fish emulsion or liquid kelp, following package directions.

PRUNING

Begin harvesting **asparagus** as soon as the spears are the length you prefer. With a sharp knife, cut the spear just above ground level. With enough plants, you can have **asparagus** every other day for at least a month.

Did You Know?

All About Chives

Chives are must-haves in any garden, both for their grasslike, oniony leaves and their lilac-pink pompom flowers. Keep cutting the flowers of these perennial plants, and they'll keep blooming intermittently for months. When you're cooking with the flowers, break them into florets (the individual flowers that make up the large flower head), or the flavor can be too intense (one flower can be the equivalent of an entire bulb of **garlic**). Rub the flower around the inside of a wooden bowl to release its essence when making a salad of mixed greens. Add some fresh-squeezed orange juice and balsamic vinegar for a quick and easy, flavorful, fat-free salad dressing. Include chive florets in marinades for meat, fish and chicken. Brush on marinade during cooking (craft a "brush" from **chive** stems and flowers), and sprinkle a few florets on the finished dish.

PROBLEMS

Walk around the garden and look closely at the plants—stems, leaves (top and bottom), flowers, fruit—with an eye to any critter that may be lurking, or signs that something has been nibbling.

Identify the pest; some, like slugs and snails, are nocturnal; if you can't find the culprit in the daytime, go out hunting at night with a flashlight.

Decide whether the damage is enough to warrant control. Handpick what you can.

JUNE
Herbs & Vegetables

PLANNING

In a moist, boggy area you can grow the best **celery** you will ever eat. **Watercress** flourishes in a small stream. There are a surprising number of edible aquatics, including **wild rice**, **lotus** (unripe seed and tubers), **water mint**, **taro** (tubers), **water cilantro water chestnuts**, and more.

Surprisingly, It is not too early to start thinking about a fall garden. First and foremost, take a hard look at the garden, realizing that the existing plants will fill in a lot of the bare space. If there is room or if there are plants that will be completely harvested by early July, start making your wish list. The best fall crops are the same as the early spring crops—greens of all sorts and *Brassicas* species. For a splash of color, include some **pansies**.

Find out if your local nursery, garden center, or home store carries starts of any of the plants you want. Right now, you can only find a few at select merchants. Get out the catalog and order seeds now, unless you have seeds left-over from spring planting.

PLANTING

Plant some herbs, salad greens and one or more **tomatoes** in containers near your kitchen door. Easy accessibility means you are likely to open the door and pick them for immediate use, no matter what the weather—very hot, rainy, and even a delightfully comfortable day. Yield on these plants is very high; as you keep picking, you are encouraging new leaf and fruit formation.

Make successive plantings of summer greens; change to **New Zealand spinach**, which can take the heat, and **lettuces** labeled for summer. They will get ample light and stay cooler in dappled sun or a place that has morning sun with shade from noon on.

CARE

Stake or cage **tomatoes**, if you didn't do it when they were planted. **Tomatoes** are one of the few vines that cannot climb on its own. You can let it run along the ground, but put some straw or other material under the vine to improve air circulation and to keep it from touching damp soil, which can lead to fungal diseases.

To train **tomatoes** to a single stem, pinch out any side shoots (they emerge between the main stem and a branch).

Cloth or old pantyhose are ideal for tying **tomatoes** and other plants to supports. Make a loose figure-eight that goes around the stem and support, crossing between the too. These are loose-fitting materials, so there's less danger of them cutting into the vine as it grows and expands. Tie every eight to twelve inches.

After a heavy rain or storm, go out into the garden and assess the damage. Restake plants, if necessary, using a stronger stake set deeper into the ground.

WATERING

Get a good rain gauge and set it in your garden. It will keep an accurate check of the amount of precipitation each week. Remember to empty the gauge at the end of each week. If the gauge measures less than one inch, supplement with sprinkler, hoses, or hand watering.

FERTILIZING

Give the Mediterranean herbs one foliar feeding early in the month. Foliar feed everything else twice a month.

PRUNING

Stop harvesting **asparagus** and let some of the stalks grow out into delicate, ferny foliage. Plants are dioicus, the females will bear red berries during summer.

Depending on how temperate the winter and spring were, you may be starting getting something besides salad and other leafy vegetables out of your garden.

Pick **snow peas** before the pods inside start to enlarge. **Sugar snap peas** are best once the pods are about half to three quarters filled out, although they are fine for cooking when completely ripe. Harvest **English**, or **garden peas**, when the pods are completely filled out

As the herb plants grow, cut off what you need. Pick **chive** blossoms, crumble them and use them like **onion**. Keeping the flowers picked off results in more flowers for a longer time.

Check the **broccoli** and other *Brassicas* species, except for the **Brussels sprouts**, which won't be harvested until fall. If the weather is turning hot for an extended period of time, harvest **broccoli** and **cauliflower** even if they have not reached mature size. Give the **cabbages** another few days, and if the mercury is still soaring, cut them too. Pull **carrots** and **radishes** when they are fairly young as they can get pithy as the temperature rises.

Did You Know?

Surprising Colors

There are a multitude of colors of familiar vegetable that might surprise you. The list shows the most common color first, followed by the vegetable's lesser known colors:

Name	Color	Other Colors
Beans	Green	Yellow, cream, purple
Cucumber	Green	Yellow
Eggplant	Deep purple	White, yellow, red-orange, purple & white
Peppers	Green	Brown, violet, purple, red, yellow, orange
Summer Squash	Green	Yellow, orange, green and white
Tomatoes	Red	Orange, yellow, white, green, pink, striped yellow and green or green on green, darker or different color shoulder (top part of the tomato) than the rest of the tomato.

 PROBLEMS

Did you know that some garden caterpillar pests metamorphose into beautiful, prized butterflies and moths that flit through the garden gathering nectar. The striped parsleyworm or celeryworm, which voraciously eats **parsley, celery, dill,** and **carrots,** eventually turns into the lovely black swallowtail butterfly. Unaware of this transformation, you could unwittingly kill off the potential butterflies by spraying the plants with (Bt *(Bacillus thuringiensis)*. Plant extra **parsley** in another space for the hungry larva; if they get out of control in your veggies, handpick and move them to the new feeding ground.

JULY
Herbs & Vegetables

 ## PLANNING

It's not too early to start thinking about a winter garden. You can eat fresh greens through much of winter if they are grown in a cold frame. You can buy fancy ones, or make a cold frame yourself. There are different kinds from very basic manual ones to preconstructed frames with automatic vents. Have it electrified or not. It depends on how much time and money you want to spend.

 ## PLANTING

Start the seeds for your autumn garden. Start those that take the most time first, followed in two weeks by the plants with the shorter growing period. (See Planting Chart on page 119.)

Although you can direct seed fall plants, germination may not be very good as the soil is quite warm, and you're trying to get these cool-season plants started. Instead, start them indoors or outside. Outdoors, start them in full shade; once the seeds have germinated, move them to dappled shade.

 ## CARE

By this time of year, **chives** tend to get a bit tough. Cut back your **chives** within an inch of the ground to spur a new spurt of growth of tender, young leaves.

If you are growing **tomatoes** on stakes or in a cage, pinch out the side shoots that grow out at an angle between a branch and the stem the as soon as you see them. This practice does limit your harvest a bit. You may have less fruit, but it will be larger than on plants that grow wild.

Cathy started pinching **tomatoes** weekly in spring and the plants were vigorous yet manageable. After being away for a week, it was too late to undo the great growth the **tomatoes** had put on. I have to prune the plants as they threaten to grow over the sidewalk in my front-yard garden. It is challenging to get into the mass of shrubbery to find the **tomatoes.**

Pinch flower spikes from **basil** as they appear. The small flowers are edible, but if the plant goes into full flower the leaves change flavor—and not for the better.

 ## WATERING

As the temperature climbs, keep the vegetables and all herbs (except the Mediterranean herbs) well-watered. A long slow watering is ideal as it allows the water to be drawn deeper into the soil, encouraging the plant to grow deeper roots. That, in turn, keeps the plant from wilting as soon as it would with shallow roots.

The exception to slow watering directed at the root area is when the temperatures are in the 90s or above. A midday spritz from a sprinkler or a good misting from a hose helps to cool down the plants. As perspiration aids us in keeping our bodies cool through evaporation, the evaporation of the water from a plant's leaves cools it down. Cathy often restricts herself to the plants that prefer cool weather, such as **lettuces**, **broccoli**, **cabbage**, **Brussels sprouts**, and other leafy greens.

 ## FERTILIZING

Skip the foliar feeding for the Mediterranean herbs this month. Foliar feed all other herbs and vegetables.

Although you can direct seed fall plants, germination may not be very good as the soil is quite warm, and you're trying to get these cool-season plants started. Instead, start them indoors or outside in full shade.

Some plants need a lot of energy to keep growing and fruiting, so foliar feeding by itself is not enough. Spread about two to three inches of compost or humus around the base of the plant. Avoid smothering the stem by keeping the compost/mulch an inch away from it. **Tomatoes**, **squash**, **melons**, **peppers**, **eggplants**, and **cucumbers** all benefit from a nutritional boost. Unlike many commercial fertilizers which give the plant a big meal all at once, compost enriches the soil, so the plant is getting a constant supply of nutrients.

PRUNING

Cut handfuls of herbs—with as long a stem as possible. Gather them (a single variety at a time) with a rubber band and hang them upside down in a dry area. Once they are dry, you can keep them in bunches or remove the leaves and store them in a glass bottle for use all winter.

Keep picking vegetables as they ripen. Don't forget about your root crops, such as **beets, carrots,** and **radishes.**

Did You Know?

A Winter Spa for Plants

Constructing a cold frame can be very basic, or more challenging but more aesthetic, with a few bells and whistles. The basic shape is rectangular, commonly with a 1:2 ratio of depth to width (2 x 4 feet, 3 x 6 feet, etc).

The very simplest cold frame is created with bales of hay, straw, or whatever is available and inexpensive), stacked up two or three high. Make sure that you and anyone who might be helping can easily lean into the cold frame, touch bottom, and reach to the back without having to lean so hard against the front bales that they could get knocked into the frame. Set the lid on the bales; for strength, it should rest on the outsides of the bales.

If you construct the cold frame from wood, you can angle the sides so the back of the frame, where the top attaches, is higher than the front. This allows better access to the plants inside.

The top of the frame needs to be clear—glass or some type of plastic. Old windows or glass doors make excellent tops.

PROBLEMS

If you had covered some of your plants with floating row covers to prevent insects from eating your plants or laying their eggs so their larvae can feast on tasty veggies, it's time to remove it. At this time of year, it can get too hot under the cover. Put it away until you need it again in fall.

AUGUST
Herbs & Vegetables

 PLANNING

Think ahead to spring and start planting with edibility in mind. Order and plant some **tulip** bulbs. The petals of yellow, orange, and red **tulips** are the best tasting.

Grow **dandelions** on purpose? There are some wonderful French and European varieties that were bred for the flavors of the leaves and young flowers.

Most **daylily** flowers are delicious. 'Stella de Oro' is outstanding for its smaller flowers and constant bloom through summer. In spring, cut the leaf shoots (do this only once or you risk weakening or killing the plant) when they are less than 8 inches high. Use them in salads or stir-fries. Dried flowerbuds are a standard ingredient in Chinese hot and sour soup. The flower petals are a low-carb solution to chips with dips. Place a whole flower (pistils and anthers removed) in a wineglass and drop a scoop of ice cream, sherbet, or sorbet in the glass. What a simply elegant and easy dessert that is sure to wow guests.

 PLANTING

Around the middle of the month, start transplanting the fall vegetables you started earlier into the garden. They may need a few days of partial shade to adjust to the sun's brightness.

Sow seeds for **lettuces**, **chard**, **kale**, **spinach**, **mizuna**, and other greens that you will enjoy throughout fall by the second week of the month. With some protection, they might keep going through winter as well. Sow the seeds in the garden or in a cold frame if you have one.

If you are trying to grow seeds in a hot, dry area, there's a trick that's guaranteed to get you good germination. Make a small 2-inch furrow and water it until the soil is saturated, but not muddy. Scatter the seeds in the bottom of the furrow and then cover the furrow with burlap—secure it to the ground or it will blow away. The warm, moist environment is just what seeds need to germinate. Sprinkle with water—through the burlap—twice a day until the seeds germinate. Water daily until the seedlings have six leaves. After that, water as needed.

Plant some **ornamental kale**; it's beautiful and edible. There are a number of varieties, some with fringed leaves, others with curled leaves, and some that look like an open **cabbage**—in mixtures of green and white, rose and green.

 CARE

August can be so unbearably hot that it's hard to want to be in the garden. Take a break from it. Curiously, many other gardeners get a case of the August doldrums (Cathy coined the name in honor of the Dog Days of August, when there is no breeze and everything becomes slack). I ignore the garden for a couple of weeks (watering when necessary), take a break from it all, and relax. In one garden, Cathy rigged up a hammock in a lovely shady glen; she was surrounded only by the many shades of green of the trees and shrubs. What made it a "vacation" environment? She couldn't see the garden from there—no guilt. You've been nurturing plants all season, you need to nurture yourself as well.

WATERING

Keep up the July watering plan on page 131.

FERTILIZING

For the last big push of the season, follow the July information for fertilizing. In addition, foliar feed young transplants weekly.

PRUNING

August is often the most bountiful month in the garden. Graze through the garden, eating **tomatoes** still warm from the sun.

Is your harvest overwhelming? If you're like me, you plant way too much and have too little time to deal with bumper crops (canning, freezing, drying, or making sauces and soups). There are a lot of people and places (homeless shelters, nursing homes, food banks, soup kitchens) who would be happy to receive your extra fresh produce

See the Fair

Make time to go to your state fair! Head for the horticulture competition. You'll see some amazing fruits and vegetables. You'll no doubt discover a new variety of **tomato**, **corn**, **eggplant**, or other veggie that you hadn't seen before. Unfortunately, you can't taste the produce—it would be gone in less than five minutes if you could do that. Yet you can get the variety name from the entrant's card. When you come across a must-have, call the person who grew it and garner as much information as possible before ordering the seeds. For example, one gorgeous **tomato** that was about the size of a beefsteak looked so flavorful and luscious to Cathy. The grower saved her time, money, and space in her garden because the **tomato** was all show. It was watery and mealy inside (he'd won numerous blue ribbons entering that variety over the years).

In the future, you might want to become part of the nationwide Plant a Row for the Hungry (PAR) campaign sponsored by the Garden Writers Association. Last year, through PAR, people across the country raised 2.2 million pounds of food, which translates into 8.8 million meals. You don't have to plant an entire row—even one **zucchini** or other **summer squash** plant can produce enough food to make a difference. For information, contact visit the web site http://www.gardenwriters.org/par/

PROBLEMS

Do you have **tomatoes** with black spots on the bottoms? That's blossom end rot and it's caused by a deficiency of calcium and magnesium in your soil. Water tomatoes monthly with a solution of half a cup of Epsom salts diluted in a gallon of water. Give each plant a full gallon drink. Scratch one half-cup of pelleted lime around each plant and then water them well.

SEPTEMBER

 PLANNING

Spend some time doing research now that will benefit next year's garden. Go to the grocery store and note which vegetables and fruits are your favorites, paying special attention to the prices. Then take a realistic look at your garden and budget. It's smarter to grow **raspberries**, costing more than $3.00 a half pint or **asparagus** that rarely dips below $2.99 a pound than **zucchini** which can be as low as 20 cents a pound. Besides, in my opinion, one **zucchini** is pretty much like the rest; with **carrots**, **tomatoes**, **lettuces**, **cucumbers**, and more, the range of varieties seems limitless—shape, size, color, and flavor can vary greatly from one to another.

 PLANTING

There's still a little time to sow fall vegetables (greens and **radishes**) in a cold frame. Or, make a hoop house with a floating row cover. Although that does not provide ample protection for the big chill, it will give you a few weeks more harvest.

A few weeks before your first fall frost date, sow seeds of some of the hardier greens, such as **escarole**, **radicchio**, **spinach**, and **kale** in a raised bed (or any other area that you won't disturb during winter or spring). These greens are for a very early spring harvest. Even though they are small going into late fall and winter, most of them will just stop growing once the mercury plummets only to start growing again as the weather warms.

Look for **pansies** at your local nursery, garden center, or home store. Although they are touting "new fall varieties," such as the **Icicle** Series, any **pansy** will do. Cut off any flowers and plant them now in a place that you can easily see them. They will put out more blooms this fall (edible, with a slight wintergreen flavor) and continue into winter. Let the snow and ice come, and when it melts there will be your **pansies**, cheery faces to greet you. They will really start growing bigger in spring. Ironically, these cold-weather **pansies** can stand the heat better than ones you plant in spring. They can last well into summer.

 CARE

Time to pot up **rosemary** to bring indoors. Choose a pot that's about as wide as the width of the lowest branches. **Rosemary** grows best in "lean" soil you can blend at home by mixing equal parts of potting and cactus soils (available anywhere you buy plants).

Dig the plant up—digging down about a foot and around the plant at the tips of the branches. Shake most of the soil off the roots, untwine any ensnarled roots, and cut off overly long roots. Give it a quick shower in water that is slightly cool to the touch and then repot it and put it in a sunny place.

 WATERING

Continue to water weekly if the plants need it.

 FERTILIZING

You're done feeding plants for the season.

PRUNING

If you have the time, "put up" vegetables—today that ranges from old-fashioned canning to freezing and making dishes ahead of time or drying. When you look at a small jar of **basil** for $4.79, you realize that you can make dozens of jars of dried **basil** yourself with much better flavor and at a minimal cost.

Continue picking and harvesting vegetables and herbs. Do not harvest all of the stems on the Mediterranean herbs as most will come back next year.

A few weeks before your first fall frost date, sow seeds of some of the hardier greens, such as escarole, radicchio, spinach, and kale in a raised bed

Wait until after the first frost to pick **Brussels sprouts**; the cold enhances their flavor. Starting at the base of the plant, twist off only as many sprouts as you need at a time. The garden provides free refrigeration for the rest. And, most of us don't have enough refrigerator space for even one stalk of sprouts, much less any more.

Kale also benefits from a freeze. Extend the **kale** harvest (you can eat **ornamental kale** too, provided it wasn't sprayed before you bought it) into winter by picking only as many outer leaves as you need at a time. As long as the temperature is in the 40s, it will keep producing more leaves at the center of the plant.

If you still have green **tomatoes** on the vine, bring them indoors to ripen. Pick them off the vine and set them in a cool place where they won't get any direct or indirect sun. Lay them in a shallow box on the dining room buffet making sure that none are touching each other. Some folks bring in the entire vine and hang it upside down in the basement or attic to let the **tomatoes** ripen.

Did You Know?

Raised Beds Elevate the Garden

Nothing improves plant growth in clay soil better than a raised bed. Because they are raised, the soil warms up earlier, and you can start planting—and harvesting—earlier.

Prepare beds now for spring planting. Dig out the soil to a depth of six to twelve inches, breaking clods as best as you can. Move the soil onto a tarp.

On top of the soil, spread a two-inch layer of sharp sand or granite meal, two inches of lightly moistened peat moss, and three inches of compost or well-rotted manure.

Mix it all together and fill the hole, making a planting area above that gently slants inward from the soil up.

You don't even have to wait till spring to plant. Get the bed off to a good start by planting cloves of garlic an inch into the soil. Water well and let nature take its course through the winter and spring.

PROBLEMS

Japanese beetles have crossed the Mississippi and are here. If you see any of these $1/2$-inch, shiny green-black varmints, shake them off the plant into a plastic bag; it easy to do in early morning, as the beetles are not early risers. If they have been a problem throughout this growing season, attack them where they overwinter. Apply milky spore to lawn and garden areas—about a teaspoon every four feet, creating a grid pattern. Water it in. As the beetle grubs eat, they ingest some of the bacteria, which will kill them and only them. One application can last twenty to thirty years. But there's a catch: If you use chemical herbicides or pesticides, they will kill off all bacteria, which is another reason to go organic.

135

OCTOBER
Herbs & Vegetables

 ## PLANNING

As plants are completely harvested, collect the plant labels. Make any last-minute notes on the labels right after you pull them out of the ground. Otherwise, by the time you look at the labels again, it's likely that you won't remember the information. Cathy says, "I learned my lesson after throwing all the markers in a plastic bag and taking them into the house. A week or so later, I quickly jotted the notes I could remember on the labels. When I finally had time to scrutinize the labels, I found that I had put down info for the wrong cultivar, and in two instances that I caught, the wrong plant entirely."

Do not remove markers from any plants that are still in the ground—annuals that are still growing, and all the perennials, including herbs that stay outdoors for winter.

 ## PLANTING

If you don't have an evergreen and a deciduous shrub growing in or near the vegetables, take advantage of the fall clearance sales and buy them now and get them planted ASAP. They will give much needed winter protection. Be sure to use plenty of transplanting solution to encourage new roots so the plants can get established before winters comes blowing in.

Did You Know?

Tasty, Beautiful, and Perennial

Use **rhubarb** and **asparagus** as the backbone of a small perennial border. In spring, cut and cook the stems of each, freezing some to enjoy in fall and winter. After the harvest, the true beauty of both plants emerges. **Asparagus** grows tall with fernlike foliage, bearing small red berries in autumn.

Rhubarb's handsome red stalks are somewhat hidden by large, poisonous leaves. In summer, it sends up a tall stalk of small cream-colored flowers. Later, the seed heads are attractive—each dark seed surrounded by a semitransparent pod— excellent when used in flower arrangements. Order these plants for spring planting.

 ## CARE

Nothing improves plant growth in clay soil better than a raised bed. Because they are raised, the soil warms up earlier, and you can start planting—and harvesting—earlier.

 ## WATERING

Provide at least an inch of water a week to any plants still in the garden.

 ## FERTILIZING

No feeding is necessary.

 ## PRUNING

Check the **tomatoes** you brought indoors to ripen every couple of days. Remove any bad or overripe ones immediately. If you need ripe **tomatoes** soon, put a few in a brown paper bag with an apple. Close the bag, and lay it on its side so the fruits don't touch. The ethylene gas that the **apple** gives off encourages fast ripening. You may have noticed that when you have **apples** in the refrigerator, other fruits and vegetables will spoil faster than normal.

 ## PROBLEMS

Check any plant you bring indoors for any sign of pests. It's the ideal time to pot or repot the herbs and other plants. Shake off most of the soil from the roots and then give them a quick shower in tepid water (slightly cool to the touch). Repot and keep them separated from other houseplants for about three weeks. After that time, if they are still clean, let them join the other plants.

NOVEMBER
Herbs & Vegetables

 PLANNING

See the "Did You Know" on this page for information on rotating vegetable familes.

 PLANTING

Begin your winter break early—at least from outdoor planting.

If you want to grow **lettuce** and other salad greens in time for the holidays, you need to get started around the middle of the month. To have Thanksgiving greens, start on the 1st of the month; although that's cutting it close if Thanksgiving is earlier rather than later in the month. Refer to the Janurary "Planting" section for complete directions.

 CARE

Harvest any vegetables and herbs that are still left in the garden. Remember to take leaves of perennial herbs, such as **sage, thyme, oregano** to dry or freeze for winter use. Continue to clean up garden as neighbor's leaves blow into it.

 **Did You Know?**

Rotating Vegetables

• Don't pull out **parsley** plants after their first year. They are biennials and, even if the leaves discolor over winter, they'll send out new leaves in spring.

• Some plants are heavy feeders, while others actually enrich the soil. By changing the plants growing in one area the first year to a new space the second year, and yet someplace else the third year, you will have fewer pests and diseases than if you grew the same vegetable in the same place year after year. Grouping these plants by families makes it easier to see which crops should or shouldn't follow in succession. This is not critical if you are only growing one or two plants in the same family, but when you grow a "patch of **tomatoes**," be sure to plant something else there the following year.

 WATERING

Take care not to over water the indoor plants. Don't let them sit in a saucer of water.

If the ground hasn't frozen, continue watering outdoor plants; cut back a little on the water—to about three quarters of an inch a week

 FERTILIZING

Nothing to feed this month except yourself at Thanksgiving.

 PRUNING

Pick a few branches of **rosemary** to flavor your Thanksgiving stuffing. Add a bit of **parsley** if you have some.

Remember to use the **tomatoes** you are ripening.

PROBLEMS

Keep an eye on the indoor plants for any signs of pest or disease.

DECEMBER
Herbs & Vegetables

 PLANNING

Many long-time organic gardeners and immigrants who bring with them their gardening traditions steadfastly believe that plants are healthier and yields greater when they are planted in sync with the moon. Although this has not been scientifically proven or disproven, it adds an interesting twist to planning the garden.

The premise is based on the great influence that the moon exerts on the earth, as evidenced by the pull of the tides. It's easy to remember; plant annuals that produce their yield (flowers, vegetables) above the ground during the increasing light from the new moon to full moon. From full moon to new moon, during the decreasing light, plant biennials, perennials, bulbs, trees, shrubs and annuals which produce their yield (such as **potatoes, beets, turnips**—the root crops) underground.

 PLANTING

Unless you want more salad greens, take a holiday from planting.

 CARE

Make herbal bath salts for yourself by infusing **lavender** or **basil**, even **rosemary** (use whole branches rather than just the leaves), in 2 parts sea salt, one part dried milk powder, and 3 tablespoons of Epsom salts. Place the stems in a glass, and pour in the salt mixture. Store it in a dark place for about a month. Open the jar, remove the herbs and sniff; you don't want to be overwhelmed with fragrance, you want a lilt of perfume. If the scent is too strong, add proportional amounts of dried milk powder and salt until you get just the right fragrance for you. This can be a lovely holiday gift; put it in a fancy bottle or jar with a big bow.

 WATERING

Continue the directions given last month.

 FERTILIZING

Nothing to feed.

 PRUNING

Make use of the herbs you're growing indoors:

Stuff a sprig or two of **rosemary** (or **thyme**) under the chicken's skin when roasting a chicken.

Add **oregano** to any dish or sauce with **tomatoes.**

Chop some **chives** and toss them into a salad

Pretend it's still summer. Buy some fresh mozzarella cheese, Cut slices of your ripened **tomatoes,** and make a ring by overlapping a slice of cheese, a slice of **tomato,** and a large **basil** leaf. Drizzle with extra virgin olive oil and balsamic vinegar. This makes a tantalizingly colorful appetizer course for a holiday meal.

 PROBLEMS

Keep a watchful eye out for any intruders on your plants; often a strong shower of tepid, not cold or hot water will do the trick.

CHAPTER FIVE

Houseplants

Indoor gardens are the perfect way to make gardening a year-round avocation. When the rest of your garden is buried under snow, you can get some much-needed green relief from your houseplants.

Do not worry if you have been unsuccessful in the past. Most good gardeners have killed their share of houseplants along the way to developing green thumbs. The key to success is finding the right plant for your growing conditions and gardening style.

PLANNING

Start by evaluating the growing conditions in your home. Look at the available light, temperature, and humidity. Select plants that can tolerate the existing conditions. You will need to adapt your watering schedule to the plant's needs. This varies somewhat with each plant and each growing location.

Helping plants adapt to the growing conditions relates to your gardening style. If you like to water, groom, and generally fuss over your plants you can select **orchids**, **ferns**, and other houseplants that need a little extra care. If you prefer the benign-neglect plan, you need to select plants, such as **cactus**, **cast-iron plant**, and **snake plant,** that thrive with limited care. The plant must also fit in the space

available. Some houseplants grow into trees, while others crawl their way across the room. Select plants that fit your indoor décor, your personal style, and the available space.

Purchase a healthy plant. Investing a little extra money up front can save you a lot of frustration as well as money spent on replacement plants. Purchase plants that are acclimatized and are free of pests and signs of neglect.

Most houseplants are raised outdoors in southern, more tropical areas. They need to be acclimated to the lower light of indoor growing conditions. Quality plant growers have done this for you. Check with the florist, nursery, home store, or garden center where you regularly purchase your plants to see if they have plants suited for the indoors.

Avoid plants that show signs of insects or disease. Choose plants with lots of leaves with good color that are free from spots, blotches, and insects. Be sure to look under the leaves, on the stem, and the bottom of the pot. If you see roots coming out the drainage hole, put the plant back—it is rootbound. You do not need to pay for

added challenges. Gardening indoors offers challenges enough on its own. Avoid plants with:

- Sticky leaves from honeydew secreted by mites, aphids, whitefly, or scale.

- Fine webs in the leaf joints from spider mites.

- Small, hard-shelled bumps (scale insects) on stems and leaves.

- A small cloud of tiny white, flying insects (whitefly) that waft from the plant when you move it briskly through the air.

- Soft spots on leaves and stems from rot.

- Yellow leaves and brown tips from pest damage or poor care.

THE GROWING ENVIRONMENT

Light is usually the key factor in raising healthy plants. Unfortunately light is not always plentiful indoors. Select plants that will thrive in the available light, or consider growing some plants

Houseplants

under artificial lights. Here are some general categories for light requirements. You will have to monitor and experiment with the plants and lighting in your home to make a good match.

High-light plants must be in or next to a south-, east-, or west-facing window. Make sure there are no trees, buildings, awnings, or other structures diffusing the light.

Medium-light plants need bright (less direct) light all day. Place them within 3 feet of an unobstructed south-, east-, or west-facing window. Move plants closer to the window if the light is somewhat obstructed. Low-light plants need to be within 6 feet of a well-lit (south-, east-, or west-facing) window or next to a north-facing window. It is rare to find any houseplants suffering from too much light.

Temperature can also be difficult to control. Matching the needs of plants and people can be challenging. Most houseplants survive in normal household temperatures—they just do not like the low humidity that goes with them. Cooler temperatures increase humidity and help slow down plant growth to match the lower light conditions. Keep houseplants in cool, bright locations during the winter. Avoid drafts of hot or cold air (check where your heating ducts and returns are; keep plants away from them).

Humidity, like light, is a difficult environmental factor to change. You can help increase the humidity near your plants with one of these techniques. Group plants together. As one plant loses moisture from the leaves and soil, nearby plants benefit. Place pans of water on radiators. The added moisture is also good for the people in the house. Place plants on saucers filled with pebbles and water. The pot sits on the pebbles above the water. As the water evaporates, it increases the humidity around the plant. Create a terrarium for your plants. Buy one—yes they are back in style—or create your own. Use an old aquarium or other large glass container. Cover for high humidity lovers, but leave open for most plants.

Soil

Soil provides support and is the reservoir of nutrients and water for your plants. Select a sterile, well-drained potting mix. Soil-less mixes are the most common potting mixes on the market. They contain a mixture of peat moss, vermiculite, and perlite. These mixes are lightweight and well drained—perfect for gardeners who tend to overwater. Once these mixes dry, however, they are difficult to rewet. Your plant will be sitting in a block of hard, dry peat. Place it in a tray of

water and let it gradually absorb the moisture. Many gardeners concoct their own potting mix. Start with $1/3$ sterile soil, $1/3$ peat moss, and $1/3$ vermiculite or perlite. Adjust the proportions to your gardening style. Once you find a blend you like, mix extra. Store the soil in sealed 5-gallon buckets in a cool place for later use.

Watering

Always water plants thoroughly and allow the excess to drain out the bottom. Keep pebbles in the plant saucers so that the plants sit above, not in, the excess water. Growing conditions, the container, and the plant itself influence how often you need to water. Plants growing in bright light, high temperatures, and low humidity need to be watered more frequently than those in low light and cool temperatures. Plants in glazed ceramic or plastic containers dry out more slowly than those in porous clay or terracotta pots. The bigger the container, the slower it dries out.

The potting mix you use also influences watering. Soil-less mixes need to stay slightly moist. Their built-in drainage makes it difficult to overwater. Potting mixes containing soil are less forgiving. Waterlogged soils can mean death to your plants.

Houseplants

Water plants when:

- The top few inches of the soil-less mix are slightly moist. Wait to water until the top few inches of the soil-based mix are slightly dry. Use your finger to monitor soil moisture; it is the best moisture meter on the market.

- The container is lightweight due to the decrease in moisture.

- The leaves turn a bluish-green.

Fertilizing

Consider growing conditions, plant needs, and your growing goals when fertilizing plants. Houseplants in difficult conditions grow slowly and need little fertilizer. Increasing the fertilizer without improving the growing conditions can harm the plant. Most fertilization should be done in spring and summer when the growing conditions are better and the plants are actively growing.

Do not fertilize new plants for at least four months. Give them time to adjust to their new, often less than ideal, growing conditions. Plants growing in soil-less mixes need to be fertilized regularly. These mixes do not hold the nutrients like mineral soils. Some mixes come with slow-release fertilizers added, or you can add them yourself at planting time. Different types of slow-release fertilizers can provide needed nutrients for several months or the whole fertilizing season. Check label directions. Some gardeners prefer to have a little more control. Use a dilute solution of houseplant fertilizer once or twice a month. The more often you fertilize, the bigger and faster your plants will grow. Reduce fertilizing frequency to control plant growth.

Repotting

Do not be anxious to repot your houseplants. Most plants can spend months and even years in the same container. Plants like **African violets**, **hoyas**, **spider plants**, and **clivia** actually flower better when they are slightly potbound. Let the plant tell you when it needs to be moved.

Repot houseplants when:

- The roots fill the container. Carefully slide the plant out of the pot. If you see nothing but roots, it is time to transplant.

- Water runs right through the soil and out the drainage holes. This can also occur when soil-less mixes dry out.

- The new growth is stunted. Undersized growth and pale leaves can be caused by a lack of nutrients or lack of soil to hold those nutrients.

Move plants to a slightly larger (1 to 2 inches larger in diameter) container with drainage holes. Avoid over-potting (replanting in a much larger pot—more than 2 inches in diameter than the current pot). Many gardeners like to transplant once and be done. Unfortunately this is not best for the plant. Over-potting can cause a decline in growth coupled with waterlogged soil that lead to root rot and the eventual death of the plant.

Transplant in early spring when the light is increasing, days are lengthening, and plants are beginning to grow.

1 Select a clean container with drainage holes. Use a pot that is no more than 1 to 2 inches larger in diameter than the original container.

2 Use a sterile potting mix. Select or mix one that best suits your gardening style. Do not put gravel or clay pot chips in the bottom. They actually decrease drainage and lead to waterlogged soils. Cover the drainage hole with a coffee filter if you are concerned about soil spilling out the bottom.

3 Massage the sides of the pot to loosen the roots. Tip the pot over and slide the plant out of the container. Do not pull on the stem as this can damage the roots.

Houseplants

4 Free up potbound roots. You can lightly massage the rootball of slightly potbound plants; otherwise, use a knife to make shallow cuts on opposite sides and the bottom of the rootball. This frees up the roots, allowing them to grow into the new soil.

5 Put about 1 inch of fresh potting mix in the new container. Place the plant in the pot. Adjust the height by adding or removing some of the mix under the rootball. The soil level (same as crown of the plant) should be 1 inch below the rim of the container.

6 Fill in around the sides with fresh mix. Gently firm the soil in place with your fingers or by tapping the pot on the tabletop.

7 Water thoroughly to encourage root growth, settle the soil, and remove air pockets. Do not fertilize for at least one month.

8 Adjust the watering schedule to accommodate the change in potting mix, larger size container, and additional soil.

CARE

Clean and groom your houseplants regularly. It improves the plants' health and appearance. Wipe dust off smooth leaves with a damp sponge or cloth. Use a soft cosmetic brush to dust **African violets** and other fuzzy-leafed plants. Check under the leaves and along the stem for any unwelcome insects. It is much easier to control a few aphids than the large colony that can quickly develop. Remove any dying, damaged, or diseased leaves that will look pale green, yellow, brown, or full of holes. The plant will look better, and that reduces the risk of further problems.

Move the plants for even exposure to the sun. Turn the pot so that all sides eventually face the window. Every week Cathy gives each houseplant a quarter turn clockwise. Exchange plants in poor light conditions with those growing in more suitable conditions. A monthly switch can keep both plants growing despite the less than desirable conditions.

PRUNING

Houseplants, like any other plants, benefit from pruning. Save the majority of pruning for late winter or early spring before new growth begins. Remove broken, dead, or damaged stems or leaves as soon as they are found. Fall pruning should be reserved for plants that outgrew their home during summer vacation outdoors.

To prune houseplants:

1 Remove damaged, diseased, or dead branches.

2 Remove crossing and rubbing branches. This prevents injury and opens up the center of the plant for better light penetration.

3 Pinch out growing tips or cut back the stems of leggy plants to encourage branching and fuller growth.

4 Cut back stems just above a healthy bud or leaf, where one branch joins another or where the branch joins the main stem.

5 Play it safe and never remove more than $1/3$ of the total growth.

6 Air-layer severely overgrown plants. This technique is used to start new plants and rejuvenate old overgrown specimens.

PESTS

A healthy plant is your best defense against pests. Select the plant that is most suited to your home and provide it with proper care. Check frequently for insect sand diseases. Small infestations can often be picked off by hand or pruned off and destroyed. See the monthly "Pests" sections for common houseplant pests and their control.

Houseplants

Common Name (Botanical Name)	Light	Moisture	Comments
African Violet (*Saintpaulia*)	High to medium	Moist	Needs bright light or artificial light to flower. Warm temperature. Keep cold water and soil salts off leaves.
Aloe (*Aloe vera*)	High	Dry	Tolerates neglect as long as it receives good light. Plant juices soothe burns.
Asparagus Fern (*Asparagus densiflorus* 'Sprengeri')	High to medium	Slightly moist	Good bright light and cool temperatures. Often loses leaves in winter, but will recover if moved outdoors for summer.
Begonia (*Begonia* species)	Medium	Moist	Likes warm temperatures, high humidity, and moist organic soils.
Boston Fern (*Nephrolepsis exaltata* 'Bostoniensis')	High to medium	Moist	Bright light and high humidity. Summer outdoors if plant declines over winter.
Bromeliad (*Bromelia, Tillandsia,* and more)	High to medium	Moist to slightly dry	See August "Helpful Hints" (page 161)
Cactus (*Cereus, Mammillaria, Opuntia,* and more)	High	Dry	Summer outdoors or in a sunny south-facing window inside. Cool, bright location for winter to encourage bloom.
Cast-iron Plant (*Aspidistra elatior*)	Medium to low	Well drained to dry	Tough plant that tolerates a lot of abuse. May be hard to find.
Chinese Evergreen (*Aglaonema* species)	Medium to low	Well drained	Tough plant. Avoid wet soils and drafts.
Christmas Cactus (*Schlumbergera* species)	High to medium	Well drained	See October "Helpful Hints" (page 165) for reblooming information.
Clivia (*Clivia miniata*)	High	Moist, well drained	Blooms best when potbound.
Dracaena (*Dracaena* species)	Medium to low	Moist, well drained	Lots of varieties. Water and light needs vary with species. Brown leaf tips due to fluoride and chlorine in water. Keep soil slightly moist.
Dumb Cane (*Dieffenbachia* species)	High to medium	Moist, well drained	Needs bright light to maintain even bottom leaves. Air-layer to renew. Keep out of children's reach. It's poisonous.
English Ivy (*Hedera helix*)	High to medium	Moist	Watch for mites. Keep soil slightly moist and wash leaves occasionally.
Grape Ivy (*Cissus rhomifolia*)	Medium to low	Moist, well drained	Tough plant. Be careful not to overwater in low-light situations

Houseplants

Common Name (Botanical Name)	Light	Moisture	Comments
Hibiscus (*Hibiscus rosa-sinensis*)	High to medium Prefers high to flower	Moist, well drained	See September "Did You Know" (page 163)
Jade (*Crassula ovata*)	High	Well drained to dry	Summer outdoors or in a southern window. Bright light, cool temperatures, and dry soil for winter for blossoms.
Norfolk Island Pine (*Araucaria heterophylla*)	High to medium	Moist	Needs bright light and high humidity to keep lower branches and prevent drying.
Orchids (*Cattleya, Dendrobium, Phalaenopsis*)	High	Moist	Blooms over long period with little care.
Palm (*Areca, Chamaeodorea, Howea*, and more)	High to medium	Moist	Tough plant. Watch for mites and brown leaf tips if soil goes too dry.
Peace Lily (*Spathiphyllum* species)	Medium to low	Moist	Check often; this plant dries out fast. It will forgive you the first few times and then leaves start yellowing and browning.
Philodendron (*Philodendron* species)	High to low	Well drained	Tough plant. Prefers benign neglect; usually killed with kindness.
Pothos (*Epipremnum aureum*)	High to low	Well drained	Tough plant. Avoid overwatering.
Rubber Tree (*Ficus elastica*)	High to medium	Well drained	Loses leaves when adjusting to new location. Pinch out growing tip to encourage branching.
Schefflera (*Schefflera actinophylla*)	High	Moist, well drained	Avoid wet soggy soils and drafts. Watch for mites.
Snake Plant (*Sansevieria* species)	Medium to low	Well drained to dry	Tough plant that is difficult to kill. Will bloom when grown potbound in bright light.
Spider Plant (*Chlorophytum comosum*)	High to medium	Moist	Avoid brown tips (caused by chemicals in the water) by keeping soil slightly moist.
Wax Plant (*Hoya carnosa*)	High	Well drained	Summer outdoors to encourage blooming. Leave long, leafless stems intact for flowering. Watch for mealybugs.
Weeping Fig (*Ficus benjamina*)	High to medium	Moist	Drops leaves with any change in the environment. Can lose 95 percent of its leaves and still recover. Watch for scale insects.

Houseplants Notes

PLANNING

The short, dark days of January are hard on gardeners and houseplants alike. Consider moving your houseplants south for the winter to a south-facing window where the plants receive the most sunlight. Move low-light plants closer to the window and those near east- or west-facing windows to a south-facing window. Or move them under artificial lights. A combination of natural sunlight supplemented with artificial lights helps your houseplants survive the dark days of winter. Avoid drafts of hot and cold air. Cold drafts from patio doors and windows can chill the foliage and lead to root rot. Drafts of hot air from heating ducts unevenly heat and cool the plant and they lower humidity. The drier air is hard on the plants, but is a great environment for mites and aphids.

 ## PLANTING

Pot up purchased or stored **amaryllis** bulbs. See January "Planting" in the chapter on bulbs for details. Wait until the light increases, days lengthen, and temperatures warm to propagate and transplant other houseplants.

 ## CARE

The holidays may be over but your **poinsettia** and other holiday plants are still blooming. Keep these in a cool, bright location to prolong flowering. Once the bloom cycle is complete, remove faded flowers, decrease the watering, and move to a sunny window.

You may need to sacrifice some sunlight during extremely cold weather. Move plants away from the window or keep the curtains and blinds between the cold window and the plants. Never trap plants between the curtain and the window where they can suffer cold damage. Increase the humidity around your plants. Group plants together, place them on gravel trays, or place pans of water on your radiator. See "The Growing Environment" on page 139 in the introduction to this chapter for more details.

Some gardeners like to move their plants to a cool room for winter. The cooler temperatures slow the plants' metabolism and allow them to better tolerate the low light.

Clean your plants. Removing dust and debris increases the light reaching the leaves and helps remove any insects that may be present. Use a damp cloth or sponge to clean smooth leaves. Brush dust off fuzzy-leafed plants using a soft cosmetic brush.

Plants growing under fluorescent lights need 12 to 16 hours of light each day. Give plants at least 6 hours of dark each night. Use a timer to automatically turn lights on and off. It makes your job easier and eliminates the problem of forgetfulness.

 ## WATERING

Adjust your watering schedule to meet the needs of the plants. Always water thoroughly until water runs out of the pot. Pour off the excess. Wait until soilless mixes are slightly moist and soil-based mixes are slightly dry to water again.

Plants growing in a warm house with low humidity need to be watered more frequently than those growing in a cool house. Light intensity also influences watering. The more light plants receive, the more often you need to water.

 ## FERTILIZING

Do not fertilize. Most houseplants are in a resting stage for winter.

Plants growing in soil-less mixes under artificial lights may benefit from a dilute solution of fertilizer. Use the same dilute solution to fertilize holiday plants that have finished blooming.

PRUNING

Remove the faded flowers on holiday plants. Prune off insect-infected, broken, or wayward branches. Save major pruning for late February.

PROBLEMS

Insects. Indoor growing conditions are tough on plants, but they are great for all the insects that like to feed on them, such as fungus gnats, aphids, mites, mealybugs, and scale.

Check under the leaves and along the stems for signs of problems. Look for speckling, yellowing, spots, or a clear, sticky substance on the leaves. Handpick or prune off small populations of insects. See January and February "Helpful Hints" for more details.

Diseases. Powdery mildew, leaf spot, and root rot can affect houseplants. See February "Pests" for more information on the diseases and their control.

Animals. Curb your cat's love for your indoor garden by planting him a garden of his own. Plant a 6-inch pot with untreated **ryegrass** for your feline to munch. If this does not work, contact your vet or try one of the commercially available cat and dog repellents.

Helpful Hints

Insects: Part I

Fungus gnats are often misidentified as fruit flies. These insects feed on the organic matter in moist soil. They do not harm the plants, but they can be annoying. Tips for controlling fungus gnats include:

• Try living with them. The populations rise and fall and eventually disappear.

• Allow the soil to dry slightly between watering. Fungus gnats thrive in moist, organic soils; keeping it dry helps reduce their population.

• Try an environmentally friendly product sold as Gnatrol. The active ingredient is *Bacillus thuringiensis israelensis*. This particular bacteria only kills the larvae of fungus gnats and mosquitoes. Check your local garden center, home store, or catalogs for this product.

• As a last resort, you can use an insecticide labeled for indoor use. I find the smell of some of these more offensive than the gnats. And as always, be sure to read and follow all label directions before purchasing and using any pesticide. Spray in an area with good air circulation. If your pets are still eating any of your houseplants, do not use a pesticide

• Speckling or bronzing of leaves means you have aphids or mites. Aphids are small (1/8-inch), teardrop-shaped insects that suck out the plant juices. Their feeding can cause yellowing and distorted growth. Mites are much smaller but cause similar damage. Use the white paper test to discover if mites are present. Shake a leaf over a sheet of white paper. If you see small specks moving, your plants have mites. Even though these are different types of pests, both aphids and mites require the same control.

• Regular cleaning helps remove small populations.

• Spray plants with a strong blast of water to dislodge these pests. Place the pot in a bag and secure it around the stem. Place it in the sink or shower and spray with water; you can wash off the plants without washing the soil down the drain.

• Treat with insecticidal soap. You may need several applications to get these pests under control.

FEBRUARY

PLANNING

Sit down, grab your journal, and start writing. Make notes on the winter survival strategies that you tried this year. Record pest problems, controls used, and the results. This will help reduce guessing and improve results next winter. Now is also a good time to prepare for all the grooming and transplanting activities that start next month.

Locate, clean, and sharpen your hand pruners or garden scissors. Use a solution of one part bleach to nine parts water to clean and sterilize the pots you plan to use. Rinse and store pots for later use.

Purchase or mix your own potting mix.

PLANTING

Force some **paperwhites** for indoor bloom.

1 Fill a shallow container with pea gravel. Add enough water to reach the top of the gravel. Place the bulbs on the gravel and cover with just enough gravel to hold them in place. Or plant them in a container of any well-drained potting mix. Leave the tops of the bulbs exposed. Keep the planting mix moist, but not wet.

2 Place the potted bulbs to a cool location for rooting.

3 Move them in a cool, bright location as soon as the leaves start to grow. It takes just a few weeks to get fragrant flowers. This is a great project for kids—or any anxious gardener!

CARE

Continue cleaning plants once a month. Wipe off smooth leaves with a damp sponge or cloth. Use a soft cosmetic brush to dust **African violets**, **gloxinias**, and other fuzzy-leafed plants.

Dry winter air is hard on tropical plants. Increase the humidity around your plants by grouping plants together, placing them on gravel trays, or placing pans of water on your radiator. See "The Growing Environment" on page 139 in the introduction to this chapter for more details.

WATERING

Water plants as needed. Always water thoroughly until water runs out of the pot. Pour off the excess water. Wait until soil-less mixes are slightly moist and soil-based mixes are slightly dry to water again. Plants growing in a warm house with low humidity need to be watered more frequently than those growing in a cool house. Light intensity also influences watering. The more light plants receive, the more often you need to water.

FERTILIZING

Do not fertilize plants.

Those growing under lights in a soil-less mix can be fertilized with a dilute solution of houseplant fertilizer.

Check plants for salt buildup. This appears as a crusty, white substance on the soil surface or as white ring stains on clay pots. Scrape off the crusty salt buildup on the soil, then leach the soil by watering thoroughly. Wait 20 minutes and water thoroughly again. This helps dilute and wash the salts out of the soil.

PRUNING

Remove faded flowers, brown leaves, and pests. The end of the month is a good time to prune **hibiscus**. Cut stems 1/2 inch above a healthy bud or leaf, where one branch joins another, or back to the main stem. Remove crossed, inward growing, and damaged branches first. Next, thin out the branches and shape. Remove only one-third of the plant.

Light intensity also influences watering. The more light plants receive, the more often you need to water.

 PROBLEMS

Insects. Continue to monitor plants for pest problems. Consult January and February "Helpful Hints" for details on insects and their controls.

Diseases. Powdery mildew (looks like someone sprinkled baking powder on your leaves) problems should be decreasing with the increase in light. Continue to remove infected leaves and provide plenty of space for air circulation.

A variety of leaf spot diseases attack houseplants, especially those that have been overwatered. Reduce watering frequency and remove infected leaves. This is usually enough to correct the problem. Root rot can also infect overwatered houseplants. Correct your watering habits. As a last resort, you can use a fungicide labeled for use as a soil drench on houseplants. If rot continues, remove the infected plant from group plantings or discard rotted plants. If you decide to use a pesticide, be sure to read and follow all label directions carefully. Spray in an area with good ventilation. Don't spray if pet munch on leaves.

Animals. Cats love indoor gardens—for eating, digging, and other inappropriate purposes. Here are some tips for discouraging your feline friends:

Helpful Hints

Insects: Part II

Mealybugs look like little pieces of cotton and are found in the leaf joints and on the stems of a variety of houseplants. **African violets**, **hoya**, **jade plants**, and **cactus** are favorites of this pest. Treat with alcohol. Dip a cotton swap in rubbing alcohol and apply it to each mealybug. The alcohol dissolves the fuzzy covering and kills the insect below. Insecticidal soap can be used to treat the immature mealybugs that have not formed the cottony covering. Repeated applications are needed.

Scales are hard-shelled insects. They suck out the plant juices causing stunting and poor growth. The immature stage is translucent and hard to see. The hard shell develops as the insect matures. This shell protects it from insecticides. Gently scrape off the scale using an old toothbrush or your thumbnail. Spray the plant with insecticidal soap to kill any immature scale. Persistence is the key to success. It takes several treatments and lots of scraping to get this pest under control.

Whitefly is a descriptive name for this insect. The tiny whiteflies suck out the plant juices and cause stunting. Use yellow sticky traps to reduce the population to a tolerable level. Buy traps at your local garden center or make your own. Spread Tanglefoot tm on a small piece of yellow poster board. Place several traps in your houseplant collection. You may choose to treat high populations of whiteflies if they are causing significant damage. Use an insecticide containing Resmethrin or Permethrin that is labeled to control whiteflies on houseplants. Make three applications, five days apart. If you miss an application, start over.

Train cats to stay away from houseplants. Use a squirt gun to discourage plant-damaging activities.

Try one of the commercially available cat and dog repellents. Use large chunks of mulch or wire screening to keep cats from digging in the soil.

Plant a pot or tray of **ryegrass** or **oats** (be sure the seed has not been treated with any chemicals) for your cats. Let them eat these greens and hopefully they won't eat your plants. Consult your vet if they still prefer a more varied diet.

PLANNING

Houseplants are beginning to show signs of life. Start preparing them for their growing season. It is time to take action on all the observations that you have made throughout the winter.

 PLANTING

Start repotting houseplants that have outgrown their containers. Potbound plants have stunted growth or roots growing out of the bottom of the pot. See the "Repotting" section in the introduction to this chapter.

Use kitchen tongs or a strip of newspaper to transplant a **cactus**. Gently grasp the **cactus** with tongs or wrap the paper around it. Tilt the pot and slide the plant out of the container. Be careful not to crush the stem or spines.

Pot up any annuals such as **geraniums** that were kept in dormant storage for winter. Cut the stems back to 4 inches above the soil surface. Water thoroughly and repeat when the soil starts to dry. After growth begins, fertilize with a dilute solution of any flowering houseplant fertilizer.

This period of new growth is a great time to propagate houseplants.

1 Fill a container with moist vermiculite, starter mix, or soil-less potting mix.

2 Use a sharp knife, pruners, or garden scissors to take a 4- to 6-inch cutting. Cut just above a leaf.

3 Remove one or two lower leaves. This is where the roots will form.

4 Dip hard-to-root cuttings in a rooting hormone. This product contains hormones that promote root development and fungicides to prevent rot. Be careful not to get rooting hormone in your eyes.

5 Stick cuttings into the rooting mix so at least one node (leaf joint) is buried. Water until the excess drains out of the bottom of the pot.

6 Place the pot in a loose plastic bag. Do not seal it, and move it to an area away from direct light.

7 Once the roots develop, transplant rooted cuttings to a small container of potting mix.

 CARE

Monitor changes in the growing conditions. The light is improving and the days are getting longer. By late March, you may be able to move plants back to their original locations.

Continue cleaning plants once a month. Wipe off smooth leaves with a damp sponge or cloth. Use a cosmetic brush to dust **African violets**, **gloxinias**, and other fuzzy-leafed plants.

 WATERING

Adjust your watering schedule for recently repotted plants. The increased amount of soil usually means you need to water less frequently. The type of soil used can also either increase or decrease frequency.

You also need to adjust your watering schedule to match the changes in light, temperature, and humidity.

 FERTILIZING

You can start fertilizing plants. Fertilize if the plants show signs of nutrient deficiencies, or if you want to promote growth. Use a diluted solution of any houseplant fertilizer. Do not fertilize newly repotted plants. Give them a month or so to adjust to their new container.

Start repotting houseplants that have outgrown their containers. Potbound plants have stunted growth or roots growing out of the bottom of the pot.

PRUNING

Use hand pruners or garden scissors to shape plants and reduce their size. Cut stems above a healthy bud or leaf, where one branch joins another, or back to the main stem. Remove crossed, inward growing, and damaged branches first. Next, thin out the branches and shape. Remove no more than one-third of the plant.

Overgrown and leggy vines in hanging baskets can be pruned back severely. Cut above a healthy set of leaves. Cut trimmings into shorter pieces (4 to 6 inches long) and use to start new plants.

Sterilize pruners after each use to avoid spreading diseases. Use rubbing alcohol or 1 part bleach to nine parts water.

PROBLEMS

Continue to monitor and control insects and diseases as needed. A spring cleaning under the shower helps wash away the dust and some of the insects. See January and February "Helpful Hints" and "Pests" (on page 148).

African violets do not always age gracefully. As the oldest leaves yellow and drop, a bare-stem "neck" develops. This leafless stem is topped with healthy leaves and beautiful flowers. You can save the plant and improve the appearance.

Short-necked **African violets** can be planted deeper by following these steps:

1 Remove the plant from its container. Cut away the bottom half of the rootball.

2 Position the plant in the container so that the lower leaves are just above the soil. Add soil below and above the rootball as needed. Water thoroughly so that the excess runs out the drainage holes in the bottom of the pot.

African violets with longer necks (3 inches or more of bare stems) can be propagated.

1 Cut off the rosette of leaves with 1 to 2 inches of stem attached. Stick the stem in an African Violet or well-drained potting mix.

2 Water and place the pot in a loose plastic bag. The bag helps to trap moisture without causing rot that often occurs in sealed bags.

3 Grow in indirect light until the plant is well rooted. Then remove the bag and provide normal care.

4 Save the original plant. Cut the stem back to 1 inch above the soil surface. Keep the soil moist and wait. In several weeks, you will see new leaves sprouting from the stem.

Animals. Curb your cat's love for your indoor garden by planting him a garden of his own. A 6-inch pot of untreated **ryegrass** or **oats** is fine. If this does not work, contact your vet or try one of the commercially available cat and dog repellents.

PLANNING

Summer is on its way. Start evaluating where your plants will spend the summer. Moving houseplants outdoors often revives winter- weary and declining plants. It also increases the risk of insects infesting your indoor garden. These unwelcome guests often hitch a ride with the houseplants when they move back indoors. See September "Pests" on page 163 for tips.

PLANTING

Finish repotting plants that have outgrown their containers. Large plants with nowhere to go (they have reached the maximum pot size) can be topdressed or root-pruned.

Topdressing—a short-term solution—is done by carefully removing the top 1 to 2 inches of soil. Replace it with fresh soil and water.

Root pruning gives longer-lasting results. It is a bit riskier but can be done successfully. Post-transplanting care is critical to success. Move plants to the best possible growing location to encourage new root growth.

1 Take cuttings from valuable specimens, just in case this process does not work.

2 Massage sides of the container and slide the plant out of the pot.

3 Prune off a thin layer of roots around the sides and bottom of the rootball.

4 Repot in the same or similar container. Make sure the container is clean and free of pests. Water until the excess runs out the drainage holes in the bottom of the pot.

Divide and plant divisions of large plants that spread by increasing in diameter or by rhizomes. **ferns**, **snake plants**, and **peace lilies** are just a few plants that can be divided.

1 Loosen and remove the plant from its container.

2 Use a sharp knife to cut the rootball in halves or quarters.

3 Repot divisions in smaller containers that are slightly larger than their rootballs.

4 Water and move plants to a location with the best available growing conditions.

Finishing planting any Annuals that were kept in dormant storage for winter. See March "Planting" on page 150 for details.

Continue propagating houseplants. Stem cuttings described in March "Planting" are the most common and successful ways to start new plants.

Leaf cuttings of **African violets**, **begonias**, and **snake plants** require a little more effort and some patience.

Cut 3-inch sections of **snake plants**. Notch the bottom of the stem. Bury the bottom inch in vermiculite or a well-drained potting mix. Keep it slightly moist and out of direct sun. Wait for a new plant to develop.

Remove a healthy leaf from an African Violet plant. Bury the leaf stem in vermiculite or a well-drained potting mix. Keep it moist and out of direct sun. New plants will develop in one to two months.

Remove a **begonia** leaf. Slice through several large veins. Lay the leaf (top side up) on the soil surface. Use hairpins or small stones to anchor the leaf in place. Keep the soil moist. Cover with a loosely tied plastic bag to increase humidity and chance of success. Be patient; this process takes one to two months. Plant rooted cuttings started last month. Plant in a small container filled with a well-drained, sterile potting mix.

CARE

Continue cleaning plants once a month. Wipe or brush off dust.

Prune back poinsettias to 4 to 6 inches above the soil surface. This encourages branching and help control the growth for the coming season.

WATERING

Adjust your watering schedule to match the change in growing conditions. Use your finger to measure soil moisture. Soil-less mixes should be watered when they are barely moist. Soil-based mixes should be allowed to go slightly dry before watering. Keep in mind the differences in individual plant requirements.

Reduce brown tips on **spider plants**, **dracaenas**, and **prayer plants** by keeping the soil slightly moist. This dilutes the fluoride and chlorine in the water, preventing tip burn. Or use rainwater, dehumidifier water, or distilled water for these plants.

FERTILIZING

Do not fertilize recently repotted, divided, or propagated houseplants. Give them time to establish new roots. Established houseplants can be fertilized as needed.

PRUNING

Prune back **poinsettias** to 4 to 6 inches above the soil surface. This encourages branching and help control the growth for the coming season. You can root the trimmings to start new plants.

Clip off brown tips of **spider plants**, **dracaenas**, and **prayer plants**. Change watering practices to reduce this problem.

Shape and reduce the size of overgrown and leggy houseplants. See March "Pruning" for directions.

PROBLEMS

Continue to monitor plants for pest problems. Check under the leaves and along the stems for hidden pests. Remove insects and infected leaves as soon as they are discovered. See January and February "Pests" for more details.

Insects. Mites and aphids cause speckling on the leaves. Aphids can be seen with the naked eye. You need a hand lens or the paper test to detect mites. Shake an infested leaf over white paper. If you see specks moving, the plant has mites. Several applications of insecticidal soap will control these pests.

If you find holes in the leaves of outdoor plants but no insects are present, the culprit is probably slugs, caterpillars, or earwigs. Check for these pests at night. A few insects can cause significant damage. Remove and destroy any offenders you discover. High populations may need additional treatment. Use beer bait for slugs and insecticides for earwigs and other beetles. Select a product labeled for use on tropical plants. As always, read and follow all label directions carefully.

MAY
Houseplants

 PLANNING

Start making plans for moving. Survey your indoor garden and decide which houseplants will stay inside and which ones will move outside for the summer. Wait until the daytime and nighttime temperatures are warm before moving these tropical plants outdoors. This is usually the end of May in the southern parts of the Prairie Lands states and early June in the northern parts. Do not let a few warm days in early May coax you into a premature move.

Plan for new additions to the outdoor patio garden. Tropicals are quite popular and readily available at many nurseries, home stores, and garden centers. **Bougainvillea**, **oleander**, **hibiscus**, and other tropicals can add beauty to the landscape. Just make sure you have indoor space, a friend with a greenhouse, or another alternative if you plan on keeping these large plants over winter.

 PLANTING

Continue repotting and dividing plants. See "Repotting" (p. 141) in the introduction to this chapter and April "Planting" (p. 157) for detailed directions.

Plant rooted cuttings in a small container filled with a well-drained potting mix.

Use a few tropical plants as accents in your flowerbeds. A **banana plant** or an **ornamental taro** growing in a bed of annuals can really attract attention. Wait until the weather warms—late May or early June—to plant these outdoors. Leave the plants in the container and sink the pot into the garden. This makes it easier on you and the plant when it is time to move the plant indoors for winter.

Smaller tropical plants, such as **rex begonias** and **ferns**, make great companions for more traditional Annuals and Perennials. Treat these like bedding plants. Space them so that the plants have room to mature, and plant them directly in properly prepared soil. No need to leave them in the pot if you do not plan on digging them up and moving them indoors for winter.

 CARE

Harden off (acclimatize) the houseplants you plan to move outdoors. Hardening off allows the plants to gradually adapt to the outdoor environment—just like Northerners must do when they travel to Florida for the winter. Melinda keeps her houseplants in a shady spot all summer. The slight increase in light and humidity still revives the plants, but the change is less drastic. This is less stressful for

plants moving outside and then back inside in fall.

Indoor plants may also need some relocating. Some collections of houseplants stay put—many are too large, heavy, or unwieldy.

Move plants away from air conditioner vents. Blasts of cold air can be drying and can cause damage to houseplants.

Adjust location according to heat and light. A south- or west-facing window may be too warm or sunny for some low-light plants. Move them away from the windows or into an east-facing window. Sheer curtains can also be used to reduce the intense heat and sun.

 WATERING

Check the soil moisture before watering. The changing environment will change your watering schedule. Air conditioning, higher humidity, and more sunlight all influence how quickly the soil dries out.

Soil-less mixes should be watered when they are barely moist. Soil-based mixes should be allowed to go slightly dry before watering. Keep in mind the differences in individual plant requirements.

Check houseplants moved outdoors daily. These plants dry out quickly and

Helpful Hints

Moving Houseplants Outside for Summer

Summering plants outdoors can help rejuvenate declining plants. It also adds some challenges to your gardening efforts. You need to monitor and control insects that catch a ride on the plants when they move back indoors. Small populations of mites, aphids, and whiteflies can quickly grow into infestations and damage your indoor plants. Gradually acclimate the plants to the change in environment when moving outdoors for summer and indoors for fall.

Move plants outdoors to a shaded location once the temperatures stay above 50 to 55 degrees Fahrenheit. Bring plants inside the house or garage on cold nights. Gradually increase the amount of sunlight these plants receive each day. By the end of two weeks, the plants should be ready to stay in their permanent location.

Some of our favorite spots to summer our plants include:

• Under the filtered shade of a honeylocust or other tree that casts light shade. The high humidity and diffuse light is perfect for reviving houseplants.

• On a screened-in porch. Even in the shade, the light is better than indoors and the plants are protected from harsh weather and are somewhat protected from insects.

• Displayed with other container gardens. Tropical foliage can add lots of interest and variety to the garden.

• On the front porch, where there is full sun, full shade, and part shade—lighting to suit any plant, Plants are also protected from strong winds and storms.

• In existing gardens or container plantings for added interest. Burying the pot makes the plant look like it is part of the garden and reduces watering frequency.

may need to be watered every day. Water plants when the top few inches of soil are just starting to dry.

 ## FERTILIZING

Continue to fertilize indoor plants as needed. Do not fertilize recently repotted, divided, or propagated houseplants. Give them time to establish new roots. Houseplants summering outdoors benefit from regular fertilization. Use a dilute solution of houseplant fertilizer or foliar feed once or twice a month, according to label directions.

 ## PRUNING

Do minimal pruning on flowering houseplants. Most of them will be blooming soon. Pruning now can delay or eliminate the bloom period. Prune off only broken, dead, or wayward branches.

Pinch out the growing tips or prune back the stems of leggy foliage plants to promote branching.

 ## PROBLEMS

Continue monitoring pests on houseplants located inside and outside. Outdoor houseplants are exposed to many more problems and should be monitored more closely. Cover the bottoms of buried pots with a piece of old nylon stocking to prevent slugs, centipedes, and sow bugs from moving in through the drainage holes.

JUNE
Houseplants

PLANNING

As the outdoor gardening season becomes our primary focus, it is easy to neglect our houseplants. Take advantage of rainy days to catch up on your indoor garden care. Keep writing in your journal. Make notes on how things are growing indoors and out. Note planting locations and the use of tropical plants in your landscape. Record how the plants looked and how well they thrived in their outdoor location. This will help you repeat or improve plant placement next season. There is still time to make changes and additions to your indoor and outdoor gardens. Be sure to consider the winter growing space needed for your existing plants and the new additions.

PLANTING

It is usually safe to move tropical plants into the outdoor landscape in early June. They need to be protected or moved indoors if cold or frost is predicted. Use large tropical plants as accents in your flowerbeds. Leave the plants in the container and sink the pot into the garden. This makes it easier on you and the plant when it is time to move them indoors for winter. Cover the pot with an old nylon stocking to help keep slugs, sow bugs, and other soil-residing insects from

entering through the drainage hole. Smaller tropical plants, such as **Boston ferns**, **pink polka-dot plants**, and **asparagus ferns** make great companions for more traditional annuals and perennials. Mix **rex begonias** with **Japanese painted ferns** and **New Guinea impatiens** for a nice shade garden combination. Treat the smaller tropicals like bedding plants. Space them so that the plants have room to mature, and plant them directly in properly prepared soil. No need to leave them in the pot if you do not plan on digging them up and moving them indoors for winter.

CARE

You can move houseplants outdoors when the temperatures are at least 50 to 55 degrees Fahrenheit and the danger of frost has passed.

Move indoor plants away from air conditioner vents. Blasts of cold dry air can be drying and damaging to houseplants.

Monitor the growing conditions. The increased light and temperatures outdoors affects plant growth indoors. South- and west-facing windows can get pretty warm on sunny days. Low-light plants may need to be moved away from the window or into an east-facing location. Sheer curtains and awnings also

reduce the available light. Match plants to their growing requirements.

Clean smooth-leafed houseplants with a damp sponge or cloth. Brush dust off hairy-leafed plants with a soft cosmetic brush.

WATERING

Water indoors as needed. Improved growing conditions usually mean you need to water more often. Plants in an air-conditioned or low-light environment need less frequent watering.

Check outdoor plants daily. The soil dries quickly, and the plants use more water in these good growing conditions. Shade plants need to be watered less often than those in full sun. Water as the top few inches of soil begin to dry. Check twice a day in extremely hot, dry weather.

FERTILIZING

Continue to fertilize indoor houseplants as needed. Those growing outdoors for the summer also benefit from regular fertilization. Apply a diluted solution of any houseplant fertilizer or foliar feed once or twice a month. Use a flowering plant fertilizer, one higher in phosphorus, for flowering houseplants. Consult label

Take advantage of rainy days to catch up on your indoor garden care. Make notes on how things are growing indoors and out.

directions for specific information. Those planted in the ground can be fertilized with the other annuals and perennials in the garden.

PRUNING

Remove faded flowers on blooming plants.

Pinch out the growing tips or prune back the stems of leggy foliage plants to promote branching and give you a fuller plant in the future.

Prune off any broken, dead, or wayward branches.

PROBLEMS

Monitor both indoor and outdoor houseplants. Insects can move indoors through screens, on gardening tools, and with new plants. Isolate insect-infested plants as soon as they are discovered. This reduces the risk of them spreading to other plants. Control insects and monitor for several weeks before returning the plant to its permanent location.

Holes in the leaves of outdoor plants can be caused by slugs, earwigs, caterpillars, or beetles. Check for these pests at night. Remove any offenders. Use beer to trap slugs or insecticides to treat high populations of earwigs, caterpillars, and beetles. Read and follow all label directions.

Animals often damage houseplants summering outdoors. Birds often try to nest in and chipmunks often dig in hanging baskets. Cover the planter with bird netting to discourage this behavior. Remove the netting once the animals find another gardener to bother.

Weed seeds may blow in and sprout in houseplants summering outdoors. Pull weeds as soon as they appear.

JULY
Houseplants

PLANNING

Keep monitoring and evaluating houseplants growing indoors and out. Record the plants' response to their summer environment. This information will help you decide where to place plants next summer.

PLANTING

Continue propagating plants. Overgrown **dumb canes** (*Dieffenbachia* spp.) can be air-layered and propagated by cane cuttings. To make cane cuttings:

1 Fill a flat with a mixture of 1/2 peat and 1/2 vermiculite or perlite.

2 Cut long, leafless stems of **dumb canes** into 3-inch sections (must contain bud).

3 Lay the cane sections, lengthwise, on the soil surface so that a bud is facing up. Press the bottom half of the stem into the potting mix.

4 Store the flat of cuttings in a bright location out of direct sun. Keep the potting mix moist, but not wet.

5 Watch for new shoots to develop. It takes four to eight weeks for canes to root and new plants to develop.

6 Move the new plants to a small container filled with any well-drained potting mix. Give small plants the same care as the parents—bright light and slightly moist soil.

Take cuttings of **poinsettias** now so you will have more to give and enjoy this Christmas. See March "Planting" on page 150 for details on starting plants from stem cuttings.

CARE

Keep grooming and cleaning both indoor and outdoor plants. Indoor plants collect dust, pet dander, and other airborne particles on their leaves. Cleaning removes it, allowing more light to reach the leaves. Outdoor plants may need an occasional cleaning from dust, splashing soil, and such. Use a damp sponge or cloth to wipe off glossy leaves. A soft cosmetic brush works well for removing debris from hairy-leafed plants. The heat of midsummer often means houseplants, indoors and out, need a break from the heat. Make sure plants are well watered. Outdoor containers may need

to be watered twice a day, or move them into a partially shaded area until the extreme heat has subsided. Indoor plants may need to be moved away from hot locations as well. Adjust watering to adapt to the changes in the environment.

Hibiscus plants should be in full bloom. Late pruning, excess nitrogen, or lack of light can prevent flowering. Plants pruned after the middle of March eventually bloom, just be patient. Fertilize **hibiscus** and other blooming tropical plants with any flowering houseplant fertilizer. These fertilizers are higher in phosphorus (the middle number on the container) and promote flowering.

WATERING

Water plants as needed. Check plants growing outdoors every day. Indoor plants do not need to be watered as often. Check these plants once or twice a week. Remember the bigger the container, the less often the plants need watering.

Double pot houseplants when using decorative containers or baskets that lack a drainage hole. Fill the bottom of the decorative container with pebbles. Place your houseplant (in a plastic pot) on top of the pebbles inside the decorative container. Mask the plastic pot with sphagnum moss. The pebbles collect the excess water while keeping the plant from sitting in the water and rotting. Occasionally pour off the excess water that collects in the pebbles.

 # FERTILIZING

Continue fertilizing as needed. Plants with stunted growth may benefit from fertilization. Fertilizer also promotes faster growth. This may not be what you really want for some of the bigger plants that barely fit in your home.

Outdoor houseplants benefit from regular fertilization. Frequent watering and the good growing conditions outdoors increase the need for nutrients.

 # PRUNING

Remove faded flowers on blooming tropical plants. Prune off damaged, diseased, or wayward branches.

Pinch and prune **poinsettias** and **azaleas** to the desired size and shape.

Helpful Hints

It is difficult, sometimes impossible, to find a dependable sitter for your plants when going on vacation. Melinda and Cathy are lucky enough to have green thumb neighbors to water and tend our gardens. If this is not the case for you, try these suggestions:

• Fill the sink or tub with an inch or so of water. Elevate houseplants on empty containers so that they sit above, not in, the water. Water the plants thoroughly. Cover the sink or tub with plastic sheeting. This creates a moist, humid environment reducing the plants' need for water.

• Double pot houseplants. Plant your houseplants in a clay pot. Set the clay pot in a larger plastic container. Fill the empty spaces with damp peat moss. Water the peat moss. Moisture will move from the moist peat moss, through the clay pot, and into the soil.

• Make your own self-watering container. You will need an old margarine container; a strip of felt, string, nylon stocking, or other wicking fabric; and a houseplant. The margarine tub serves as the water reservoir, and the wick moves the water from the container to the potting mix for the plant to use.

• Frequent travelers might want to invest in self-watering pots or switch to growing only **cactus** and **succulents** .

 # PROBLEMS

Monitor all your houseplants, indoors and out, for pests. Check under the leaves, along the stems, and throughout the plants for signs of pests.

Diseases. Yellow, brown, or spotted leaves are common symptoms of fungal disease. Remove infected leaves as soon as they appear. Adjust watering so that the plants are watered thoroughly, but not so often that the soil stays wet. Pour off the excess water that collects in the plant saucer.

AUGUST
Houseplants

 PLANNING

Fall is quickly approaching. Soon it will be time to move all your houseplants and tropicals indoors. Take inventory and make a list of what you plan to bring indoors and possible indoor growing locations. If you are like most gardeners, you probably have more plants coming indoors than you moved out in the spring.

Find an area to quarantine plants as they move indoors. It should be an area with good, bright light but separate from your indoor houseplants. Keep plants in this area for several weeks. Check along the stems and under the leaves for insects. Control any pests found and continue to monitor. Once the plants are free from insects, it is safe to move them in with the rest of your houseplant collection.

 PLANTING

Take cuttings of **coleus**, **geraniums**, **vinca**, and other annuals you want to overwinter indoors. This method reduces the space needed and the risk of bringing insects indoors with the plants. Here's how to start new plants from cuttings:

1 Fill a container with moist vermiculite, starter mix, or soil-less potting mix.

2 Use a sharp knife, pruners, or garden scissors to take a 4- to 6-inch cutting. Cut just above a leaf.

3 Remove one or two lower leaves. This is where the roots will form.

4 Dip hard-to-root cuttings in a rooting hormone. This product contains hormones that promote root development and fungicides to prevent rot.

5 Stick cuttings in rooting mix so that at least one node (leaf joint) is buried. Water thoroughly, allowing excess water to drain out of the bottom of the pot.

6 Place the pot in a loose plastic bag—do not seal—and move to an area away from direct light.

7 Once roots develop, transplant rooted cuttings into a small container of potting mix.

 CARE

The hot days of early August can cause heat stress and may result in scorch. Move plants to a partially shaded area and keep the soil moist during times of extreme heat.

Going on vacation means you need to find a plant sitter or set up your plants to be self-sufficient. Make the plant sitter's job easier by writing down directions for care. You may want to spend some time showing and telling your friend how to water. It will reduce your concern and his or her anxiety over this responsibility. See July "Helpful Hints" for more details.

Reduce brown tips on **spider plants**, **dracaenas**, and **prayer plants** by keeping the soil slightly moist. This dilutes the fluoride and chlorine in the water, preventing tip burn. Or use rainwater, dehumidifier water, or distilled water for these plants.

 WATERING

Check outdoor plants daily. Indoor plants do not dry out as quickly. Water as often as needed to keep the soil slightly moist. You need to water more often in hot, dry weather. Plants in small containers dry out faster than those in large containers. Water plants growing in a soil-less mix often enough to keep the soil slightly moist. Those growing in a soil-based mix should be allowed to dry slightly between waterings.

FERTILIZING

Continue fertilizing plants as needed. Over-fertilization can damage plants or cause unwanted growth on already large plants. Those growing outdoors or in soil-less mixes need more frequent fertilization. Soil-less mixes do not retain the nutrients like soil-based mixes do, so they need to be replenished more frequently. Nutrients are leached out of the soil by frequent watering on outdoor plants.

 ## PRUNING

Remove faded flowers to improve appearance and flowering. Use a hand pruner or garden scissors to remove damaged or pest-infested stems. Clip off brown tips common on **spider plants**, **dracaenas**, and **prayer plants**.

 ## PROBLEMS

Monitor both indoor and outdoor houseplants. Insects can move indoors through screens, on gardening tools, and with new plants. Isolate insect-infested plants as soon as they are discovered. This reduces the risk of them spreading to other plants. Control insects and monitor plants for several weeks before returning them to their permanent locations.

Weed seeds may blow in and sprout in houseplants summering outdoors. Pull weeds as soon as they appear.

Helpful Hints

Bromeliads are fun and beautiful plants that can brighten up any indoor garden. Add these members of the pineapple family to your collection. Purchase a healthy, flowering **bromeliad** from a garden center or florist. The flowers are so large and colorful some people think they are artificial.

Grow **bromeliads** in a bright location indoors. Keep the soil evenly moist for all but those **bromeliads** that have thick, fleshy leaves. Water the soil until the excess runs out the drainage hole. Water again as the top 2 inches begin to dry.

Fertilize spring through fall with any dilute solution of a flowering houseplant fertilizer. Only fertilize in winter if the plants are growing but showing signs of nutrient deficiency. Apply fertilizer if the leaves are yellow and stunted.

Enjoy the **bromeliad** flower—it can last a month or more! Remove the faded flower, but leave the foliage intact.

Soon the mother plant may begin to fade as small plants (pups) form around its base. Remove and plant the small offshoots individually in smaller containers.

Force the offspring to flower once they reach full size and their roots fill the pot. Place a piece of Apple in the plant and cover with a plastic bag. Keep the bag sealed and the plant out of direct light for three days. Remove the bag and apple. Now wait for your flowering reward. It takes weeks.

SEPTEMBER
Houseplants

PLANNING

Identify an area in which to isolate plants as they move indoors. This reduces the risk of contaminating your indoor houseplant collection. Select a well-lit location that can accommodate all the plants moving indoors.

Review your garden journal to see where your houseplants thrived last year. Avoid or alter problem areas. You may need to invest in artificial lights if your houseplant collection has outgrown the available windows.

Record the highlights, both successes and failures, from the summer season. Note pest problems, plant locations, and maintenance strategies. This will help you plan and care for your houseplants next summer.

PLANTING

You can still take cuttings of annuals that you want to overwinter indoors. Impatiens, **coleus**, **vinca**, and others can be started from cuttings and grown as houseplants for winter. See August "Planting" for more details.

Pot up rooted cuttings of annuals. Plant them in small containers filled with a well-drained potting mix. Grow them under artificial lights or in a sunny win-

dow. Even shade plants such as **impatiens** prefer a sunny window indoors in winter. Keep the soil slightly moist.

Plant cane cuttings that have developed roots and shoots. These also prefer a well-drained potting mix. Plant single cuttings in small containers or several cuttings in a larger (6 to 8 inch), pot. Extras make nice gifts for friends or trading material to use with other gardeners. Move these to a bright location and keep the soil slightly moist.

CARE

Isolate and acclimatize your plants as you move them indoors. Plants summered outdoors have developed sun leaves. They are not efficient at capturing the available sunlight. These leaves cannot support the plant in the low-light conditions found indoors.

Isolate plants from your indoor houseplant collection. Monitor and control insects.

Place plants in the sunniest south- or west-facing window available, or grow them under artificial lights. Leave plants here for several weeks.

Next, move them into an east-facing or well-lit north-facing window. Leave them here for several weeks. Gradually decrease the light until the plants reach

their final locations. This helps the plants develop new, shade-tolerant leaves that are more efficient at capturing what little light is available. Failure to acclimatize plants results in yellow leaves and massive leaf drop. This is stressful on the plants—and most gardeners as well!

Move **amaryllis** indoors before the first fall frost. Store the bulb in a cool, dark location or continue to grow it indoors. See the January "Did You Know" in the "Bulbs" on page 77 chapter for information on reblooming your **amaryllis**.

WATERING

Adjust your watering schedule to accommodate the changes in climate and location. Plants moved indoors need less frequent watering. Check the soil moisture on all your plants before watering.

Soil-less mixes should be watered when they are barely moist. Soil-based mixes should be allowed to go slightly dry before watering. Keep in mind the differences in individual plant requirements.

FERTILIZING

Cut back or stop fertilizing houseplants. This is a time of adjustment. Plants are adapting to their new indoor location and the change in the climate. Fall means

Cut back or stop fertilizing houseplants. This is a time of adjustment. Plants are adapting to their new indoor location and the change in the climate.

shorter days and less intense sunlight. Houseplants will grow less and need less frequent fertilization.

Plants growing in soil-less mixes may benefit from an occasional dilute solution of fertilizer. These mixes do not retain nutrients like the soil-based potting mixes. Fertilize plants that show signs of nutrient deficiencies.

 # PRUNING

Limit pruning to broken, damaged, or pest-infested branches. You may need to prune large plants to fit their indoor location. Cut stems above a healthy bud or leaf, where one branch joins another, or back to the main stem.

 # PROBLEMS

Quarantine houseplants moving indoors. Maintain the plants in a well-lit location away from your indoor plants. They may need to stay here for several weeks or months.

Helpful Hints

Overwintering **hibiscus** can be challenging and often frustrating. Evaluate the available growing space. **hibiscus** plants prefer a sunny window, moist soil, and the same care as your houseplants. They even tolerate less than ideal conditions and survive, though not thrive, over the winter. For the best results, follow these tips:

Acclimatize (see the "Care" section) the plants to their winter location. This gradual reduction in light helps to minimize leaf loss.

Hibiscus growing in an unobstructed south-, west-, or east-facing window should be watered often enough to keep the soil slightly moist, not wet.

Hibiscus moved to a cool, low-light location need much less water. The goal is survival, not growth. Water often enough to prevent the soil from drying. Prune as needed in February. Move the plants back outdoors in late May or early June. You will be amazed by their recovery and bloom. Melinda places her **hibiscus** in an east-facing basement window in the laundry room. It is cool, and she's there often enough to remember to water. Her plants lose some leaves but bloom profusely all winter. This makes laundry a little less of a chore!

Check under the leaves, along the stems, and throughout the plant for signs of insects.

Remove and destroy any insects that are found. Insecticidal soap controls aphids, mites, immature scale, and other soft-bodied insects. See January and February "Helpful Hints" for specifics of controlling houseplant insects.

Evaluate the success of your treatment and continue to monitor for additional pest outbreaks.

Move plants to their permanent location once they have been acclimatized and pests are under control.

PLANNING

This month marks the beginning of the most difficult growing period for indoor plants. The short days, low light, and decreasing humidity make it hard to create a plant-friendly environment. Add to this the addition of holiday decorations that may occupy some prime indoor growing space.

Now may be the time to consider installing artificial lights. A standard, two-bulb fluorescent fixture will provide additional indoor growing space. Look for existing tables, benches, or other areas where a light garden can be installed. Check garden catalogs for some of the new and different lighting options. New plant stands and clip-on light fixtures allow greater flexibility even where space is limited.

PLANTING

Plant rooted cuttings. Place one cutting in a small pot, or several cuttings in a larger container, filled with a well-drained potting mix. Move plants to a sunny window or under an artificial light. Water often enough to keep the soil moist, but not wet.

CARE

Yellow falling leaves are a common sight on houseplants and tropicals that have been moved indoors for the winter. The plants are shedding their sun leaves and soon will start producing more shade-tolerant leaves. Reduce leaf drop by acclimatizing plants to their indoor location. See the September "Care" section for details.

Your **weeping fig tree** may also be losing leaves. These plants are sensitive to any change in their environment, including the decrease in day length and light intensity. As the light intensity outdoors decreases, so does the light reaching indoor plants. This causes leaves to drop. Fortunately, **weeping figs** can lose up to 95 percent of their leaves and still recover. Adjust watering for the change in light and wait for new, more shade-tolerant leaves to appear.

Wipe off glossy leaves with a damp sponge or cloth. Dust hairy-leafed plants with a soft cosmetic brush. This improves the appearance and health of your plants.

Now is the time to begin forcing **poinsettias** and **Christmas cactus** into bloom for the holidays. These plants need several months of specific growing conditions to initiate flowering. See "Helpful Hints" for details.

Move **azaleas** to a cool (40 to 50 degrees Fahrenheit), sunny location for the fall. The cooler temperatures help promote bloom. Keep the soil slightly moist. They need less frequent watering in this cooler environment. Move them to a warmer location after the first of the year. Or try finding a cool, sunny window to grow them year round. Melinda has been rewarded with a scattering of flowers year round under these conditions. Move **cactus** and **succulents** to a cool location for the winter. Grow them under artificial lights in a cool basement or in a sunny window in a cool, vacant room. The cooler conditions help them adapt to the low light and encourage flowering.

WATERING

Adjust your watering schedule to fit the plants' needs in their new growing conditions. Cooler temperatures, decreasing humidity, and lower light all impact watering.

Water soil-less mixes often enough to keep the soil slightly moist. Soil-based mixes should be allowed to dry slightly before watering. Keep the individual plant needs in mind.

Cactus and **succulents** in cool locations need little water. Water these plants thoroughly, but only often enough to prevent shriveling.

FERTILIZING

Stop fertilizing. Plants growing under artificial lights or in soil-less mixes may benefit from an occasional application of a dilute solution of houseplant fertilizer. Only fertilize actively growing plants that show signs of nutrient deficiency.

PRUNING

Limit pruning to the removal of dead, damaged, or pest-infested branches. Wait until February or March for major pruning work.

PROBLEMS

Watch all your houseplants for uninvited guests that may have hitched a ride on plants that were moved back inside.

Helpful Hints

Reblooming **poinsettias** and the **Christmas cactus** can be a fun family activity. The challenge and sense of accomplishment is something the cost of a new **poinsettia** cannot replace. Rebloom **poinsettias** by modifying the growing conditions.

1 Provide plants with 10 hours of light and 14 hours of total darkness each night.

2 Move plants to an unused closet or room each night. Even a reading light or streetlight can interfere with the dark treatment and delay flowering. Or cover the plant with a cardboard box to keep out any artificial light.

3 Cool night temperatures and slightly dry soil help stimulate bloom.

4 Continue dark treatments until the bracts (upper leaves) are fully colored. Then move to an area for everyone to enjoy.

5 Each missed or interrupted dark period delays the blooms by one day. Do not give up if this happens to you. Keep up the event and enjoy your flowering **poinsettia** for Valentine's Day.

Christmas cactus are usually treated like **poinsettias** to initiate flowering. There has been some recent debate as to whether or not they really need the dark treatment. Melinda finds that keeping the plants cool and dry in fall helps promote bloom. You may want to do both to ensure success.

Isolate pest-infested plants as soon as they are discovered. This reduces the risk of infesting nearby plants.

Remove insects. A strong blast of water followed by insecticidal soap helps control aphids, mites, and immature mealybugs and scale. Repeated applications may be necessary. See January and February "Helpful Hints" on pages 147 and 149 for details on insects and their control. Always read and follow all label directions carefully. Never apply pesticides indoors without adequate ventilation. Remove spotted and yellow leaves as they appear. These fungal diseases often occur when plants are overwatered, overcrowded, or growing in low light. Improving the growing conditions is often enough to eliminate the problem.

NOVEMBER
Houseplants

 PLANNING

Cut flowers and flowering plants are traditional hostess and holiday gifts. Use the following suggestions to add a new look to plant gifts: Dress up a houseplant with cut flowers. Place cut flowers in water picks and stick these into the soil. When the flowers are gone, the houseplant will continue to add beauty.

Fill a large basket with a collection of potted houseplants and flowering plants. The flowering plants can be replaced as the seasons change or the plants decline.

Create a changeable planter. Plant several compatible houseplants in a large container. Sink a small, empty pot in one area. Set a small, potted, flowering plant inside this empty container. Replace it occasionally with fresh flowering plants.

Consider giving a terrarium or dish garden. These are both back in style.

Consult your local professional florist for other new and creative gift-giving suggestions.

 PLANTING

Purchase and plant **amaryllis**, **paperwhites**, and **hyacinths** for holiday bloom. See the January and February "Planting" sections in the "Bulbs" chapter for details on forcing **amaryllis** and **paperwhites**. **hyacinths** need a cold period in order for them to bloom. Follow the planting directions included with the bulbs.

 CARE

The light and humidity are decreasing, and it is time to move plants to the best possible growing conditions. Move low-light plants closer to the window and those near east- or west-facing windows in front of a south-facing window. Or move them under artificial lights. A combination of natural sunlight supplemented with artificial lights will help your houseplants survive the dark days of winter. Avoid drafts of hot and cold air. Cold drafts from patio doors and windows can chill the foliage and lead to root rot. Drafts of hot air from heating ducts create lower humidity. The drier air is hard on the plants, but great for mites and aphids.

Continue giving your **poinsettia** and **Christmas cactus** 14 hours of total darkness each night. Uncover or move plants into the sunlight each day. Increase the humidity around your plants. Group houseplants together so that as one plant loses moisture the others benefit. Or use gravel trays, terrariums, and other techniques described in "The Growing Environment" section on page 139 in the introduction to this chapter.

 WATERING

Water houseplants as needed. Always water plants thoroughly. Overwatering is caused by watering too often or allowing houseplants to sit in excess water. Here is a simple way to deal with the excess water that collects in the plant saucer:

1 Place a few pebbles in your plant saucers.

2 Water plants thoroughly so that the excess collects in the pebble-filled saucer. The pot should sit on the pebbles, not in the water.

3 As the water evaporates, it increases the humidity around the plant. This creates a better environment for your plants and make less work for you.

Group houseplants together so that as one plant loses moisture the others benefit.

Underwatering plants is common during the hectic holiday season. Soil-less mixes turn into a solid block of peat when they are allowed to dry out completely. To re-hydrate, place the pot in a container of water. It takes several hours for the soil to rehydrate. Check plants more often, and water when the soil is slightly moist.

Helpful Hints

Always protect houseplants, flowering plants, and cut flowers being moved from one location to another during cold winter weather. Wrap plants in paper or plastic. Remove plastic sleeves as soon as the plants move indoors.

Move plants in a warm car and never leave them in the car while you run errands. Move chilled plants into warmer locations. The cold temperature injury usually appears later as a graying or blackening of the foliage. Remove dead leaves and wait to see if the plants recover.

 ## FERTILIZING

Do not fertilize plants. Those growing under lights in a soil-less mix can be fertilized with a dilute solution of houseplant fertilizer. Check plants for salt buildup. This appears as a crusty, white substance on the soil surface or as white stains on clay pots. Scrape off the crusty salt buildup on the soil, then leach the soil by watering thoroughly. Wait 20 minutes and water thoroughly again. This helps dilute and wash the salts out of the soil.

 ## PRUNING

You can trim off brown tips on **spider plants**, **dracaenas**, and **palms**. It is not necessary, but it improves the appearance and makes many gardeners feel better.

 ## PROBLEMS

Continue to monitor and control pests as needed. A shower helps wash away the dust and some of the insects. Place the pot in a plastic bag before hosing plants down in the sink or shower. This keeps the soil in the pot and out of the drain. See January and February "Helpful Hints" on page 147 and 149 for common insects and their controls.

Diseases. Powdery mildew problems may start appearing with the decrease in light and poor air circulations. Move plants to a sunnier window or under artificial lights. Increase the space between plants to increase air circulation. Remove infected leaves to reduce the spread of this disease.

A variety of leaf-spot diseases attack houseplants, especially those that have been overwatered. Reduce watering frequency and remove infected leaves. This is usually enough to correct the problem. Root rot can also infect overwatered houseplants. Correct your watering habits. As a last resort, you can use a fungicide labeled for use as a soil drench on houseplants. If the rot continues, you need to remove the infected plant from group plantings or discard rotted plants.

Animals. Curb your cat's love for your indoor garden by planting him a garden of his own. A 6-inch pot of untreated **ryegrass** or **oats** is fine. If this does not work, contact your vet or try one of the commercially available cat and dog repellents.

DECEMBER
Houseplants

 PLANNING

Do not worry if you are tired of red **poinsettias**. You are in luck. You can find curly and variegated **poinsettias**, speckled and marbled, as well as pastels and even yellow-flowered varieties.

 PLANTING

You still have time to purchase, plant, and force **amaryllis** and **paperwhites** into bloom for the holidays. Flowering plants or "bloom-it-yourself" kits make great gifts for others. See the January entry on page 59 in the "Bulbs" chapter for details.

 CARE

Continue dark treatments for your **poinsettia** and **Christmas cactus** until they are in full bloom. Then move them to a cool, bright location where you can enjoy the colorful display.

Wipe dust and insects off glossy leaves with a damp sponge or cloth. Use a soft cosmetic brush to dust off hairy leaves.

 **Helpful Hints**

December often means a houseful of flowering holiday plants. Get the most out of your holiday plants by following these simple guidelines:

1 Remove plants from protective sleeves as soon as they arrive.

2 Bend foil edges down so that light can reach all of the leaves, or remove the foil altogether.

3 Punch holes in the foil to allow excess water to drain out the bottom. Be sure to place the plant on a saucer to avoid water damage.

4 Pour off excess water or place pebbles in baskets and saucers to prevent plants from sitting in excess water. Keep soil moist and plants in a cool, bright location.

 WATERING

Water as needed. Keep the soil moist for holiday plants. **poinsettias** and **Christmas cactus** like to be slightly dry during the dark treatment. Once flowering, you can keep the soil slightly moist.

Water **cactus** and **succulents** growing in cool locations only as often as needed to prevent shriveling.

 FERTILIZING

Do not fertilize. The low light and poor growing conditions mean plants need very few nutrients.

 PRUNING

Only remove dead, damaged, or pest-infested branches. Pinch out growing tips of houseplants and Annuals that are growing tall and leggy.

PROBLEMS

Keep watching plants for signs of insects. Fungus gnats often move in with holiday plants and new additions to the indoor garden. They are annoying but not harmful to the plants. See January "Helpful Hints" for details on controlling these and other insects.

CHAPTER SIX

Lawns

Whether you view your lawn as a matter of pride or as something to keep your feet from getting muddy when it rains, a healthy lawn will give you the results you want.

Lawns have long been viewed as a status symbol. In ancient times the amount of lawn (cut grass) you owned reflected your wealth. The more money you had, the more sheep you owned; and therefore, the more "mowed" grass you had on your property. Lawns made their way from the castle grounds to urban and suburban landscapes. Now, instead of sheep, we have mowers, weedwhips, and bagged fertilizer. We spend our weekends mowing, watering, and fertilizing.

Some gardeners feel like slaves to their lawns while others find great satisfaction in managing the turf. Minimize your efforts and maximize your results by matching mowing, fertilizing, and watering to the grass's needs, your quality goals, and especially the time you really spend on your lawn. Keep the grass healthy and you will reduce the time and chemicals needed to rid it of insects, diseases, and weeds.

The amount of effort needed to manage your lawn depends somewhat on the level of quality desired and the amount of use your lawn receives. A golf course quality lawn will require more care than a lawn maintained at a lower level of quality. A well-used lawn, with space for kid's play and sports, will also require more care than one merely viewed from the porch or only occasionally walked upon. Look at how you use your lawn and what quality level you desire to determine your yearly care schedule.

High-quality lawns with dense weed-free grass will receive the maximum number of fertilizations, four or five times per year, and the most pesticide use. Those interested in a nice looking, less-than-perfect lawn can get by with fewer fertilizer applications and no pesticide. No matter what quality level you desire, proper care and properly timed management are the keys to building a healthy and attractive lawn.

SELECTING THE RIGHT GRASS

Putting the right plant in the right location applies to lawns as well as to other garden plants. Cool-season grasses are the best choice for Prairie Lands landscapes. These grasses provide some of the first and last glimpses of green in our cold northern climate.

Kentucky Bluegrass is a favorite lawn grass in our region. It has a fine texture (thin leaf) and a good green color. It is best suited for sunny locations.

Fine Fescues are more shade- and drought-tolerant than **Kentucky Bluegrass**. They look similar to and are generally mixed with **Bluegrass**.

Turf-type Perennial Ryegrass is quick to germinate and sometimes short-lived in the Prairie Lands. It is blended with other grass seeds to provide quick cover until the other grasses germinate. Newer cultivars are hardier; they make up a large percent of most grass seed mixes.

Tall Fescue is a tall, coarse-textured (wide leaf) grass used for high-use areas in full sun to part shade and in dry soils.

STARTING A LAWN

A healthy lawn starts from the ground up. Investing time and effort now will save you a lot of frustration in the future. Both seeding and sodding require proper soil preparation for good results. Seeding a lawn takes more time, but it

Lawns

saves you money and increases your selection of grass-seed mixtures. Sodded lawns give you instant beauty at a price. See April "Planting" for directions on installing sod.

Most people think of lawns separately from gardens, like the ever popular "lawn and garden show." When you get right down to it a lawn *is* a garden—a garden of grass. However, folks don't respect it like a real garden. Especially when you are putting in a new area of lawn, take the time to work the soil and feed the lawn appropriately so that you can reduce the amount of time and chemicals you'll need to keep it green and thrivng. Leave grass clippings on the lawn, they will decompose and feed the soil that feeds the lawn. As with any plant, the secret's in the soil.

To seed a lawn:

1 Take a soil test to determine what nutrients and soil amendments should be added to the soil prior to planting. See "General Horticultural Practices" in the book introduction or contact your local county office of the Cooperative Extension Service for soil testing information.

2 Kill the existing grass and weeds with a total vegetation killer such as Roundup or Finale. Old fields, neglected, or extremely weedy areas may benefit from two applications made two weeks apart. Read and follow label directions exactly. Increasing the concentration will burn off the tops and not kill the roots. Lower rates will not kill the weeds and make additional applications (more product in the long run) necessary. You must wait four to fourteen days after treatment before tilling the soil. Or, if you have the time, simply cover the area with black plastic for 3 to 4 months— overwinter works well. You'll have killed the existing grass and weeds without chemicals.

3 Cultivate the top 6 inches to loosen compacted soil and turn under dead weeds and grass. This is your rough grade. But remember, only work the soil when it is moist. Grab a handful of soil and gently squeeze. Tap it with your finger. If it breaks into smaller pieces it is dry enough to till. Working wet soil results in compaction and clods, while working dry soil breaks down the soil structure.

4 Rake the area smooth, removing any rocks and debris. Allow the soil to settle. Time, rainfall, or a light sprinkling with water will help the soil to settle.

5 Fill in any low spots. Slope the soil away from the house and make the final grade 1 inch lower than adjacent sidewalks and drives.

6 Till the recommended amount of fertilizer, organic matter, and any other needed amendments into the top 6 inches of the soil. In general, new lawns need 1 pound of actual nitrogen per 1000 square feet and several inches of organic matter such as peat moss or compost. See chart on page 172.

7 Rake the soil smooth and make any final adjustments to the final grade.

8 Spread grass seed at a rate of 3 to 4 pounds per 1000 square feet for sunny mixes and 4 to 5 pounds per 1000 square feet for shade mixes. (See August "Helpful Hints" on page 187 for seed selection tips.) Using a drop-type or rotary spreader. Sow half the seed in one direction and the remainder at right angles to the first.

9 Lightly rake seeds into the top 1/4 inch of soil. Roll the seeded area with an empty lawn roller to ensure good seed-to-soil contact. Borrow an empty lawn roller from a friend or rent one from a local tool rental center.

Lawns

10 Mulch the area to conserve moisture and reduce erosion. Use weed-free straw, hay, or floating row covers sold as GrassFast or ReeMay for mulch. Cover the area with the row cover and anchor the edges with stones, boards, or wire anchors. Or spread the straw and hay over the soil surface. Apply a thin layer so some of the soil is still visible through the mulch. Thin layers of these materials can be left on the lawn to decompose naturally.

11 Water after seeding and frequently enough to keep the soil surface moist, but not soggy. You may need to water once or twice a day for several weeks. Once the grass begins to grow, you can reduce the watering frequency. Established seedlings should still be watered thoroughly, but less frequently.

12 Mow the grass when it is one-third higher than your normal mowing height of 2½ to 3½ inches tall. Cut 4-inch-tall seedlings back to 3 or 3½ inches and continue mowing as needed.

CARING FOR YOUR LAWN

Proper care is the best defense against weeds, disease, and insects. The three major practices include watering, fertilizing, and mowing. Manage these properly and you will be rewarded with a beautiful, healthy lawn.

Established lawns need about 1 inch of water per week from rain or irrigation. On clay soils, apply the needed water once a week. Sandy soils should receive ½ inch of water twice a week. See July "Helpful Hints" for watering tips.

Your soil test results will tell you what type of fertilizer to use and the amount to apply for every 1000 square feet. High-quality and high-use lawns require more fertilizer than most residential lawns.

Keep the grass 3 to 3½ inches high. Taller lawns will be healthier and better able to fight off weeds and disease. Mow frequently enough so that you remove no more than one-third (about 1 inch) of the total height. Leave these short clippings on the lawn. Rake and compost longer clippings, run the mower over long clippings or use a mulching mower to cut them down in size.

FERTILIZER GUIDELINES

Most **Prairie Lands** lawns are a blend of **Kentucky Bluegrass**, **Fine Fescues**, and **Perennial Ryegrass**. These lawn areas need 1 to 3 pounds of nitrogen (N) per season. Most soils have high to excessive levels of phosphorus (P) and potassium (K) and need little or none of these nutrients. Select the fertilizer recommended by your soil test or use one high in nitrogen with little or no phosphorus and potassium. Avoid midsummer fertilization on non-irrigated lawns as it can damage turf and encourage weed growth.

To calculate your fertilizer needs:

Calculate your lawn area by measuring the length and width of each section. Multiply the length times width to find the square footage of that portion of lawn. Approximate the area of irregularly shaped parcels.

Highly managed and frequently-used lawn areas should receive several applications of fertilizer. Nice looking lawns with less activity can get by with just one or two applications of fertilizers.

Calculate the fertilizer needed. Most fertilizer spreaders' settings are based on applying 1 pound of actual nitrogen per 1000 square feet. You can calculate the amount of fertilizer needed with this formula:

Divide 100 by the percentage of nitrogen in the fertilizer that you are using. Multiply that number by the amount of actual nitrogen recommended by the results of your soil test or Fertilization Schedule. This will give you the amount of fertilizer needed per 1000

Lawns

Helpful Hints

Fertilization Schedule

Dates and Rates (Actual Nitrogen Per 1000 Square Feet) of Application

Total Number of Applications	May/June	July	September	Late October
1				1
2	1/2			1
3	1/2		1	1
4	1/2	1/2	1	1

Common Fertilizers

Fertilizer Analysis (N-P-K) sq. ft.	Pounds of Fertilizer Needed to Supply		
	1/2 lb. N*/1000 sq. ft	1 lb. N*/1000 sq. ft.	1 1/2 lb. N*/1000
45-0-0	1.1 (100/45 × 0.5)	2.2 (100/45 × 1)	3.3 (100/45 × 1.5)
24-8-6	2.1 (100/24 × 0.5)	4.2 (100/24 × 1)	6.3 (100/24 × 1.5)
16-4-8	3.1 (100/16 × 0.5)	6.25 (100/16 × 1)	9.4 (100/16 × 1.5)
6-2-0	8.3 (100/6 × 0.5)	16.7 (100/6 × 1)	25 (100/6 × 1.5)

square feet. Or use the "Common Fertilizers" chart.

Use low-nitrogen or slow-release fertilizers to avoid burning the lawn.

Apply half the needed fertilizer in one direction and the remaining half in the other direction. This will reduce the risk of striping and fertilizer burn. Be careful not to overlap or leave the spreader open when making your turns.

PESTS

A healthy lawn is your best defense against weeds, insects, and diseases. Mow high, fertilize properly, and water during droughts to keep weeds and other pests under control. If a problem is discovered, find out why it has developed. Correcting the cause, not just killing the pest, will give you better long-term results.

Lawn Notes

JANUARY
Lawns

 PLANNING

January is the time for resolutions, and maybe one of yours is to hire someone to care for your lawn.

Selecting the right lawn care professional is not just about price. Here are some additional factors to consider:

• Know what services you want performed and contact several companies for cost estimates.

• Ask friends and relatives for their recommendations.

• Get a written service agreement. Ask about automatic renewals and penalties for discontinuing the service.

• Pesticides, including herbicides, insecticides, and fungicides, should only be applied as needed. Ask what chemicals they plan to use and why. You can ask to see the paper that describes the chemical, note warnings (many lawn chemicals can kill fish), and any side effects, as well as its toxicity. Be assertive, it's your lawn.

• Make sure the company will provide advance notice—at least 24 hours—of chemical applications. This will allow you to get the dog, toys, and lawn furniture away from the areas to be treated.

• Tell them they need verbal authorization to do anything except mow, if you are concerned about unnecessary chemical applications.

• Seek a company that belongs to a professional organization, such as the Professional Grounds Management Association.

• Ask about the staff's training and qualifications. Do they have any Certified Landscape Technicians? These are individuals who have demonstrated a standard of competency through a voluntary certification program.

• Ask the company for references from local customers and check with the Better Business Bureau.

 PLANTING

Still in our dreams for now—so sit back, relax, and enjoy the peace and quiet!

 CARE

Shovel walks and driveways before using deicing salts. This will help reduce damage to lawns and other valuable plants.

 WATERING

No need to water; the grass is dormant and the ground is usually frozen or covered with snow.

 FERTILIZING

Do not fertilize. Applying fertilizer to frozen soil can pollute the water. Melting snow and winter rains wash the fertilizer off the frozen soil surface and into nearby storm sewers, rivers, and lakes.

 MOWING

Nothing to cut, so enjoy the break!

 PROBLEMS

Make a note of areas where snow and ice tend to linger. These are prime candidates for snow mold. Damaged turf will be matted and covered with a gray or pink fungus in spring.

Watch for vole activity. These rodents scurry beneath the snow eating weeds, chewing on bark, and wearing trails in the lawn. Be prepared to do a little raking and overseeding in the spring.

FEBRUARY

PLANNING

Draw a sketch of the lawn. Mark areas where water and ice collect, snow is slow to recede, and deicing salts may cause damage. Plan on filling low spots in spring to reduce future drainage problems. Areas where ice and snow collect will benefit from a light raking soon after the spring thaw. Raking also helps reduce snow mold disease. Grass along the driveway and sidewalks will benefit from a thorough watering in the spring to leach (wash) the salts through the soil. Consider using magnesium chloride, calcium acetate or other more plant-friendly deicing compounds.

Helpful Hints

Nothing beats a nice stand of shade trees when it comes to beating the summer heat—unless you are trying to grow grass under those trees. The lack of sunlight and competition for water make it difficult, if not impossible, to grow grass under some shade trees. But you do not have need to sacrifice the shade or give up on the lawn. Here are some tips for getting both the shade and the lawn you want:

Plant shade-tolerant grass seed mixes in these areas. They contain a high percentage of **fine fescue** grass. This shade- and drought-tolerant grass is the best choice for shady locations.

Plant shade-tolerant groundcovers in heavily shaded areas. **hostas, pachysandra, deadnettle** (*Lamium* spp.), or **variegated archangel** (*Lamiastrum* sp.) are just a few of the shade-tolerant groundcovers you can try. Start with just a few plants to make sure there is enough sunlight and moisture for the groundcovers.

Mulch densely shaded areas. Spread 3 to 6 inches of woodchips under the tree. Keep the woodchips away from the tree trunk. The woodchips improve the growing conditions, while keeping the lawn mower and weedwhip away from the trunk of the tree.

PLANTING

Do you plan on expanding any planting beds this season? The sod removed (with a sod cutter) to create these beds can be used to repair problem areas in other parts of the lawn. Look at the season ahead. Tentatively plan a block of time when you can do both tasks.

CARE

This is a great time to take your lawn mower to the repair shop and beat the spring rush.

WATERING

Watering now is not practical and usually not needed.

FERTILIZING

Do not fertilize. Applying fertilizer to frozen soil can pollute the water. Melting snow and winter rains wash the fertilizer off the frozen soil surface and into nearby storm sewers, rivers, and lakes.

MOWING

Mowing is not needed in February.

PROBLEMS

Prairie Lands landscapes, especially those in the southern half of the region, often experience a winter thaw. Use this break to survey the lawn for signs of winter damage.

MARCH
Lawns

PLANNING

In March, spring still seems far away. Those up north may still be staring at an endless expanse of snow, while the rest of the region is being teased with a mixture of spring days and snowstorms. Now is a good time to get your lawn mower ready for the season ahead. Take it to a repair shop, or get out the owner's manual and do it yourself. These are a few of the things that will need your attention:

• For safety's sake, if you are new at this job, consider asking an experienced friend or relative for help. Always disconnect the spark plug wire when working on your mower.

• Clean or replace the spark plug and air filter.

• Drain the oil from the crankcase of a mower with a four- cycle engine (not needed for two-cycle engines). Refill with the type and amount of oil recommended by the manufacturer.

• Replace bent, cracked, or damaged blades. Sharpen or have a professional sharpen the mower's blades.

• Check the tires for wear and replace them as needed.

• Check for loose nuts, bolts, and screws, both now and throughout the season.

PLANTING

Try to contain your enthusiasm. It is still a little early to plant grass seed, and sod is usually not available until April.

CARE

Get out the rake and start work as soon as the snow and ice melt. Use a leaf rake to fluff and dry the grass to reduce the risk of snow mold. Remove any leaves and debris that may have collected prior to the snowfall. Never work on frozen or waterlogged soils. This can lead to damage and death of the grass.

WATERING

Watering is usually not needed. In dry springs, water areas exposed to deicing salts. This will help wash the salts through the soil and reduce damage caused by the salt. Water grass along sidewalks, drives, and steps. Salt damaged grass won't green up in spring. Water areas of the lawn that were seeded or sodded at the end of last season. This will reduce the stress on the young, developing root systems. Water only if the top 4 to 6 inches of the soil are starting to dry. Make sure any recently seeded repair jobs are kept moist.

FERTILIZING

This is a good time to take a soil test. See "General Horticultural Practices" for tips on taking a soil test. Contact your local Cooperative Extension Service for details on taking and submitting soil for testing.

MOWING

Mowing is usually not needed. Wait until the grass greens and starts to grow.

PROBLEMS

Lightly raking the lawn helps dry out the grass and reduce problems with snow mold. Tamp down runways formed by vole activity over winter. A light tamp is often enough to get the roots back into the soil, allowing the grass to recover. Severely damaged areas may need to be reseeded. Fill in any holes dug by animals or created by winter activities.

Helpful Hints

Dethatching Your Lawn

Should you core aerate or dethatch your lawn this season? All the neighbors are doing it, so how about you? These practices have become a common part of the lawn care scene. Make sure you have a problem that these practices will solve before renting the equipment or hiring a professional. Dethatching and core aeration are both used to control thatch.

Thatch is a layer of partially decomposed grass plants. (It is not caused by short grass clippings left on the lawn to decompose.)

A thin layer, 1/2 inch or less, of thatch is good for the lawn. It conserves moisture and reduces wear.

Thick layers, greater than 1/2 inch, should be removed.

Dethatching machines, called vertical mowers, are used to physically remove the layer of thatch. These machines cut through the thatch and pull it to the surface. This is stressful on the lawn and should only be done in early September or May when the lawn is actively growing. Rake and compost the thatch removed during this process. This is also a good time to overseed thin lawns. Spread the seed over the recently dethatched lawn. The disturbed lawn provides a good surface for the seed to contact the soil and germinate. See September "Helpful Hints" on page 189 for tips on renovating the lawn.

Core aerators remove plugs of soil from the lawn. They open up the soil surface, allowing the thatch to decompose. Breaking up the cores and spreading the soil over the lawn surface helps speed up the process.

Aeration also reduces soil compaction. Compacted soils are poorly drained, limit root growth, and result in thin, unhealthy lawns. Lawns growing in clay soils or in high traffic areas are subject to compaction. Make sure the aerator cores through the thatch layer and several inches into the soil. This process opens up the soil, allowing air, water, and nutrients to reach the plant roots. Aeration is less stressful on the lawn than dethatching, but it is most effective when done in early September or May.

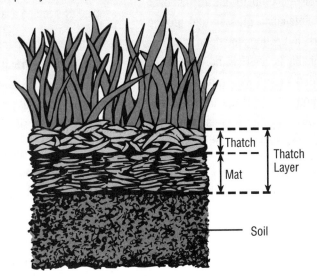

To prevent thatch from becoming a problem:

Do not overwater or overfertilize the lawn.

Avoid excessive use of insecticides that may reduce earthworm populations. Earthworms are nature's aerating machines.

Leave short clippings on the lawn to decompose. Mulch, or remove and compost long clippings (only those free of herbicides).

PLANNING

Depending on the weather, mowing can begin anytime this month. Make sure your lawn mower is ready to go. See March "Planning" for details on preparing your mower for the season.

You should have a schedule and strategy for accomplishing your lawn maintenance tasks throughout the growing season. Use your gardening journal to record successes, failures, discoveries, pests, and significant weather events encountered this year. This information will help you or your lawn care professional revise and improve your lawn maintenance program in the future.

Do not succumb to ads for fantastic, no-maintenance grasses and groundcovers. If it sounds too good to be true, it probably is. Every living thing, plants included, requires some care and attention. Those that can manage on their own are often aggressive or invasive and can take over your landscape and nearby native areas.

PLANTING

This is a good time to repair damaged areas in the lawn. As the grass greens, it will be easier to spot these problems. You can purchase lawn repair kits. These contain the seed and mulch needed to repair problem areas. Remove the dead turf, loosen and amend soil as needed, and then apply the patch. You can make your own lawn patch by mixing a handful of a quality grass-seed mix into a bucket of topsoil. Prepare the soil and spread the seed and soil mixture. Mulch to conserve moisture.

Start laying sod as soon as the snow disappears and the sod is available for sale. Site preparation is the same whether seeding or sodding a lawn.

1 Prepare the planting site and soil as directed in "Starting a Lawn" in the introduction to this chapter. Soil preparation is just as critical for sodding as it is for seeding.

2 Calculate the square footage of the area to be sodded. A roll of sod is usually $1^1/_2$ feet wide by 6 feet long. It will cover 9 square feet.

3 Order sod to be delivered or plan on picking it up just prior to installation,

4 Select freshly cut sod with a good green color. Be sure it is free of weeds and pests. Use sod that has a blend of several grass varieties and is grown on a soil similar to yours.

5 Keep sod in a cool, shady place to prevent it from overheating and drying out. Lay it as soon as possible.

6 Use a driveway, sidewalk, or curb as your starting point. Lay the first row of sod next to the longest of these straight edges. Butt sod ends together and make sure the roots contact the soil. Stagger the seams, as if you were laying bricks. Use a knife to trim the sod to fit.

7 Lay the sod perpendicular to the slope on steep hills. Use wooden stakes to hold it in place.

8 Run an empty lawn roller over the sod. Push it perpendicular to the direction that the sod was laid. Rolling removes air pockets and ensures good root-to-soil contact.

9 Water immediately. Moisten the sod and the top 3 to 4 inches of soil. Keep the sod and soil surface moist until the sod has rooted into the soil below. Continue watering thoroughly, but less frequently once this happens. Mow the sod once it is firmly rooted in place.

Do not succumb to ads for fantastic, no-maintenance grasses and groundcovers. If it sounds too good to be true, it probably is.

 CARE

Rake out any dead grass and be patient. Wait for grass roots to resprout and surrounding grass to fill in these areas.

 WATERING

Water newly sodded or seeded areas of the lawn. Keep the soil surface moist in these areas. In dry springs, water areas exposed to deicing salts. This includes the grass along walks, drives, and roadways. Spring irrigation helps wash the salts through the soil and reduces the damage caused by the salt.

 FERTILIZING

Wait until late May. Fertilizing now means more grass to cut. Lush, succulent spring growth increases the risk of disease and creates more work for you.

 MOWING

Start mowing as soon as the grass greens up and starts to grow. Keep the

Helpful Hints

Proper mowing is one of the keys to a healthy lawn. Set your mowing height at 3 or 3$\frac{1}{2}$ inches tall. Taller grass forms a deeper root system. The stronger plants are better able to fight off insects, disease, and weeds. Mow often enough so that you are removing no more than $\frac{1}{3}$ of the total height. This reduces the stress on the plants and results in shorter clippings that can be left on the lawn. These short clippings add nitrogen, moisture, and organic matter to the soil. Vary the direction and pattern of mowing. It reduces the wear and tear on the lawn.

grass at least 2$\frac{1}{2}$ inches tall, but preferably 3 to 3$\frac{1}{2}$ inches tall. Mow often enough so that you remove no more than $\frac{1}{3}$ of the total height. You may be cutting the grass several times a week in the spring.

 PROBLEMS

Prevent crabgrass problems with proper care. Keep the grass tall, and water during droughts. If this has not worked, you may choose to use a crabgrass pre-emergent. Apply it to problem areas, about the time that bridalwreath **spirea** flowerbuds start to swell or bloom. This is usually mid to late April. Do not use these products if you plan to seed or overseed the lawn this spring. Pre-emergents will kill the desirable grass seeds

as well as the weed seeds. Corn gluten based pre-emergents provide some crabgrass control in a more environmentally friendly manner.

Prairie Lands lawns seldom suffer severe insect damage. Always make sure insects are causing damage before using an insecticide. Unnecessary use of pesticides kills the beneficial insects that help create a good growing environment for the lawn.

This is the time to watch for adult billbugs. These small insects can be seen on the sidewalks. Treat them only if your lawn has suffered from browning or dieback damage that you know was caused by this insect.

MAY
Lawns

PLANNING

The pace is picking up with time spent mowing, trimming, and planting. Monitor the health and vigor of your grass as you work your way through the landscape. Watch for changes in color, density, and overall vigor. Problems caught early are easier to control. Contact a lawn care professional or your local county Cooperative Extension Service for help diagnosing problems.

PLANTING

This is the second-best time to seed or overseed lawns in the Prairie Lands states. (Mid-August through mid-September is the best time.) Proper soil preparation is the key to creating a healthy lawn that can withstand pests and the rigors of our weather. See "Starting a Lawn" in the introduction on page 169 for details on preparing the soil and seeding.

Use a grass mix suitable for your light conditions. Use a grass mix containing about 60 percent **Bluegrass**, 30 percent **Fine Fescue**, and 10 percent **Turf-type Perennial Ryegrass** for sunny areas. Use a mix with 60 percent **Fine Fescue**, 30 percent **Bluegrass**, and 10 percent **Turf-type Perennial Ryegrass** for shady areas. Select a quality grass seed that contains several varieties of each type of grass.

This is still a good time to install sod. See April "Planting" for details.

CARE

May is also the second-best time to control thatch and soil compaction. (The best time is in the fall.) Thatch is a brown, spongy layer of partially decomposed grass. Thick layers prevent water and nutrients from reaching the grass roots. Dethatching physically removes this layer of organic matter. Core aeration removes plugs of soil, allowing the thatch to break down. The openings also help repair soil compactions. See March "Helpful Hints" on page 177 for more details on thatch, core aeration, and dethatching.

WATERING

Newly planted lawns need extra attention. Keep the soil surface moist until the sod is well rooted or the grass seed has sprouted. Established lawns need an average of 1 inch of water each week. Spring rains usually provide the needed moisture. You can step in with the sprinkler as needed.

FERTILIZING

Mid May in southern areas or early June in northern areas is the first time to fertilize your lawn. Apply 1/2 pound of actual nitrogen per 1000 square feet. This is equal to 5 pounds of a fertilizer containing 10 percent nitrogen or 3 pounds of a fertilizer with 16 percent nitrogen. See the "Common Fertilizers" chart in the introduction to this chapter for details. Consider using a low-nitrogen slow-release fertilizer to reduce the risk of burn on non-irrigated lawns.

MOWING

Keep the grass at least 2 1/2 inches tall, preferably 3 to 3 1/2 inches tall. Mow frequently so that you remove no more than 1/3 of the total height at each mowing.

PROBLEMS

A healthy lawn is the best defense against weeds. Broadleaf weedkillers can be used to get problem areas under control. **Creeping Charlie,** also known as **ground ivy,** is one of the more common and perhaps most irritating of these weeds. It has round scalloped leaves that smell somewhat minty when crushed.

Helpful Hints

Common Diseases

Helminthosporium leaf-spot and melting-out diseases cause irregular patches of brown and dying grass. A close look at nearby blades reveals brown to black spots on leaves. As the disease progresses, the patch gets larger and the grass begins to disintegrate and disappear (melt away). Overseed areas with resistant grass varieties. Heavy infestations can be treated with a fungicide labeled for use on turf and melting-out disease. Read and follow label directions.

Snow mold is most evident in the spring as the snow and ice melt. Infected lawns have small to large patches of white or gray matted turf. The grass thins and is slow to recover in spring. Rake the lawn in early spring, and avoid overuse of nitrogen in the spring.

Powdery mildew looks as though someone has sprinkled baby powder on the leaves. It is most common on shady lawns in the fall, but it can appear anytime during the growing season. Over-seed shady areas with **Fine Fescue**, or increase the sunlight by thinning the crowns of trees.

Rust-infected lawns have brown, orange, or yellow spots on the leaves. A walk through a rust-infected lawn will result in red shoes. This is a common problem on newly seeded lawns due to the high percentage of rust-susceptible **Ryegrass**. As the **Bluegrass** and **Fescue** increase, the rust usually becomes less of a problem in the future. Proper care increases turf health and allows it to tolerate the damage. Treatment is usually not needed.

Necrotic ring spot (formerly known as "fusarium blight") appears as circles or irregular patches of dead grass with tufts of green grass in the center. All **Bluegrass** and **Fescue** varieties appear to be susceptible. Overseeding with **Perennial Ryegrass** may help mask symptoms. Proper care and time for the disease to run its course is usually the most successful treatment.

Fairy ring is not life threatening, but it can cause aesthetic concerns. Infected lawns have rings of dark green, yellow, or dying turf. The rings appear for a short time, disappear, and then return—slightly larger in diameter—later or the next season. During wet periods, mushrooms will appear within the ring. No control is needed (or effective). Water fairy rings during drought to minimize the symptoms.

The purple flowers appear in mid- to late May. There is good news for those who are losing the battle. Broadleaf weed-killers containing 2-4D and MCPP will work. Timing is the key. Treat **creeping charlie** when it is in full bloom. Spot treat problem areas only. This will reduce the amount of pesticide used. It may take several years to eliminate the offspring of these weeds.

Insects are not usually a major threat to Prairie Lands lawns. Sodwebworm feeding can cause thin patches, brown trails, or patchy lawns. Treat these insects only if you find more than 1 per square yard. See June "Helpful Hints" for more information on monitoring turf insects.

Cool, wet springs often increase the risk of lawn disease. Helminthosporium leaf spot and necrotic ring spot (formerly known as fusarium blight) are probably the most common diseases of home lawns. Proper care and over-seeding with resistant grass varieties can minimize the damage. See this month's "Helpful Hints" for more information on these and other turf diseases.

JUNE
Lawns

 PLANNING

As the temperatures rise, grass growth slows. Keep monitoring the lawn for weeds, insects, and disease. Draw a sketch of the lawn area, and record any problems that may require further evaluation or treatment.

 PLANTING

You can still lay sod. Lawns installed now will need a little extra water as the weather turns hot and dry.

 CARE

A spongy lawn surface may mean you have a thatch problem. Confirm your suspicions with this simple test. Remove several 3- by 3-inch plugs of grass. Take these samples from several areas throughout the lawn. Measure the thatch layer. If it is greater than 1/2 inch you should consider taking action in the fall. See March "Helpful Hints" for more details on thatch prevention and control.

 WATERING

Be sure to provide new lawns with adequate moisture. Established lawns generally need 1 inch of water each week. June rainfall often provides enough moisture. Water established lawns only as needed. If your footprints remain in the lawn, the color turns a dull bluish-gray, or the leaves start to roll, it is time to water the lawn. Water thoroughly, but less frequently to encourage deep roots for drought tolerance.

 FERTILIZING

Apply 1/2 pound of actual nitrogen per 1000 square feet, if it was not done in late May. This is equal to 5 pounds of a fertilizer containing 10 percent nitrogen or 3 pounds of a fertilizer with 16 percent nitrogen. See the "Common Fertilizers" chart on page 172 in the introduction to this chapter for details. Consider using a low-nitrogen slow-release fertilizer to reduce the risk of burn, especially on non-irrigated lawns.

 MOWING

Mow often enough so that you remove only 1/3 of the total grass height at each cutting. Removing less leaf surface minimizes the stress on the plant. Keep the grass 2 1/2 to 3 1/2 inches tall. The taller grass shades the soil, keeping grass roots cool and preventing weed seeds from sprouting.

 PROBLEMS

Check for symptoms and monitor the occurrence and spread of disease. A cool, wet spring means you will be seeing more problems. Proper care and drier weather often are sufficient to stop or slow down the spread of disease. Keep cutting the grass high, water during droughts, and overseed damaged areas in late August or early September. See May "Helpful Hints" for more details.

Insects are not usually a severe problem in Prairie Lands lawns.

Greenbugs, a type of aphid, occasionally feed on the grass under trees in the southern region. If you find 30 or more aphids on each grass blade, it is time to treat. Spray the infested areas and the surrounding 6 feet with insecticidal soap.

Sodwebworm feeding can cause thin patches, brown trails, or patchy lawns. Treat these insects only if you find more than one insect per square yard.

Turf-damaging grubs are the immature larvae of several different beetles. They feed on grass roots, causing the turf to be uniformly thin, droughty, or dead. Treat only if three or four grubs are found per every 1 square foot of turf sampled.

Keep the grass 2½ to 3½ inches tall. The taller grass shades the soil, keeping grass roots cool and preventing weed seeds from sprouting.

Anthills may sporadically appear throughout the lawn. They generally do not harm anything, but just annoy some home owners. If their activity is damaging the turf roots, or if your family cannot abide their presence, you may chose to use an insecticide. Spot treat to minimize the use of pesticides. Remember, insecticides also kill or reduce the population of the good insects living in the soil. Select an insecticide labeled for use on lawns to control the problem pest. And as always, be sure to read and follow all label directions carefully.

The warm weather is perfect for most weeds. As grass growth slows, the weeds seem to appear and grow overnight. Do not use herbicides (weed-killers) in the summer. They can damage your lawn when applied in hot, dry weather. New weeds will fill the voids left by the dead weeds faster than the grass. Dig small numbers of weeds or those in bloom. Removing their flowers will help reduce future weed problems. You may be able to convince the neighborhood kids it is fun to pull or "decapitate" weeds. No? Then how about a penny or two for each weed removed?

Helpful Hints

Insects do not generally pose a threat to lawns in the Prairie Lands. Before reaching for the can of insecticide, make sure insects are really the problem. Here are some easy tests you can conduct to determine if insects are damaging your lawn:

Flotation Test: This test is used for chinch bugs. Remove both ends of a coffee can or similar container. Sink the can in the grass at the edge of the dead area. Fill the can with water and agitate the grass. Chinch bugs will float to the surface. Test several areas. Treatment is needed if you find two or three of these insects per test.

Irritation Test: This test will detect sodwebworm larvae. Mix 1 tablespoon of dishwashing detergent in 1 gallon of water. Sprinkle the soapy water over 1 square yard of lawn. Conduct the test in several areas, both damaged spots and areas adjacent to the damaged grass. Check the treated areas several times over the next 10 minutes. Treat if one or more sodwebworm larvae are present.

Turf Removal: This is done to confirm the presence of grubs. Cut out and remove 1 square foot of turf. Check the top 4 to 6 inches of soil for white grub larvae. Replace the sample and keep the soil moist until it re-roots. Treat if three or four grubs are found per 1 square foot of turf.

Dogs often cause brown spots of dead grass in the lawn. Their nitrogen-rich urine acts just like fertilizer burn. The treatment is the same. Thoroughly water the area to dilute the urine and wash it through the soil. Some gardeners have trained their dogs to go in a specific area. They may have several mulched areas for this purpose. The surrounding grass will eventually fill in these brown areas. Nature and time do heal many landscape problems. There are mixed reports on some of the new urine-neutralizing products. Several people have reported great success while others find the watering works just as well.

JULY
Lawns

 PLANNING

Keep evaluating your lawn. Make notes on the areas that need work. Late summer through early fall is the best time to repair, over-seed, and start a new lawn. Use the summer months to find ways to reduce your workload or to make it more enjoyable. Consider creating beds around groups of trees and shrubs to reduce mowing and hand trimming. Eliminate tight areas that are hard to reach with the mower. Write down these ideas in your journal. You can implement them as time allows.

Make plans for lawn care while on vacation. If you plan on being gone more than a week, you will need someone to cut the grass. Vacationing during the hot, dry months of July and August may mean you need someone to water the lawn—or you could just let it go dormant for this portion of the growing season.

 PLANTING

You can still lay sod. Use fresh sod and install it as soon as possible. Stored sod can overheat and damage or kill the grass plants. Once installed, the new lawn will need extra care during this often hot, dry month. Make sure the soil surface stays moist until the sod roots into the soil below. Once rooted, it will still need thorough, though less frequent watering.

 CARE

Right now, you just want to sustain your lawn. As the heat increases and the weather turns dry, you will need to decide how you will manage your lawn through droughts. Some gardeners prefer to let their lawns go dormant. They stop watering and let the lawns shut down and turn brown during this stressful period. As the weather cools and the rains return, the lawn will green up and begin to grow again. Others choose to keep watering to prolong the growth and green in their lawn. The choice is yours.

 WATERING

Growing lawns need 1 inch of water per week. You may need to step in and give nature a hand during July and August. In clay soils give lawns a good soaking once a week. Lawns in sandy soils should be watered $1/2$ to $3/4$ an inch twice a week. During an extended drought of three or more weeks, water dormant lawns $1/4$ inch. This is enough water to prevent the plants from drying, while still keeping them dormant. Once the rain returns, the lawn will turn green. Do not water and bring the lawn out of dormancy unless you can maintain a regular watering schedule throughout the drought. Allowing the lawn to go in and out of dormancy several times during the season stresses and can even kill the grass.

 FERTILIZING

Only irrigated and highly managed lawns can be fertilized this month. Use $1/2$ pound of actual nitrogen per 1000 square feet. This can be accomplished by using 5 pounds of a fertilizer containing 10 percent nitrogen. See the "Common Fertilizers" chart on page 172 in the introduction for more details. Do not fertilize dormant or non-irrigated lawns. This can damage and even kill the grass.

 MOWING

Keep the grass 3 to $3^1/2$ inches tall. Taller grass is more drought-tolerant and better able to compete with pests. Remove no more than $1/3$ of the total height with each cutting. The warmer, drier weather means you will probably be mowing less frequently.

Allowing the lawn to go in and out of dormancy several times during the season stresses and can even kill the grass.

PROBLEMS

Proper care is the best defense against pests. Always properly identify the pest, determine if control is needed, and evaluate your options before treating. Nature is the best pest manager for your lawn.

Insects. Grub damage becomes obvious during the dry months of July and August. Their feeding causes the turf to be uniformly thin, appear droughty, or die. Only treat in spring or late summer if you find three or four grubs per 1 square foot of turf.

Small patches (2 to 4 inches) of dead grass may indicate billbug damage. Check the soil for the larvae before treating.

Watch for pale or yellowing turf under trees. Greenbugs, a type of aphid, can cause this type of damage. Treatment is only needed when you find 30 or more greenbugs per grass blade. Always read and follow label directions before purchasing or using any pesticide.

Helpful Hints

Correct Watering Practices

Improperly watered lawns suffer more problems than those that depend on rainfall as the sole source of water. Make the most of your efforts by watering properly.

Lawns need to be watered when your footprints persist, the grass turns bluish-gray, or the leaves start to roll.

Lawns will typically need 1 inch of water each week. Water lawns on clay soils once a week. Water lawns on sandy soils with about 1/2 inch of water twice a week.

Set several straight-sided cans under the sprinkler to measure the water applied. Once filled with the required amount of water, turn off the sprinkler and move it to the next location. Note the pressure used and the time it took to apply the needed water. Now you have an idea of how long you need to water.

Water early in the day for best results. Watering early reduces disease problems and water lost to evaporation.

Diseases are usually less of a concern on home lawns at this time of the year. See May "Helpful Hints" on page 181 for more information.

To help control weeds, continue to mow high. Taller grass is better able to out-compete the weeds. Continue to dig offensive weeds as time allows. Crabgrass is just starting to appear. Mark locations of problem areas on your lawn map. This will make it easier to target pesticide applications next spring, reducing the amount of chemical you will have to use.

AUGUST
Lawns

PLANNING

Early August is often the peak of hot, dry weather. Keep monitoring the health of your lawn. By mid- to late-August, the weather usually begins to cool in northerly areas. This is a good time to review your journal entries, evaluate needed repairs, and make plans for the remainder of the season. Mid-August through mid-September is the best time to repair, replace, or start a new lawn. Consider replacing lawns when 50 percent or more weeds should be replaced. Those with compacted soils, some weeds, or bare spots would benefit from some renovation and repair. See September "Helpful Hints" for details on renovating lawns.

PLANTING

Begin seeding lawns in mid- to late-August or when the weather starts to cool. This is the best time to seed lawns. The soil is warm, so the seeds germinate quickly. The temperatures are cooling and perfect for growing grass. See "Starting a Lawn" on page 169 in the chapter introduction for details on seeding.

This is also a good time to lay sod. The cooler temperatures promote root-ing and mean you will need to water less frequently than lawns sodded in July. See April "Planting" on page 178 for details on installing sod.

Bare areas can also be repaired. Remove dead grass, amend soil as needed, and roughen the soil surface. Purchase a lawn patch kit or make one yourself. Mix one handful of a quality lawn-seed mix into a bucket of topsoil. Sprinkle this over the soil surface, rake smooth, and mulch. Water often enough to keep the soil surface moist.

Overseed thin lawns. Creating a denser stand of turf will help reduce weeds, fight pests, and improve the overall appearance. See September "Helpful Hints" for details.

CARE

The early part of the month is focused on sustaining the lawn. Proper care, whether the grass is dormant or growing, will help the lawn survive the heat and drought often experienced in early August. As temperatures cool, you will notice the improvement in the health and appearance of your lawn.

WATERING

Established lawns should receive 1 inch of water when it shows signs of wilting. Use a rain gauge or coffee cans to measure the amount of water applied (see July "Helpful Hints").

Grub-infested, disease-damaged, or stressed lawns should be watered. Watering helps reduce stress and mask pest damage.

Dormant lawns should be left dormant until the drought conditions pass. Give them 1/4 inch of water during extended (three to four weeks) drought periods. This is enough moisture to keep the grass alive while still allowing it to remain dormant.

New lawns should be watered often enough to keep the soil surface moist. Reduce watering frequency once the sod has rooted into the soil and the grass seed begins to grow.

FERTILIZING

Wait until September to fertilize established lawns. Incorporate fertilizer into the soil prior to seeding or sodding new lawns.

As temperatures cool, you will notice the improvement in the health and appearance of your lawn.

 ## MOWING

Keep the grass 3 to 3$^1/_2$ inches tall. Taller grass is more drought-tolerant and better able to compete with pests. Remove no more than $^1/_3$ of the total height with each cutting. Start cutting newly sodded lawns as soon as they are well rooted.

 ## PROBLEMS

Insects may be more of a problem if the summer has been hot and dry. Continue monitoring for grubs, billbugs, sodwebworms, and greenbugs. Make sure the insects are present and the damage is severe enough to warrant treatment.

Skunks, raccoons, and moles can damage lawns with their digging and tunneling. These critters are searching for big, fat, tasty grubs. Continual damage means they have found a food source and plan to stay. Get rid of the food—the grubs—and you will solve the problem. Squirrels can also be found digging in the lawn. They are storing nuts and seeds for future meals. The damage is irritating, but not a threat to the health of the lawn. Gently tamp down disturbed areas.

Helpful Hints

A quality lawn starts with good soil preparation and a quality lawn seed.

Use a mixture of approximately 60 percent **Bluegrass**, 30 percent **Fine Fescue**, and 10 percent **Turf-type Perennial Ryegrass**.

Seed shady areas with a mixture of approximately 60 percent **Fine Fescue**, 30 percent **Bluegrass**, and 10 percent **Turf-type Perennial Ryegrass**.

All grass seed mixes should contain several varieties of each type (**Bluegrass**, **Fescue**, and **Ryegrass**) of grass. This increases disease resistance and reduces the risk of losing your whole lawn to a pest infestation.

Purchase a high quality seed. Select seeds with a high rate of germination. The higher the germination rate, the more viable (living seeds) the mix contains. The purity rate tells you what percentage of the mix is desirable grass seed. The remainder includes other grass seeds, weed seeds, dirt, and chaff. A high percent of purity means you are paying for seeds and not unwanted "other ingredients."

Seed sunny grass seed mixes at a rate of 3 to 4 pounds per 1000 square feet. Apply shady mixes at a rate of 4 to 5 pounds per 1000 square feet.

Grass	Minimum Seed Germination	Minimum Purity
Kentucky Bluegrass	75-80%	90-95%
Fine Fescue	80-85%	95-97%
Perennial Ryegrass	90-95%	95-98%
Tall Fescue	85-90%	95-98%.

Newly seeded lawns are often infected with rust. This fungal disease causes the grass to turn yellow, orange, or brown. The symptoms will soon disappear and the grass will begin to recover on its own. Treatment is usually not needed.

Powdery mildew often appears in August. Like rust, it is more of an aesthetic problem than a threat to the lawn's health. See May "Helpful Hints" for more information on turf diseases.

SEPTEMBER
Lawns

 PLANNING

Labor Day marks the beginning of increased lawn care activity. Cooler temperatures and regular rainfall make this a good time to start a new lawn or repair an existing one.

 PLANTING

Whether you are renovating an existing lawn, starting a new one, or just patching bare spots, early to mid-September is the best time to plant grass seed. The warm soil speeds up germination while the cooler air temperatures aid in growth and development. Do not seed after September 20th. Late plantings do not have time to establish and may be winterkilled. You still have time to sod. The good growing conditions speed up the root development of newly laid sod.

 CARE

Now is the time to correct compacted soils and thatch problems. Both problems interfere with root growth and result in thin lawns. Removing the thatch or removing plugs of soil allows water and fertilizer to reach the roots. The actively growing grass will quickly recover from the stress of these opera-

tions. (See March "Helpful Hints" on page 177 for more information on dethatching and core aeration.)

 WATERING

Water new plantings often enough to keep the soil surface moist. Reduce watering frequency once the grass seeds have sprouted or the sod has rooted into the soil below.

 FERTILIZING

Apply 1 pound of actual nitrogen per 1000 square feet. This is equivalent to 10 pounds of a 10 percent nitrogen fertilizer. The September fertilization helps lawns recover from the stresses of summer.

Incorporate fertilizer in the soil prior to seeding or sodding a new lawn.

 MOWING

Things should start slowing down. See August "Mowing" for more information.

 PROBLEMS

A healthy lawn is your best defense against pests. Review your maintenance

practices to be sure you are mowing, fertilizing, and watering correctly. If not, make needed adjustments. This should always be your first step in pest control.

Weeds. Fall is the best time to control perennial weeds, such as dandelions and plantain. The chemicals are usually more effective, and the actively growing grass will quickly fill in the empty spaces.

Consider replacing lawns that contain more than 50 percent weeds. Starting over gives you quicker and more effective results. Reclaiming a weed-infested lawn often requires more pesticides and gives poor results over a long period of time. Kill the existing lawn and reseed or sod.

Add a wetting agent or dishwashing detergent to liquid herbicide mixtures. The wetting agent breaks down the surface tension of the water, providing better coverage. Even pesticide coverage helps in the control of waxy leafed, hard-to-eliminate weeds, such as clover and violets.

Control violets in the lawn with a broadleaf weedkiller containing triclopyr, such as Weed-B-Gon for difficult weeds. Make the first application in mid-September. Repeat in late October if weeds are still present. Wait to treat Creeping Charlie. Late fall applications, after a hard frost, of broadleaf weedkillers will kill this weed. Do not be alarmed if the weed begins to grow next spring. Fall-treated Creeping Charlie often starts to grow but quickly dies. Keep in mind there are hundreds of seeds just waiting to sprout. It may take several years to get this pest under control.

Insects. Grubs are starting to move deeper into the soil for winter. Complete all grub treatments by September 15th. Only treat lawns that have been diagnosed with a problem that needs control.

Diseases. The cool, wet weather of fall increases the risk of disease. Watch for leaf spot, mildew, and rust. Fall fertilizations and proper care are usually enough to control these diseases. See May "Helpful Hints" on page 181 for more on turf diseases.

Animals. Skunks, raccoons, and moles damage lawns in their search for food. Continual damage means they have found some tasty grubs and plan to stay. Get rid of the food—the grubs—and you will solve the problem. Squirrels can also be found digging in the lawn. They are storing nuts and seeds for future meals. The damage is irritating, but is not a threat to the health of the lawn. Gently tamp down disturbed areas.

Helpful Hints

September is a great time to renovate poor quality lawns. Renovation is the last step before replacement. Use this method on lawns that are thin, have lots of bare spots, or are full of weeds. Consider hiring a professional for large jobs. They have the equipment, training, and staff to get the job done efficiently. To renovate your lawn:

1 Cut the grass as short as possible. It will act as a living mulch. Rake off and compost clippings.

2 Remove the thatch layer if it is greater than $1/2$ inch thick. Use a vertical mower to lift the thatch. Set the revolving blades to slice into the top $1/2$ inch of soil. This will remove the thatch while creating grooves or slits in the soil surface. These slits make a good seedbed. Rake up and compost the debris.

3 Core aerate compacted soil to improve drainage. Core aerate in several directions. See March "Helpful Hints."

4 Spread grass seed over the renovated area using a broadcast or drop-type spreader. Use 3 to 4 pounds per 1000 square feet of sunny grass-seed mixes or 4 to 5 pounds per 1000 square feet of shady mixes. Apply half the total amount in one direction and the remainder at right angles to the first. Rake for good seed-to-soil contact.

5 Fertilize renovated lawns next month.

6 Raise the mower back to the recommended 3 or $3^1/2$ inch mowing height. Cut the grass once it reaches 4 inches.

OCTOBER

PLANNING

Many plants are shutting down for the season, but your lawn is still growing full force. Fall is the time when lawns use their energy to spread and develop deeper root systems instead of top growth. This is good for the grass and even better for the mowing crew.

PLANTING

You can still lay sod to establish new lawns or to repair existing ones. Weed removal and soil preparation are important whether you are repairing a small area or installing a 1-acre lawn. See "Starting a Lawn" on page 169 in the introduction to this chapter and April "Planting" on page 178 for detailed tips on preparing the soil and laying sod. Once in place, water the sod often enough to keep the soil surface moist. Reduce watering and begin mowing the sod once it has rooted into the soil below.

CARE

Fall has arrived, and you may be tired of raking all those leaves. And, of course, there is that **Norway maple** that just will not let go of its leaves. Put away the rake and break out the mower. Shredded leaves make a great amendment for gardens and lawns.

Shred leaves with the mower the next time you cut the grass. You may need to make several passes with the mower during peak leaf drop. As long as you can see the grass blades, the lawn will be fine. In fact, the leaves add nutrients and organic matter to the soil.

Mow and collect the clippings (herbicide-free) and leaves. This makes a great addition to the compost pile or vacant garden. Spade this mix into the top 6 inches of an annual or vegetable garden this fall.

Or use them to mulch the soil around your perennials. Don't use them as a winter mulch over the plants. They mat down, hold moisture, and lead to disease. Save this for straw and evergreen branches, which work better than leaves as a winter mulch over the plants. Store dry leaves in bags over winter for use

next spring. Do not store wet leaves. The weight can be difficult to manage and the smell that develops in the bag will turn most gardeners' noses. You can tuck the leaf-filled bags behind the bushes next to your home's foundation. This is an out-of-the way storage area that provides added insulation for winter.

Gardeners in the southern part of the region can still core aerate the lawn. You get the best results when the lawn has at least four weeks of good growing weather to recover. Do not dethatch the lawn using a vertical mower at this time of the year. The lawn will not have enough time to recover before winter.

WATERING

Make sure new plantings are watered. Keep the soil surface moist under newly laid sod. Continue to water thoroughly, but less frequently, once the sod is rooted into the soil below.

Established lawns should be watered when they show signs of wilting.

Shred leaves with the mower the next time you cut the grass.
The leaves add nutrients and organic matter to the soil.

 # FERTILIZING

Late October is the most important fertilizer application for your lawn. Apply 1 to 1½ pounds of actual nitrogen per 1000 square feet. This can be obtained by applying 2.2 pounds per 1000 square feet of sulfur-coated urea (45-0-0) or 6¼ to 8 pounds per 1000 square feet of an 16 percent nitrogen fertilizer.

Use a slow-release nitrogen fertilizer for best results. The actively growing plants will use some of the nutrients now. The unused nitrogen will remain in the frozen soil over winter. As soon as the ground thaws, the grass will begin growing. This fertilizer will be available for the grass early in the season. Avoid winterizing fertilizers that are high in phosphorus and potassium. Most Prairie Lands soils have high to excessive levels of these nutrients. Have your soil tested if you are not sure.

 # MOWING

Keep cutting the grass as long as it keeps growing. Remove no more than ⅓ of the total height at each cutting.

Helpful Hints

Mushrooms and moss can drive turf enthusiasts to distraction. There is no miracle cure for either. Like all weeds, once we find the cause of the problem, we have also found the cure.

Mushrooms are the fruiting bodies of fungi. They typically appear after a period of cool, wet weather. The underground fungus feeds on decaying tree roots and wood in the soil. Once the food source is gone, the fungus disappears. Rake and break up the mushrooms to prevent kids and pets from eating them. Time is the only cure. Moss also thrives in moist conditions. It is commonly seen in shaded areas with compacted and poorly drained soils. Change the poor growing conditions, and you will eliminate the moss.

Increase the sunlight by having a certified arborist thin out the tree canopies. Add organic matter to improve drainage and try shade-tolerant grass and groundcovers.

If the moss returns, you may have to look for alternatives to grass. Try mulching the area with woodchips or shredded bark. Or better yet, add a few stepping stones and call it a moss garden!

PROBLEMS

Apply a broadleaf herbicide (weedkiller) to Creeping Charlie and other difficult to control weeds in mid- to late October after a hard frost. Make a second application to violets if needed. The triclopyr-containing herbicide will also work on Creeping Charlie and other broadleaf weeds. Spot treat problem areas to reduce the amount of chemicals needed. Squirrels are still stashing their nuts and bulbs in the lawn for safekeeping. Enjoy all the surprises that appear in the lawn next spring.

NOVEMBER
Lawns

 ## PLANNING

It is almost time to pack away your lawn care equipment. Our work is about done, even though the grass keeps growing until the ground freezes. Though we do not see much happening, there is a lot growing underground. Take one last look at the lawn. Make notes on any needed changes, improvements, or repairs. Purchase a good snow shovel or snow blower and plant-friendly deicing salt. Removing the snow before salting saves you money and reduces salt damage to the lawn.

 ## PLANTING

Dormant seeding is risky. You might want to risk a little seed and some time on small areas, but think twice before seeding large areas or new lawns.

Sprinkle seed over bare or thin areas of the lawn.

The fluctuating winter temperatures will help work the seed into the soil.

Don't worry about the snow, it makes the best winter mulch. Hope for consistently cold weather until spring.

Unseasonably warm weather can extend the landscaping season. Sod can be laid as long as the ground is not frozen and the sod is available. Keep the soil surface moist until the sod roots into the soil below. Make sure it is well watered before the ground freezes. Poorly rooted sod is subject to winter drying. Snowfall is the best protection for late-season plantings.

 ## CARE

Keep raking leaves. **Norway maples** and **Callery pears** are reluctant to give in to winter. Rake and remove leaves from the lawn. If left on the lawn, large leaves block the sunlight and trap moisture, increasing the risk for disease and death of turf.

1 Shred leaves with the mower the next time you cut the grass. You may need to make several passes with the mower to chop up thick layers of large leaves like **Norway maple** and **oak.** As long as you can see the grass blades, the lawn will be fine. In fact, the leaves add nutrients and organic matter to the soil. This is a great way to improve the soil while reducing time spent on lawn care.

2 Mow and collect the clippings (herbicide-free) and leaves in your mower's bag. This makes a great addition to the compost pile or vacant garden. Spade this mix into the top 6 inches of an annual or vegetable garden this fall. See October "Care" for additional ideas for using fallen leaves in the landscape.

 ## WATERING

Newly planted lawns benefit from regular watering throughout the fall. Established lawns should only be watered in dry falls when they show signs of wilting. Drain and pack away the garden hose after the final watering.

 ## FERTILIZING

Didn't get the fertilizer applied in October? There is still time to apply fertilizer in early November before the ground freezes and snow begins to cover the ground. Apply 1 pound of actual nitrogen per 1000 square feet. This is equal to 2 pounds per 1000 square feet of sulfur-coated urea (45-0-0) or $6^1/4$ to 8 pounds per 1000 square feet of an 16 percent nitrogen fertilizer.

Avoid winterizing fertilizer that are high in phosphorus and potassium, the last two of the three numbers on the fertilizer bag. Our soils tend to be high to excessive in these nutrients. Adding more can pollute the ground water and interfere with the uptake of other needed nutrients. Consider using a slow-release

There is still time to apply fertilizer in early November before the ground freezes and snow begins to cover the ground.

nitrogen fertilizer for best results. The actively growing plants will use some of the nutrients now. The unused nitrogen will remain in the frozen soil over the winter. As soon as the ground thaws, the grass will begin growing. This fertilizer will be available for the grass early in the season before we can get out and fertilize. Have your soil tested if you're not sure. Contact your local Cooperative Extension office and see "General Horticultural Practices" at the beginning of the book for more information.

Helpful Hints

Tying Up Loose Ends

Now that the mower is safely stored, it is time to locate, organize, and safely store fertilizers and pesticides.

Always leave pesticides in their original containers. It is illegal—and unwise—to transfer them to a different container.

Pesticides should be stored in a locked area, away from pets and children.

Store granular formulations in cool, dry locations.

Liquids should be kept out of direct sunlight and freezing temperatures. Freezing and UV light can diminish their effectiveness.

MOWING

Keep cutting the grass as long as it keeps growing or until the snow starts flying. Your final cut does not need to be shorter. Once the mowing season is over, you can clean up and pack away the mower until next spring.

Empty the gas tank, or fill it with a gas preservative. The tank can be emptied by running the engine until it stalls. Or add a gas preservative and run the engine for a few minutes to distribute it throughout the gas. Disengage the spark plug wire for safety.

Drain and replace the oil. This should be done at least once a year. Check the owner's manual for specific information.

Clean off any dirt and matted grass.

Sharpen the blades or make a note in your journal to do that before the next mowing season begins.

Buy replacement belts, spark plugs, and an air filter as needed and store them for spring.

PROBLEMS

Work on your journal. Record all pest problems encountered this season. Evaluate the possible cause and the solutions tried. Do a little research over the winter to try to reduce future problems.

Watch for voles. These small rodents are active all winter. They scurry across the turf and under the snow in search of seeds, bark, and roots to eat. Protect trees and shrubs from these critters. Lawn damage can be repaired in the spring.

DECEMBER
Lawns

 PLANNING

This is a good time to make a Christmas list. Maybe you need a new fertilizer spreader, an environmentally friendly push mower to work off the winter bulge, or just the promise of a helping hand.

 PLANTING

Dormant seeding is risky. You might want to risk a little seed and some time on small areas, but think twice before seeding large areas or new lawns.

Sprinkle seed over bare or thin areas of the lawn.

The fluctuating winter temperatures will help work the seed into the soil.

Do not worry about the snow; it makes the best winter mulch. Hope for consistently cold weather until spring.

 CARE

All of your hard work can be damaged with a quick toss of deicing salt. A little care now will eliminate the frustration and time needed next spring to repair winter-damaged turf.

Did You Know?

Before Salting...

Winter, snow, and deicing salts have a major impact on our landscape. Identify any lawn areas that are killed each year by deicing salt. Then evaluate your snow removal technique. Consider alternatives such as adding a border of annuals, expanding the walk, or incorporating some other landscape feature instead of grass in these areas.

Shovel before applying deicing salt. This reduces the amount of salt needed to control ice on walks and drives. It also eliminates salt-laden snow from ending up on the lawn.

Use plant-friendly deicing compounds. Calcium chloride is more expensive, but it is easier on your plants. Calcium magnesium acetate is also safe for both concrete and plants. Watch for new, more plant-friendly products entering the market.

Apply deicing compounds down the middle of walks and drives, avoiding the grass.

Consider using sand or kitty litter to provide traction and reduce the use of salt.

Note the areas most impacted by deicing salts. Water these areas in spring to dilute the salts and wash them through the soil.

 WATERING

No need to water. Drain and store the hose for winter.

 FERTILIZING

Do not fertilize frozen lawns. Winter rains and melting snow can wash the fertilizer off the frozen soil surfaces and into our waterways.

 MOWING

The mowing season is over. (There are some good things about winter!) Clean and store your mower if you have not done so already.

 PROBLEMS

Take a break!

CHAPTER SEVEN

Perennials & Ornamental Grasses

Although perennials don't bloom from spring through fall, a well-planned garden can provide year-round interest from foliage, flowers, and seedpods. Some gardeners mix a few annuals in with their perennials, filling in voids left by winter damage, empty spots between new plantings, and planning mistakes.

Perennials are moving in and taking over many landscapes in the Prairie Lands states. People are converting their annual gardens and lawn areas to large perennial gardens. English cottage gardens, filled with a collection of colorful blossoms; the New American Gardens, composed of masses of ornamental grasses and perennials; and mixed borders are filling landscapes in the Prairie Lands.

No matter the garden style, everyone's ideal garden is filled with season-long blooms that need no maintenance. Although many perennials need less attention than other plants, they do require some care: Pruning back in fall or spring, and dividing occasionally. Also, some need fertilizing, deadheading, and winter protection.

Although perennials don't bloom from spring through fall, a well-planned garden can provide year-round interest from foliage, flowers, and seedpods. Some gardeners mix a few annuals in with their perennials, filling in voids left by winter damage, empty spots between new plantings, and planning mistakes.

PLANNING

Growers are now producing perennials blooming when you purchase them at the nursery, garden center, or home store. Annuals have been marketed that way for a number of years. Most perennials have a limited flowering season and although a few will rebloom if you cut them back, the majority will not. What that means is that when you buy all your perennials in midspring—in bloom—they will look pretty in the garden for a short time (most have bloom times from 2 to 6 weeks). However, when summer comes or whatever the normal bloom time is for the plant, it has already put on its show and you have to wait until the next year to see flowers.

The joy of flower gardening is personal expression. Melinda likes the subtleties of a mixed border, while others prefer dynamic masses of bloom. Both are fine. Select the style that fits your landscape, interest, and desires. Try a few of these design ideas to make maintenance easier:

● Select and plant the right perennial for your growing conditions. A healthy plant looks more attractive, flowers longer, and needs less care.

● Start small and expand your garden as time allows. It is better to end the season wanting more than to be overwhelmed with weeds and work in August.

● Consider using fewer species, but more of them. A garden with 10 different types of perennials is easier to maintain than one with 30. In spring, you'll only have to differentiate weeds from 10 plant types.

● Plan for year-round interest; there are options. Interplant spring-, summer-, and fall-blooming perennials in your gardens. Or design individual gardens that peak at different times: Place the spring garden outside the kitchen window, the summer garden next to the deck, and the fall garden outside the family room. Select a design strategy that best fits your family's likes and habits. Include some perennials that provide winter interest and food for wildlife. Add **ornamental grasses**, **rudbeckias**,

coneflowers, and other plants that have attractive seedpods.

Consider the foliage, as well as the flowers, when planning your garden. Some plants, such as **coralbells**, have attractive foliage all season long. Others, such as **poppies** and **bleeding heart**, fade away in midsummer. Don't overlook fall color. Many perennials, such as **willow amsonia**, **evening primrose**, and some **sedums**, have colorful fall foliage.

CONTAINERS ADD VERSATILITY

It is important to choose the right plant for the right place. Trying to grow a woodland plant like **Jack-in-the-pulpit** (*Arisaema triphyllum*) that requires moist soil and part shade next to **black-eyed Susan** (*Rudbeckia fulgida* 'Goldsturm') that likes well-drained soil and full sun is a recipe for failure—if you plant them in the ground next to each other. Yet you can grow them side by side—in separate containers. There you can control the soil type, moisture level, and place it where it gets the sun it needs. In that example, place the pot with **Jack-in-the-pulpit** where it is shaded by a taller plant, an ornamental grass, or even the shade cast by a bigger container.

SOIL PREPARATION

Taking time to properly prepare the soil before planting is an investment in the health and welfare of the plants that will grow there. Begin preparing soil in the spring or fall prior to planting.

1 Remove the grass from the area to be developed. Cut it out with a sod cutter, kill it off with a total vegetation killer, or cover the area with clear plastic for a season. Select the technique that best fits your time frame and gardening style.

2 Take a soil test if you plan on gardening in the existing soil. Wait to take the test if you are creating a garden with purchased topsoil. Contact your county Cooperative Extension Service for soil test information.

3 Mix 2 to 4 inches of compost, peat moss, well-rotted manure, or other organic matter in to the top 12 inches of soil. The organic matter improves drainage in heavy clay soils, increases water-retention in sandy soils, and adds nutrients.

4 Only add fertilizer if it is recommended by your soil test report. Recent research has found that organic matter usually provides sufficient nutrients for perennials. Excess fertilizer can cause poor flowering, leggy growth, and stunted root systems. Use no more than 1 pound of a 10 percent, or 2 pounds of a 5 percent, nitrogen fertilizer per 100 square feet if your plants need a boost.

5 Level and rake the soil smooth. Lightly sprinkle with water or wait several days for the soil to settle.

PLANTING

Purchase perennials as bare-root plants from catalogs or garden centers in 4-inch, 1- gallon, or 2-gallon containers. The smaller plants may look a little sparse at first, but give them enough room to grow.

Plant bare-root perennials as soon as they arrive in spring.

If the weather is bad, store them in a cool location, such as a root cellar or refrigerator, until they can be planted outdoors. Keep the packing material around the roots lightly moist.

Perennials & Ornamental Grasses

Pot up any bare-root perennials that have begun to grow. Keep them in a cool, bright location free from frost. Gradually introduce them to the outdoors.

Plant container-grown perennials anytime from spring through fall, but the best time is spring and early summer. This allows plants to become established before the heat of summer and the cold of winter.

Loosen potbound roots on container-grown plants prior to planting. Use a sharp knife or hand pruners to slice through the rootball in several places to encourage the roots to grow into the surrounding soil.

Place the plant in a hole the same depth but at least twice as wide as the root system. Avoid shallow planting—it causes plants to dry out, and deep planting that leads to crown rot and plant death. Fill with soil, and gently tamp.

Water thoroughly with transplant solution, wetting the top 6 to 8 inches of soil. Water the planting hole and the surrounding soil to encourage rooting beyond the planting hole.

WATER

Give special attention to new plantings. Check them every other day for the first few weeks. Water thoroughly when the top 4 to 6 inches of soil start to dry. Gradually increase the length of time between waterings. Provide young plantings with 1 inch of water per week.

Established perennials can get by with less water. Water thoroughly so that the top 8 inches of soil are lightly moist to encourage deep, more drought-tolerant roots. Water thoroughly when the top 3 inches of soil is crumbly and dry.

Water early in the day to reduce the risk of disease and water lost to evaporation. Consider using a watering wand or drip irrigation system to keep the water off the plants and a soil level where it is needed.

Mulch the soil surface to conserve moisture and reduce the watering frequency. Use a thin layer of compost, leaf mold, well-rotted manure, shredded leaves, or twice-shredded bark.

ONGOING CARE

Overgrown perennials fail to bloom, open in the center, and tend to flop. Dig and divide overgrown perennials in early spring as new growth is emerging or in early September. Most perennials are tough and can be divided at other times during the season as long as proper post-transplant care is provided. To divide perennials:

1 Cut the plant back by one-half to two-thirds to reduce transplant stress.

2 Use a shovel or garden fork to dig up the perennial. Dig out the clump and place it next to the hole. Use a knife or two shovels to divide the clump into several pieces.

3 Prepare the new planting location. Amend the existing area by working compost, peat moss, or other organic matter into the soil. Plant one of the divisions in the original location. Use the remaining pieces in other gardens or for trading with friends.

4 Water thoroughly. Check every few days, and water whenever the top 4 inches of soil begin to dry.

PRUNING

Control plant height, reduce floppiness, and delay flowering with proper pruning. Cut back **sedum**, **coneflower**, **asters**, and **mums** early in the season to encourage shorter, stiffer branches. Stop pruning in July; otherwise the plant might not bloom until frost.

Pinch out the growing tips on small plants or prune back taller plants halfway down the stem. Prune above a set of healthy leaves. See May and June "Pruning" on page 211 and 213 for details on pruning specific perennials.

Deadhead—remove faded flowers—to lengthen bloom time and improve the appearance of some perennials. Deadheading allows the plant to put energy into forming new flowers instead of setting seed. Stop dead-heading at the end of bloom time to encourage seed formation if you want bird food or winter interest.

Use a garden scissors or hand pruners to make the cuts. Remove the flower stem just above the first set of leaves or sideshoots.

Prune back lower on the stem after the second flush of flowers. This encourages branching and new, more attractive foliage.

PESTS

Perennials are fairly pest free. Minimize problems by doing the following:

- Select the most pest-resistant species and varieties available. Plant them in a location with the right type of soil and light conditions as specified on the label.

- Provide proper care to keep the plants healthy and better able to resist plant damage.

- See May through August "Pests" for more information on pests and their control.

- To keep weeds under control, try the following suggestions:

- Start with a weed-free garden. Take time to control weeds before they take control of your garden. Eliminate quackgrass, ground ivy, and other perennial weeds prior to planting. Spray the actively growing weeds with a total vegetation killer. Wait four to fourteen days (check label) before tilling and preparing the soil. Or, hand dig the weeds. Make sure you remove all the weeds to prevent their return. If you have the time, cover the area with clear plastic for several month; that will kill the weeds without chemicals.

- Spot treat invasive weeds as they appear. See July "Helpful Hints" on page 215 for tips on controlling perennial weeds in an established garden.

- Mulch the soil with shredded leaves, compost, leaf mold, well-rotted manure, or twice-shredded bark to suppress weed seeds.

- Be careful using pre-emergent weedkillers to control weed seeds. They can prevent some perennial reseeding and may injure some plants.

- Pull or lightly cultivate young weed seedlings as soon as they appear. Remove all weeds before they go to seed. This means several hundred fewer weeds to pull next season.

Perennials

Common Name (*Botanical Name*)	Hardiness	Light	Bloom Time	Comments
Artemisia (*Artemisia* species)	3 to 7	Full sun	Summer	Grown for foliage, not flowers. Needs well-drained soil.
Aster (*Aster* species)	4 to 8	Full sun	Late summer to fall	2 to 5 feet tall. Prune back to 6 inches through June to control height. Good fall interest.
Astilbe (*Astilbe* species)	3 to 7	Part to full shade	Summer	1 to 4 feet tall. Good color for shade garden; attractive foliage fall season. Needs moisture.
Balloon Flower (*Platycodon grandiflorus*)	3 to 8	Full sun	Midsummer to early fall	2 to 3 feet tall. Balloon-like flower buds. Pinch back in early June to encourage branching. Plant is late to emerge in spring.
Black-Eyed Susan (*Rudbeckia* species)	3 to 7	Full sun	Summer and fall	2 to 3 feet tall. Attractive flowers and seedpods for winter. Quickly fills in available space.
Bleeding Heart (*Dicentra spectabilis*)	3 to 6	Full to part shade	Spring	2 to 3 feet tall. Foliage dies back in midsummer. *D. eximia* is smaller with good foliage all season; it repeats bloom throughout the season.
Bugbane (*Cimicifuga* species)	3 to 7	Part shade	July	4 to 6 feet tall with white bottlebrush blooms. Nice summer bloomer for shade. *A. simplex* is a fall-blooming species.
Butterfly Weed (*Asclepias tuberosa*)	4 to 8	Full sun	Summer into fall	18 to 30 inches tall. Plant in well-drained soil. Slow to establish from ransplants. Allow seedlings to develop where they decide to thrive.
Columbine (*Aquilegia* species)	3 to 7	Full to part sun	Late spring to early summer	1 to 3 feet tall. Attracts butterflies and hummingbirds. Prune back miner-infested foliage after bloom for a fresh look.
Coralbells (*Heuchera* species)	3 to 8	Full to part sun	Spring to summer	12 to 15 inches tall and wide. Nice foliage and small, bell-shaped flowers. Purple foliage types scorch in full sun.
Coreopsis (*Coreopsis verticillata*)	3 to 8	Full sun	Mid-June to frost	2 to 3 feet tall. Attractive foliage and yellow blooms. Low maintenance; no deadheading needed on young plants.
Corydalis (*Corydalis lutea*)	4 to 7	Part shade	Late May to frost	Nonstop yellow bloom. Either thrives and spreads or fails to survive. Invasive.
Daylily (*Hemerocallis* species)	3 to 9	Full to part sun	Summer to fall	1 to 4 feet tall. Tolerates a wide range of soils. Select repeat bloomers or a variety of cultivars for season-long blooms.

Perennials

Common Name (*Botanical Name*)	Hardiness	Light	Bloom Time	Comments
Gayfeather (*Liatris* species)	3 to 7	Full sun	Midsummer to fall	2 to 3 feet tall. Prefers moist, well-drained soils to dry soils. Attracts birds and butterflies.
Geranium (*Geranium sanguineum*)	3 to 7	Full to part sun	Summer	6 to 15 inches tall. Deadhead or clip back by 4 inches after main bloom.
Hosta (*Hosta* species)	3 to 7	Full to part shade	Summer or fall	Grown for foliage. Watch out for slugs, earwigs, rabbits, and deer.
Oriental Poppy (*Papaver orientale*)	3 to 8	Full to part sun	Late spring to early summer	2 to 4 feet tall. Feathery foliage and paperlike flowers. Foliage dies early in the season; cut back for regrowth or mask with nearby plantings
Peony (*Paeonia* hybrids)	3 to 7	Full sun	Early to late spring	3 feet tall. Good foliage all season with red to purple fall color. Flowers for fragrance and cutting.
Phlox (*Phlox* species)	3 to 7	Full sun	Spring or summer	Creeping, running, or upright types. Well drained soils. Deadhead for repeat blooms.
Purple Coneflower (*Echinacea purpurea*)	3 to 7	Full sun	Summer to fall	2 to 4 feet tall. Good for well-drained to dry soils. Good winter interest and food for birds.
Russian Sage (*Perovskia atriplicifolia*)	4 to 7	Full sun	Midsummer to fall	3 to 5 feet tall. Silvery gray foliage and blue flowers; fragrant. Cut back to 4 to 5 inches in late March.
Salvia (*Salvia* species)	3 to 8	Full to part sun	Summer	2 to 3 feet tall. Deadhead for continuous bloom. Prune back to prevent floppiness. Leave standing for winter hardiness.
Sedum (*Sedum* species)	3 to 8	Full to part sun	Summer to fall	3 inches to 2 feet tall. Various foliage colors and textures. Some have fall color and winter interest.
Shasta Daisy (*Chrysanthemum superbum*)	4 to 8	Full to part sun	Summer to frost	1 to 3 feet tall. Divide every other year for improved hardiness and vigor.
Veronica (*Veronica* species)	3 to 7	Full to part sun	Late spring to summer	4 to 36 inches. Deadhead for repeat blooms. Divide floppy and over-grown plants every two to three years.
Yarrow (*Achillea filipendulina*)	3 to 8	Full sun	Early summer to early fall	6 to 36 inches. Clump forms. Long-lasting blooms. Excellent for drying.
Yucca (*Yucca filamentosa*)	4 to 9	Full sun	Summer	2- to 3-foot-tall foliage and up to 12-foot-tall blooms. Evergreen foliage; often a biennial bloomer.

Ornamental Grasses

Common Name (*Botanical Name*)	Hardiness	Light	Bloom Time	Comments
Blue Fescue (*Festuca cinerea*)	4 to 7	Full sun	Midsummer	12-inch clump grass with blue-green foliage; evergreen. Needs well-drained soil. Salt tolerant.
Blue Oat Grass (*Helictotrichon sempervirens*)	4 to 8	Full sun	Summer	2 to 3 feet tall; wide clump grass. Blue-green foliage; evergreen. Tolerates clay soil.
Feather Reed Grass (*Calamagrostis acutiflora* 'Stricta')	4 to 8	Full to part sun	Midsummer	4 to 5 feet; upright clump. Prefers well-drained soils, but tolerates moist soils. Salt tolerant. Has winter interest.
Japanese Forest Grass (Hakone Grass, Hakonechloa) (*Hakonechloa macra* 'Aureola')	4 to 8	Part shade	Late summer	2 feet tall and wide. Small mound of variegated foliage that combines well with **Hostas.**
Little Bluestem (*Schizachyrium scoparium*)	3 to 6	Full sun	Fall	1/2- to 3-foot-tall native grass. Needs well-drained soils. A fine-textured.grass that is good for naturalized and perennial gardens.
Miscanthus (*Miscanthus sinensis* cultivars)	4 to 8	Full sun	Fall	3 to 7+ feet tall. Good vertical and winter interest in any landscape.
Moor Grass (*Molinia caerulea*)	4 to 7	Full to part sun	Midsummer	1- to 2-foot-tall foliage and 5- to 8-foot-tall blooms. Light, airy, see-through blooms.
Spike Grass (*Spodiopogon sibiricus*)	3 to 6	Full sun	Summer	4 to 5 feet tall. Fall color. Falls apart in winter.
Switchgrass (*Panicum virgatum*)	3 to 7	Full to part sun	Mid- to late summer	5- to 6-foot-tall native grass. Tolerant of a wide range of soil conditions. Spreads quickly by roots and seeds. Consider using one of the tamer cultivars for small areas.

PLANNING

Pack away the holiday decorations and break out the photos, video, and journal of last year's gardens and landscape. Review these materials before you start planning this year's additions. Look for areas to convert to perennial gardens as well as locations for adding a few new plants. See February "Planning" for more ideas on designing perennial gardens.

PLANTING

Start perennials from seed indoors the way you start annuals. Some seeds need to be stratified (a cold treatment) for weeks, soaked in tepid water overnight, or scarified (the seed coat scratched) prior to planting. Check the label directions for seed treatment, timing, and planting directions. See the January and February "Planting" sections in the "Annuals" chapter for details on starting plants from seed.

CARE

Winter mulch helps protect plants from fluctuating temperatures. Nature provides the best mulch, snow, for much of the Prairie Lands. Lend nature a hand if this is not the case in your area.

Apply winter mulch after the ground freezes. Some years the ground freezes by Thanksgiving, while other years it does not freeze until January. The goal is to prevent temperature extremes caused by winter thaws and fluctuating spring temperatures—not to keep the soil warm.

Recycle your holiday trees and trimmings by converting them into windbreaks and mulch. Cut branches off the trees and lay them over your perennials.

Relax and enjoy the scenery if nature mulched the garden with snow. Keep a few branches handy in case of a winter thaw and nature's mulch disappears. Melinda often places a few holiday trees in a snow bank for storage. They provide shelter for the birds and easy storage, just in case she needs to convert them into mulch.

WATERING

The ground is frozen, so there is no need to break out the watering can.

FERTILIZING

Perennials and other outdoor plants should not be fertilized while the ground is frozen.

PRUNING

No need to prune. Enjoy the seedpods, form, and winter interest provided by the perennials. Note areas that need a little lift. Perhaps you need a few more perennials or the addition of dwarf conifers, small trees, or ornamental shrubs.

PROBLEMS

Check for tracks, chewed bark, and other signs of vole (meadow mouse) damage. High vole populations may start nibbling on the roots of **Siberian iris** and **hostas**. Chipmunks and squirrels can also damage perennials by digging up the plants and leaving the roots exposed to cold winter temperatures. There is not much you can do when the plants are buried in the snow. Next year, plan ahead and try to prevent the damage. See November "Pests" for information on managing voles.

Recycle your holiday trees and trimmings by converting them into windbreaks and mulch. Cut branches off the trees and lay them over your perennials.

Helpful Hints

Consider adding a few of the Perennial Plants of the Year. These plants were selected by members of the Perennial Plant Association for their low maintenance and easy propagating, multi-season interest, and suitability to a wide range of climates. See www.perennialplant.org for more information. Past winners of the Perennial Plant of the Year include:

1993   **Sunny border blue speedwell** (*Veronica* 'Sunny Border Blue'): The dark green, wrinkled leaves make a nice contrast to the blue spike flowers on this **speedwell**. The plant produces flowers throughout the summer in Zones 3 through 8. Divide every three or four years to keep it vigorous and long blooming.

1994   **Sprite astilbe** (*Astilbe* 'Sprite'): This **astilbe** has lacy leaves and a late bloom of pale pink flowers that make it a nice addition to the shade garden. Hardy in Zones 4 through 8, it grows 20 inches tall and up to 36 inches wide.

1995   **Russian sage** (*Perovskia atriplicifolia*): The fragrant silvery foliage combined with the airy blue summer flowers makes this plant a good addition to many perennial gardens. The plant is hardy in Zones 4 through 9 and reaches heights of 4 to 5 feet. Grow in full sun with well-drained soil.

1996   **Husker red beardstongue** (*Penstemon digitalis* 'Husker Red'): The maroon foliage of this winner is topped by white flowers, tinged pink in midsummer. It is hardy throughout the state and should be grown in full sun and well-drained soils.

1997   **May night salvia** (*Salvia* 'May Night'): This **salvia** was selected for the deep indigo flowers produced in summer on 18-inch-tall plants. It is hardy in Zones 3 through 8 and grows best in full sun.

1998   **Magnus purple coneflower** (*Echinacea purpurea* 'Magnus'): This winner has large, rosy purple flowers with non-drooping petals. It grows to 4 feet tall and is hardy throughout the state. Grow in full sun for best results.

1999   **Goldsturm black-eyed Susan** (*Rudbeckia fulgida* var. *sullivantii* 'Goldsturm'): This variety is a nice compact (24 inches tall), powdery mildew resistant **rudbeckia** with bright yellow flowers. Blooms through fall and is hardy throughout the state.

2000   **Butterfly blue pincushion flower** (*Scabiosa columbaria* 'Butterfly Blue'): This season-long bloomer tends to bloom itself to death. Not reliably hardy in the Prairie Lands states, it does put on a good show in its first and possibly only season. Grow this 12-inch-tall plant in full sun and well-drained soils.

2001   **Karl foerster feather reed grass** (*Calamagrostis aculiflora* 'Karl Foerster'): This winning grass is a nice grass for small and large landscapes. It grows 4 to 5 feet tall and 2 feet wide and flowers in early summer. This tough grass grows best in full sun and is hardy in Zones 4 through 8.

2002   **David Garden Phlox** (*Phlox paniculata* 'David'): This long bloomer produces fragrant white flowers on mildew resistant plants. It grows 36 to 40 inches tall and wide and is hardy in zones 4 to 9.

2003   **Becky Shasta daisy** (*Lecanthemum* 'Becky' or *Chrysanthemum* 'Becky'): produces lots of bright white flowers for a long period of bloom. The sturdy stems resist flopping while reaching heights of 40 inches. It is hardy in zones 4 to 9.

2004   **Japanese Painted fern** (*Athyrium niponicum* 'Pictum'): This short shade lover grows 15 inches tall forming clumps 2 feet wide. The green fronds are highlighted with silvery gray and red veins. Hardy throughout most of the Prairielands through zone 3.

FEBRUARY

PLANNING

Continue to review photos and videos of last year's landscape. Start sketching areas that you might want to turn into perennial gardens. Site the gardens in areas that have good soil drainage and that receive sufficient sunlight for the plants you want to grow. Some additional tips for developing the plan for your perennial garden include:

- Create perennial borders by designing planting beds in front of hedges, walls, or buildings. Island beds are surrounded by turf or pavement.

- Make sure all parts of the garden can be reached for maintenance chores. Add stepping stones or walkways in large gardens for easier access.

- Check out catalogs for newer and harder to find perennials. Catalogs are also a great source of information. If you do not currently receive catalogs, surf the Internet or look through the book *Gardening by Mail*. Once you order a few catalogs, a hundred others will follow.

- Plan for year-round interest. Try using a variety of perennials that bloom at different times in one garden or create several different gardens that each peak at different times of the season.

- Create dramatic impact by massing perennials in drifts or in large clusters. These large sweeps of color will be visible from great distances.

- Use a mixture of bulbs, perennials, shrubs, and small trees to take advantage of all planting and vertical space.

- Once you have a plan, you can start ordering plants and seeds. Talk to friends to see if they want to share an order. This is a great way to get the benefits of quantity discounts without having to order more perennials than you can fit into your landscape.

PLANTING

Start perennials from seed indoors the same way you grow annuals. The soil needs to be warm and lightly moist. Check seed packets and garden catalogs for specific information on starting times and seed treatment requirements. Grow seedlings under lights for stronger and stouter plants. See January and February "Planting" in the "Annuals" chapter for details on building your own light stand and growing plants from seeds.

CARE

Transplant seedlings from flats into individual containers as soon as the first set of true leaves appear. Adjust your watering schedule to fit plant needs. Continue to keep the soil lightly moist, but not wet.

Check winter mulch if the snow has disappeared. You can always add mulch after snow melts. Remember, the goal is to keep the soil temperature consistent and avoid those January and February thaws.

Monitor plantings for frost heaving caused by the freezing and thawing of unmulched gardens. The fluctuating temperatures cause the soil to shift and often push shallow-rooted perennials right out of the soil. Gently tap these back into the soil as soon as they are discovered. Make a note to mulch these areas next fall after the ground lightly freezes.

WATERING

Check perennial seedlings growing indoors every day. Keep the soil lightly moist, but not wet. Insufficient water can stunt and kill seedlings while excess moisture can cause rot.

FERTILIZING

Fertilize young seedlings with a dilute solution of a complete fertilizer every other week. Cathy likes to foliar feed with a dilution of fish emulsion or liquid kelp (following package directions).

PRUNING

Be patient. Wait for the worst of winter to pass before cleaning out the garden. Many borderline hardy perennials, such as **Salvias**, seem to survive better when the stems are left standing. The standing plant stems and the snow help provide extra winter insulation.

PROBLEMS

Avoid damping off (a fungal disease) of seedlings by using sterile containers and seed starter mix—not potting soil. Infected plants suddenly collapse and rot at the soil line. Remove any diseased seedlings as soon as they appear. Apply a fungicide as a soil drench to infected plantings. Make sure the product is labeled to control damping off disease on perennial seedlings. Cathy generally starts seeds in small pots or peat pots, so if damping off does occur, she just throws out the individual infected pot.

Helpful Hints

Melinda's planting list always seems small until it is time to plant. At that point, she seems to have more plants than available space! Luckily, she's always find a willing gardener to take the extras off her hands.

Avoid overbuying and the temptation to overplant by buying the right number of plants for the available space. Consider planting groups of odd-numbered plants (one, three, five) for a more informal appearance. Use larger groupings for a bolder display of color. To calculate the number of plants you will need:

1 Measure the length and width of the garden. Multiply these numbers for the total square footage of the perennial garden. This will give you an idea of the total space available for planting.

2 Now review your garden design. Calculate (length times width) the planting area of each drift, mass, or cluster of plants. Then evaluate the area you have for each plant.

3 Check the space requirements of the individual plants. Use the spacing chart below to calculate the number of plants you will need.

4 Multiply the square footage of the planting area times the number of plants needed per square foot to get the number of plants needed for your garden. For example, if your garden is 100 square feet, and you decide to cover 9 square feet with **Spike Speedwell** at 18 inches apart, then your calculation would be:

9 square feet x 0.45 = 4 plants of **Spike Speedwell**

Plant Spacing	Number of Plants Per Square Foot
12 inches	1.0
15 inches	0.64
18 inches	0.45
24 inches	0.25
36 inches	0.11

Continue monitoring for rodent and animal damage. See January "Pests" for more information.

MARCH

 PLANNING

Get out your garden journal and start watching for the first signs of spring. Take one last look at the winter garden and make notes on any changes that should be made. Now check this against your planting plans for this year. Make any needed adjustments.

Remember to keep your plans simple if you are either a beginner gardener or one with limited time. Gardens with fewer species, but more of each species, are easier to maintain. Those with botanical zoos (that's both Melinda and Cathy!) need to spend a little more time giving the wide range of plants the care they need.

Finalize your plant list. Include the number of each plant species that you need. See February "Helpful Hints" for details on calculating this number. A plant list is like a grocery list: they both keep you from buying the wrong items or more than you need. You may still succumb to the temptation of new plants, but the list will help you keep overbuying to a minimum.

 PLANTING

Starting plants from seeds may be the only way you can get some of the newer and harder-to-find perennial varieties. You can mailorder some of these plants,

but they are likely to blow up your entire garden budget for the year. Check the catalogs and seed packets for starting times. Continue planting seeds and transplanting seedlings.

Take a soil test of new garden areas. Follow the test results to ensure that you are adding the right amounts and types of fertilizer and organic matter to your garden. Soil test information is available from your local office of the Cooperative Extension Service.

Wait until the soil thaws and dries before getting out the shovel. Working wet soil causes damage that takes years to repair. Be patient; keep looking at those garden catalogs and planting plans and envision the garden as it will look in three years when the plants fill in and mature.

Most catalogs send bare-root plants just prior to the planting time for our area. Dormant plants can be planted directly outdoors if the soil is workable.

Sometimes the plants arrive early or winter stays late. Store dormant bare-root plants in a cool, dark location. A root cellar or refrigerator works fine. Keep the roots lightly moist.

Pot up bare-root plants that started to grow during shipping or storage. Grow these plants indoors in a sunny window or under artificial lights. Move outside after the danger of frost has passed.

 CARE

Continue to check unmulched gardens for signs of frost heaving. Replant any perennials that were pushed out of the soil.

Wait until temperatures consistently hover above freezing before removing the mulch. This can be anywhere from late March to early April, depending on Mother Nature's whims.

Remove the mulch if plants are starting to grow. Keep some mulch and floating row cover handy to protect the tender tips of early sprouting **Hostas**, **Primroses**, and other early bloomers that may be damaged by a sudden drop in temperature.

WATERING

Check seedlings every day. Keep the soil lightly moist, but not wet. As the plants grow and develop larger root systems they will need less frequent watering.

Water potted bare-root perennials often enough to keep the soil lightly moist, but not wet. Continue to water thoroughly but less frequently as the plants grow.

Keep the packing material around the roots of stored bare-root plants lightly moist.

Starting plants from seeds may be the only way you can get some of the newer and harder-to-find perennial varieties. Check the catalogs and seed packets for starting times.

FERTILIZING

Take a soil test of new garden areas as soon as the ground thaws. Retest the soil in established gardens every three to five years or when problems develop.

PRUNING

Get out your pruners, loppers, hedge shears, rake, wheelbarrow and other tools you'll need as you start getting the garden ready for emerging plants and new arrivals. The winter vacation from gardening is over. It's time to get your garden—and yourself—in shape.

Be sure you have room, in your compost pile for all the trimmings. If not, it's time to start another pile.

Remove any stems and seedpods you left in the ground for winter interest.

Cut back **ornamental grasses** before the new growth begins. Use a weedwhip, hedge shears, or hand pruners to clip the plants back to several inches above the soil. Smaller grasses, such as **blue fescue** and **blue oat grass**, can be clipped back or left intact. The new growth will quickly cover the old leaves in the spring.

Prune back **Russian sage** and **butterfly bush** to several inches above the soil. Both plants (often classed as sub-

Cleanup of large perennial gardens can be a fair amount of work. Melinda finds it comes in late March when most of us are anxious to get busy outdoors and are not yet bored with maintenance tasks. Spring cleanup is also a great uncovering and discovery of the first signs of life in the garden.

Use the proper tool to make the cleanup job easier on your back.

Hand pruners will take care of most of the cleanup jobs. Use these to cut back perennials and sub-shrubs such as **Russian sage** and **butterfly bush**. Use loppers on some of the larger and harder-to-reach stems, rather than ruining a good pair of hand pruners by trying to cut something too big.

Use an electric hedge shear, or weedwhip with a rigid plastic blade for mass planting of perennials and grasses. Wear safety glasses when working with any power tool.

Compost pest-free materials. See "General Horticultural Practices" at the beginning of the book.

shrubs) usually die back in winter. Use a lopper or hand pruners to cut stems at 45 degree angle just above an outward facing bud.

Cut back only the dead tips of **candytuft**, **lavender**, and **thyme**. Cut them back even more in late spring if the plants become leggy.

Remove dead foliage and stems of all perennials. Be careful not to damage the leaves of early emerging perennials during the cleanup process.

Remove only the dead leaves on evergreen perennials, such as **lungwort** (*Pulmonaria*), **barrenwort** (*Epimedium*), and **coralbells** (*Heuchera*). This makes a more attractive display as the new foliage fills in.

Remove dead foliage on **lamb's ear**. The old leaves tend to mat down over winter and will lead to rot if not removed.

PROBLEMS

Continue to monitor for damping off in seedlings. Watch for collapsing seedlings and stem rot at the soil line. See February "Pests" for management strategies.

PLANNING

Take a walk through your landscape. Note what survived and what may need replacing. Adjust your landscape plans to accommodate these changes.

Start a bloom chart in your garden journal. Record the name and bloom time of various plants in the landscape. This will help you fill any flowering voids when planning next year's additions. After a few years, you'll have a picture of what will bloom where and when.

PLANTING

Start the planting process for a new garden or bed by properly preparing the soil.

1 Remove the existing grass with a sod cutter. Use this to patch problem areas in the lawn. Or treat the grass with a total vegetation killer. The grass and weeds must be actively growing for these chemicals to be effective. Wait four to fourteen days (check the label) before completing soil preparation. If you anticipate that you'll want to use this garden at a later time, cover the area with black plastic—weight or pin down the edges. The weeds and grass will die, without the use of chemicals.

2 Work the soil when it is lightly moist, but not wet. Grab a handful of soil and gently squeeze. Open your fist and tap on the clump. If it breaks into smaller pieces, the soil is ready to be worked. If it stays in a clump, it is too wet; wait a few days and do the "fist test" again.

3 Add 2 to 4 inches of organic matter to the top 8 to 12 inches of soil. Use compost, peat moss, leaf mold, or well-aged manure to improve the drainage of clay soil and to increase water retention of sandy soil.

4 Follow soil test recommendations for fertilizer. Recent research indicates that amended soils need little if any fertilizer. Use a transplant solution on each individual plant; wait to see if more fertilizer is needed. If you feed the soil (adding lots organic matter and using an organic mulch that will eventually break down), the soil will feed the plants.

5 Rake the garden smooth and allow the soil to settle. Lightly sprinkle the prepared site with water to speed up settling.

Begin planting once the soil is prepared and the plants are available. This is usually the middle to the end of the month in southern areas and late April to early May in the northern areas. Purchase plants as bare root, field grown in pots, or greenhouse plants. See May "Planting" and this month's "Helpful Hints" for tips on transplanting.

CARE

Continue removing winter mulch. Let the weather and plant growth be your guide. Remove mulch as temperatures consistently hover above freezing. Look under mulch for plant growth. Remove mulch as soon as plants begin growing. Keep some mulch or floating row cover handy to protect semi-hardy plants from sudden and extreme drops in temperature. Use a cold frame for starting seeds outdoors and hardening off transplants. Check the cold frame daily. Vent by opening the lid when temperatures get too warm. Close the lid in late afternoon to keep plants warm during the cold nights. Water plants as needed. See March "Helpful Hints" in the "Annuals" chapter for more details on making and using a cold frame.

Watch for late-emerging perennials, such as **butterfly weed**. Use a plant label or consider adding spring-flowering bulbs next fall to mark its location to avoid damaging the **butterfly weed** in the spring.

WATERING

Cathy recommends that you thoroughly water in transplants and divisions with transplant solution (follow label instructions) at the time of planting. Water when the top few inches of soil begin to dry. Always water thoroughly enough to wet the top 4 to 6 inches of soil. Reduce watering frequency as the plants become established.

FERTILIZING

Perennials grown in properly amended soil need very little fertilizer. Always follow soil test recommendations. Transplant solution (follow label directions) gives new transplants a bit of a boost and encourages root formation.

Spread several inches of compost or aged manure over the surface of existing gardens. Lightly rake this into the soil surface. Use organic matter as a mulch and most perennials will thrive. Replenish the mulch as it breaks down.

PRUNING

Finish cleanup early in the month. Cut dead stems back to ground level and remove dead leaves on evergreen plants. See March "Pruning" and "Helpful Hints" for more specifics.

Helpful Hints

Divide perennials that had poor flowering, open centers, or floppy growth last season. Some plants, such as **shasta daisy** and **moonshine yarrow**, benefit from transplanting every few years. Others, such as **purple coneflower** and **perennial geraniums**, can go many years without division. Let the plant, not the calendar, be your guide.

To divide perennials:

Begin digging and dividing existing plants just as new growth appears. Try to move them when they are less than 3 to 4 inches tall. Cut back taller plants to reduce the stress of transplanting.

Early spring is a good time to transplant summer- and fall-blooming perennials. Transplanting spring-blooming perennials now may delay or eliminate this year's flowers.

Dig and divide spring-flowering plants in late August or early September. You can dig and divide most perennials anytime as long as you can give them proper post-planting care.

Use a shovel or garden fork to dig the clump to be divided. Lift the clump and set it on the ground. Use a sharp knife or two shovels or garden forks to divide the clumps. Carve up the plant into smaller pieces. Plant one division in the original hole. Use the others in new and existing gardens, or share them with your friends and neighbors.

Amend the soil when dividing and transplanting perennials. Add several inches of compost, peat moss, or other organic matter into the soil. Plant the division at the same depth as it was growing originally. Gently tamp the soil, and water in with transplant solution to remove any air pockets and stimulate root growth.

PROBLEMS

Complete garden cleanup. Sanitation is the best defense against pest problems.

Inspect new growth for signs of pests. Remove insects and disease-infested leaves as soon as they are found. Make this a regular part of your gardening routine.

Use netting and repellents to protect emerging plants from animal damage. Start early to encourage animals to go elsewhere to feed. Reapply repellents after severe weather or as recommended on label directions.

PLANNING

Use your landscape and garden design as a working document. We all make changes to our plans. Sometimes the plants we wanted are not available—and then there are those few unplanned additions that we just could not resist at the garden center.

Continue to check your garden for losses and voids that need filling. Look at these losses as an opportunity to try something new.

Record bloom times in your journal. This will be useful in planning future gardens—and fighting the winter blues next January.

List all your new additions to the garden in your journal or on your landscape plan. Ideally, you'd do it in both places.

PLANTING

Complete soil preparation. Invest time now to ensure many years of success with your perennial garden. See April "Planting" for soil preparation information.

1 Plant dormant bare-root plants as soon as they arrive or when the weather permits.

2 Soak the roots for 2 hours—no more.

3 Trim off any broken roots.

4 Dig a hole large enough to accommodate the roots.

5 Place the plant in the hole and spread out the roots.

6 Fill the hole with soil, keeping the crown of the plant (where stem joins the roots) just below the soil surface.

7 Gently tamp and water thoroughly.

Move field-grown container plants right into the garden. See "Planting" on page 196 in the chapter introduction.

Harden off plants started indoors or in a greenhouse before planting outdoors. Use a cold frame or protected location for this process. Stop fertilizing and reduce watering as you harden off the plants. Move transplants outdoors on warm, frost-free days. Cover or bring them indoors when there is danger of frost. Start in a shaded location. Gradually increase the amount of light the plants receive each day for two weeks.

Cut back any overgrown and leggy transplants. Prune the stems back by one-third to one-half at planting. This encourages new growth and results in a fuller, sturdier plant.

Label plants and record the planting information on your landscape plan and in your journal. Make a note of the cultivar (variety), planting date, and plant source.

Dig and divide overgrown perennials or those you want to propagate.

Spring is the best time to divide summer- and fall-blooming perennials. Wait until after flowering or late August to divide spring-flowering perennials. See April "Helpful Hints" for specifics.

Dig and divide your woodland wildflowers after blooming. Do this only to move existing plants or to start new plantings; otherwise, leave your wildflowers alone.

CARE

Move or remove unwanted perennial seedlings. **coneflowers**, **black-eyed Susans**, and other prolific seeders may provide more offspring than needed. Dig and share with friends or donate surplus plants to nearby schools, community beautification groups, care facilities, and master gardeners.

Put stakes, **peony** cages, and trellises in place. It is always easier to train young plants through the cages or onto the stakes than manipulate mature plants into submission.

Wait for the soil to warm before adding mulch. Apply a thin layer of compost, leaf mold, well-rotted manure, twice-shredded bark, or chopped leaves to the soil surface. Do not bury the crowns of the plant. This can lead to rot.

 # WATERING

Check new plantings several times a week and water only as the top few inches of soil start to dry. Established plants need less frequent watering.

 # FERTILIZING

Perennials need very little fertilizer. Incorporate organic matter at the time of planting. Topdress established plantings with several inches of compost as the mulch breaks down and becomes incorported into the soil.

Use a starter solution of fertilizer (transplant solution) per label directions at planting to give transplants a boost.

 # PRUNING

As the garden comes to life, so does the opportunity to spend time in the garden. Deadhead (remove faded flowers) of early blooming perennials.

Shear **phlox, pinks,** and **candytuft** to encourage a new flush of foliage. Use hand pruners or pruning shears.

Pinch back **mums** and **asters**. Keep them 4 to 6 inches tall throughout the months of May and June.

Pinch back **shasta daisy**, **beebalm**, **garden phlox**, and **obedient plants** to control height and stagger bloom times.

Disbud (remove side flower buds) **peonies** if you want fewer but larger flowers.

Thin **garden phlox**, **beebalm**, and other powdery mildew-susceptible plants when the stems are 8 inches tall. Remove one-fourth to one-third (leaving at least four to five) of the stems. Thinning increases light and air to the plant, decreasing the risk of powdery mildew.

Trim any unsightly frost-damaged leaves.

 # PROBLEMS

Monitor the garden for pests. Remove infected leaves when discovered. Watch for four-lined plantbug, slugs, and aphids. See July "Pests" on page 215 for more identification guides and control information.

Check **columbine** plants for the following specific pests:

Check for leafminer. The leafminer causes white, snake-like lines in the leaves. Prune back badly infested plants after flowering. The new growth will be fresh and pest free.

Watch for columbine sawfly. This worm-like insect eats holes in the leaves so quickly that it seems to devour the plants overnight. Remove and destroy any that are found. You can use insecticides labeled for controlling sawflies.

Check wilted **Columbine** plants for stalk borer. Look for hole- and sawdust-like droppings at the base of the plant. Remove infested stems and destroy the borer.

Pull weeds as soon as they appear. dandelions, thistle, and quackgrass are among the first to appear. Removing weeds before they set seed saves pulling hundreds more next year.

Continue to minimize animal damage by fencing and using repellents on susceptible plants.

PLANNING

Summer is a great time to plan next year's garden. Evaluate the success and beauty of your spring garden. Be sure to take photographs or videotape your ever-changing landscape.

Record visitors to your garden: Note in your journal the birds, butterflies, and beneficial insects stopping by to nest or feed. You may want to add water, birdhouses, and butterfly houses to encourage your welcomed guests to stay.

Visit botanical and public gardens to see new and different plants. Participate in the local garden tours. This is a great way to support community beautification efforts and charities while getting a peek into fellow gardeners' backyards. Record planting combinations that you want to use in future gardens.

Harvest flowers for arrangements and drying. Experiment with different flower combinations. If they look good in the vase, they will probably look good as planting partners in the garden.

Start a wish list for new plants for future gardens. Add to this throughout the season. Record the name, bloom time, size, hardiness, and other features of the plant. This will help when planning new additions.

PLANTING

Keep planting. The soil is warm, and there are still lots of perennials available at local garden centers, home stores, and perennial nurseries. Label new plantings, write their locations on your garden design, and record critical information. See the plant tag for any specific planting and care information. Consider saving the tags for future reference. Write the plant name, variety, source, and planting date in your garden journal. This will help you track the plant and its success in your garden.

This is a good time to transplant **Bleeding Heart**.

Dig and divide overgrown perennials. Dig a hole slightly larger than the plant. Lift the plant out of the hole. Amend the soil with organic matter. Cut the plant into several smaller pieces. Replant one of the divisions in the original hole and use the other pieces to fill in voids, start new gardens, or share with friends. Cut back taller plants to 3 to 4 inches, and provide shade for those showing signs of transplant stress.

CARE

Put stakes and cages in place. Tuck plants in place or carefully tie them to the support as needed. Twine or other soft bindings work best. Loop the twine around the stem and then around the support in a figure-eight

Thin **Garden Phlox** and other overgrown perennials subject to mildew and leaf spot diseases. Remove one-third of the stems.

Remove dead or declining foliage on spring-blooming perennials. Add it to the compost pile—unless it died from pests or disease.

Mulch perennials with compost, leaf mold, well-rotted manure, twice-shredded bark, or shredded leaves. Apply 1 to 2 inches of these materials to conserve moisture and reduce weeds—but be careful not to bury the plant with mulch.

WATERING

As a general rule, perennials need 1 inch of water per week.

Check new plantings several times a week. Water thoroughly whenever the top few inches of soil start to dry. Established plants can tolerate drier soils.

Do not overwater new or established plantings. Perennials, like other plants, often wilt in the heat of day. This is their way of conserving moisture. As soon as the temperatures cool, the plants recover.

Keep planting. The soil is warm, and there are still lots of perennials available at local garden centers, home stores, and perennial nurseries.

FERTILIZING

Perennials usually get enough nutrients from the soil and need very little supplemental fertilization. Let the plants be your guide. Spray the leaves with a dilution of fish emulsion or liquid kelp (following package instructions). You can foliar feed once a month, but most perennials don't need it. Or use a liquid fertilizer for plants needing a quick boost. Topdress established beds once every two to four years by working several inches of compost into the soil surface.

PRUNING

Continue deadheading plants to prolong bloom, prevent unwanted seedlings, and improve the overall appearance.

Deadhead **columbine**, **valerian**, and other heavy seeders to prevent unwanted seedlings.

Do not deadhead **Siberian iris**. Leave seedpods to provide added interest in the summer, fall, and winter garden.

Consider removing the flowers of **lamb's ear** as soon as they form. This encourages better foliage while removing the flowers that lead to open, less attractive growth.

Pinch back perennials to control height or delay bloom. Keep **mums** and **asters** 6 inches tall throughout the month.

Cut back **willow amsonia** and **wild blue indigo** (*Baptisia* spp.) by one-third to prevent sprawling, open centers.

Pinch or cut back an outer ring of stems or scattered plants of **purple coneflower**, **heliopsis**, **garden phlox**, **balloon flower**, and **veronica**. The pinched-back plants will be shorter and bloom later. They act as a living support for the rest of the plant and extend the bloom period.

Pinch out the growing tips or cut back 8-inch stems to 4 inches on **autumn joy sedum** that may have tended to flop in your garden. Or try moving it to a sunnier location with less fertile but well-drained soil.

Shear dead or miner-infested foliage on Columbine. The new growth will be fresh and pest free.

Cut back unsightly foliage on **bearded iris** and **perennial geraniums** after bloom.

Cut back **bleeding heart** as the flowers fade. This reduces reseeding and encourages new growth that may last all season. Mulch the soil and water to help preserve the leaves.

PROBLEMS

Cool, wet springs mean lots of diseases. Remove spotted, blotchy, or discolored leaves as soon as they are found. Sanitation is the best control for disease problems.

Watch for leafhoppers, aphids, mites, and spittlebugs. These insects all suck out plant juices, causing leaves to yellow, brown, and die. Control high populations with insecticidal soap. Repeat weekly as needed. See July "Pests" for more details on controlling these pests.

Get out the flashlight, and check your garden for nighttime feeders. Slugs and earwigs eat holes in leaves and flowers at night. See Annuals "Did You Know?" on page 31 for more information.

Check the garden for signs of wildlife. Deer and rabbits love **hostas**, **phlox**, and other perennials. Apply repellents or use scare tactics such as noisemakers and whirligigs. Fence gardens to discourage feeding.

Pull weeds as soon as they are found.

JULY
Perennials & Ornamental Grasses

PLANNING

Continue evaluating the garden—yours and other gardeners'. Take pictures, or record with a movie camera so that it will be easier to recreate good ideas and avoid repeating mistakes.

PLANTING

Keep planting as long as you have space, time, and plants. Give July transplants extra attention during hot dry spells. Mulch new plantings to conserve moisture and keep soil temperature cool. Label, map, and record all new plantings. This will make spring cleanup and weeding much easier.

Dig and divide or take root cuttings of spring-blooming **poppies**, **bleeding heart**, and **bearded iris**.

CARE

Mulch bare soil. A thin layer of compost, well-rotted manure, twice-shredded bark, or leaves will help keep the soil cool and moist during hot, dry weather.

Finish staking. Carefully maneuver plants around trellises and into stakes.

Evaluate the light and growing conditions in your perennial gardens. Note the plants' response and any future changes you need to make.

WATERING

Check new transplants several times per week. Water thoroughly anytime the top few inches start to dry. Established plants need less frequent watering.

Reduce the need to water by planting the right plant for your growing conditions. Apply a thin layer of organic mulch to help conserve soil moisture. Water thoroughly, but less frequently, to encourage deeper, more drought-tolerant roots.

FERTILIZING

Avoid overfertilizing your plants. Most perennials can get all the nutrients they need from the soil. Give stunted, less vigorous plants a boost with a foliar feeding (See "Fertilizing" June for specifics).

Consider fertilizing heavy feeders and those cut back for rebloom. Use a low-nitrogen, slow-release fertilizer to avoid burn.

PRUNING

Continue deadheading and pinching back straggly plants, such as **lavender**.

Prune back **silvermound artemisia** before flowering. Prune back to fresh new growth to avoid open centers.

Cut back old stems of **delphiniums** to the fresh growth at the base of the plant. This encourages new growth and a second flush of flowers.

Prune back yellow foliage of **bleeding heart** to ground level. This is normal and no cause for concern—the plants go dormant and will be back next spring.

Stop pinching fall-blooming perennials at the beginning of the month.

Remove insect-infested, diseased, or declining foliage. This reduces the source of future infection.

PROBLEMS

Continue removing spotted and diseased leaves as soon as they are found.

Deadhead plants during wet weather to further reduce the risk of disease.

To control insects:

Check the upper and lower leaf surfaces and stems for aphids and mites. These pests suck out plant juices, causing leaves to yellow and brown. Spray plants with a strong blast of water to dislodge these insects. Use insecticidal soap to treat damaging populations. This is a soap formulated to kill soft-bodied insects, but it is not harmful to the plant or the environment.

Check for plantbugs whenever you see speckled and spotted leaves and stems. These insects suck out plant juices, causing leaves to discolor and brown. Insecticidal soap or other insecticides labeled for controlling plantbugs on flowers can be used.

Monitor for spittlebug, earwigs, and slugs. See "Annuals" "Helpful Hints" on page 31 for additional information.

Watch for lacy leaves caused by Japanese beetles and rose chafers. Handpick and destroy these pests. Insecticides labeled for controlling these pests on flowers can also be used to reduce their damage.

Helpful Hints

Perennial Weeds

Ground ivy, quackgrass, and bindweed are perennial weeds that can quickly take over your garden. Hand pulling does not usually work on these deeply rooted plants. Cultivation just breaks the plants into smaller pieces that can start lots of new plants. Use a total vegetation killer to control these pesky weeds. These products kill the tops and roots of the weeds and any growing plant they touch. Several applications may be needed to control Bindweed, as well as other tough and established weeds.

Paint, sponge, or wipe the total vegetation killer on the weed leaves. The chemical moves through the leaves, down the stems, and into the roots. Be careful that none of the weedkiller touches your perennials-the herbicide will kill them as well. Here is a quick tip for making the job easier:

1 Remove the top and bottom of a plastic milk jug.

2 Cover the weed with the plastic milk jug.

3 Spray the total vegetation killer on the weed inside the milk jug. The jug will protect the surrounding plants from the harmful weedkiller. Remove the jug after the herbicide on the weed dries.

They Are Not Weeds

Save yourself the headaches and frustration caused by accidentally removing **butterfly weed**, **balloon flower**, and other late-emerging perennials by making a note to mark their spot with spring-flowering bulbs. Next fall, plant bulbs next to these plants. As the bulbs fade in spring, the perennials will begin to grow. You will get twice the beauty and less risk of digging up your perennials.

AUGUST
Perennials & Ornamental Grasses

 PLANNING

Continue evaluating your garden. Take pictures and videotape both the good and bad parts of your landscape. These records will help you correct problems and duplicate successes in next year's landscape.

Take advantage of the heat. Grab a cold drink, find a little shade, and write in your journal. Make sure you have recorded all your new plantings, pest problems, and other useful information.

Create or add to your planting wish list. Write down the plant name, variety, bloom time, and other features that caught your attention. Use this list when planning changes and additions to next year's garden.

Look for bare areas for new plants or planting beds. Late summer is a great time for adding new plants or preparing the soil for new perennial gardens.

 PLANTING

Keep making additions. Be sure to label, map, and record the location of all new plantings.

Dig and divide overgrown **iris**, **poppies**, and other spring-blooming perennials.

 CARE

Mulch perennial gardens if you have not yet done so. Apply a thin layer of compost, leaf mold, well-rotted manure, twice-shredded bark, shredded leaves, or other organic matter. This will help keep perennial roots cool and moist.

Lightly rake mulch during wet periods to prevent slime mold. This fungus develops and feeds on the mulch. It looks disgusting—in fact, its common name is dog vomit fungus—but it does not harm the plants. Cathy is overjoyed that she's never seen it, and hopes she never does.

 WATERING

Check new plantings several times a week. Water when the top few inches of soil start to dry. Apply enough water to wet the roots and surrounding soil. New plantings need about 1 inch of water per week. Water clay soils in one application and sandy soils in two applications. Water established and mulched plantings thoroughly but less frequently. They can last several weeks with very little water. Pay special attention to moisture-loving plants. Use a watering wand to spot water these plants. Consider moving them to areas that tend to stay wet for longer periods.

Water your gardens early in the morning to reduce the risk of disease and water loss to evaporation. Use a soaker hose or watering wand to get the water to the soil and roots where it is needed.

 FERTILIZING

Do not fertilize. Late-season fertilization encourages problems with winter survival. Use this time to evaluate the health and vigor of your plantings. Make note of those areas that need topdressing or fertilization next spring.

 PRUNING

Continue deadheading for aesthetics, to prevent reseeding, and to prolong bloom. Leave the last set of flowers intact to allow the formation of seedpods that add interest to the winter landscape.

Cut back declining plants to improve the overall appearance of your perennial garden. Remove insect-damaged, declining, and dead foliage.

Do not prune sub-shrubs such as **butterflybush** (*Buddleia* spp**.), blue mist spirea** (*Caryopteris* 'Blue Mist'), and **Russian sage** (*Perovskia atriplicifolia*). Enjoy the late-season blooms and allow plants to start hardening off for winter. Prune these only once a year, in late March, and enjoy a long flowering display and attractive seed set for winter.

Try cutting back short-lived perennials, such as **blanket flowers** (*Gaillardia* spp.). Late-season pruning will stimulate new green growth and may help extend the plant's life.

Harvest flowers to use fresh and dried.

Harvest flowers in the morning for fresh use. Take a bucket of water with you to the garden. Place cut flowers in the water while collecting the remaining flowers. Remove the lower leaves and recut the stems just prior to arranging them in the vase. Keep the vase full of fresh water to extend your enjoyment.

Wait until midday to harvest flowers used for drying. Remove leaves and combine in small bundles. Use rubber bands to hold the stems together. As the stems shrink, the rubber bands will contract, holding the stems tight. Use a spring-type clothespin to attach drying flowers upside-down to a line, nail, or other support.

 PROBLEMS

Continue monitoring perennial gardens for disease and insect problems. Catching the problems early may mean the difference between removing a few sick leaves and spraying the whole garden.

Check **beebalm**, **garden phlox**, and other perennials for signs of powdery mildew. Look for a white, powdery substance on the leaves. This fungal disease causes leaves to eventually yellow and brown. Consider moving infected plants into an area with full sun and good air circulation.

Substitute mildew-resistant cultivars of mildew-susceptible plants in next year's garden. Use 'Bright Eyes', 'David', or 'Starfire' cultivars of **garden phlox** (*Phlox paniculata*). Or substitute the mildew-resistant **wild sweet William** (*Phlox maculata*).

Try 'Marshall's Delight', 'Gardenview Scarlett', 'Vintage Wine', and other mildew-resistant cultivars of **beebalm** (*Monarda didyma*).

To control weeds, try these tips:

- Continue pulling weeds as soon as they appear. Remove weeds before they set seed to avoid adding hundreds of new problems to next year's garden.

- Remove or kill perennial weeds such as quackgrass, bindweed, and creeping charlie. Be sure to remove all roots and stems when pulling these weeds. Any little piece that remains can start a new plant. See July "Helpful Hints" for ideas.

SEPTEMBER
Perennials & Ornamental Grasses

 ## PLANNING

Fall is for planting and planning. Evaluate your fall perennial garden. Do you need more **mums**, **asters**, or fall-blooming **anemone**? Record bloom and fall color. **hosta** leaves turn a beautiful yellow, while **evening primrose** and **peonies** add a touch of purple and red to the fall perennial garden.

Continue evaluating the bloom and performance of the perennials in your landscape and gardens. Note the results of pinching back **sedum** 'Autumn Joy', **coneflower**, and other fall bloomers. Make a list of changes you want to implement in next year's garden.

Add to your wish list of plants for next year's garden. Record bloom time, care, and other plant features that will help you plan.

Take pictures and videotape of the fall garden. These will make for nice memories and easier planning during winter.

 ## PLANTING

Keep adding perennials to your garden and landscape. The warm soil and cooler air temperatures are great for planting and establishing new perennials.

Move self-sown biennials to their desired location. Transplant early in the month so the seedlings will have time to get re-established before winter.

Finish transplanting **Iris** early in the month. This gives them time to put down roots and prepare for winter.

Transplant **peonies** now until after the tops are killed by frost. Dig and divide, leaving at least three to five eyes per division. Replant so that the eyes are no more than 1 to 2 inches below the soil surface.

Add **mums** to the fall garden. Fall planted **garden mums** are not always hardy in our area. Many botanical gardens and estates use them as an annual for fall interest.

Consider planting your bulbs and **mums** at the same time. Dig a hole for the bulbs in mid to late September.

Place the bulbs in the bottom of the hole and lightly cover with soil. Set the **mum** in the same hole above the bulbs. Make sure the **mum** will be planted at the same depth as it was growing in the container. Backfill with soil and gently tamp. Water in with transplant solution (following label instructions) and enjoy the fall display.

Or consider using the sunken-pot technique. Sink empty planting pots, with drainage, in groundcover and other planting areas. Set potted **mums** in the sunken pot. This method eliminates the need to dig and disturb surrounding plant roots. Replace the **mums** with Pansies, summer annuals, or other seasonal displays.

Finish digging and dividing perennials as soon as possible. Northern Prairie Lands gardeners should try to finish this task early in the month. Those in the southern region should try to finish by the end of the month. Wait until spring to divide **Siberian iris**, **astilbe**, **delphinium**, or other slow-to-establish, less hardy perennials.

Winter is quickly approaching, especially for those in the north. Make note of new and semi-hardy plantings that will need winter protection. Look for sources of straw, marsh hay, evergreen branches, or other winter mulch materials.

Consider preparing the soil for new garden areas. Kill or remove the grass, take a soil test, and amend the soil as needed. Shredded fallen leaves make a great soil amendment. Spade several inches of this free material into the top 12 inches of soil. The leaves will disintegrate over the winter and will improve the drainage and water-holding capacity of your soil. Starting now gives you a jump on next season.

 ## CARE

Winter is quickly approaching, especially for those in the north. Make note of new and semi-hardy plantings that will need winter protection. Look for sources of straw, marsh hay, evergreen branches, or other winter mulch materials. Wait until the ground freezes to apply them to the soil.

 ## WATERING

Water as needed. As the temperatures cool, you will need to water less frequently. Check new plantings several times a week. Keep the top 4 to 6 inches lightly moist. New gardens need about 1 inch of water every seven to ten days. Water established plantings when the top few inches of soil are dry.

 ## FERTILIZING

Do not apply fertilizer. This is a good time to take a soil test if your plants are showing signs of nutrient deficiencies. Poor flowering, discolored leaves, and generally poor growth may indicate a need to fertilize. Start with a soil test before adding fertilizer. Excess nutrients can cause floppiness, poor flowering, and other problems. Contact the local county office of the Cooperative Extension Service for more information.

 ## PRUNING

Stop deadheading plants you want to develop seedpods for winter interest, such as fall-blooming **sedums**, **astilbes**, **coneflowers**, and **rudbeckias**.

Continue deadheading to prevent seed set on perennials that are overtaking your garden; share the seed with friends.

Or plan to invite gardening friends over for a digging party next spring.

Cut back faded summer-blooming plants as needed. This improves their appearance and opens up space for the fall flower display.

 ## PROBLEMS

Continue weeding all your gardens. Removing weeds now can reduce the amount of weeds you will have to pull next year.

Monitor plants for insects and disease. Fewer harmful insects are present during the cool temperatures of fall. See July "Pests" on page 215 for more details on pests and their control.

Continue removing spotted and diseased leaves as soon as they are found. Water early in the day or use a watering wand or drip irrigation to reduce moisture on the leaves. This helps reduce disease problems. Make note of mildew-infested plants. Consider thinning young plantings to reduce mildew, moving susceptible plants to a sunnier location, or replacing them with mildew-resistant plants such as *Phlox maculatum* and **beebalm** 'Gardenview Scarlet'.

Remove plants with rotting roots and stem. Amend the soil to improve drainage, adjust watering, and replace with a plant more suited to the location.

OCTOBER

PLANNING

Make your final review of the garden during the growing season. Take a few minutes to record what worked and what needs improvement for next season. Don't put your notes away; you'll want to evaluate the garden during the coming winter months.

Review your wish list. Add some outstanding fall bloomers and evaluate some of the early bloomers on your list. Remove any that have not lived up to their early season performance.

Evaluate future planting sites and look at next year's landscape plans. Consider preparing new perennial gardens now, when there are fewer garden chores.

PLANTING

Finish planting early in the month. The later you plant, the less time your perennials will have to get established, and the greater the risk of winterkill. Try to limit planting to hardier perennials that are suited to our cold winters.

Locate a place to overwinter less hardy transplants and those scheduled for spring planting. Melinda always has more plants than time left in the fall. She finds vacant space in a protected location for these and other transplants slated for spring planting. Sink the pots into the ground. Once the soil freezes, mulch with evergreen branches or straw for extra protection.

Collect and sow seeds of **coneflowers**, **rudbeckias**, and other late summer- and fall-blooming perennials. Spread the seeds outdoors on well-prepared soil.

Dig and divide **peonies** after the tops have been killed by frost. Use a spading fork to dig the rhizomes. Dig a hole wider than the plant to avoid damaging the root system. Cut the clump into smaller pieces, leaving at least three to five eyes per division. Prepare the planting site by adding several inches of compost into the top 12 inches of soil. Replant the divisions, keeping the eyes no more than 1 to 2 inches below the soil surface.

CARE

Clean up, remove, and destroy any diseased or insect-infested leaves, stems, and flowers.

Decide what "look" you want for your winter garden. Some gardeners like the neat and tidy look and prefer not to have standing "dead stuff." Both Melinda and Cathy prefer to leave perennials standing for winter interest and improved hardiness. Cathy adds some whimsical touches with dried alliums—the large heads that look like a starburst—*au naturale* or spray painted purple—their spring color, attached to a stake in the garden. She resprays them silver or gold for the holidays and changes colors whenever the mood strikes. Most passersby her front yard garden are fooled and think they are alive!

Overwinter plants, such as **salvia** and **mums,** without removing their dead stems; they seem to perform better the next year. (While reading, Melinda's friend thought she was just lazy. But he followed suit and discovered that the perennials not only provided visual relief for the winter garden, but they also attracted birds to his landscape. He still claims it is laziness, but with a purpose!)

Carefully blow or rake tree and shrub leaves off your perennial gardens. Large leaves get wet, mat down, and provide poor insulation for your plants. Shred fallen leaves and use them as a soil mulch or amendment for new plantings. Or rake and bag them for use in next year's garden, or compost them into leaf mold.

Collect dried pods, grasses, and other materials for fall and winter arrangements.

Remove stakes and supports as plants decline. Clean and store for next year's garden.

Start preparing the soil for next year's

Decide what "look" you want for your winter garden. Some gardeners like the neat and tidy look and prefer not to have standing "dead stuff."

gardens. Remove or kill the grass and weeds. Take a soil test. Add organic matter such as compost, aged manure, and shredded leaves to the top 12 inches of soil. Wait until spring to add the fertilizer recommended by your soil test report.

WATERING

Water established plants thoroughly before the ground freezes.

Keep watering until the ground freezes. New plantings and transplants need your attention throughout the fall. Make sure they get 1 inch of water every seven to ten days. Adjust your watering schedule to fit the weather and soil. Give plants the needed water in one application in clay soils and in two applications in sandy soils.

FERTILIZING

Take a soil test of new and existing gardens. Test older gardens every three to five years or whenever you suspect a nutrient problem. Alternate years for testing to help spread out the cost.

Wait until spring to fertilize. You can top-dress the soil with compost or organic matter. Consider shredding fallen leaves and using them as a soil amendment for new plantings. Work the shredded leaves

Helpful Hints

Winter interest is not just "dried stuff" peeking through the snow. It can also be a way of attracting birds that brings color, motion, and life to the winter landscape. Break out the journal and start recording the plants that feed and attract songbirds to your garden. Here is a start for your list:

Black-eyed Susan	*Rudbeckia* spp.
Gayfeather	*Liatris* spp.
Hosta	*Hosta* species
Little bluestem	*Schizachyrium scoparium*
Purple coneflower	*Echinacea purpurea*
Switchgrass	*Panicum virgatum*

into the top 12 inches of soil in empty gardens. These will break down over winter and improve the soil for future planting. Or spread the shredded leaves on the soil surface for mulch. Do not use leaves to cover the plants for winter protection.

PRUNING

Leave stems, flower heads, and seedpods standing for winter interest. Remove only those infected by pests or those that tend to reseed more than you desire.

Cut back the foliage of **peonies** and **hostas** to reduce the risk of fungal leaf disease in next year's garden. Melinda leaves the flower stems of **purple coneflower** standing for winter interest. In

fact, you may find birds feasting on the seeds over the winter.

PROBLEMS

Remove and destroy diseased or insect-infested foliage, flowers, and stems. A thorough fall cleanup reduces the risk of pest problems next season.

Check last winter's notes on wildlife damage. Consider control options if voles have been a problem in the past. Some gardeners choose to cut down their gardens in fall to eliminate the vole's habitat. Others depend on nature, hawks, owls, temperature extremes, and the neighbors' cats to control these rodents. See November "Pests" for more details.

221

NOVEMBER
Perennials & Ornamental Grasses

 PLANNING

You have spent the season evaluating the beauty of your garden. Continue doing this through the winter, but take some time now to evaluate the amount of work you had to spend to keep the garden looking good.

Keep adding to and amending your wish list. Consider maintenance and year-round interest as you add to your list.

 PLANTING

It really is too late to plant. Every gardener occasionally pushes the limit and plants later than they should, but you know you are taking a risk. Increase success by overwintering transplants for spring planting.

1 Find a vacant planting space in a protected location. Look for areas near your house, shed, or fence that are sheltered from winter wind and sun.

2 Sink pots into the soil in this protected location. The soil will insulate the roots from our cold winter temperatures.

3 Wait until the ground freezes to add winter mulch. This usually occurs after a week of freezing temperatures.

4 Use evergreen branches, straw, or marsh hay as winter mulch for added insulation.

Collect and save seeds of **coneflowers**, **black-eyed Susans**, and other perennials you want to plant next spring. Remove seeds from the seedpod and allow them to dry, then place the seeds in an envelope. Write the seed name and the date they were collected on the outside of the envelope. Place the envelope in an airtight jar in the refrigerator. This gives the seeds their needed cold treatment (stratification) while storing them at a consistent temperature. The seeds will be ready to plant next spring.

 CARE

Soil preparation can be done until the ground freezes. In some years, November is the end of the season, and in other years, we can still work in the gardens into December or even January. Here are some tips for preparing your soil and plants for the coming cold weather:

Spread a 2- to 3-inch layer (topdressing) of organic matter on the soil of your perennial gardens now or in the spring. Do this every three to four years to keep your perennials healthy and beautiful.

Add winter mulch to your perennial gardens after the ground freezes. This occurs after a week of freezing temperatures. The goal of winter mulch is to prevent the freezing and thawing of the soil and heaving of plants out of the ground. Mulch anytime after the ground freezes and before a winter thaw occurs. Waiting until after the soil freezes also gives the wildlife a chance to find another place to spend the winter—as opposed to under your mulch and near your plants.

Do not worry if it snows before you put the mulch in place. Snow is the best mulch. Keep the other materials handy for late applications needed when the winter thaw melts the snow. Apply the mulch after the snow melts and before the soil thaws.

Give your perennials growing above-ground extra care for the winter. Place planters in an unheated garage, porch, or other protected area where temperatures hover near freezing. Insulate the roots with packing peanuts or other material. Water whenever the soil is thawed and dry.

Or sink the containers into a vacant garden area for the winter. This is perfect for double-potted containers. Slide the ugly inner pot out of the decorative planter. Bury the ugly pot in a protected area of

Collect and save seeds of coneflowers, black-eyed Susans, and other perennials you want to plant next spring.

the landscape. Next spring, lift the pot out of the soil, repot or divide as needed, and place in the decorative container. Or add potted perennials to the garden. Store decorative containers in the potting shed or garage. Now you have an excuse to buy new plants next season!

Leave the stems or place markers by **butterfly weed**, **balloon flower**, and other late-emerging perennials. Plant bulbs next to these perennials to marks their locations and to prevent accidental damage in early spring.

WATERING

Water the perennial garden thoroughly just before the ground freezes. Monitor poor drainage and ice buildup.

FERTILIZING

Do not fertilize. Fertilizing frozen soil can lead to groundwater pollution.

Helpful Hints

You may have used **garden mums** for a burst of color in the fall garden; however, these late additions often fail to survive the winter. Most botanical gardens and professionals treat them as annuals. They add them to the fall garden and replace them each year. Following are some suggestions for overwintering **mums**:

Improve hardiness by planting **garden mums** in spring. Check with your favorite garden center, nursery, or home store. Many now sell **mums** for spring planting.

Leave the **mums** standing for winter. The dried stems help catch snow and hold winter mulch in place. Cover plants with evergreen branches after the soil freezes.

Increase winter protection by mounding 6 to 8 inches of soil over the dormant plants. Remove in spring as the temperatures hover near freezing.

Try planting 'My Favorite Mum'™, a new cultivar hardy in zones 3 to 7, or its similar hardy relative *Chrysanthemum rubellum*. 'Clara Curtis', 'Duchess of Edinburgh', and 'Mary Stoker' are popular cultivars.

PRUNING

Finish cleanup and enjoy the winter interest.

Remove seedpods from heavy seeders that procreate more than you want. Consider saving some for birds.

Leave semi-hardy perennials—those subject to winterkill—standing for winter. The standing stems will catch the snow for better winter insulation. This, along with the intact plant, seems to increase winter hardiness.

PROBLEMS

Monitor for animal and rodent damage. Fall cleanup may help reduce the damage. Try trapping voles (meadow mice) with snap traps baited with peanut butter and oats. Tuck the traps in a pipe or under cover to prevent birds and desirable wildlife from accidentally being injured. Keep in mind there may be more than 400 voles per acre. That's a lot of peanut butter and snap traps!

Cut back, remove, and destroy disease- and insect-infested perennials.

DECEMBER

 ## PLANNING

The holidays are quickly approaching, and all thoughts are turning to preparation for the holiday season. Help make gift giving easier for your family and friends by making a wish list—a new journal, plant labels, hand pruners, flower scissors, a harvest basket, a new shovel, a gift certificate to your favorite garden center or catalog, a load of manure (to be delivered at a later date!), and much more.

 ## PLANTING

Pull out your garden pictures and dream of the planting season. Keep exercising and stretching to keep those planting muscles toned until spring returns.

 ## CARE

Finish garden cleanup. Do not worry if you have waited too long and the snow has buried all your good intentions. Wait until the first thaw or spring to finish garden cleanup.

Use evergreen branches, straw, or marsh hay for winter mulch to protect semi-hardy perennials and prevent frost heaving.

 ## Helpful Hints

Don't throw away that holiday tree. Use it in your winter landscape. Cathy and Melinda both collect all the discarded trees in their neighborhoods to use as mulch in their gardens. Prune off the branches and cover perennial and bulb gardens. The soil is usually frozen by the holidays and we have not yet had the damaging winter thaw.

Or leave the tree intact and use it as a windbreak for other plants in the landscape. In snowy winters, Melinda props her trees in a snowdrift for winter interest. The trees provide shelter for the birds that like to feed on the seeds of **coneflower**, **rudbeckia**, and **gayfeather** in the perennial garden.

 ## WATERING

Make sure the garden hose is safely stored for winter. Turn off the water or insulate outside faucets to prevent freezing.

 ## FERTILIZING

Review soil tests and make a list of fertilizing and soil amendment needs. Make a note on next year's calendar so that you will not forget to implement your soil improvement plans.

 ## PRUNING

Sit back and relax. Enjoy the winter interest your perennial garden provides. Make notes about which plants add to and which ones detract from your winter landscape.

PROBLEMS

Wildlife can be a wonderful addition to the landscape. Their movements and antics can be entertaining. Make a list of the visitors to your winter garden. Note what plants helped bring them into the landscape.

Unfortunately, some wildlife do more damage than we want to tolerate. Watch for tracks, droppings, and their other signs. Monitor for damage done by squirrels digging and voles eating roots.

Repellents may discourage squirrels and deer. Treat before feeding and digging begins. Reapply repellents as needed. Check label for more specific directions.

CHAPTER EIGHT

Roses

Roses are considered by many to be the "Queen of Flowers." Their popularity is evidenced by the fact that they are our national flower.

Within the Prairie Lands states, roses are a popular choice for state flower chosen by both Iowa, **wild prairie rose** (*Rosa pratincola*), and North Dakota, **wild prairie rose** (*Rosa arkansana*). Common names can be regional, as here when the same common name is shared by two different plants. Also, one plant can have several different common names. This is why it is best to use the botanic name when talking plants so there is no doubt as to the plant's identity.

KNOW THE DIFFERENT TYPES OF ROSES

There are a number of different classes of roses. In this region, people tend to grow **hybrid tea, floribunda, grandiflora, shrub, miniature, landscape,** and **species** roses such as the two state flowers above.

When you think of roses, the vision you are most likely to see is a **hybrid tea rose**; the many cultivars are the most widely grownn. Hybrid teas epitomize the ideal rose: Long pointed buds open to reveal elegant, high-centered, fragrant flowers of diverse colors on long, straight stems. However, despite their sales figures, they are the least likely to survive in our frigid winters and hot summers. Perhaps that is why they sell so well; many die back and need replanting every year.

Floribunda roses were developed to grow in the colder climates of northern Europe. They bloom constantly through the summer and require little or no special attention. Unlike **hybrid teas** with their long stems, **floribundas** produce beautiful flower clusters.

Grandiflora roses are crosses between **hybrid tea roses** and **floribundas**—bred to include the best characteristics of both. They bloom consistently all season with an abundance of 3- to 5-inch double flowers borne singly or in clusters. Their stems are a compromise: longer than **floribundas** but shorter than **hybrid teas.** They did not get the genes for cold hardiness, however, and don't reliably survive winter without protection.

The group called **shrub rose** comprises true **shrub-form roses, landscape roses, old-garden roses** (hybrids introduced before 1867 which is the year 'La France', the first hybrid tea rose, was introduced) and **Modern English roses** (the roses that David Austin developed that resemble old-fashioned roses in their appearance and fragrance). The common characteristic of the **shrub roses** is their toughness. Choose from among this diverse group if low maintenance is a priority.

Species roses occur naturally in the wild. Most self-pollinate; their fruit—called rose hips—are eye-catching in hues of orange and red. Plant a seed and it will grow into a plant just like its parent (do that with **hybrid roses,** and the result is highly variable). Organically grown rose hips make delicious tea and jelly and are high in vitamin C. Today you can find named hybrids as well as the straight species.

It may come as a surprise that **miniature roses**, with their diminutive form, are among the toughest, most hardy roses you can grow. One reason is that they are generally grown on their own roots. Being lower to the ground may help them as well, receiving more consistent snow cover in winter and offering more protection from wind—both hot and cold—that can easily desiccate a plant.

Roses

PLANNING

Before you buy a rose, read the three guidelines below. Otherwise, you may end up with an expensive annual that may bloom the first season, but is unlikely to come back in future years. It is easy to grow great roses when you follow these steps.

Location, location, location—first and foremost choose a space that gets at least six hours of direct sun a day. Give the plant(s) room to breathe. Select a spot that allows for good air circulation (not up against a walk or hemmed in by hedges or taller plants). Don't crowd roses. Keep them away from trees and large shrubs that shade the plants and compete for nutrients in the soil. None of the plants benefits when they share too small a space. Provide well-drained, fertile soil; if the soil is less than optimal, amend it. Add compost, well-rotted manure, or leaf mold to make it richer. Mix in builder's sand, peat moss, and a little vermiculite to enhance drainage.

The right plant for the right place. Choose the sturdiest, healthiest plant you can find that is in sync with your current outdoor conditions. For example, don't buy a **container-grown rose** that has leafed out if the soil is still frozen and you can't plant it. Look for a plant with at least three healthy canes

(main branches) broader than a pencil. When possible, purchase a rose grown on its own rootstock. **Grafted roses** often seem to change color in the second or third year (look for a "knob" near the base of the main stem—the bud union where the flowering rose was grafted to hardy rootstock). That's because the less vigorous top died back and the flowering canes are growing up from the rootstock. Make sure the plant is rated hardy for your zone.

TLC works every time. Give the plant tender loving care. This includes mulching, feeding, watering, weeding (often not necessary if the plant is mulched well), pruning, preparing the plant for winter dormancy, and controlling pests and diseases.

SELECTION

Whether you buy a rose on-line, through a mail-order catalog, at a specialty nursery, at a home and garden store, or in the parking lot of your local supermarket or hardware store, you will find roses packaged in two distinct ways. Learn the difference so you can start giving the plant TLC as soon as you arrive home or when it is delivered. The time of year that you purchase the rose should also impact your choice.

The rose you receive from a mail-order or Internet company is a **bare-root rose**. There is no soil around the roots; there may be moist newspaper, sawdust, or excelsior around the roots to keep them from drying out. Unless a **bare-root rose** is dormant—no signs of buds breaking or leaves emerging on the canes—do not buy it. These roses are kept in cold storage and sent to you at the proper time for planting (you hope). Some local nurseries also have some **bare-root roses** in early spring. Check the canes (stems) to be sure they are healthy; they should have green or reddish color and be firm to the touch. Do not buy one with dry or broken canes. Nor should you buy a **bare-root rose** with a lot of new growth; it will need special handling early in the season. Did you know that some of the roses you see in stores in waxed cardboard boxes ("plant the box and all") are bare-root, just wrapped with wood shavings, newspaper, or other moist packing material? You can judge by the weight whether the cardboard-boxed roses are bare root or have their roots in soil.

You can often find **container-grown roses** locally throughout the growing season. The choice of **container-grown roses** is very limited compared to bare-root plants. However, they are available later in the season—even in bloom—so you can truly judge the

Roses

vigor of the plant. Containerized roses are not available through mail order, as the weight of the soil makes shipping costs prohibitive. Potted roses are **bare-root roses** recently planted in a container; be sure to handle these with care since their rootball is not thoroughly developed.

PLANTING

Roses are heavy feeders and need good, rich, well-drained soil. If you are planting an entire bed of roses, it is best to prepare the soil in the fall and then it will be ready to plant in the spring. Amend the soil before planting: Mix in plenty of compost and about 1 cup of superphosphate per cubic foot of soil and mix in well. Roses prefer slightly acid soil with a pH between 6.0 and 6.5.

Consider spacing before you plant: Allow a foot between **miniature roses,** 2 feet between **hybrid tea roses,** 1 ½ feet between **grandifloras,** 3 feet between **floribundas,** 4 feet between **standards** (roses grown in tree form; plant them as an annual in the Prairie Lands), and 7 feet between **climbing roses.** Adequate spacing allows for good air circulation that prevents fungal diseases and keeps plants from touching to prevent the possible spread of any disease or pest. Spacing is most important to give you access to the plant.

Bare-root roses

These tough plants can be put in the ground before the last frost date as long as the ground is workable and not too wet and the plant is dormant. When you receive a bare-root plant, Cathy recommends that you unwrap it and soak it in muddy water with a capful of transplant solution added for at least eight hours before planting. If you cannot plant it within 24 hours, wrap it in wet burlap or newspaper and store at about 40 degrees Fahrenheit in a dark place (a refrigerator or cool, dark basement) for up to a week. If it still cannot be planted, soak it again and heel it in a trench at a 45-degree angle. Cover completely with several inches of moist soil and it can remain entrenched for up to six weeks. If it has already leafed out, keep it in a cool, bright place until danger of frost has passed, and then plant it. Otherwise, the tender leaves and buds could freeze.

To plant:

1 Dig a hole several inches deeper and wider than the root system. Fill the hole with transplant solution and give it an hour to soak in. If there is still solution in the hole, dig deeper and wider. Mix in builder's sand and organic matter to increase drainage.

2 Mix the soil from the hole with equal parts of compost; add a cup each of rock phosphate, bonemeal and bloodmeal. Put amended soil back into the hole, forming a cone to support the roots.

3 Take a good look at the rose. Prune out any small canes (thinner than a pencil), leaving three or four healthy canes. Cut back any damaged or disproportionately long roots.

4 Place the rose so that the roots fan out over the cone and the bud union (bump on stem above roots where hybrid was grafted onto rootstock) is about 2 inches below soil level. Add amended soil until the hole is two-thirds full. Add 2 to 3 quarts of transplant solution and let it soak in.

5 Fill in the rest of the hole; firm the soil gently with your hands. Water in with transplant solution.

6 Cover two-thirds of the exposed plant with moist soil to protect it from wind and weather. The extra moisture allows the plant to develop properly.

7 Keep an eye on the rose. When the new growth is 1 to 2 inches long, gently remove the extra soil, smoothing it out to soil level. Mulch well.

Roses

Container-grown roses are easy to plant.

1 Dig a hole a few inches wider and deeper than the container. Amend the soil from the hole with several handfuls of organic matter (compost, leaf mold, humus, or well-rotted manure), and a cup each of rock phosphate, bonemeal, and bloodmeal.

2 Add about 6 inches of amended soil to the hole.

3 Remove the rose from the container (even cardboard boxes that say to plant the entire thing). Keep the surrounding soil intact unless the plant appears rootbound (then gently tease the roots apart).

4 Pour a quart of transplant solution in the hole and let it absorb into the surrounding soil.

5 Position the rose at the same soil level it was in the container unless it is a **grafted rose.** You can distinguish a graft by the knob-like protrusion on the stem—the bud union where the rootstock and main plant were joined. For the growers' convenience, the bud union is above soil level on container-grown plants—ideal for mild winter climates, but not here. Make sure that bud union is 2 to 3 inches below soil level once planted.

6 Fill the hole halfway with soil and gently firm to eliminate air pockets. Water with a quart of transplant solution. Add soil to fill the hole; water in with 2 quarts of transplant solution.

7 Gently tamp the soil down with your hands (do not step on it, or it becomes too compacted). Top off with additional soil, if necessary.

8 Mulch the planting area with 2 to 3 inches of organic matter. Keep the mulch 1 inch away from the stem.

WATERING

In addition to food, roses need plenty of water—the equivalent of at least an inch of rain a week. The best way to measure accurately is with an inexpensive rain gauge.

Several factors influence the amount of water needed. When it is hot and humid, roses get by with less water than when it is hot and dry. Factor in our Prairie Lands "breezes," which increase evaporation (and the water bill). Newly planted roses require more water than those that have been established in the garden for a few years.

How can you tell if a rose needs water? Stick a finger into the soil; it should feel lightly moist—not wet. If the soil feels dry an inch or more down, water immediately. Adding a thick layer of mulch around the roses in spring not only keeps the weeds down and moderates the soil temperature, it also conserves water and keeps the soil from quickly drying out.

Water at ground level to avoid wetting the leaves. There are several options. The easiest and least costly way is to use a leaky hose, also known as a soaker hose, that steadily releases beads of water from its surface. In spring, weave it around the outer root zone of the plants. Cover it with mulch, so it's invisible. Calculate the hourly output of the hose, set a timer or turn on the hose for the allotted time needed, and the roses are watered. Our winters are too cold to leave the hose out (another reason for choosing leaky pipe over emitter or other plastic piping systems which are more complicated). Take it up and store inside for the winter.

FERTILIZING

To thrive, roses need to be well fed. Treat your plants as you would your children or pets. Provide food that is as close to its natural state as possible that is able to break down into a form the plants can use.

Roses

Traditional Rose Food–When choosing an all-purpose rose fertilizer, read the label carefully. Find one that does not have additional ingredients that will kill pests and weeds at the same time. If you don't want a fertilizer formulated specifically for roses, you can use a granular, general-purpose fertilizer with an N-P-K—Nitrogen-Phosphorus-Potassium (also known as potash)—ratio of 5-10-5. Spread a handful or cupful around the base of each plant, taking care to avoid getting fertilizer on the stem or leaves. Always follow package instructions.

Even though roses are heavy feeders, it's not necessary to feed a newly planted rose for at least three months. Think about all the good nutrients you added to the soil before you planted the rose.

Hybrid teas, floribundas, and grandifloras need at least three feedings a year; the first feeding as early in spring as the rose starts to leaf out. Give it a second feeding the moment it starts to bloom, and round out the feeding season in early August. Although it's as tempting to over feed a rose as to give extra treats to pets, in the Prairie Lands states feeding after the middle of August only encourages new growth that won't harden off before frost and will subsequently die back. **Species, shrub roses, ramblers** and **climbers** need only be fed once in spring, before they leaf out.

A more natural approach to feeding:

It is up to you to decide how you want to feed your roses. In Cathy's experience, she has better success with roses when she gives them a spring tonic (see recipe on page 239) followed by monthly foliar feedings (spraying the leaves tops and bottoms of leaves early in the day with a solution of liquid rose food). Following the natural path, Cathy uses liquid kelp, fish emulsion, or compost "tea" brewed from her own compost. You could use a dilution of MiracleGro or another fertilizer. Be sure to follow the package directions for mixing it for foliar feeding; fertilizer that you water into the ground is more concentrated than what you spray on leaves. Too strong a solution can burn the leaves. If they need a final feeding in early August, use a formulation without nitrogen, such as 0-10-10. Nitrogen promotes foliar growth. In late summer and autumn, you want to encourage root growth, not new leaves.

PRUNING

Pruning is intimidating to many folks. Don't be afraid of killing the plant, it is tougher than you. In fact, pruning is beneficial. Without pruning, most roses would become a jungle of tangled stems bearing fewer and smaller flowers—like the **wild roses** at the edges of woodlands.

By pruning, you can remove diseased or dead wood and train a plant to grow so that the crown area is as open as possible, allowing for optimal air circulation. Cutting off dead or broken stems, faded flowers, or nipping off fresh flowers to enjoy indoors are all forms of pruning. If you are pruning to remove disease (blackspot, powdery mildew), dip the pruners in isopropyl alcohol between each cut. Wipe your hands and pruners well with alcohol when you have finished pruning a diseased plant and are moving on to another—healthy or diseased—to avoid spreading the problem to other plants.

What many folks don't realize is that pruning encourages new growth. When you cut back the faded blooms of many modern roses (wait for the last in the cluster to finish blooming), you are often rewarded with a new flush of flowers. Whether pruning or cutting a bloom, make the cut just above an outward-facing five- to seven-leaflet leaf at a 45-degree angle. This makes the new branch grow outward from the shrub, rather than crowding the center.

Roses

A good pair of pruners (also called secateurs) is well worth the investment, as they will make clean cuts and can last for decades. To gain confidence with pruning, practice on a dead branch. Make a 45-degree cut ¼ to ½ inch above an outward-facing leaf or branchlet. If the practice branch is bare, make some dots on it with an indelible marker to use as pruning guides.

In the Prairie Lands states, do not prune roses after August 15th. Don't even cut back faded flowers. After a flower dies, you can remove just the flower if it is unsightly, but don't cut the stem. Late in the season, any new growth will not have time to mature and harden off enough to endure the cold of winter. The result—not seen until the following spring—is heavy dieback even lower than the original cut. Let the spent flowers develop into the bright orange fruit (rose hips). Most **species** and some **hybrids** will produce a plethora of hips, which attracts birds and other creatures. You can cut the hips and use them in making rose hip tea or rose hip jelly—both high in vitamin C.

Wait until late winter/early spring to do major pruning. **Floribundas, hybrid teas, grandifloras,** and **miniature roses** respond to a good spring pruning, rewarding you with a healthier, more floriferous plant. As you prune, look for bud eyes—small nubs on the stems. They can be a bit hard to see in the early part of the season, but once the plant is growing, they are easily found in the crotch between the leaf attachment and the stem. Always prune at a 45-degree angle just above an outfacing bud or leaf; each bud can produce up to three branches. In early spring, you can cut these roses down as low as 8 to 12 inches, if necessary.

Shrub roses and **climbers** only need minimal pruning to keep them in shape.

PROBLEMS

Caterpillars of different kinds can roll up in a leaf and eat it from inside out, skeletonize leaves, and even feast on flowers. Aphids can suck on some particularly succulent buds, and a pair of Japanese beetles could eat, sleep, and breed all on a single rose blossom. Blackspot can kill a rose after a few years. Don't let naysayers spook you with tales of all the pests and diseases to which roses succumb.

Nor should you let them try to convince you that lots of sprays and powders and noxious chemicals are the only lines of defense. Have an armament of good bugs at the ready to seek and destroy any bad guys. Encourage beneficial insects—lacewings, ladybugs, praying mantises, and spiders—to make your garden their home.

First and foremost, remember that a healthy plant is not a lure for diseases and pests; a weak, malnourished, or stressed plant attracts them. If you follow the tenets described above, your roses should be happy and vigorous.

Perhaps it is because roses are all too often planted in their own separate gardens that they seem to have more "bad guys" out to get them. It's like planting an acre of tomatoes; you're sending the message loud and clear: "Tomato hornworms, come and get us!" If your garden is a mixture of different types of plants—annuals, perennials, herbs, vegetables, shrubs, trees, vines, and roses—the variety hosts innumerable good bugs (beneficial insects) that can attack any bad guys that come along.

Viral or bacterial diseases, fungi, or pests cannot wreak havoc if the plant of choice is surrounded by different plants. Any problem that does occur is likely to be isolated to one plant. Until recently, Japanese beetles were unheard of—and unseen—west of the Mississippi. Now that they have made the jump, we can only anticipate their arrival in our gardens and plant accordingly. Since they love roses (they can eat, sleep, and mate all in the same flower), don't offer them a buffet of rose varieties. Instead, mix roses in

Roses

with herbs, plant them in the perennial border, pair them with bulbs or evergreens and they very well might just fly over your garden. Bolster your knowledge. If you understand the lifecycle of the pest, you can determine the best method and time to control it.

Blackspot is a fungal disease that manifests itself as small black spots on the leaves. It is spread by spores when rain or overhead watering sprays on the leaves. Blackspot begins on the lowest canes; when a droplet of water connects with mature spores, the fungus spores are launched upward to land on the leaves above.

GETTING READY FOR WINTER

The main reason to grow **Griffith Buck** and hardy **Canadian roses** like the **Explorer** and **Brownell Subzero series** is that they were bred to withstand tough winters. They need no special treatment in the fall to ready them for the cold.

Hybrid teas and **grandifloras** need the most attention. Check their hardiness relative to your Zone and microclimate. In autumn, after the first light front, mound up 4 to 6 inches of light soil around established roses. After

Helpful Hints

Tasty Roses

Have you ever eaten a rose? All roses are edible—if grown organically (no chemicals, systemics, orthene, pesticides, or herbicides used on or near them). The petals of some taste much better than others. Generally, the roses with the richest scents have the best flavor. There are always exceptions; the most notable is Flower Carpet™ Pink. It has no aroma, yet the petals are sweetly rose-flavored. Remove the petals from the flower and tear or cut off the white base of the petal, which tends to be bitter. Use the petals in a fruit cup, chopped and mixed with sweet butter to make open-faced tea sandwiches, as a garnish with ice cream, or boiled with sugar and used as a base for rose sorbet or ice cream.

- 'Buff Beauty' (Sh)
- 'Cherish' (F)
- 'Double Delight' (Ht)
- Flower Carpet™ Pink
- 'Gertrude Jekyll' (Sh)
- 'Gold Medal' (G)
- 'Love' (G)
- 'Magic Carrousel' (M)
- 'Mirandy' (Ht)
- 'Mister Lincoln' (Ht)
- 'Perfume Delight' (Ht)
- *Rosa rugosa* 'Alba' (Sp)

the first hard frost, when that layer freezes, add another few inches of soil. Continue adding soil, allowing each layer to freeze before adding another. Top off at about a foot. You'll see a broad cone of soil with rose canes sticking up from that. In Zone 4 and below (and for any success with **hybrid teas**), cover the frozen mound with leaves. Cover any new plant completely or the extreme cold will kill the tender canes.

Plastic and styrofoam cones are available, but their success is limited unless you vent or remove them during the warm fall days that are likely to occur after the first frost. Venting is also necessary during January thaw and the occasional balmy days that crop up during the otherwise frigid winter. They are unattractive and often blow away or are disturbed by critters burrowing beneath their warmth.

Roses

Name	Type	Zone	Color	Fragrance	Bloom	Comments
'Alba Meidland'	L	4 to 7	White	Light	Late spring to frost	Graceful; disease-resistant
'Alchymist'	Sh/Cl	4 to 8	Apricot blend	Bold rose	Early summer	Grows in poor soil; shiny leaves
'Bonica'	Sh	4 to 7	Light pink	—	Summer	Good as hedge; disease-resistant
'Carefree Beauty'	Sh	3 to 8	Pink	Moderate	Late spring to frost	Best-known Buck rose, lives up to its name; long-lasting hips
'Cecile Brunner'	Cl	5 to 9	Pale pink	Light	Late spring to frost	Sweetheart rose; disease-resistant
'Climbing America'	Cl	3 to 8	Coral pink	Spicy, clove	Early summer to frost	One of the best climbers
'Dainty Bess'	Ht	5 to 7	Soft pink	Light	Summer to frost	Unique Ht: single flowers w/prominent yellow stamens
Flower Carpet™ Pink	L	4 to 8	Deep pink	None	Late spring to frost	Low-growing; grows in any soil; covered w/blooms, shade tolerant
Flower Carpet™ Yellow	L	4 to 7	Sunny yellow	None	Late spring to frost	Handsome shiny leaves; lights up the landscape; great ground cover
'Fragrant Cloud'	Sh	4 to 8	Deep peach	Strong tea/honey	Summer to frost	Good cut flower
'Gertrude Jekyll'	Es	4 to 7	Clear pink	Sweet rose	Late spring to frost	Excellent flavor; good cut flower
'Hansa'	Cl	4 to 7	Purplish red	Moderate	Early and late summer	Short stems; disease-resistant
'Harison's Yellow'	Cl/Sh	2 to 7	Brilliant yellow	Strong rose	Mid-spring	Earliest bloomer; grows in any soil; thrives in partial shade
'Heirloom'	Sh	4 to 8	Pale lavender	Sweet rose	Late spring to frost	Old-fashioned look; glossy leaves
Knockout™	Sh	4 to 7	Cherry red blend	Mild tea	Early spring to hard frost	Disease-resistant; continuous bloom, drought-tolerant
'Lambert Close'	Sh	2 to 6	Pink	Sweet rose	Late spring; reblooms	Canadian Explorer rose; disease resistant
'Mister Lincoln'	HT	5 to 8	Deep red	Sweetly spicy	Late spring to frost	Deep velvety red, good cut flower
'Peace'	HT	4 to 7	Pale pink w/yellow	Lightly rose	Late spring to frost	Arguably the most popular rose off all time

Roses

Name	Type	Zone	Color	Fragrance	Bloom	Comments
'Prairie Fire'	Sh	4 to 8	Bright red	None	Summer to frost	Vigorous, disease-resistant
'Prairie Princess'	Sh	4 to 7	Orange-pink blend	Moderate	Late spring to frost	Buck rose; disease-resistant, profuse blooms
'Queen Elizabeth'	G	5 to 8	Pale pink	Delicate	Late spring to frost	Elegant; the first grandiflora rose
Rosa eglaniteria	Sp	4 to 8	Small, light pink	Apple/spicy	Early summer	Sweetbrier; fragrant leaves; good hips
Rosa glauca	Sp	2 to 7	Small single; pale pink	None	Fleeting-late spring	Bluish-green foliage & stems; burgundy hips in summer; carefree
Rosa rugosa	Sp	4 to 7	Deep rosy pink; single	Sweet rose	Late spring to frost	Large red-orange hips; tasty
Rosa spinossima 'Altaica'	Sp	3 to 7	White	Strong	Late spring	Handsome thorny stems
'Shooting Star'	M	4 to 8	Red/orange/yellow	Light	Late spring to frost	Shade tolerant, color fades in heat
'Sir Thomas Lipton'	Cl	4 to 7	White	Good rose	Late spring to frost	Disease-resistant, vigorous
'Sunsprite'	Fl	5 to 8	Yellow	Sweet rose	Late spring to frost	Good in containers
'White Lightnin'	G	4 to 8	White w/ruffled pink edge	Sweet	Late spring to frost	Floriferous; disease-resistant
'William Baffin'	Cl	2 to 7	Deep rosy pink	Light	Summer	Disease-resistant floriferous; cascading form; Explorer rose
'Zephirine Drouhin'	Cl	4 to 7	Rose-pink	Rich rose	Late spring	Thornless; an old-garden rose

* with winter protection in colder zone

KEY:
Cl – Climber; Es – Modern English Shrub; F – Floribunda; G – Grandiflora; Ht – Hybrid Tea; L – Landscape; M – Miniature
Sh – Shrub; Sp – Species

JANUARY
Roses

PLANNING

Check out roses on the Internet. Thumb through catalogs. Get out the magazine clippings from last summer. Resist the allure of the photographs (especially colorful in the bleakness of winter) and look first at the Hardiness Zone. If the rose is listed as hardy to Zone 7 or above, don't even think about it. Zone 6 plants may do well in some of Kansas or in warm microclimates in other areas. To be confident that the rose will grow and prosper in the Prairie Lands states, seek those hardy to Zone 5 and lower. Then you can look at their pretty photos.

Make a master list to keep track of everything you order (plants, tools, books, anything plant-related) so that you don't accidentally order the same plant more than once.

PLANTING

In preparation for the planting season, be sure you have the tools you will be using; everyone has his/her preferences. If you haven't sharpened and oiled them, it's not too late. Tools include: spade, shovel, garden fork, rake, trowel, and hand pruners. You'll also want heavy garden gloves, a 5-gallon bucket, and a waterproof tarp.

CARE

Walk around the garden every once in a while, especially after a snow or ice storm. Tie a piece of brightly colored yarn or ribbon on any plants that need attention. Later, you can come back and attend to them—cut off broken canes, tie up canes that are blowing in the winds, or add more mulch around the plant.

WATERING

If the temperature rises above freezing and there has been little or no snow, give the roses (and other shrubs and trees) a good drink of water. Avoid wetting the leaves; water slowly at ground level, allowing the water to seep slowly into the soil.

FERTILIZING

During the winter, the action in the compost pile slows down tremendously. Unlike other times of the year, when it can keep up with whatever you add, in winter the pile just grows and is frozen and immovable. Consider indoor vermiculture—raising worms, using a pound of red wigglers and a fancy three-tiered worm bin (or make it yourself with Rubbermaid storage bins with air/drainage holes punched in the sides and bottom). It does not smell, and it's amazing how much worms can eat and turn into castings in a few days. A bonus is that they happily eat the colored pages of the newspaper and all the slick magazines.

PRUNING

It is vital to use the right tool for the size of the cane or stem. It is equally important to invest in a good pair of hand pruners (also called pruning shears or secateurs) that are comfortable for your hand. High-grade pruners actually come in sizes to fit delicate or burly hands. Bypass pruners cut cleaner than anvil-type pruners. Hand pruners work well on canes up to $1/2$ inch in diameter.

For canes up to an inch in diameter, use long-handled loppers. If you are pruning a very old rose with a larger diameter, use a fine-toothed saw. Wear leather or rubber-reinforced gloves to protect your hands from thorns.

PROBLEMS

Study your insect book so you know what is visiting your garden come spring.

FEBRUARY
Roses

 PLANNING

Get out your master list and get your planting plan organized. Which roses stay and which become compost? Realistically, how many new roses can you plant this year? Sometimes it is easier if you can visualize it. If you photographed the garden, look at the images, and, if possible, literally "x" out the plants that have died or that you want to move or discard.

Place your Internet and mail orders for roses (and other plants) by the middle of the month to be assured of getting the varieties you want. To be safe, make a list of alternates in case any roses are sold-out.

Most companies will ship at the proper planting time (a few weeks before the last frost date). To be on the safe side, clearly mark on the order form the week that you want to receive the bare-root plants. Mark it on your calendar so you don't schedule an out-of-town trip without having someone to rescue your roses from the cold and snowy front stoop.

 PLANTING

Climbers bloom best on horizontal canes. To get the best show from them, consider training one or more along a fence, across a broad arbor, on a wide pergola, or splayed out on a fan lattice. Get the sup-

Helpful Hints

If you're new to gardening or growing roses, start off with some of the tried and true, easy to grow roses:

- 'America' (CL)
- 'Carefree Beauty' (Sh)
- 'Charlotte Armstrong' (Ht)
- 'Europeana' (F)
- Flower Carpet™ series (Sh)
- 'Fragrant Cloud' (Ht)
- 'Gertrude Jekyll' (Sh)
- 'Green Ice' (M)
- Knockout™ (S)
- 'Mister Lincoln' (Ht)
- 'Queen Elizabeth' (G)
- 'Popcorn' (M)
- 'Rise n' Shine' (M)
- 'Shreveport' (G)
- 'The Fairy' (Sh)
- 'William Baffin' (Cl)

plies you will need; you can start building the project inside.

 CARE

If you use Styrofoam or plastic cones to protect your roses, keep an eye on the weather. On those suddenly balmy days when you go outside in a light jacket, think of the roses that are steaming in their impenetrable, airless prisons. Remove the brick or whatever you use to weight it down and let the plant breathe. Remember to close it in the afternoon before the light begins to fade.

 WATERING

If the temperature stays well above freezing for several days and there has been little or no snow, it wouldn't hurt to water the garden.

 FERTILIZING

Be prepared. Shop now for fertilizers and soil amendments to avoid the crowds.

 PRUNING

Canes can break from the wind whipping them. Secure these and prune off any broken part of the cane.

 PROBLEMS

Keep an eye out for deer. If it has been a rough winter, they like nothing better than some nice roses to nibble—and they can nibble all the way down to the ground if there's no snow. The best way to keep them out of the garden is with an 8- to 10-foot high electric fence. Deer netting of the same height may be equally effective and more pleasant to the eye.

MARCH
Roses

 PLANNING

Be sure to lay in some salt or barley hay in case of a late freeze. A light covering can make the difference between a plant that thrives and one that succumbs to a late winterkill. Start a master list of the roses you have. Include the basics: name (botanic if it's a species), type (**hybrid tea, shrub, floribunda,** etc.), when planted, and color (use the description from the catalog or tag; change it later if it's not accurate). Add new varieties as you plant them. Cross plants off if they die.

Once you have a master list, it's easy to chart progress. Keep it simple: date of bloom, repeated bloom (if applicable), overall look and health (vigorous, spindly, well-branched, many flowers), fragrance (none, mild, strong and a descriptive word—rose, spicy, apple, etc.), any pests and/or diseases and treatment. Include a space for comments: great, lots of flowers, must have more, dig up and toss, etc.

As it can be challenging to draw a landscape plan, and even more challenging to remember what is where, document the garden with photographs. Nothing fancy, a Polaroid shot or print from a point-and-shoot camera or a digital image will do. Date-stamp the image if your camera has that feature; otherwise, write the date on the photo. Get some overall shots that show the gardens progress from month to month. Jot down plant names; the more information you can add, the better.

 PLANTING

A **bare-root rose** can be put in the ground before the last frost date as long as the ground is workable, not too wet and the plant is dormant. Heel it in if you don't have the time or place to properly plant it. If the rose has already leafed out, keep it in a cool, bright place until danger of frost has passed, and then plant it. Otherwise, the tender leaves and buds could be frozen. If it is likely to be more than a few days before you can plant it, temporarily pot it up in a large container filled with potting soil. The roots will take up water and nutrients from the soil, keeping the plant from getting stressed.

 CARE

Spring is capricious; light frosts can kill tender growth. Play it safe and don't remove winter protection too early. Look under the mulch to see if there is evidence of new growth. When danger of frost has passed, gently remove the mulch. Avoid injuring tender (and small) new growth. If a freeze threatens, cover the plant with salt or barley hay.

You can see why mulching roses with soil and leaves is more satisfactory than using a cone; it saves time and money. If you have used a cone, be sure to vent the roses during the sunny hours of the day. Slowly harden off the rose, removing the cone for a few hours each day and keeping it on at night, until gradually, over a period of two weeks, the cone can remain off.

 WATERING

Keep newly planted **bare-root roses** evenly moist until they are established.

As the soil thaws, if it is dry and there is no rain in the forecast, begin to water with an inch a week.

Spring is capricious; light frosts can kill tender growth. Play it safe and don't remove winter protection too early. Look under the mulch to see if there is evidence of new growth.

Set a rain gauge in the garden so you can accurately measure rainfall.

FERTILIZING

Save used coffee grounds. Dry them completely and then store them in the freezer in a zipper storage bag. Add them to our alkaline soil to provide nourishment, give it more friability, and lower the pH.

PRUNING

Begin by cutting off any dead or broken canes. Cut down to live wood. Scratch the cane lightly with your thumbnail. If the area is green, it is living tissue; if it is brown, it is dead. As you do late winter/early spring pruning, look for bud eyes, which are small nubs on the stems.

Helpful Hints

Roses Resistant to Blackspot

- 'Angel Face' (F)
- 'Europeana' (G)
- 'First Edition' (F)
- Flower Carpet™ Pink (Sh)
- 'Gene Boerner' (F)
- 'Queen Elizabeth' (G)
- 'Peace' (Ht)
- 'Mister Lincoln' (Ht)
- Knockout™ (Sh)

They can be a bit hard to see in the early part of the season, but once the plant is growing, they are easily found in the crotch between the leaf attachment and the stem.

PROBLEMS

Some gardeners swear by using dormant oil in early spring to ward off blackspot and powdery mildew; it will smother any overwintering insects on the plant. If you are spraying the trees and shrubs, spray the roses as well. Make sure that you are using plain horticultural oil with no insecticide or pesticide additives. Spray only when the temperatures are 40° Fahrenheit or above, otherwise you can damage the plants.

APRIL
Roses

PLANNING

To some, a rose is not a rose if it has no scent. Aromatic roses to consider growing include:

- 'Alchymist' (Sh)
- 'Angel Face' (F)
- 'Apricot Nectar'(F)
- 'Beauty Secret' (M)
- 'Blossomtime' (Cl)
- 'Candy Stripe' (Ht)
- 'Chrysler Imperial' (Ht)
- 'Don Juan' (Cl)
- 'Double Delight' (Ht)
- 'Europeana' (F)
- 'Harison's Yellow' (Sh)
- 'Iceberg' (F)
- 'Mirandy' (Ht)
- 'Mister Lincoln' (Ht)
- 'Perfume Delight' (Ht)
- *Rosa eglanteria* (Sp)
- *Rosa rugosa* (Sp)
- 'Royal Sunset' (Cl)
- 'Sterling Silver' (Cl)
- 'Sundowner' (G)
- 'Sunsprite' (F)
- 'Tiffany' (Ht)
- 'White Lightnin' (G)

Key:

Cl – Climber	M – Miniature
F – Floribunda	Sh – Shrub
G – Grandiflora	Sp – Species
Ht – Hybrid tea	

PLANTING

If, after digging deeper and amending the soil, a planting hole still does not drain, you can install French drains (a time-consuming and expensive project). It is easier to find a better-draining area for the roses. If the whole yard is clay, consider building a raised bed for your roses. Make the bed as large or small as you want—for an entire garden or a single rose bush. Raise it at least 2 feet from the ground. Work the base soil and amend it before adding good soil to the bed. For older gardeners and those with bad backs, an added benefit of a raised bed is that you don't have as far to bend to reach the ground.

CARE

For a bare-root rose planted earlier in the season, gently remove the extra soil above ground level when the plant begins to break dormancy (showing the first signs of leaves and bud). Add a 3- to 5-inch layer of organic mulch around the plant; keep the mulch at least an inch away from the stem. However, if there is a threat of a freeze after the soil has been removed and the plant is still relatively tender, cover it with a floating row cover or a light blanket for the night. Remember to remove the covering the next day, midmorning is ideal, as you don't want to overheat the plant during the day.

WATERING

Water if the season is dry. You don't want to start the season with roses stressed out from insufficient water.

If you have an automatic watering system, make sure it includes a rain sensor. Too much water is wasted watering gardens in the midst of rain storms.

FERTILIZING

Cahty remommends foliar feedings as soon as leaves appear. Get nutrition to the plant by spraying liquid fertilizer. Follow package instructions for dilution; make sure it is the right formula for foliar feeding, not watering into the soil. Foliar feed with fish emulsion or seaweed. Don't spray if the temperature is over 80 degrees Fahrenheit or if rain threatens. Wait three months before foliar feeding newly planted roses.

If you want to stick to conventional feeding, give the roses food three times during the growing season, starting now. However, if you use the Cathy's Spring

Tonic described in this chapter's "Did You Know," omit the first traditional feeding. The second feeding is when flower buds appear; the final meal comes after the first flush of bloom is over. As always, follow package instructions.

PRUNING

Prune ever-blooming shrub roses if they get too large. Simply shear the previous year's growth back by about one third. You can shear older canes to the ground.

Finish spring pruning of **hybrid teas, floribundas, grandifloras,** and **miniatures.** If you didn't get around to pruning before they leafed out, it is easier to spot the deadwood. Prune them as soon as you can; you don't want to be cutting off flower buds.

PROBLEMS

If Japanese beetles are destined to threaten our roses, be ready to nip them in the bud. The best, longest-lasting way to control them is with milky spore disease (*Bacillus popillae*). Japanese beetles overwinter in the garden and lawn in the form of grubs. In spring, they emerge transformed into beetles. Although grubs are most commonly found in lawns, they are also in the garden soil. As soon as

Helpful Hints

Cathy's Spring Tonic

Strong plants are less likely to become infested with insects or disease—it's the survival of the fittest. Give your roses a springtime boost to get them off to a good start. Do not give the tonic to newly planted roses.

2 to 3 cups compost or other well-rotted organic matter
    (leaf mold or manure)
$1/2$ cup bonemeal
$1/2$ cup bloodmeal
$1/2$ cup rock phosphate
$1/2$ cup greensand (optional)
1 cup all-purpose organic fertilizer (optional)

Sprinkle around base of each plant in a circle about a foot in diameter. Keep it several inches from the canes. Water in with a solution of 1 to 3 tablespoons of Epsom salts dissolved in 1 gallon of water. It is helpful when spreading the ingredients to alternate between a dark-color and light-color amendment. The Epsom salts help to strengthen the canes (it is also beneficial for tomato plants). Top it all off with 4 to 6 inches of organic mulch (shredded bark, cocoa hulls, ground leaves, coffee grounds, or others). After finishing this spring chore, run a warm bath, add half a cup of Epsom salts, and immerse yourself in a languid tub; it will ease away any aches from a good day's work.

the soil is workable, inoculate the soil and lawn: Put 1 teaspoon of the powder every 4 feet—making a checkerboard pattern. Water it in lightly. Milky spore infects any grubs in the soil, killing them, which releases new spores. Although it may take three years or more to establish, the bacteria can thrive in the soil without reinoculation for 25 years. However, any pesticide will kill the milky spore bacteria—all the more reason for keeping the lawn and garden organic.

For problem caterpillars, get help from another bacteria, Bt (*Bacillus thuringiensis*), available commercially from a number of companies. It comes in powder and liquid form. Spray it on the caterpillars as well as the tops and bottoms of leaves. When ingested by a caterpillar in the feeding stage, the bacteria paralyzes the digestive tract, and the caterpillar dies of starvation.

MAY
Roses

 PLANNING

Walk around the garden and take a good look at the roses. After their spring pruning and feeding, they should be looking great—healthy and vigorous, getting ready to bloom. If any aren't up to snuff, look closely to see what's wrong. Did the graft die and the rootstock has taken over? Is the plant weak and spindly? Are there signs of major pests or disease this early in the season? Decide whether it is worth the time and effort to coddle the plant. If it was a plant from grandmother's garden, do whatever needs to be done to save it. Otherwise, this is a perfect time to pull it up and replace it. If the problem was pests or disease, choose a different planting place for the replacement. Plant onions, chives, or garlic in the space.

If you buy roses at a large home and garden chain store, find out when they get their shipments of plants. Plan to go to the store that day or the next when the plants are at their best and least stressed. Some stores take good care of their plants (they have real gardeners who understand plants' needs), so they thrive despite the harsh conditions, but too many others neglect the plants once they are off the truck.

 PLANTING

The soil should be warm and dry enough to start planting **container-grown roses.** When purchasing roses, look for ones that are breaking dormancy (with leaves). Avoid those that are in bloom. Too often they are stressed from being forced into an early flowering.

 CARE

Take a breather this month and enjoy your new plantings.

If you planted garlic in the fall, cut off the flowering stems when they appear so the energy of the plant is channeled to making the bulb bigger and better. Use the stems (and flowers, broken into individual florets) in salads, marinades, or stir-fries.

 WATERING

Avoid creating the conditions that encourage blackspot. Watering at ground level early in the day gives the leaves time to dry before the cool of the evening. Problems increase if the shrubs are watered too often.

 FERTILIZING

Cathy recommends you foliar feed with fish emulsion or seaweed; follow package instructions. Don't spray if the temperature is over 80 degrees Fahrenheit or if rain threatens. Wait three months before foliar feeding newly planted roses.

 PRUNING

The major pruning should be done by now. As the plants start to bloom, cut some flowers to bring into the house and enjoy. Cutting a long stem (45-degree angle just above to the lowest out-facing five- or seven-leaflet leaf) is good for you—longer stem for arrangements— and the plant—encouraging new growth and another bloom.

 PROBLEMS

Stroll around the garden at least every other day. Stop and smell the flowers and take a good look at the leaves, stems, and blooms with an eye out for any early signs of insect or disease problems. "If it's not broken, don't fix it." Routine spaying is unnecessary unless pests or disease are seen.

When purchasing roses, look for ones that are breaking dormancy (with leaves). Avoid those that are in bloom. Too often they are stressed from being forced into an early flowering.

At the first sign of blackspot, or if it has been a problem in the past, spray with baking soda solution (see recipe in "Did You Know") as soon as the plant leafs out. The baking soda changes the pH slightly so conditions are not optimal for fungal growth. Spray the entire plant, including leaves and canes, every seven to 10 days. It will not eliminate blackspot that already exists but can keep other leaves from being affected. Remove affected leaves and clean up around plant.

Attack insect pests early, while they are young, to avoid an infestation. Insecticidal soap works well for whitefly, aphids, caterpillars of many kinds, and Japanese beetles. You can purchase the concentrate or "ready-to-spray" solution (more expensive concentrate lasts for a long time), or you can make your own (see Helpful Hints below).

Helpful Hints

Two Remedies for Blackspot on Roses

1 tablespoon baking soda
3 drops Ivory Dish Liquid
1 gallon water

or

1 tablespoon baking soda
1 teaspoon light horticultural oil
1 gallon water

Mix well.

Spray at first sign of blackspot; spraying the tops and bottoms of the leaves and stems.

Do not spray if the temperature is over 80 degrees Fahrenheit.

Soap Spray

Concentrate:

Mix equal parts of vegetable oil and Ivory Dish Liquid.

Shake well to mix. Cap and store in a cool, dry place.

Working Solution:

Mix 1 to 2 teaspoons concentrate in 1 cup of water

Or Mix 1/4 to 1/2 cup concentrate in 1 gallon of water.

Spray on affected plants, making sure to spray all surfaces. Spray early in the day, once the dew has dried. Never spray if the temperature is rising above 80 degrees Fahrenheit.

JUNE
Roses

PLANNING

Get inspired by other gardens. Visit a nearby botanic garden or arboretum where you know all the plants will be labeled correctly. Go on garden tours; walk around the neighborhood and look at other gardens. Take a notebook with you to jot down notes. Note any interesting combinations you see of roses with other flowers. Ask questions. People are flattered to have their garden admired. Offer to swap something from your garden in exchange for a cutting or division of a coveted rose companion.

PLANTING

If there are any "holes" in the garden, now is the time to fill them with roses. Give the rose a head start by soaking the container overnight in transplant solution. Take care to gently loosen or tease any roots that may be encircling the rootball.

CARE

Look for a sale on bird feeders, bird-baths, and bird food. Encourage birds to come into your garden. The sight and sound of them are mesmerizing. You can count on them to help with pest patrol. To keep birdseed from germinating, place the bird feeder on a 3 feet square area of stone, wood, cement, or other inorganic material.

If you are growing garlic in the garden, begin to harvest it when the leaves start to yellow. Choose a dry sunny day, with a three-day forecast of more of the same. Gently pull or dig the bulbs out of the ground, lay them on top of the ground for one to two days. Braid them or store the garlic in a cool, dry area. Be sure to put some bulbs away for planting in fall.

WATERING

Water weekly or as needed.

If you are going on vacation and don't have an automatic sprinkling system, your roses can still get watered. This is not the most aesthetically pleasing solu-tion, but it will keep the plants going. First, water the garden well. Take a plastic, 2-liter soda bottle and make small holes on the bottom and around the lower 2 inches of the bottle, using an awl or other sharp object. About a foot away from the crown, dig a 3-inch-deep hole wide enough to hold the bottle. Fill the bottle with water and recap it. Place it in the hole and pack the excess soil around it. That should quench any thirst for at least a week—up to two weeks in cooler temperatures.

FERTILIZING

Foliar feed with fish emulsion or sea-weed; follow package instructions. Don't spray if the temperature is over 80 degrees Fahrenheit or if rain threatens. Feed early in the day so that leaves can dry. You don't want to be setting the up for fungal problems. Start foliar feeding roses planted in March; wait on those planted more recently.

If using traditional fertilizer, give plants their second feeding when the flowers are in bud just before they open. For granular fertilizer, remove the mulch from around the plant, sprinkle the fertilizer evenly around the plant, water well, and then replace the mulch. Or you can spread fertilizer over mulch and water and rake it through the mulch and into the soil. Add more mulch if it has broken down (feeding the soil) and there is less than 3 inches left (also see "Did You Know"). If using liquid fertilizer, follow package instructions for dilution. No need to remove the mulch, just water around the plant with the diluted food.

Helpful Hints

If the weather has been warm and damp, your mulch may be turning into compost faster than you realize. Check the mulch around plants; the level may be different in various locations. If there is less than 3 inches left, you need to add more. To save money—and help the environment—use your shredded junk mail (nothing glossy, black-and-white only), the excess printed matter your computer generates each day, and black-and-white newsprint.

Attack a small area (up to 4 feet x 4 feet) at a time. Pull back the existing mulch and spread a 6-inch layer of shredded paper around and between plantings. Water it well. Cover it lightly, just so ribbons of paper do not show through, with the mulch.

PRUNING

Whether deadheading or cutting a bloom to enjoy indoors, the technique is the same as basic pruning: Make the 45-degree cut just above the lowest outward-facing branch 5 to 7 leaves down.

PROBLEMS

If blackspot persists, remove and destroy any afflicted leaves. Check the stems for spotting. If they are affected, cut them off and destroy. Clean up around the plant, picking up any dead leaves on the ground. Spray the entire plant, including leaves and canes, every seven to 10 days with baking soda solution.

If you are gardening without chemicals, remember that everything does not have to look picture perfect. If you see a few caterpillars, beetles, cabbage moths, or other pests, you need to decide your tolerance level. Not every pest is bad. Armed with your insect book, decide if removal or treatment is necessary. First, identify the pest and find out what they will evolve into—some caterpillars turn into monarchs, other beautiful butterflies, or moths.

Many caterpillars are easily handpicked and can be disposed of in a zippered plastic bag. Japanese beetles are also easily handpicked, especially early in the morning as they are late risers. If you're squeamish, gently shake the assaulted flower into a zippered bag. Early in the day, the beetles will just drop off. Some gardeners garner great satisfaction from squashing them.

JULY
Roses

PLANNING

On a hot day, plan a trip to the cool, air-conditioned library. Flip through the latest gardening magazines and books for new ideas: style, design, plant combinations, new plants, and using all or part of the garden as an extension of the house—a summer living room.

PLANTING

If you want to move roses or other plants around in the garden, this is not the ideal time, but it can be done now. First prepare the new planting area. Dig it out, add soil amendments, mix well, and replace soil in ground. Water it well with transplant solution so the entire area is lightly moist at least a foot down and give the plants you plan to move a good drink as well. Planting and transplanting is best done in the late afternoon when the sun is getting low in the sky or anytime on an overcast day. Dig up and move the plants, settle them in, and water once more with transplant solution.

CARE

If the weather is scorching hot, make a tent of Reemay or lightweight white fabric to lessen the transplant shock for new plantings. Don't pin it to the ground; raise it up so air can move between the plants.

WATERING

Even with a good layer of mulch, roses will need more water if the temperature reaches the three-digit mark. Take extra care with new plantings.

FERTILIZING

Cathy suggests that you foliar feed with fish emulsion or seaweed; follow package instructions. Don't spray if the temperature is over 80 degrees Fahrenheit or if rain threatens. Feed early in the day so that leaves can dry; you don't want to be setting the up for fungal problems. Start foliar feeding new roses planted in April; wait on those planted more recently.

If using traditional fertilizer, give plants their final feeding now, after they have finished their first bloom. If you mulched at the time of the last feeding, just sprinkle granular fertilizer around the base of the plant and water it in well. If you didn't mulch, you may remove the mulch from around the plant, sprinkle the fertilizer evenly around the plant, water well, and then replace the mulch. Or you can sprinkle it on top of the mulch, and water and rake it through the mulch. Add more mulch if it has broken down into compost and there is less than 3 inches left. If using liquid fertilizer, follow package instructions for dilution. No need to remove the mulch, just water around the plant with the diluted food.

PRUNING

Since **climbers** bloom on old wood (the previously year's growth), do any hard pruning as soon as the first flush of bloom has finished. Prune to keep it in bounds or train the canes. Remove any weak canes, cutting them all the way down to the base of the plant. Allow the sturdiest two or three canes to continue growing as they are, doing light cosmetic pruning only.

Keep up with deadheading **miniatures, grandifloras, hybrid teas,** and **shrub roses.** To extend the beauty of **floribundas,** which bloom in a cluster, remove the largest, central flower while it is still in bud and let the surrounding blooms show their profusion.

PROBLEMS

If blackspot persists, remove and replace the mulch; spores may have lodged in it. Continue to spray the entire plant, including leaves and canes, every seven to 10 days with baking soda solution. Remove affected leaves. If you end up with a leafless scarecrow, you have two choices: If blackspot has been a persistent problem (more than one year), dig up the rose and toss it in the garbage. Otherwise, you can plan on doing the spray routine every year. Get rid of the soil as well, since it is probably contaminated. Never add diseased plants to the compost pile. If it's a new plant, an existing plant that never had blackspot before, or an heirloom or rare rose that you feel you must save, give it a severe pruning. Cut it back to 12 to 16 inches tall. Now you are taking advantage of the

fact that each bud can produce three sets of leaves or branches over time.

The inconsistency of our weather can wreak havoc in the garden—and create the ideal conditions for some pests. Keep an eye out for aphids, small insects (green, black, brown, or orange in color) that suck the juice out of buds, stems, and leaves. Before you do anything, be

Helpful Hints

Roses, especially **miniatures,** make great container plants. Grow them alone or combine them with other plants, such as **Wave™ petunia, blue lobelia, peach alyssum,** or even **lettuce.** Choose a mate that offsets the shape and form of the rose; a trailing plant does that well.

In the heat of summer, a container can easily dry out despite daily watering. If it does dry out, water it with a solution made of three drops of Ivory Dish Liquid in a quart of tepid (not ice-cold) water. If you can, put the container in a pan of the liquid so it can hydrate from top and bottom. Slowly water the soil with the soap solution over a period of a few days. The soap allows the water to stick to the soil rather than running through it.

sure that you know what you have. Once identified, try hosing them off the plant(s) with a strong stream of water. Repeat every other day for a week. If they persist, squirt them with insecticidal soap. (See page 241 for directions on how to make your own). It is available commercially as a concentrate or in a ready-to-use squirt bottle.

AUGUST
Roses

PLANNING

If the roses aren't as perky as they were earlier in the season, you might want to add some pizzazz in the form of autumn-blooming bulbs. Order **autumn crocus** (*Colchicum autumnale*) bulbs now and plant them as soon as you they arrive. Keep one and put it on a sunny windowsill. It will bloom in a few weeks, without water, soil, or food, sending up clusters of pale lavender crocus-like flowers. The ones in the garden will bloom quickly and last longer. They'll add a bright color accent near ground level. Mark their spot so you don't plant over them. In spring the leaves emerge rich green, broad, and growing about a foot high. Even the leaves are ephemeral; they'll disappear within six weeks, and there will be no sign of the plant until the leafless flowers arise in late summer.

PLANTING

Even though nurseries and plant growers are touting "Fall is for Planting," August is the cut-off for planting **container-grown roses.** (**Bare-root roses** are generally available only in late winter and early spring, while the plants are still dormant.) Some nurseries, home and garden stores, and garden centers may have special sales. If you find a "must-have" rose that's a bargain price, get it—unless there is any indication of pests or disease (check under leaves and on stems). Although it is probably stressed, an overnight soak in transplant solution before planting should re-energize it. Loosen any packed roots. Remember that the bud union needs to be under at least 2 inches of soil.

CARE

For a spectacular cutflower finale, disbud some of the **hybrid tea** and **grandiflora roses.** Remove all but one (the biggest and sturdiest looking) flower bud on each stem soon after the flower buds appear. By doing this, you are guaranteed long-stemmed roses elegant enough to please a queen. Instead of expending energy on multiple flowers, the plants' resources are channeled into the single flowers. The result is a larger, more robust flower.

WATERING

Continue to be vigilant about watering.

The measurements in a rain gauge may be misleading. An inch of more of rain might fall during a severe weather event, such as thunderstorms, hail, and tornado threats. However, it falls so fast and furious that none of the water is absorbed into the soil; it all runs off. When in doubt, stick your finger in the soil to feel the moisture—or lack thereof.

FERTILIZING

Continue Cathy's monthly foliar feeding schedule. Remember: Don't spray if the temperature is over 80 degrees Fahrenheit or if rain threatens. Feed roses planted in May. Roses planted after May don't need any supplemental feeding until next spring.

For a spectacular cutflower finale, disbud some of the hybrid tea and grandiflora roses. Remove all but one (the biggest and sturdiest looking) flower bud on each stem soon after the flower buds appear.

Do not fertilize any roses after August 15th. You don't want to encourage new growth that won't have time to harden off before the temperatures drop to freezing and below.

PRUNING

Last call for pruning this season. August 15th is the cutoff date in Hardiness Zones 5 and 6. For each subsequent zone (moving down the scale to colder), subtract one week from the August 15th date to determine the last pruning date for your area. Remember to factor in your microclimates, colder or warmer, for the most accurate gauge of time.

# PROBLEMS

Continue to control blackspot by spraying the entire plant, including leaves and canes, every seven to 10 days with a baking soda solution. Take a hard look at the plant(s) you have had to treat all season. Is it worth it? Blackspot can also be a product of the weather. A summer that is warm, cloudy, and humid sets the perfect stage for blackspot and other fungi. If many of your roses that had been healthy in years past suddenly have blackspot one year, look to the weather as a causative factor. Don't rush to pull out the entire garden.

Helpful Hints

Enjoy the Garden at Night

Put out a comfortable chair or bench facing or in the garden. It can take up to 15 minutes for your eyes to adjust to the darkness on a moonlit night. As you are sitting, be aware of the sights, sounds, and smells of evening. White roses, such as **'White Lightnin'** and **'John F. Kennedy'** appear to float in midair. You can't see dark colors at night, so green stems and leaves seem to vanish. Pale colors, such as the pinks of **'Queen Elizabeth'** and **'Peace'**, stand out well. Notice that some roses are more fragrant at night (that can vary due to temperature and humidity). **'White Lightnin'** and **'Mirandy'** perfume the air around them. As you sit and relax, you might hear the whirr of a sphinx moth (it looks more like a brown hummingbird than a moth) or catch a glimpse of the elusive, exquisite Luna moth.

Organizing Your Tools

After sharpening your hand pruners and other cutting tools, consider painting the handles of each the same bright color. Not only will this help you to see them in the garden, it enables you to find the necessary tools easily. If you have a new garden assistant, he/she can quickly help you if you ask for the purple-handled tools instead of naming and describing each one. Take this a step further, and paint all the handles in a color code. Group the tools in the way that is most logical to you. For instance all the digging tools together, lawn tools, hand tools, etc. If all the tools have brightly colored handles, you'll never lose another pair of pruners, a trowel or hand fork in the garden again. It may cut down on accidents, too; hopefully you'll see the rake's bright handle before you step on the tines, causing the handle to knock you in the head.

SEPTEMBER

 PLANNING

Create a new garden just for cutting. There are other flowers you may want to include as well. In preparation for the spring and planting, take advantage of the long cold winter to do much of the work for you. Cathy likes to make a no-dig bed. Mark out the garden in chalk or flour (if it's on existing lawn). Water well. Put down three layers of cardboard over the entire garden, moistening each piece as you lay it down. Add about a dozen pages of black-and-white newspaper, wetting them as well. Cover that with a 2- to 3-inch layer of peat moss; water it. Continue watering as you add each subsequent 2- to 3-inch layer: compost, peat moss, shredded leaves, peat moss, if you have any red wiggler worms, put them in between these two layers (don't water the worms), shredded paper (junk mail, black-and-white computer printouts), well-rotted manure (direct from the farm or bagged), peat moss, partially decomposed compost, and peat moss, decomposed, bread, egg shells, coffee grounds, and tea bags. No oily food or animal products, no human or pet waste (farm animals are okay), and more shredded leaves as they fall. To keep it from blowing and hasten the decomposition, you can throw a black tarp over the whole thing. By spring, this will have shrunk drastically in height, but what remains is a thick layer of rich soil—perfect for roses.

 PLANTING

The time for rose planting has passed. There's time to plant some companion plants, however, especially minor spring-blooming bulbs such as **glory-of-the-snow, Siberian squill, crocus, grape hyacinth, miniature daffodils,** and **snowdrops.** These will add color interest before the roses leaf out and bloom. More important, they will not take necessary nutrients away from the roses.

 CARE

Unless you are growing only the hardy **floribunda, species,** and **shrub roses**—especially any **Griffith Buck** hybrids or the any of the roses in the **Canadian Explorer** and **Brownell Subzero series,** it's time to think about winter protection. After the ground lightly freezes, mound up 4 to 6 inches of light soil around established **hybrid tea** and **grandiflora roses.** After the first hard frost, when that layer freezes, add another few inches of soil, allowing each layer to freeze before adding another.

If you prefer to use the Styrofoam or plastic "cones" around your roses, be sure to use the ones that have either a removable top or no top. This allows you to vent the roses on warm days. When the night is chilly, recover the cone. If you cannot vent the cone, you can all too easily roast the roses when the mercury climbs for several days. If you can mound dry shredded leaves all around the rose and place the cone over it, the leaves would help stabilize the temperature inside.

If you are still considering the cone, look at its height. To fit a rose inside, you would have to give it a major pruning—not a good idea at this time of year. In addition to the pruning stimulating new growth, so would the warmth inside the cone. There is no room for new growth.

An alternative is a rose collar. It is a large rectangular piece of green plastic with vent holes cut into it. Stand it up and it can encircle a rose. You can put shredded leaves inside the collar, but they will get wet (there is no "top"), freeze, and thaw. The best protection is mounded soil, frozen in layers—and it's free.

 WATERING

Even though many of your garden tasks are done for the season, do not neglect watering.

After the first hard frost, when that layer freezes, add another few inches of soil, allowing each layer to freeze before adding another.

Does your rain gauge have the capacity for measuring snow? If not, you can always use an old-fashioned yardstick to measure the depth.

 # FERTILIZING

No need to fertilize.

If you eat bananas, which are high in potassium, bury the peels around your roses. Over time they will break down and turn into rich organic matter. The added potassium strengthens the canes. Dig in banana peels any time of year that the ground isn't frozen. To keep from planting the bananas in the same place twice, start with one rose (front, back, side of garden). Bury up to six peels, staggering them to make a circle at least 1 foot out from the base of the rose. Then move on to the next rose. By the time you bury the last peel by the last bush, those around the first will be well composted, and you can start all over again.

Helpful Hints

Rose Hips

If the birds have not gotten to them, pick the large colorful hips (the fruit) from species roses like *Rosa rugosa* and its cultivars. You can make rose hip jelly, simply by boiling the hips in fresh apple cider for about an hour. Process the mixture in a blender or food processor. Strain it through a sieve. Follow your favorite jelly recipe, using the strained "hip juice." You can cut the sugar at least by half. You'll need less pectin, as the cider is a good source. Start your day with a slice of toast slathered with rose hip jelly for more vitamin C than in a glass of orange juice. If you have used systemics or other chemicals, do not eat the hips.

 # PRUNING

Pruning is finished for the year except for cutting off any storm or wind damage.

Keep the Japanese handsaw, loppers and pruners sharp. Put them in a basket, bucket or other container with sturdy gloves so you don't have to be hunting down tools and gloves out of season.

 # PROBLEMS

Continue to control blackspot by spraying the entire plant, including leaves and canes, every seven to 10 days with baking soda solution. This should be the last month of spraying.

Clean up leaves as they fall. Oak leaves in particular mat together when wet, not allowing water to get through them. Run dry leaves through a shredder and use them for winter mulch, add them to the compost pile, or make a leaf mold pile (leaves will disintegrate in about a year).

Save money by sharing. A group of neighbors can jointly own pieces of more expensive garden equipment—shredder, blower, tiller, snow plow, sometimes even mulching mowers. It is rare that two people want to use the machinery at the same time. Instead of joint ownership, each person could own a single piece of equipment with the agreement to share with all.

OCTOBER
Roses

PLANNING

Catch up on your master list before the snow flies in and buries the roses. Add any notes and comments you may have about specific roses. If you have chronicled the garden in photographs, be sure to caption them while it's still fresh in your memory. Include date of photo, plant names, and area of the garden (if it's a close-up shot rather than an overview).

PLANTING

Plant some helpers that will strengthen your garden the following season. Garlic, for example, deters many garden pests. If you have planted bulbs, garlic will help keep the squirrels from digging up the newly planted bulbs and storing them for a midwinter snack. Break the garlic bulb apart. With the pointed end up, push the clove into the ground so the top is at least an inch below soil level. Plant the cloves at least 6 inches apart. Water well.

CARE

Top off soil mounds around the roses at about a foot. It may look strange—a broad cone of soil with rose canes sticking up. In Zone 4 and below (and for any success with **hybrid teas**), cover the frozen mound with leaves. Cover any new plant completely or the extreme cold will kill the tender canes. If you live in an area with little winter snow cover, add 6 inches of mulch (shredded leaves are good) around the roses to reduce the freeze/heave cycle that can damage the plants. It doesn't hurt to mulch hardy roses, such as the **Canadian Explorer** and **Griffith Buck roses,** in Zones 4 and colder that has relatively dry winters,

WATERING

Until the ground freezes, continue watering if there is insufficient rainfall.

If you had any sort of drip or leaky hose irrigation system and the layout worked well, photograph or make a rough sketch of the placement. Pull back the mulch so you can see the system. This will save time and aggravation next spring. Blow all the water out of the pipes and hoses. Take a large box along with you to the garden to hold all of the many pieces of the drip irrigation, so you don't risk accidentally leaving some attachment or emitter on the ground. Start at one end of the drip system and remove sections (as large as can easily fit into the box) one at a time. Wrap a piece of tape around each section and loop it over itself so it makes a tab label that won't come off the plastic while it's in winter storage. Number each section sequentially using a waterproof marker. Move mulch back into place. Once you and the box are back in the house, get another box and replace the sections into it so that come spring, tube or pipe #1 is on the top, covered by the map of the layout, and you are ready to go.

FERTILIZING

Don't feed your roses until next spring.

PRUNING

No scheduled pruning this month; clean up and prune any branches broken in storms or hurt by animals.

PROBLEMS

If you haven't already done so, remove and discard all mulch and fallen leaves within a 2- to 3-foot radius of any diseased rose. Pick any remaining leaves off the plant and destroy them as well as the old mulch. If your town has a recycling project, avoid sending any diseased or pest-infested plant material to them. You wouldn't want to be bringing diseases and pests into the garden when you get free compost or mulch. Instead, throw the tainted material in a large black plastic bag and add it to your regular garbage.

NOVEMBER

Roses

PLANNING

Take some time before the craziness of the holidays to read over your master list. Start thinking about next year's garden. Don't write it down yet; just visualize it as it will be with new additions, subtractions, multiplications, and divisions. As life gets more hectic with the approaching end-of-year celebrations, take a moment or two to bring your new garden scheme to mind. Feel free to edit it at any time; it's your garden and your fantasy.

PLANTING

Plant some small bulbs before the ground freezes. Put in the last of the fall **pansies**. Surprisingly, if you keep them deadheaded, they will keep blooming right through winter, spring and on into next summer. Whenever the snow or ice melts and the sun shines on them, the plants will grace you with one or two flowers—hardly a bouquet, but the bright face is sure to put a smile on yours. As the weather warms, **pansies** produce more blooms.

CARE

In case of a heavy, wet snow, gently brush the snow off exposed branches and canes, especially on **climbers** and any tall roses

Helpful Hints

• Does the garden look too bleak and barren? Plant a few well-placed **silk flowers;** they are amazingly durable. **Freesias** and **forsythia** add bright highlights. Choose flowers with height so they are covered after the first snow.

• Holiday decorations can extend beyond the house. Create a winter fairyland with strings of white fairy lights draped in and around the roses. Imagine the rose arbor or trellis all aglow. Hang small (1-inch) glass ornaments from canes or branches more than 1/2 inch in diameter. Drape sparkling garlands on the shrubs. Wherever you decorate, be sure you can see it from inside so you can relax in a comfortable chair and enjoy the fantasy of the garden in winter.

using a soft broom. Get out and brush it before too much accumulates, or you risk both broken canes and supports. However, don't try to remove frozen snow; this could cause greater damage.

WATERING

Keep watering, 1 inch weekly as rain or from your hose or watering can.

Drain water from all hoses, coil them, and move them inside to a cool (not below freezing) dry storage space.

Shut off the valves to outside water spigots. You can put a Styrofoam form around the spigot and knob to protect it from freezing, a good idea if you water during the winter.

FERTILIZING

No fertilizing is necessary until spring.

PRUNING

Keep an eye out for any storm damage. Prune it off as soon as you can, especially if it is not completely severed. Even if it is broken off, keep disease and water away by making a smooth, neat cut below the break. Look closely and you can see dark-colored dots that will develop into buds in spring and eventually become leaves or branches. Make the 45-degree cut just above an outward-facing dot.

PROBLEMS

If a **climber** breaks free of its support, tie it back with an old pair of pantyhose. Not the most aesthetically pleasing look, but pantyhose provide more support than a narrow piece of string or a twist-tie. In addition, they give and stretch so you don't have to worry about the cane being girdled.

DECEMBER

 PLANNING

You encouraged birds in your garden during the growing year, don't abandon them now. Get a heater for the birdbath to keep it from freezing over. Birds always need fresh water. Plan on giving them some holiday treats. Tie half a bagel to a string, cover it with peanut butter and hang it nearby.

Other "tweet" treats to hang include a pine cone rolled in a mixture of peanut butter and birdseed or suet mixed with birdseed, raisins, or other small pieces of dried fruit. Melt the suet slowly in a saucepan over low heat, add the birdseed, fruit or nuts (or a mixture of all). Stir well. As it cools, form it into whatever shape you want, either freehand or using an ice-cream or chocolate mold for form.

 PLANTING

Although it is too late in the season to plant roses, it's the perfect time plant the idea by giving roses as gifts to friends and family. Order a **miniature rose** (usually packaged in a cute container) for immediate pleasure, or give a gift certificate to a nursery, mail-order or online rose company. Make the certificate "good for one rose" rather than a dollar amount if you can. If there is a special rose that you know they want or that you want them to have, make the certificate specific "good for one 'Prairie Princess' rose," for example.

An alternative is fresh or dried roses. As elegant as fresh roses can be, they won't last long. Consider an arrangement of dried roses in a special container, a dried wreath with roses to hang indoors, or a pot or hanging sachet of dried rose buds. If you're creative and handy with a glue gun, you can make this yourself. Otherwise, you will find rose gifts in many of the plant and catalogs that are filling your mailbox.

 CARE

If there hasn't been a freeze yet, begin to mound soil around tender roses. The freeze will not be gradual; if it has waited this long, it will be fast and furious.

Take care of yourself. Indulge in something rose: a long soak in a bath with rose salts or rose bubble bath, a massage with rose oil. Get a spray bottle of rose water; a spritz on your face is relaxing and invigorating at the same time. You'll enjoy the rose water year-round. In summer keep it in the refrigerator for a cooling mist.

 WATERING

If the soil is dry, water it.

 FERTILIZING

Don't worry about fertilizers until spring.

 PRUNING

If snow or ice damages tree limbs, prune them back as soon as you can. If you need to cut back to the main cane, graft or root, leave about an inch of cane to allow the cut to heal properly.

 PROBLEMS

Ask Santa for a good insect identification book. Tell him you want a book that shows both the good bugs and the bad bugs in all their life stages. After reading this book during the rest of the winter, you'll be somewhat familiar with the most likely candidates to visit or take up residence in your garden in the upcoming seasons and will be able to make informed decision about if and how you want to deal with them.

CHAPTER NINE

Shrubs

Many people confuse a tree with a shrub. One of the easiest ways to tell the difference is that most have a multiple main stems, while a tree has a single trunk. Another differentiation is size. A shrub is generally less than 20 feet tall, while a tree is over 20 feet.

As with trees, there are evergreen and deciduous shrubs. Variety is the spice of life and adds life to the garden, so include both types in the garden. When choosing a deciduous shrub, it is a bonus if it has an interesting or unique architectural form that will lend draw the eye in winter when there is less in the typical garden or landscape. One of Melinda's favorite plants, Harry Lauder's walking stick, has such marvelous twisted branches that it looks better in winter than in summer when they are hidden by the leaves.

Think of shrubs as the icing on the cake in the garden. They can accentuate and highlight the other plantings, especially perennials and trees. Shrubs tie the garden together.

Unfortunately, shrubs have long been shoved up against home foundations or strung out along the lot line. Consider expanding the use of shrubs in your landscape. Look for opportunities and spaces that could use the facelift shrubs can provide.

- Mix both deciduous and evergreen shrubs with perennials to create year-round interest.

- Use single plantings as specimens and focal points in the garden.

- Strategically plant large shrubs for screening a bad view.

- Add low-growing shrubs to areas around trees to create attractive and healthy planting beds.

- Increase the year-round interest in the landscape by including shrubs with colorful flowers, fruit, and bark.

- Attract birds and butterflies by planting shrubs that provide food and shelter.

PLANNING

Now that you see the possibilities, break out the landscape plan. Select the shrubs that are best suited to the growing conditions and your design goals. Proper planning will give you an attractive landscape with a lot less work.

Evaluate the light, soil, wind, and other environmental factors that affect plant growth. Plant shrubs suited to the growing conditions. Use raised planting beds to improve drainage in poorly drained soils.

Measure the area. Make sure the plants will still fit once they reach full size. Choose a shrub with a mature height of three feet rather than one that has a mature height of twenty feet that requires pruning twice a year to keep it in bounds.

Consider the ornamental value of the shrubs selected. Include evergreens for year-round foliage, **lilacs** and other flowering shrubs for an added splash of color, or plants such as **red twig dogwoods** with decorative bark that adds winter interest.

Match your gardening style with the plant's maintenance requirements. Minimize your workload by planting drought-tolerant and pest-resistant shrubs. Avoid fast-growing shrubs that will grow too large for the location and require frequent pruning.

PURCHASING

Once the plan is complete, you are ready for the trip to the nursery, home store, or garden center.

Shrubs

Hook up the trailer or clear out the trunk to make room for your purchases. Throw a couple of tarps in the car. Use them to protect the seats and carpet in your vehicle or to cover leafed-out shrubs transported in the open air of a pickup truck or trailer.

Purchase healthy plants free of damaged stems, discolored or brown leaves, or other signs of pests and stress. Avoid unhealthy bargain plants that can end up costing you more money and time when they need replacing.

Planting

The planting process starts with a call to your utility-locating service. These free services mark the location of all underground utilities. Working with utility-locating services can prevent costly damage to underground utilities and may save your life.

Most shrubs are sold in containers. The majority of these are grown in the container, but others are dug out of the field and placed in the container. We will call these potted plants. The remainder, mostly evergreens and a few select flowering shrubs, are sold as balled-and-burlapped plants.

All types of shrubs benefit from proper planting.

1 Adjust planting locations to avoid conflicts with both underground and overhead utilities.

2 Dig a hole that is the same as or slightly shallower than the depth of the rootball. Make it at least two times as wide as the roots. See shrub planting illustrations.

3 Roughen the sides of the planting hole to avoid glazing. Smooth-sided holes prevent roots from growing out of the planting hole and into the surrounding soil. Use your shovel or garden fork to nick or scratch the sides of the planting hole.

4 Remove the plant from container. Potted plants need special care since their root systems may not be well established in the container. Minimize root disturbance by using this technique: Cut off the bottom of the pot and place it in the planting hole. Slice the pot lengthwise and peel it away.

5 Loosen the roots of potbound container-grown shrubs. Use a sharp knife to slice through the rootball. Make several shallow slices (running top to bottom of the rootball) through the surface of the roots to encourage roots to grow out into the surrounding soil.

Use a similar technique with balled-and-burlapped plants.

1 Place the shrub in the hole. Remove the twine and peel back the burlap. Cut away the fabric.

2 Fill the hole with the existing soil. Use water, not your foot or a heavy tool, to settle the soil.

3 Water the planting hole and surrounding soil with transplant solution. Cover the soil surface with shredded bark or woodchips to conserve moisture, insulate roots, and reduce weeds.

To care for your new plantings:

Check new plantings once or twice a week. Water shrubs in clay soil every seven to ten days. Those growing in sandy soils should be checked twice a week. Water when the top 6 inches begin to dry. Water thoroughly enough to moisten the top 12 inches of soil.

Container plants grown in soil-less mixes need special attention; potting mixes dry out faster than the surrounding soil. Keep the root system moist, but take care not to overwater the surrounding soil.

Wait until next year to fertilize new plantings. Fertilizer can damage the young tender roots and interfere with the plant getting established.

Shrubs

Remove only the branches damaged in the transport and planting process. The more branches left on the plant, the more leaves will be formed and the more energy will be produced for the plant.

Add the plant name to your landscape plan. Enter the planting information in your journal. Include the plant name, place of purchase, and planting date.

PRUNING

No other gardening chore evokes such a wide range of emotions as pruning. Feelings range from pruning paranoia (fear of killing or maiming the plant) to visions of a chainsaw massacre. Before breaking out the tools, make sure there is a reason to prune.

Prune to maintain size, improve flowering and fruiting and bark color, or remove damaged or disease branches. When and how you prune are equally important.

Prune spring-flowering shrubs, such as **lilacs** and **forsythia**, in spring right after flowering. Spring bloomers flower on the previous season's growth. Pruning in late summer or winter cuts off the flower buds and eliminates the spring display.

Trim summer-blooming plants during the dormant season. **hills-of-snow hydrangeas**, **potentilla**, and summer-blooming **spireas** flower on the current season's growth.

Remove dead, damaged, or disease-infected branches whenever they are found. Disinfect tools between cuts to prevent the spread of disease. Use rubbing alcohol or a solution of one part bleach to nine parts water as a disinfectant.

The "how" of pruning is a little trickier. Match the type of pruning to the plant and your landscape goals. Some plants, such as **cotoneasters** and **barberries**, need very little pruning, while **forsythias** and common **lilacs** need regular attention. Use thinning cuts and renewal pruning to contain plant size while maintaining the plant's natural appearance. Shearing transforms shrubs into rectangular hedges or spheres of green, (sometimes called meatballs and lollipops for their unnatural shapes that need continuous pruning) is less healthy for shrubs than letting them grow in their natural form. Choose the right form and shape before you buy the plant.

Where you make the pruning cut is equally important. Prune on a slight angle above a healthy bud, where one branch joins another, or where a branch joins the trunk. These cuts

close quickly and reduce the risk of insects and disease entering the plant. No need for paint or glue on the wounds—they can be more problematic than helpful.

The location of the pruning cut also influences the plant's appearance and future growth.

Use thinning cuts to open up the plant and reduce the size while maintaining its natural appearance. Prune off branches where they join the main stem or another branch. Thinning cuts allow air and light to penetrate the plant improving flowering, fruiting, and bark color. It also helps reduce some disease problems.

Use heading cuts to reduce the height and spread of shrubs. Limit the number and vary the location of heading cuts to maintain the plant's natural appearance. Prune branches back to a shorter side shoot or above a healthy bud. Excessive heading can lead to a tuft of growth at the end of a long, bare stem.

Reserve shearing for only the most formal settings. This technique is easy on the gardener but hard on the plant. Shearing makes indiscriminant cuts, leaving stubs that make perfect entryways for insects and disease. Prune so that the bottom of the plant is wider than the top. This allows light to reach

Shrubs

all parts, top to the bottom, of the plant.

Use renewal pruning to manage overgrown shrubs, contain growth, and stimulate new, healthy, and more attractive stems. Start by removing one-third of the older (larger) canes to ground level. Reduce the height of the remaining stems by one-third if needed. Repeat the process the next two years for overgrown shrubs. By the end of the third year, the shrub will be smaller, more attractive, and healthier. Continue to remove older canes as needed throughout the life of the shrubs.

Use rejuvenation pruning to manage the size of some fast-growing and overgrown shrubs. Make sure the plant will tolerate this severe pruning. Cut all stems back to 4 inches above the soil line during the dormant season. Late winter through early spring before growth begins is the best time. The plant will soon begin to grow and recover.

See April "Helpful Hints" on page 269 for specific pruning recommendations.

FERTILIZING

Shrubs receive most of their nutrients from fertilizers applied to nearby plantings and lawn areas. Organic mulches also add small amounts of nutrients as they decompose.

Start with a soil test to determine if fertilizer is needed. The soil test report will indicate what type and how much fertilizer you will need. See "General Horticultural Practices" in the general introduction for details on soil testing.

Apply needed fertilizer in the spring for best results. Stop fertilization by midsummer. Late-season fertilization can stimulate late-season growth that may be winterkilled.

Use a fertilizer higher in nitrogen, such as 21-0-0, at a rate of 1 to 2 pounds per 100 square feet of planting area. Two cups of synthetic inorganic fertilizer is equal to about 1 pound. Consider using a slow-release fertilizer to reduce the risk of burn and provide a more even fertilization over a longer period of time.

Spread the fertilizer on the soil surface. Keep the fertilizer off the shrubs. Rake the fertilizer into the soil surface and water well. Fertilizer can be applied over organic mulch and raked into the soil below.

Overfertilization can lead to rapid growth and increased pruning frequency. Young plants can be fertilized every few years to encourage rapid growth. Heavily mulched plantings benefit from additional nitrogen. Reduce or eliminate fertilizer applications on mature shrubs to limit plant growth.

PESTS

Pest control starts by selecting the right plant for the growing conditions. Healthy plants are more resistant to insects and disease.

Select plants hardy to your growing conditions. Plants that tolerate the temperature extremes of winter and summer will be less stressed and more able to withstand pest attacks.

Purchase and plant healthy, high-quality shrubs. Bargain plants are often not suited for the climate, stressed from improper care, or come with pest problems.

Provide plants with proper care and check frequently for pest problems.

Shrubs

When problems occur, consult your local Extension Service for proper diagnosis and control options. See monthly "Pests" and July "Helpful Hints" for details on specific pest and their controls.

PRUNING POINTERS

Get the greatest ornamental value from your shrubs through proper pruning. Match the pruning method to the shrub for increased flowering, improved bark color, and maintenance of its natural form. See April "Helpful Hints" on page 269 for details on pruning evergreen shrubs.

Barberry (*Berberis* spp.) and **cotoneaster** (*Cotoneaster* spp.) are generally slow growing. Remove only damaged and diseased stems to ground level in spring before growth begins.

Blue Mist Spirea (*Caryopteris* x *clandonensis* 'Blue Mist') is marginally hardy and usually dies back to the ground over winter. Cut the plant back to several Inches above the soil in late winter.

Burning bush (*Euonymus alatus*) needs minimal pruning, which can be done during the dormant season. Selectively remove vigorous growth to major side branches to maintain the desired size and shape. Do not use renewal or rejuvenation pruning on this single-stemmed shrub.

Butterfly bush (*Buddleja davidii*) usually dies back over winter. Prune back to 3 to 4 inches above the soil in late winter or early spring before growth begins.

Dogwoods (*Cornus* spp.) can be pruned during the dormant season. Remove old and discolored stems of the suckering type to ground level.

Wait for **cornelian cherry dogwood** to blossom before pruning. Pruning will depend on the desired form.

Forsythia (*Forsythia* spp.) flowers on the previous year's growth. Wait until after flowering to prune. Finish pruning by early June so that the plant has time to set flower buds for next spring's display. Remove three-year and older stems to ground level.

Honeysuckles (*Lonicera* spp.) are tough shrubs that can take severe pruning. Consider removing invasive species from the landscape. Renewal prune (remove one-third of the older stems to ground level) others to encourage new growth at the base of the plant. These tough shrubs will tolerate rejuvenation pruning back to several inches above ground level. Prune during the dormant season.

Hydrangea (*Hydrangea* spp.), **hills-of-snow, annabelle**, and other snowball types of **hydrangea** should be pruned back to ground level each winter. Wait until late winter if you want to enjoy the dried flowers in the winter landscape. **PeeGee hydrangeas** are often trained into small trees or specimen plants. Regular pruning is not needed but can improve flowering. Prune the plant to the desired shape. Yearly pruning cuts can be made back to the first set of healthy buds above this framework.

The **juneberry** or **serviceberry** (*Amelanchier* spp.) can be trained as multistemmed large shrubs or small trees. Do minimal pruning once the main stems are selected. Prune suckering types of **juneberries** the same way you prune **forsythia** and **dogwoods**. Remove one-third of the older stems to ground level. Prune in late winter or just after spring bloom.

Lilacs (*Syringa* spp.) bloom on old wood and should be pruned after flowering. Remove old flowers after bloom to increase next year's floral display. Prune one-third of the older canes back to ground level to encourage fuller growth at the base of the plant.

Potentilla (Shrubby Cinquefoil) (*Potentilla fruticosa*) are summer-blooming shrubs that can be pruned anytime during the dormant season. Prune plants back halfway, then

Shrubs

remove the older stems to ground level. Or prune the whole plant back to several inches above the soil line. The plant will recover but tend to be a little floppier with this technique.

Rose-of-Sharon (*Hibiscus syriacus*) is best pruned in late spring. Remove dead branches and prune out dead tips to healthy buds or side shoots. Do very little additional pruning to established plants.

Spireas (*Spiraea* spp.) are divided into spring and summer blooming types. Spring-flowering **Bridal Wreath or Vanhouttei Spirea** should be pruned right after spring bloom. Remove flowering tips to improve next year's bloom. Remove one-fourth of the older stems to ground level on established plants. Older, overgrown plants may be slow to respond to rejuvenation pruning. Prune **Anthony waterer** and **Japanese** and other summer-flowering varieties anytime during the dormant season. Wait until late winter if you want to enjoy the winter interest provided by the chestnut brown stems and dried flowers. Prune these the same as **potentilla**.

Viburnums (*Viburnum* spp.) grow at different rates. Slow-growing species need very little pruning. Remove old, damaged, and unproductive branches to ground level.

SHARING SHRUBS

Gardeners love to share special plants with friends and relatives. Tip cuttings, layering, and division can be used to pass along a piece of that special plant.

Try propagating **lilacs**, **forsythia**, **weigela**, and other shrubs by the tip cutting method.

1 Gather all the materials needed. This includes a sharp knife or hand pruners, small containers, well-drained potting mix, sand or vermiculite, and a rooting hormone for woody plants.

2 Remove several 6 to 8 inch pieces from the tips of the stems. Remove the lowest set of leaves. Dip the cut end in a rooting hormone for woody plants. Stick one or more cuttings into a pot filled with a well-drained potting mix, sand, or vermiculite.

3 Store the cuttings in a shaded location. Group it with other plants or place under trees or shrubs to increase humidity. Keep the rooting medium moist.

4 Transplant rooted cuttings as soon as the roots develop. Plant in a container filled with a well-drained soil. Check soil moisture daily and water as needed. These will be ready for planting next spring.

Try layering shrubs with long, pliable stems.

See May "Helpful Hints" in the Vines and Groundcovers chapter on page 331 for step-by-step directions.

Dig and divide rooted suckers to start new plants. **dogwoods** and other suckering shrubs send out shoots.

1 Carefully remove the soil at the base of the sucker to see if it has roots.

2 Use a sharp spade to disconnect the sucker from the parents. Some gardeners prefer to leave it in place to develop a stronger root system. Others divide, dig, and transplant immediately. For greatest success, try this in early spring before growth begins.

Shrubs

Common Name (Botanical Name)	Hardiness Zone	Light	Comments
Alpine Currant (*Ribes alpinum*)	3 to 6	Full sun to shade	Small shrub that tolerates shearing through looks attractive in its natural form. Consider the native **Clove Currant** (*Ribes odoratum*) with fragrant yellow flowers.
Arborvitae (*Thuja occidentalis* cultivars)	3 to 5	Full to part sun	Generally large upright evergreen shrubs. Select cultivars that hold their green color for winter, and fit the location and desired use. Prefers moist soil protection from snowloads.
Azalea (*Rhododendron* × 'Northern Lights')	3 to 8	Part sun to shade	Small shrub with orange, yellow, pink, white, or orchid flowers in spring. Hardiest of the **Azaleas.** Protect from winter winds and sun.
Barberry (*Berberis thunbergii* species and cultivars)	4 to 7	Full sun to part shade	Small and medium shrubs that prefer well-drained to dry soils. Attractive red fruit and fall color. Spines make them good barrier plants.
Bird's Nest Spruce (*Picea abies* 'Nidiformis')	3 to 8	Full sun	Slow-growing dwarf spreading spruce. Forms wide mound with dent in center.
Bottlebrush Buckeye (*Aesculus parviflora*)	4 to 7	Part sun	Large mounded shrub. Prefers moist soil. White flowers in July.
Boxwood (*Buxus* species)	4 to 8	Part to full shade	Small shrubs that prefer shelter from winter sun and wind. Select 'Green Velvet', 'Wintergreen', and other hardier cultivars.
Burning bush (*Euonymus alata*)	4 to 7	Full sun to part shade	Medium to large shrubs grown for attractive fall color. Avoid heavy shade and high nitrogen fertilizer for best fall display. Select hardier cultivars such as 'Nordine Strain' when looking for compact types.
Butterfly Bush (*Buddleja davidii*)	5 to 7	Full sun	Medium shrub that dies back to ground level each winter. Attracts butterflies with its fragrant, long-lasting bloom.
Chokeberry (*Aronia* species)	3 to 6	Full sun to shade	Small and medium shrubs that tolerate moist to wet soils. White flowers in spring. Produces red or black fruit with red fall color.
Cotoneaster (*Cotoneaster* species)	3 to 9	Full sun to part shade	Small to large shrubs with delicate white or pink spring flowers. Produces fruit and good fall color. Form varies from low-growing and mounded to spreading or upright.
Daphne (*Daphne* × *burkwoodii* 'Carol Mackie')	4 to 9	Full to part sun	Small shrub with variegated foliage and fragrant flowers. Often short lived.

Shrubs

Common Name (Botanical Name)	Hardiness Zone	Light	Comments
Dogwood (*Cornus* species)	3 to 8	Full sun to shade	Medium to large shrubs. Many species and cultivars have decorative bark, bird-attracting fruit, and good fall color.
Forsythia (*Forsythia* species)	3 to 7	Full sun	Small to large shrubs depending on the species. Select 'Meadowlark', 'Sunrise', or one of the other flowerbud-hardy cultivars. Plant hardiness varies with species and cultivar.
Fothergilla (*Fothergilla gardenii*)	4 to 7	Full sun to part shade	Small shrub with white fragrant flowers in early spring, and yellow, orange, and red fall color.
Fragrant Sumac (*Rhus aromatica*)	3 to 7	Full to part sun	Use 'Gro-low' cultivar for a groundcover or small shrub. The straight species is a medium-sized and more upright shrub. Late to leaf out, glossy green leaves and orange-red fall color. **Staghorn Sumac** (*Rhus typhina*) should be saved for areas where it has room to spread or can be contained.
Hazelnut (*Corylus americana*)	3- to 7	Sun to shade	Medium shrub that tolerates dry soils. Native plant with orange fall color.
Hydrangea (*Hydrangea arborescens*) (*Hydrangea paniculata*)	4 to 8	Part shade	Medium to tall, summer blooming shade-tolerant shrub. The white forms bloom on new growth while most of the pink and blue types (*Hydrangea macrophylla*) flower on the previous season's growth and need winter protection.
Juneberry/Serviceberry (*Amelanchier* species)	3 to 7	Part shade	Large upright shrub, with four-season interest. White spring flowers, edible fruit in June, orange-red fall color and smooth gray bark in winter.
Juniper (*Juniper* species and cultivars)	3 to 8	Full sun	Low-growing, medium to large spreading or upright forms. Heat and drought-tolerant evergreen.
Lilac (*Syringa* species and cultivars)	3 to 7	Full sun	Medium to large shrubs. Fragrant flowers in spring attract butterflies and hummingbirds. Select most mildew-resistant cultivars.
Mockorange (*Philadelphus*)	4 to 7	Full to part sun	Medium to small shrub grown for fragrant white flowers in spring. Select for plant and flower bud hardiness. Minnesota Snowflake (*Philadelphus* × *virginalis* 'Minnesota') is rated hardy zones 3-5 while the smaller summer double-blooming Glacier (*Philadelphus* × *virginalis* 'Glacier') is hardy in zones 4 and 5.
Mugo Pine (*Pinus mugo*)	3 to 8	Full sun	Small to large mounded shrub. Select dwarf cultivars suitable to the landscape. Tolerates full sun and dry soil. Prune expanding growth in spring to control size.

Shrubs

Common Name (Botanical Name)	Hardiness Zone	Light	Comments
Potentilla (*Potentilla fruticosa*)	2 to 7	Full sun	Small shrub performs best in well-drained to dry soils. Covered with yellow or white flowers throughout the summer and fall. Red flowering types often fade in heat of summer.
Privet (*Ligustrum* species)	4 to 9	Full to part sun	Medium to large shrub usually sheared into a hedge. Select 'Cheyenne' or one of the other hardier cultivars for best results. 'Regal' is more ornamental and 'Lodense' is a small, rounded form
Rhododendron (*Rhododendron* × 'PJM Hybrid')	4 to 9	Sun to part shade	Small broadleaf evergreen turns purple in fall, flowers in spring. Protect from winter wind and sun.
Rose-of-Sharon (*Hibiscus syriacus*)	5 to 8	Full to part sun	Medium to small upright shrub with white, blue, lavender, or red flowers in late summer. Can be killed in harsh winter.
Spirea (*Spiraea* species)	3 to 8	Full sun to light shade	Small to medium, mostly mounded in form. Spring and summer blooming, low maintenance plants.
Viburnum (*Viburnum* species and cultivars)	3 to 9	Full to part sun	Small to large upright shrubs. Most provide flowers, fruit, and fall color for seasonal interest.
Weigela (*Weigela florida*)	4 to 9	Full sun	Small shrub with main flowering in spring followed by sporadic flowers throughout the summer. Compact forms available.
Winterberry (*Ilex verticillata*)	3 to 9	Full sun to part shade	Medium shrub that tolerates wet acid soils. Bright red fruit in fall and winter. Need male and female plants for fruit.
Witchhazel (*Hamamelis virginiana*)	3b to 8	Full sun to shade	Large shrub that tolerates city conditions. Yellow flowers and foliage in fall.
Yew (*Taxus* species and cultivars)	4 to 7	Sun or shade	Large upright and medium to small spreading evergreen plants. Protect from winter wind and salt to reduce winter browning.

JANUARY
Shrubs

PLANNING

Shake off the post-holiday blues and a few pounds with a walk around the block. Find out how friends and neighbors are using shrubs to add year-round interest to their yards and gardens. Expand your search to include nearby botanical gardens and arboretums. Some may even sponsor winter walks with local experts.

Evaluate the form, color, and fruit of individual plants. Consider how these can help improve your existing landscape.

Start a list of plants you would like to add to your yard. Find out their ultimate size and desired growing conditions to see if they will fit in your landscape.

Now take a walk around your landscape. Look for areas that would benefit from some new shrub plantings. Make sure there is sufficient room for the shrubs you select.

Consider the mature size as it relates to nearby buildings, existing plants, and overhead and underground utilities.

Investigate dwarf varieties for smaller areas. Always check the ultimate size; dwarf just means they are smaller than the standard species but not necessarily as small as you might imagine. A dwarf may be 15-feet tall—when the species reaches 20 feet.

Select plants suitable for the growing conditions. Matching the shrub to the existing growing conditions will result in an attractive plant that requires very little care.

PLANTING

Take advantage of this downtime to prepare your tools for the growing season. Clean and sharpen your spade. See November "Pruning" on page 283 for tips on cleaning and sharpening tools. A sharp-edged shovel will slice through the soil with much less effort.

CARE

Monitor the landscape for snow, deicing salt, and animal damage.

Do not shake or brush frozen snow off the plants. This can cause more damage than if the snow was left in place. Make a note on your calendar to prevent plant damage next season. Apply winter protection in late October or November before the heavy snows arrive.

Shovel walks and drives before applying deicing materials. This saves money and reduces plant damage caused by these products. Consider using one of the more environmentally friendly deicing products such as magnesium chloride and calcium acetate.

WATERING

No need to water plantings. The soil is either frozen or covered with snow. Check the soil moisture of all the above-ground planters you have stored in your unheated garage or porch. Water whenever the soil thaws and dries. Water thoroughly so that the excess runs out the bottom of the planter.

FERTILIZING

Review soil test information and garden notes to decide whether you need to fertilize this season. Contact your local Cooperative Extension Service for soil test information. Test results will tell you if you need to fertilize and what you need to use.

PRUNING

Prune winter-damaged branches as they are found. Wait until the snow melts and the worst of winter has passed to start major pruning. This way you can see what winter and the animals have left for you to work with.

PROBLEMS

This may be a quiet time in the landscape, yet it's a good time to spring a surprise attack on many garden pests. A little preventative pest management can help reduce plant damage, pesticide use, and your summer workload.

Check for signs of animals. Rabbits, voles, and deer will feed on stems and branches. Get busy if you find tracks, droppings, and feeding damage. Secure animal fencing and reapply repellents as needed.

Check **ornamental plums** and **cherries** for Eastern tent caterpillar egg masses. The eggs look like a shiny glob of mud on the stem. Prune and destroy all that are found.

Watch for black knot cankers on **plums** and **cherries** at the same time. This fungal disease causes branches to swell, eventually turn black, and crack open, releasing infectious spores. Prune out infected branches below the swollen areas. Burn or bury cankered branches to reduce future infections.

Check the base of **viburnum**, **euonymus**, and **spirea** stems for round, swollen growths called galls. These galls eventually girdle and kill the stem. Prune out infected stems below the gall, and discard. Disinfect your tools between cuts with rubbing alcohol or a solution of one part bleach to nine parts water.

Helpful Hints

Add a little flavor to your landscape. Include a few shrubs that produce edible fruit as well as add beauty to your yard. Many shrubs produce fruit that can be eaten fresh, sweetened and pureed into jelly, or baked in a pie. **blueberries**, **raspberries**, and **currants** quickly come to mind. But you may be surprised to find some other ornamental shrubs that have edible parts.

American cranberrybush (*Viburnum trilobum*) has long been used for preserves. Cathy uses it to make a tasty chutney; Melinda thinks that the berries need a lot of sugar to find them tasty. 'Andrews', 'Hahs', and 'Wentworth' are selected for their larger fruit. If you are like Melinda and don't like the flavor, the fruit is still attractive, provides good winter interest, and lures birds and other wildlife to the fruit.

Cornelian cherry (**dogwood**) (*Cornus mas*) produces bright red, cherrylike fruit. The elongated fruit is a little tart at first bite. Add a little sugar—or a lot—and make it into jelly or syrup. Don't worry, if you don't like the flavor the birds will take care of the fruit for you.

Rose (*Rosa* spp.) has both flowers and fruits, called hips, which add color and beauty to the landscape. Rose petals can be used fresh in salads or omelets, batter coated and fried, sugared, or made into jelly. The fruits are also edible and high in vitamin C. Most roses produce fruit but some, such as the **Rugosa Roses**, have a little better flavor. Rose hips have long been used for jelly, tea, and sauces. Only eat roses that have not been sprayed.

American hazelnut or **filbert** (*Corylus americana*). See Fruits.

Elderberry (*Sambucus canadensis*). See Fruits.

Juneberry or **serviceberry** (*Amelanchier* spp.). See Trees.

A word of caution: Do not spray plants with pesticides if you plan to eat them. Wait a year after purchasing plants from a nursery to eat any plant parts; this allows any pesticides to work their way out of the plant. Instruct children never to eat plants or plant parts unless their parents or a trusted adult says it is okay.

FEBRUARY
Shrubs

 PLANNING

Continue to update your landscape plan. Check out catalogs and visit home and garden shows to get some new ideas. The professionals at these shows can give you design and planting tips.

 PLANTING

It is still too early to plant. Make note of any shrubs that need to be moved. Transplanting can begin as soon as the ground thaws.

 CARE

Nature still drops a few white reminders that winter is not yet over. See November "Helpful Hints" for minimizing winter damage.

Monitor shrubs and other plants for winter damage. Do not shake ice or frozen snow off plants. Your good intentions can do more damage than nature. Make note of any damage that could have been prevented with winter protection.

Use any breaks in the weather to start cleaning out shrub beds. Remove debris and broken branches.

 WATERING

No need to water shrub beds. Continue to check on aboveground planters. Water them whenever the soil thaws and dries.

 FERTILIZING

It is still too early to fertilize. Check your journal and review last year's gardening successes and challenges. Take a walk through the landscape and evaluate plant growth.

 PRUNING

Continue to prune out damaged or hazardous branches as they are found. You may want to wait until the worst of winter has passed to start major pruning. Summer- and fall-blooming plants can be pruned now until growth begins in spring. Wait until after flowering to prune spring-blooming shrubs.

Try bringing a little spring indoors. Prune a few branches from spring flowering shrubs to force for indoor bloom. **forsythia**, **quince**, and **pussy willows** make nice additions to arrangements or in a vase on their own.

1 Use hand pruners to cut branches above a healthy bud or where they join another branch.

2 Place branches in cool water (60 degrees Fahrenheit) in a brightly lit location.

3 Mist as often as possible and keep the cut ends in water.

4 Move flowering stems to a cooler location at night to prolong bloom.

 PROBLEMS

Keep monitoring for animal damage. Adjust protection as needed.

Secure fencing and other animal guards. Make sure animals are not able to crawl under or over the barriers and reach the plants.

Reapply repellents after severe weather as recommended on the label. Use a variety of repellents to help increase success. Animals often get used to the repellent and start feeding on treated plants.

Scare tactics may provide additional relief. Noisemakers, coyote urine, and whirligigs may scare some animals. Vary the techniques to keep the animals wary of the area. Keep in mind that urban wildlife is used to the smell and noise of humans so scare tactics may not provide adequate control.

Insects. Check **mugo pines** for pine needle scale. Look for white flecks on the needles. A lime sulfur spray can be used now to kill the pest.

Other scale insects (hard shells attached to stems) can be treated with lime sulfur while the plants are dormant. Check the label before treatment to make sure it can be used on your particular plant. Lime sulfur can stain walks and injure Viburnums.

Check **ornamental plums** and **cherries** for Eastern tent caterpillar egg masses. The eggs look like a shiny glob of mud on the stem. Prune and destroy all that are found.

Diseases. Also look for black knot cankers on **plums** and **cherries**. These appear as knots on the twigs. The knots start out the same color as the stem and eventually turn black, crack open, and release infectious spores. Prune out infected branches below the knots. Burn or bury cankered branches to reduce future infections.

Helpful Hints

Wildlife can add color and motion to the winter and summer landscapes. Planting shrubs that provide food and shelter is a great way to bring birds into the landscape. Nature takes care of stocking the feeder, allowing you more time to sit back, relax, and watch the birds.

Shrubs That Attract Wildlife
(Hardy in Zones 3, 4, 5)

- **Arborvitae** (*Thuja occidentalis*): BS
- **Bayberry** (*Myrica pennsylvanica*): BF
- **Chokeberry** (*Aronia* species): BF, BS
- **Coralberry** (*Symphoricarpos orbiculatus*): BF, BS, HB
- **Dogwood** (*Cornus* species): B, BF
- **Elderberry** (*Sambucus canadensis*): B, BF, BS
- **Flowering Plums** and **Cherries (***Prunus* cultivars): BF and BS, HB
- **Juneberry** or **Serviceberry** (*Amelanchier*): BF
- **Lilac** (*Syringa* and cultivars: B, HB
- **Rose** (*Rosa* and cultivars): B, BF
- **Spirea** (*Spiraea*): B
- **Viburnum** (*Viburnum* species): B, BF, BS
- **Yew** (*Taxus*): BS

Key:
B—Butterflies; BF—Food for birds;
BS—Shelter for birds; HB—Hummingbird

Check the bases of **viburnum**, **euonymus**, and **spirea** stems for round, swollen growths called galls. These galls eventually girdle and kill the stem. Prune out infected stems below the gall and discard. Disinfect your tools between cuts with alcohol or a solution of one part bleach to nine parts water.

Check **dogwood** for signs of golden canker. This fungal disease is common on **dogwoods** that have suffered heat and drought stress in summer. The twigs turn gold and die. Prune out infected stems. Disinfect tools between cuts.

MARCH
Shrubs

PLANNING

Complete your landscape plan and start shopping for those unusual plants. Contact nurseries and garden centers that specialize in unusual plants. You may have to make several calls to locate new and unusual varieties.

PLANTING

Build in preparation time for planting. Contact the utility-locating service three to ten days prior to digging. This free service locates and marks underground utilities. Having this information can help you avoid costly damage to utilities and possibly save your life. Call the Diggers Hotline or your local utility companies.

Late winter through early spring is the best time to transplant shrubs. Moving large, established shrubs can be tricky and heavy work. Replacing overgrown or misplaced shrubs may be easier, cheaper, and more successful.

Start transplanting when the ground thaws and soil is moist. Complete this garden task before growth begins.

1 Loosely tie the branches to prevent damage and keep them out of your way.

2 Dig a trench around the shrub slightly larger and deeper than the desired rootball. (See this chapter's "Did You Know?")

3 Undercut the rootball with your shovel. A sharp spade will make the job easier. Use hand pruners and loppers for larger or tougher roots.

4 Slide a piece of burlap or canvas under the rootball. Have several friends lend a hand. Extra hands and strong backs will make the job easier and reduce the risk of dropping the shrub and damaging the rootball.

5 Set the shrub in the prepared site. Carefully cut away or slide the tarp away from the shrub.

6 Backfill the hole with existing soil, water, and mulch.

CARE

This month marks the start of the transition from winter to spring. Continue protecting plants from deicing salts, snow loads and animal damage. Start the repair work of leaching out salt-laden soils and pruning off broken branches.

WATERING

Continue watering shrubs in aboveground planters. Water thoroughly whenever the ground thaws and dries. Monitor soil moisture after the soil thaws. Melting snow and spring rains usually take care of the needed moisture.

FERTILIZING

Use soil tests to get the most out of your gardening efforts. The test results will tell you about your soil and fertilizer needs. It can save you time and money spent adding unnecessary nutrients. It also helps you avoid damaging the plant and environment with misapplications of fertilizer. Contact your local Cooperative Extension Service for soil test information.

Take a soil sample as soon as the ground thaws. Take samples from several locations in the planting bed. Use a trowel or shovel to obtain samples 4 to 6 inches deep. Mix the samples together and allow them to dry. Send 1 cup of soil and the complete form to the University Extension or a state certified soil testing lab.

If soil test information is not available, use these guidelines for fertilization:

Start transplanting when the ground thaws and soil is moist.
Complete this garden task before growth begins.

- Young shrubs can be fertilized every couple years to promote rapid growth.

- Shrubs growing in heavily mulched beds benefit from regular fertilization.

- Established shrubs need infrequent or no fertilizer.

- Use 1 to 2 pounds of a nitrogen fertilizer per 100 square feet. Two cups of an inorganic fertilizer is equal to 1 pound.

Helpful Hints

Recommended Rootball Size for Transplanting

Shrub Size	Rootball Size Minimum Diameter	Depth
2 feet	12 inches	9 inches
3 feet	14 inches	11 inches
4 feet	16 inches	12 inches
5 feet	16 inches	12 inches
6 feet	16 inches	12 inches

PRUNING

Wait until after flowering to prune **lilacs**, **forsythia**, **bridal wreath spirea**, and other spring-blooming shrubs. These shrubs have already set flower buds for this spring. Pruning at other times will not harm the plants but eliminates the bloom—the reason they are planted.

Prune summer- and fall-blooming shrubs now. Late winter pruning will not interfere with summer flowering and allows the plants to recover quickly.

Start by removing damaged, broken, and diseased stems. Disinfect tools between cuts to prevent the spread of disease. Rubbing alcohol or a solution of one part bleach to nine parts water will work. Clean your tools after pruning to minimize the adverse effects of bleach.

See the "Pruning" section on page 255 for specific information on pruning.

PROBLEMS

Insects. Continue to remove and destroy Eastern tent caterpillar egg masses on **ornamental plums** and **cherries**. The eggs are dark and shiny and appear to be cemented on the branch.

Complete dormant sprays of lime sulfur on overwintering scale on **mugo pines** and deciduous shrubs before growth begins. Check the label before spraying. Make sure the pest and plant to be treated are listed on the label.

Prune out and destroy brooms (fine twiggy growths) on **honeysuckles.** Removing the brooms reduces the number of leaf-folding aphids that can re-infect these plants.

Diseases. Remove and destroy black knots from twigs of **ornamental plums** and **cherries**. Destroying the knots now can reduce infection for this growing season. Remove both the black and green knots for best results.

Prune out gold-colored branches on **dogwood**. These are infected by drought-induced golden canker fungus disease. Disinfect tools between cuts.

APRIL

 ## PLANNING

Continue to walk through your neighborhood, nearby botanical gardens, and your own landscape to gather ideas on shrubs for year-round interest. Make a list of spring-blooming shrubs you have or would like to add to the landscape. Keep in mind that the flowers may only provide a few weeks of interest while the shrubs will remain all year. Consider spring-flowering shrubs that have good fruit effect, fall color, interesting shape, or other ornamental features.

Record bloom times in your journal. It is fun and informative to see the bloom time variations from one year to the next.

Check local nurseries and garden centers for the more unusual and hard-to-find shrubs.

Plan ahead so that you will have enough preparation time for planting. Contact the utility-locating service three to ten days prior to digging. This free service locates and marks underground utilities. Having this information can help you avoid costly damage to utilities and possibly save your life. Call Diggers Hotline or your local utilities.

 ## PLANTING

The growing and planting season has begun. As the soil thaws and temperatures warm, the nurseries are busy digging, transporting, and selling shrubs. You can get busy planting as well.

Finish transplanting shrubs before growth begins. See March "Planting" for details on moving shrubs.

A few catalogs and garden centers sell bare-root shrubs. These plants are cheaper, have a lower survival rate, and require your immediate attention for good results. Store bare-root plants in a cool, shaded location. Pack roots in peat moss and keep them moist. Soak overnight before planting. Place the shrubs in the planting hole at the same depth they were growing in the nursery.

Start planting balled-and-burlapped and container-grown shrubs. Plant them at the same depth they were growing at the nursery or in the container. Reduce root damage by cutting away containers, burlap, and twine. See "Planting" on page 254 for more details.

 ## CARE

Move aboveground planters out of winter storage. Wait until temperatures hover around freezing if the leaves have begun to grow.

Remove and store winter protection. Continue applying wildlife repellents if animals continue to feed on shrubs. Make notes of any changes in winter protection that need to be made for next season.

 ## WATERING

New plantings should be watered often enough to keep the top 6 to 8 inches of the soil moist. Water thoroughly and wait for the soil to start to dry before watering again. Check clay soils weekly and sandy soils twice a week. Water as needed.

Established shrubs only need supplemental water in dry springs. Water thoroughly when the top 6 to 8 inches begin to dry.

Thoroughly water shrubs exposed to deicing materials. Heavy spring showers or a thorough watering will help wash these materials through the soil and away from the roots.

New plantings should be watered often enough to keep the top 6 to 8 inches of the soil moist. Water thoroughly and wait for the soil to start to dry before watering again.

 FERTILIZING

Wait a year or two before fertilizing new plantings. Use your soil test as a guide to fertilizing existing plantings.

Apply fertilizer once in spring or early summer. Additional applications are not needed since most shrubs put out one flush of growth a year.

Apply 1 to 2 pounds of a nitrogen fertilizer per 100 square feet if soil test results are not available. Try a slow-release formulation to reduce risk and improve results.

 PRUNING

Finish dormant pruning of summer- and fall-blooming shrubs before growth begins. See "Pruning Pointers" on page 257 for more information.

Wait until after flowering to prune spring bloomers.

 PROBLEMS

Insects. Continue to locate and destroy egg masses of Eastern tent caterpillars. The eggs hatch and the caterpillars start building their webbed tents when the **Saucer Magnolias** (*Magnolia* x *soulan-*

Helpful Hints

Prune evergreens to control size, remove damaged branches, and direct growth. Select the time and method of pruning that is best suited for the plants you are growing.

Pines are terminal growers. They send out new growth from stem tips once a year. Control their size by removing one-half to two-thirds of the expanding buds (candles) in spring. More severe pruning on stems that lack terminal buds will kill the branch.

Spruce can also be pruned in spring before growth begins. Prune stem tips back to a healthy bud. Make cuts at a slight angle just above the bud. Do not leave stubs that create an entryway for insects and disease.

Arborvitae and **Yews** can be pruned in spring before growth begins or in early summer after new growth has expanded. Both plants form buds on older wood and tolerate more severe pruning than **Pines** and **Spruce**. Prune back to a bud or branch for best results. Keep the bottom of formal sheared hedges wider than the tops.

Junipers require little pruning when the right size variety is selected for the location. Prune to control growth and keep the plant within the available space. Remove selected branches in spring or early summer. Cut the branches back to side shoots to cover cuts. Tip prune in summer for additional sizing.

geana) are in the pink bud stage. Prune out and destroy tents as they are found.

Do not apply dormant sprays once growth begins. These products can cause more damage to the expanding growth than the insects you are trying to control.

Prune out and destroy the brooms on the tips of **honeysuckles.** These contain hundreds of aphids that are waiting to feed on this season's growth.

Watch for European pine sawflies on **Mugo Pine** when the **Saucer Magnolias** begin dropping their petals. These wormlike insects feed in large groups, devouring pine needles a branch at a time. Smash them with a leather glove-clad hand or prune out and destroy the infested branch.

Diseases. Finish pruning out the green and black knots on **Flowering Cherries**, **Almonds**, and **Plums**. Removing these knots will reduce the source of future infection.

MAY
Shrubs

PLANNING

Refer to your landscape plan and planting list whenever you visit a nursery or garden center. All those beautiful plants, attractive tags, and promises of beauty can be tempting. It is too easy to succumb to temptation and end up with too many or the wrong type of plants for the available space.

Remember to call your local utility locating services. Allow three business days between the call and planting. These free utility-locating services can prevent damage to underground utilities, save you money, and even save your life.

PLANTING

Keep planting. Balled-and-burlapped and container-grown shrubs can be planted all season long.

Amend planting beds in difficult planting locations. Create raised beds with existing or blended topsoil or add organic matter to the top 6 to 12 inches of the planting bed soil. Add organic matter to the whole planting bed, not just the planting hole, where shrub roots will grow.

To plant balled-and-burlapped and container shrubs:

Dig a hole twice the diameter and the same depth or shallower than the root-ball. Roughen the sides of the planting hole, using your shovel to nick or scratch the soil surface.

Reduce root damage by cutting away the pots on container plants. Remove the bottom of the pot and set it inside the hole. Slice the side of the container and peel it away. Slice through pot-bound roots in several places around the rootball. Backfill with the existing soil and water.

Set balled-and-burlapped shrubs in a properly dug hole. Remove the twine, cut away the burlap, and backfill with the existing soil. Water to help settle the soil.

Mulch the soil around the base of the plant. Be careful not to bury the crown. A 2- to 3-inch layer of woodchips or bark will help conserve moisture, insulate roots, and reduce weeds.

CARE

Gradually move shrubs outdoors that were wintered indoors. Those stored in heated garages, the basement, or other warm location need to gradually adapt to the cooler, harsher outdoor conditions.

Shrubs wintered in an unheated porch or garage should be moved outdoors before growth begins. Once growth begins, they need a little extra time for the tender new growth to adjust to the cooler outdoor conditions.

WATERING

Give new plantings special attention. Water thoroughly whenever the top 6 inches of soil are crumbly and moist. Check clay soils once a week and sandy soils twice a week.

Established plantings only need to be watered during dry springs. Water thoroughly and wait for the top 6 to 8 inches to dry before watering again.

Water aboveground planters whenever the top few inches of soil begin to dry. Water thoroughly so that the excess drains out the bottom. Check planters every few days, daily during hot weather.

FERTILIZING

Finish shrub fertilization. Only fertilize plants that are showing signs of deficiencies, those for which the soil test report indicates a need to fertilize, or young plants that you are trying to encourage to grow.

Create raised beds with existing or blended topsoil or add organic matter to the top 6 to 12 inches of the planting bed soil.

- Apply 1 to 2 pounds of a nitrogen fertilizer per 100 square feet if soil test results are not available.

- Try a slow-release formulation to reduce risk and improve results.

- See the chapter introduction for fertilizer rates.

- Wait a year or two before fertilizing new plantings.

PRUNING

Prune spring-flowering shrubs as soon as they are done blooming. Finish pruning by early June so that the plants have enough time to set flower buds for next spring.

Renewal prune suckering shrubs, such as **forsythia**, **bridal wreath spirea**, and **lilacs**. Remove one-third of the older stems to ground level. See "Pruning Pointers" in the chapter introduction for details.

Remove faded flowers on **lilacs** and **rhododendrons** to encourage better flowering next year.

Helpful Hints

A large expanse of shrubs neatly mulched in a planting bed can get a little boring. Brighten up shrub planting beds with the help of flowering bulbs and perennials.

Add some spring surprise to the shrub beds in your landscape. A mass planting of **crocus, grape hyacinth,** and **squill** can give you a carpet of color. Intersperse some **daffodils, tulips,** and **hyacinths** for height and additional color.

Consider using perennials to create seasonal interest. A mixture of spring, summer-, and fall-blooming flowers can complement the seasonal interest the shrubs provide. See the Perennials chapter or the companion book to this one: *Prairie Lands Gardener's Guide* for suitable plants.

Try perennial groundcovers, such as **deadnettle** (*Lamium* spp.), **bishop's cap** (*Epimedium* spp,), **hosta,** and **vinca** to mask the mulch and create a good growing environment. See the "Vines and Groundcovers" chapter for additional planting suggestions.

PROBLEMS

Insects. Remove Eastern tent caterpillars as soon as they are found. Knock or prune out tents and destroy caterpillars.

Continue checking **mugo pines** for European pine sawflies. Prune off infected branches or smash sawflies with a leather glove-clad hand.

Treat **mugo** and other **pines** infested with pine needle scale. Apply insecticidal soap when the **vanhouttei/bridal wreath spirea** is in bloom and again seven to ten days later.

Check and treat **lilacs, dogwood,** and other deciduous shrubs infested with oyster shell scale. These hard-shelled insects look like miniature oyster shells. Spray the stems and leaves with an ultra-fine oil or insecticide labeled for use on shrubs with scale. Spray when the **vanhouttei/bridal wreath spirea** are in bloom and again when the **hills-of-snow hydrangea** blossoms change from white to green.

Diseases. Watch for phomopsis blight on **junipers.** Infected plants have cankered branches (sunken discolored areas) with brown and dead needles. Prune out infected branches 9 inches below the canker. Disinfect your tools between cuts.

JUNE
Shrubs

PLANNING

"The only constant in life is change." This is certainly true about gardening and landscaping. No matter how well you planned, something comes up and requires a change. The unexpected helps make gardening fun—or at least a bit challenging!

Keep adjusting your plans and make notes on the changes as they occur. You may find these changes actually improve the original plan.

PLANTING

Keep planting container and balled-and-burlapped shrubs. Both are available at nurseries and garden centers.

Call the utility-locating services at least three days before planting. They will mark the location of underground utilities to prevent damage and injury. This is a free service that is just a phone call away.

Select healthy, well-shaped plants. Avoid shrubs with brown, speckled, or discolored leaves. These may have suffered drought stress or pest problems. Stressed shrubs take longer to establish and have a lower survival rate.

Cover plants on the trip home from the nursery or garden center. Load them inside the car or cover those in the truck bed or trailer with a tarp. The windy trip home can dry out the new growth, increasing the stress on the plant.

Keep roots of newly purchased shrubs moist until they can be planted. Cover balled-and-burlapped roots with wood chips if it will be a few days until planting.

Dig a hole twice as wide and the same depth as the rootball. Remove the container, twine, and burlap from the shrub once it is placed in the planting hole. Loosen or slice through potbound roots. Backfill with existing soil and water.

CARE

Consider removing grass and creating planting beds around shrubs. Grass is a big competitor with shrubs for water and nutrients. The weed whips and mowers used to cut the grass often damage the shrubs. Reduce maintenance and improve the health of your shrubs by mulching around shrubs. Kill or remove grass and cover with woodchips or shredded bark. See August "Helpful Hints" on page 277 for more details.

Replenish mulch around individual shrubs or planting beds. A 2- to 3-inch layer of woodchips and bark will help improve the growing conditions for the shrubs. Mulch insulates the soil, protecting the roots from temperature extremes. It also conserves moisture and reduces weed problems.

WATERING

Temperature, soil type, and mulching influence the need for water. You need to check plants and water more frequently during hot spells and when growing in sandy soil. Reduce your workload by mulching planting beds. Woodchips and bark help to conserve moisture, reducing the need for water.

New plantings are still a watering priority. Keep the top 6 to 8 inches slightly moist. Check shrubs planted in clay soils once a week and those planted in sandy soils twice a week. Water thoroughly when the top 6 to 8 inches are crumbly and moist.

Established shrubs only need supplemental water during dry periods. Water thoroughly when the top 6 inches of soil dry.

Cover plants on the trip home from the nursery or garden center. Load them inside the car or cover those in the truck bed or trailer with a tarp. The windy trip home can dry out the new growth, increasing the stress on the plant.

 # FERTILIZING

Fertilize only those shrubs that are showing signs of nutrient deficiency or when recommended by soil test results. Apply needed fertilizer in one application in the spring. Finish fertilization that has not yet been done. See "Fertilizing" on page 256 for more specific recommendations.

 # PRUNING

Finish pruning spring-flowering shrubs early this month. This gives the plants plenty of time to develop flower buds for next spring's display.

Shear and shape hedges after new growth has emerged. Prune so that the top of the hedge is narrower than the bottom. This allows light to reach all parts of the shrub. Better light penetration means leaves from top to bottom.

Remove damaged, dead, or insect-infested stems.

 # PROBLEMS

As the temperatures warm, the pest populations build. Healthy shrubs can tolerate most pest problems. When the numbers get too high, you may need to step in and lend nature a hand.

Insects. Check **burning bush** and other **euonymus** for signs of the euonymus caterpillar. These worm-like insects build webbed nests and feed on the leaves. Use a stick to knock out the nests and remove the insects as soon as they are found. Large populations can be treated with *Bacillus thuringiensis* var. *Kurstocki*. This bacterial insecticide kills only true caterpillars and will not harm beneficial insects, wildlife, or people.

Look for white, hard flecks on the leaves and stems of **euonymus**. Treat these scale insects with insecticidal soap when the **Japanese tree lilacs** are in bloom. The bloom time and egg hatch coincide. Repeat applications two more times at 10- to 12-day intervals.

Aphid and mite populations begin to build as the temperatures rise and the rains decline. Spray plants with a strong blast of water during extended droughts. The water dislodges many of the insects, helping to minimize their damage.

Check all plantings for signs of Japanese beetles. These small, metallic-green insects emerge in late June and feed on a variety of plants. See July "Problems" for more recommendations.

Diseases. Continue to prune out phomopsis-blighted branches on **juniper**. See May "Problems" for specific information. Cut out infected branches 9 inches below the canker. Disinfect tools between cuts. Use rubbing alcohol or a solution of 1 part bleach to 9 parts water solution.

Watch other shrubs for twig blight. The fungal diseases causing twig dieback are most common in cool, wet weather. Remove blighted, brown, and dying branches as soon as they are found. Disinfect tools between cuts.

JULY
Shrubs

 PLANNING

The middle of the growing season is usually peak pest time. The typical cool, wet weather of spring results in a variety of leaf spot, blight, and fungal diseases. The hot weather of July and August helps insect populations quickly multiply. Start monitoring your plantings for problems. Some plants seem to struggle every year no matter what you do. These may be good candidates for replacement. Make notes in your gardening journal on plants that should be replaced or the care provided to minimize future pest problems.

 PLANTING

You can still plant container and balled-and-burlapped shrubs. Select plants with healthy green leaves. Avoid plants with brown leaf edges, indicating drought stress or pest problems.

Summer plantings need special attention. The warm temperatures slow down rooting and dry out soil. Mulch newly planted shrubs with a 2- to 3-inch layer of woodchips or bark. This will help keep roots cool and conserve moisture.

 CARE

Continue to replenish mulch as needed. Maintain a 2- to 3-inch layer of mulch around shrubs and throughout planting beds. Keep the mulch away from the crown of the plant. Burying the shrubs can lead to disease problems.

 WATERING

Check soil moisture around new plantings frequently. Shrubs planted in clay soils should be checked every five to seven days. Water when the top 6 to 8 inches just start to dry. Check shrubs in sandy soils twice a week. You will be watering more frequently in the hot, dry months of summer.

Established plants may need supplemental water during the dog days of summer. Water them thoroughly when the top 6 inches are slightly dry. Mulched plantings need less frequent watering.

 FERTILIZING

Do not fertilize. Summer fertilization is less effective and can even harm the roots in hot, dry weather.

 PRUNING

Prune **arborvitae**, **yews**, and **junipers** once the new growth has expanded. Clip stems back to a healthy bud or side shoot to contain growth. See April "Helpful Hints" on page 269 for more details on pruning evergreens.

Touch up hedges and sheared shrubs when new growth expands. Prune so that the bottom of the plant is wider than the top. This allows light to reach all parts of the plant. Lightly shear summer-blooming **spirea** to remove faded flowers and encourage rebloom. Repeat this after the second flush of flowers for a third colorful show.

 PROBLEMS

Healthy shrubs can tolerate most pests in the landscape. When weather conditions favor the pests and not the plants, you may need to lend nature a hand. Always check with a local extension service, botanical garden, or garden center for help with diagnosis.

Insects. Control large populations of aphids and mites with a strong blast of water from the garden hose. Treat shrubs with insecticidal soap if the populations grow and damage is severe.

The warm temperatures slow down rooting and dry out soil.
Mulch newly planted shrubs with a 2- to 3-inch layer of woodchips or bark.
This will help keep roots cool and conserve moisture.

Check shrubs for leucanium scale. This hard-shelled insect attacks a wide range of shrubs. Treat with an ultra-fine oil or insecticide labeled for use on this pest when the **hills-of-snow hydrangea** are in full bloom and again in two weeks.

Continue monitoring and controlling Japanese beetles. Handpick and destroy small populations of these small, metallic green-brown beetles. Use an insecticide labeled for control of Japanese beetles on shrubs to control larger populations. Don't use traps to control this pest.

Most entomologists believe the traps just bring more insects into your garden.

Check the base of wilted stems for signs of borers. Sawdust and holes indicate borers are present. Prune out and destroy borer-infested branches. Regular renewal pruning is usually sufficient control for these pests.

Diseases. Look for swellings at the base of **viburnum**, **euonymus**, and **spirea**. The disease-induced galls eventually girdle and kill the stem. Prune out infected stems below the gall. Disinfect tools between cuts.

Rake and destroy spotted leaves as they fall. This helps reduce the source of disease next season.

Helpful Hints

Nature is the best pest manager. Weather, birds, and predatory insects help keep pest populations under control. Weather also increases or decreases the incidence of disease. Occasionally, we get involved when nature's controls are insufficient or the damage is more than we can tolerate.

Try these pest management tips:

• Patience is the first step in control. Give nature time to take care of the problem. Ladybugs will not move into an area if there is no food. So let the aphids graze and wait for the predators to move in.

• Sanitation is an environmentally friendly way to reduce pest problems. Remove weeds to reduce the source for insects and disease. Remove infected leaves and stems as soon as they are discovered. This provides immediate relief while reducing future problems.

• Handpick or trap insects as they are discovered. Have a bug hunt with your family or neighborhood children. Offer a prize or a treat for the best hunter in the group. Insects may give you the creeps, but they are a great way to get kids into the garden.

• Try using insecticidal soaps, *bacillus thuringiensis,* neem, and other more environmentally friendly products reduce pest problems with great success.

Monitor **lilacs** and other shrubs for powdery mildew. Look for a white powdery substance on the leaves. Infected plants will survive, but their appearance declines as the season progresses. Reduce problems by increasing the light and air circulation. Thin overgrown plantings during the dormant season to increase light and air flow and to decrease disease.

AUGUST
Shrubs

 PLANNING

Take a walk through the landscape. Look for those drab, lifeless spots found in every yard. Consider adding a summer-flowering shrub to brighten up those areas. Visit the library, garden center, or botanical gardens for ideas. Always select plants that are hardy to your area and tolerant of the existing growing conditions.

Bottlebrush buckeye (*Aesculus parviflora*) is a large shrub that produces white spikes of flowers in July.

Butterflybush (*Buddleja* x *davidii*) is a sub-shrub that dies back to the ground in most winters. Fragrant flowers in white, pink, or lavender cover this plant from midsummer to fall.

Hydrangeas (*Hydrangea* spp,) are good summer bloomers for sun and shade locations. 'Annabelle' produces white snow-ball-like flowers in July. Try 'Endless Summer™' for a reliable pink blooming Hydrangea. It flowers in July and August. The **peegee hydrangeas** offer white flowers that fade to pink and brown from August through September.

Potentilla (shrubby cinquefoil) (*Potentilla fruticosa*) is the summer bloomer that first comes to mind. Look for this shrub to be covered with yellow or white flowers from June through fall.

Spirea (*Spirea japonica*) is a popular summer-blooming plant with white, pink, or lavender blooms.

Tamarisk (*Tamarix ramosissima*) is a tall, light, airy shrub that produces light, airy pink flowers from late June through August.

 PLANTING

Continue planting spring dug balled-and-burlapped and container-grown shrubs. Select plants with healthy leaves that have been watered and properly maintained throughout the season.

Mulch the soil around the shrubs to keep the roots cool and moist. This will improve establishment during the hot days of August.

 CARE

Replenish mulch in established plantings. Maintain a 2- to 3-inch layer of bark or woodchips around the plants. Do not bury the crowns. This leads to rot and disease.

Establish planting beds around trees and shrubs. See this month's "Helpful Hints" for details.

 WATERING

This is usually the hottest, driest month of summer. Check all plantings for moisture stress. You may need to prioritize watering needs if water bans are enacted.

New plantings are your highest priority. Make sure the top 6 inches remain moist, not wet. Check new plantings twice a week. Water thoroughly when the soil begins to dry. Improper watering is just as harmful as lack of water. Overwatered plants suffer from root rot and die. Shallow watering encourages shallow rooting that is more susceptible to drought.

 FERTILIZING

Do not fertilize now. Late-season fertilization can stimulate late-season growth that can be winterkilled.

 PRUNING

Avoid late-season pruning that can stimulate late-season growth.

Finish touchup pruning on sheared plants as soon as possible. Remove only wayward branches. Save major pruning for the dormant season.

PROBLEMS

Watch for aphids and mites. Summer thunderstorms often help keep these insects in check. You can create your own summer showers with the garden hose. Spray plants with a strong blast of water to help knock many of these pests off the plants. Try insecticidal soap when the populations start damaging the plants. Read and follow all label directions carefully.

Watch for the end of the Japanese beetles. They will soon return to the soil to lay their eggs for the next generation. Handpick and destroy small populations. Larger numbers can be controlled with an insecticide labeled for use on shrubs to control Japanese beetles.

Rake and destroy spotted and discolored leaves. This will reduce damage caused by the disease this season and next. Make notes regarding problem plants. Plan on making changes in the location or pruning practices to help relieve chronic disease problems.

Pull weeds as they appear. Deep-rooted perennial weeds can be spot treated with a total vegetation killer. These products kill the tops and roots of Quackgrass, Creeping Charlie, and Bindweed. They will kill anything green they touch, so keep these chemicals off the young stems and leaves of shrubs and other desirable plants.

Helpful Hints

Reduce maintenance and improve plant health by creating large planting beds around trees and shrubs. The larger bed eliminates competition from grass and damage caused by weed whips and mowers that get a little too close to the plants.

1 Start by outlining the bed. Select the size and shape that complements your design. You can always add more shrubs, perennials, and other plants to fill in the voids.

2 Lay out the garden hose to mark the area. Use a shovel or edger to create the outline of your new planting bed.

3 Remove the existing grass. Peel it off with a sod cutter and use this grass to repair problem areas. Or cut the grass short and cover with three layers of newspapers and several inches of woodchips. The grass and woodchips will eventually decompose. Or use a total vegetation killer to kill the existing grass and weeds. Keep these chemicals off desirable plants. Cover the dead turf with mulch.

4 Mulch the planting bed. A 2- to 3-inch layer of woodchips or bark will help reduce future weed problems. Do not put plastic or weed barriers under wood mulch. As the mulch decomposes, it creates the perfect environment for weeds. Weed seeds blow in, nearby turf spreads in, and soon the garden is full of grass and weeds that are growing through the weed barrier.

5 Reserve weed barriers for use under rock. The weed barrier helps keep the rock from working into the soil. This reduces the need to replenish the settled mulch and makes it easier for you to make changes to the area. Only use fabric weed barriers that allow air and water through. Do not use plastic that prevents water and nutrients from reaching the roots.

SEPTEMBER
Shrubs

 PLANNING

Take a few minutes to record the high-lights of the growing season. Make sure you have recorded all new landscape additions, place of purchase, and plant-ing date. Evaluate and record the high and low points of the season. Good records help you repeat your successes, not failures.

Start watching for colorful signs of fall. The bright red **sumac** growing along the freeway is a good wakeup call. Record the fall display in your landscape. Note any additions that should be made to improve the fall color. Visit local botani-cal gardens or take a walk in the woods to get ideas of the plants and combinations to include for a spectacu-lar fall show.

 PLANTING

Always start with a call to the utility-locating service. Start transplanting shrubs as the leaves begin to drop and the plants go dormant. Moving large established shrubs can be tricky and heavy work. Replacing overgrown or misplaced shrubs may be easier, cheaper, and more successful.

1 Loosely tie the branches to prevent damage and keep them out of your way.

2 Dig a trench around the shrub slightly larger and deeper than the desired rootball. (See March "Helpful Hint" on page 267.)

3 Undercut the rootball with your shovel. A sharp spade will make the job easier. Use hand pruners and lop-pers for larger or tougher roots.

4 Slide a piece of burlap or canvas under the rootball. Have several friends lend a hand. Extra hands and strong backs will make the job easier and reduce the risk of dropping the shrub and damaging the rootball.

5 Set the shrub in the prepared site. Carefully cut away or slide the tarp away from the shrub.

6 Backfill the hole with existing soil, water, and mulch.

Continue planting balled-and-burlapped and container-grown shrubs. Planting can continue until the ground freezes. The sooner you get the plants in the ground, the more time the shrubs will have to adjust before winter. Complete evergreen planting this month.

 CARE

Fall cleanup begins.

Rake leaves out of shrub beds to elimi-nate unwanted animals' habitat and potential damage to surrounding plants.

Remove and destroy leaves from dis-eased shrubs. This will help reduce the source of disease next season.

 WATERING

Continue watering new plantings throughout the fall. The cooler tempera-tures mean less frequent watering. Check the top 6 inches of soil and water thoroughly as it begins to dry.

Established plants benefit from supple-mental watering during a dry fall. Check the soil and water thoroughly when the top 6 inches are dry.

Check soil moisture in aboveground planters every day. Water thoroughly anytime the top few inches of the soil begin to dry. Continue to water planters until the soil in the planter freezes. Make sure all new plantings and evergreens receive a thorough watering before the ground freezes.

Wait until spring to fertilize shrubs. Fall is a great time to take a soil test.
You will have time to read the report and plan your
shrub fertilization program for next season.

FERTILIZING

Wait until spring to fertilize shrubs. Fall is a great time to take a soil test. You will have time to read the report and plan your shrub fertilization program for next season.

PRUNING

Remove any damaged or pest-infested branches. Wait until late winter to do major pruning. This way you can take care of winter damage and regular pruning at the same time.

PROBLEMS

Watch for the last few pests of the season. Cooler temperatures usually mean fewer aphids and mites. Make notes on this year's experiences to help guide you through next season.

Contact a plant care professional or check with a garden center if your landscape suffered severe feeding damage from Japanese beetles, scale, and other pests. Professionals can use a soil-applied systemic insecticide in the fall for control next season. Read and follow label instructions. Improper use of this product can contaminate ground water and can cause an increase in other pests.

Helpful Hints

Colorful autumn foliage is nature's curtain call for the season. Improve the seasonal show in your landscape by adding shrubs with good fall color. Add this to the list of features to consider when creating a beautiful garden.

Some shrubs with good, fall color to consider:

Red to orange
- **American Cranberrybush** (*Viburnum trilobum*)
- **Barberry** (*Berberis* species)
- **Burning Bush** (*Euonymus alatus* and many of its relatives)
- **Chokeberries** (*Aronia* species)
- **Cotoneasters** (*Cotoneaster* species)
- **Fothergilla** (*Fothergilla gardenii*) with tinge of maroon
- **Koreanspice Viburnum** (*Viburnum carlesii*) with tinge of burgundy
- **Running Serviceberry** (*Amelanchier stolonifera*)
- **Spirea** (*Spiraea japonica*)
- **Sumac** (*Rhus* species)

Purple
- **Dogwood** (*Cornus* species)

Yellow
- **Roses** (*Rosa* species and cultivars)
- **Witchhazel** (*Hamamelis virginiana*)

Leaf spots and blotches are common problems in cool, wet seasons. Do not bother to spray the plants; it will not help. Remove small numbers of infected leaves as soon as they appear. Rake and destroy disease infected leaves. This reduces the source of infection next season.

Note plants covered with a white powdery substance. The powdery mildew fungus is a common problem on **lilacs** and many other plants. Fortunately the plant will survive; it just looks bad. Thin out overgrown shrubs next spring to increase light and air circulation and to reduce disease problems.

Remove weeds from planting beds. Unwanted plants can compete with the shrubs and host unwanted diseases.

OCTOBER
Shrubs

 PLANNING

Enjoy the last few glimpses of color. Soon much of the landscape will be covered in snow.

 PLANTING

Continue planting as long as shrubs are available and the ground is workable. The cool fall weather makes this a great time for planting. The good weather conditions mean less stress on the transplants and the planter. The planting process starts with a call to your utility-locating service. Call at least three working days before planting. This free service marks the location of all underground utilities. Working with utility-locating services can prevent costly damage to underground utilities and may save your life.

Transplant shrubs as soon as they are dormant. See March "Planting" on page 266 for more information. See September "Planting" on page 278 for more specifics on moving dormant shrubs.

Finish planting evergreens early in the month. This gives the plants a little more time to put down roots before winter arrives.

 CARE

Rake and compost or recycle fallen leaves. Disease-free leaves can be shredded and left on the lawn, dug into annual gardens, or added to the compost pile. Bury or discard disease-infected leaves. These are a source of infection for the next growing season.

Prepare aboveground planters for winter. Find a sheltered location in an unheated garage or enclosed porch to store the planters for winter. Use bales of hay to insulate shrubs in planters left outside.

 WATERING

Water plants as needed until the ground freezes. New plantings, evergreens, and aboveground planters need the most attention. Water thoroughly when the top 6 inches of the soil start to dry.

Give all plants a thorough watering, especially new plantings and evergreens, before the ground freezes. Well-managed plants have a greater rate of winter survival.

 FERTILIZING

Wait until spring to fertilize. Evaluate the health and vigor of shrub plantings to determine what needs to be fertilized next year. Take a soil test to be sure nutrients are needed. Fall sampling ensures you have the fertilization information needed for spring.

 PRUNING

You can begin dormant pruning, but Melinda and Cathy prefer to wait until late winter. The plants recover quicker from the pruning, and they like to leave the stems, fruits, and dried flowers intact for winter interest. Low input (not lazy!) gardeners do all their chores at one time. Late winter pruning allows us to repair winter and animal damage while shaping the shrubs. One time spent pruning versus two!

Wait until early spring to prune evergreens. Pruning now exposes the inner growth that has not been exposed to wind and sun. Fall pruning can increase winter injury.

Avoid pruning spring-blooming shrubs, such as **lilacs** and **forsythia**. Dormant season pruning removes flower buds needed for next spring's display. Remove only dead, pest-infected, or damaged branches at this time.

Prepare aboveground planters for winter. Find a sheltered location in an unheated garage or enclosed porch to store the planters for winter.

PROBLEMS

Fall cleanup is the best way to reduce and even eliminate some future pest problems. Rake and bury or destroy diseased leaves. Prune out and destroy diseased branches. Disinfect tools between cuts.

Call in a professional to manage severe and ongoing insect problems. Professionals have a soil applied systemic insecticide that is applied in fall to control a variety of leaf feeding insects next summer.

Take a few minutes to review the year. Mark next year's calendar, based on this season's problems, for potential times of peak pest activity. This will remind you to monitor your landscape for problems. Catching the problems early makes control easier and more successful.

Start putting animal barriers in place. Surround new plantings with a 4-foot high fence buried several inches into the soil. This will help keep voles and rabbits away from the base of the plants.

Visit your favorite garden center and stock up on repellents if animals have been a problem in the past. Early applications, before feeding starts, appear to be more effective. Reapply repellents after harsh weather and as recommended on the label.

Helpful Hints

As you look through your landscape and nearby woods, you may see a few summer holdouts. These few shrubs are reluctant to give up their leaves. A closer look reveals the true identity of these plants—**buckthorn** and **honeysuckles**. These invasive plants have escaped cultivation and are now taking over our natural areas.

Buckthorn and **honeysuckles** are tough plants once considered the answer for low-maintenance urban landscapes. Both tolerate a wide range of conditions and need little care. Sound too good to be true? It was. These tough plants are now crowding out our native plants and destroying food and habitat for wildlife.

Help control these invaders and preserve our woodlands with the following tips:

Cut large plants (6 inches in diameter and larger) back to the ground and treat the stumps with a total vegetation killer such as Roundup or Finale or a brush killer such as Brush-B-Gon. Use a low-pressure handheld sprayer, spray bottle, or sponge brush to apply the chemical. Treat the exposed vascular system located just inside the bark on the cut stem.

Smaller plants can be treated using the basal bark method. No need to cut the trees. Apply the herbicide to the base of the plant. Cover the stem from the soil line up to 12 to 15 inches high.

Always read and follow label directions carefully. Misapplications can damage the desirable plants and harm the applicator and the environment.

For help with identification and control of these invasive plants see:

http://www.nps.gov/plants/alien factsheets/buckthorns.htm

NOVEMBER
Shrubs

PLANNING

Pull out the journal and review problems encountered last winter. Check notes you made on winter protection needed to prevent plant damage this season. Locate and gather materials needed.

Make a visit to the garden center to purchase needed supplies. Shop now before our thoughts and their shelves are overrun with the holidays.

PLANTING

Continue planting and transplanting as long as the ground is workable. Wait until spring to plant evergreens. This gives the plants a chance to put down roots and get established before the harsh winter weather arrives.

Late purchases can be protected until spring planting season arrives. Find a protected location away from wind and sun. Sink the pots into the ground to insulate the roots from temperature extremes. Enclose plants in a cylinder of hardware cloth 4 feet high and sunk several inches into the soil. This will help protect them from voles, rabbits, and possibly deer.

CARE

Apply winter protection to shrubs exposed to deicing salts, snow loads, and winter wind and sun.

Give special attention to **rhododendrons** and other broadleaf evergreens. Use a screen of burlap to cut the winter winds and shade the plants from the drying winter sun. Or circle the plants with a cylinder of hardware cloth several feet tall and sunk several inches into the ground. Fill with straw or evergreen branches to protect the plants. Melinda prefers evergreen boughs—much more festive.

Loosely tie upright **arborvitae**, **junipers**, and **yews** that are subject to splitting. Use strips of cotton cloth or old nylon stockings to tie the multiple stems together. This prevents snow from building up on the plant, causing it to split and bend.

Do not use tree wraps on trees and shrubs. Research has found that they do not help and can, in fact, hurt the plants. If you feel you must use them, apply them in the fall and remove them in the spring.

WATERING

Keep watering as needed until the ground freezes. Cool temperatures and fall rains often eliminate the need for supplemental watering.

Make sure new plantings and evergreens are thoroughly watered before the ground freezes. Once the ground is frozen, drain and store the hose until spring.

FERTILIZING

No need to fertilize. Evaluate the health and vigor of the shrubs and the soil test results to determine if fertilizer is needed.

Store leftover fertilizers for winter. Granular fertilizers need to be kept in a cool, dry place. Keep liquid fertilizers in a dark location in above-freezing temperatures.

PRUNING

Dormant pruning can be done now until growth begins in spring. Prune summer- and fall-blooming plants, such as **hydrangea** and **potentilla**. Or wait until late winter so that you can enjoy the winter interest these plants provide.

Wait until spring, after flowering, to prune **lilacs**, **forsythia**, and other spring-flowering shrubs. Remove damaged branches as needed.

Check, clean and sharpen hand pruners while waiting for the pruning season to begin. Replace the damaged or old blades that can no longer be sharpened. High-quality pruners have replacement blades, while cheaper pruners must be replaced when damaged. Replacement blades are available through garden supply catalogs and many garden centers. Replace nicked and damaged blades.

Use a 3-cornered (tapered) metal file to sharpen the cutting edge of your hand pruners. Take the pruners apart for easier sharpening. Sharpen away from the blade for safety or toward the cutting edge for a sharp edge—just be careful. Smooth off any burrs that form along the edge. Make a test cut to check for sharpness.

Clean the blades with a light-weight oil. Spray to lubricate the working parts and prevent rust.

Helpful Hints

Winter means ice and snow and the work that goes with managing both.

Avoid dumping snow on shrubs. Heavy snow can break branches.

Reduce the damage to your landscape plants and the environment by shoveling first and salting last. Use the snow blower or shovel to remove the majority of snow.

Once the snow is removed, use sand or an environmentally friendly deicing product such as magnesium chloride and calcium acetate. This will minimize the damage to plants and our environment.

Use burlap, decorative fencing, or other structures to protect plants from roadway salts. A physical barrier can keep the salt off the plants and reduce damage.

Leach salt through the soil in the spring. Thoroughly water areas exposed to road and sidewalk salt. Heavy spring rains or a thorough watering will move the salt through the soil and away from plant roots.

Use salt-tolerant shrubs in areas exposed to roadway and sidewalk salt. Some examples are: **alpine currant** (*Ribes alpinum*), **fragrant** and **staghorn sumac** (*Rhus aromatica* and *R. typhina*), **Mockorange** (*Philadelphus* spp.), **pfitzer juniper** (*Juniperus chinensis* 'Pfitzerana'), **Rugosa Rose** (*Rosa rugosa*), **Siberian Pea Shrub** (*Caragana arborescens*), **Snowberry** (*Symphoricarpos albus*), and **Tamarisk** (*Tamarix ramosissima*).

PROBLEMS

Make sure animal fences and barriers are In place.

Ornamental plums, **euonymus**, fruit trees, and **arborvitae** are a few wildlife favorites. Monitor these plantings for animal damage throughout the winter.

Place snow fencing around desirable plants. A 5-foot fence around a small area will often keep out the deer. Make sure they cannot reach in and feed.

Use a cylinder of hardware cloth, 4 feet tall and sunk into the ground, to protect plants from rabbits and deer.

Start applying repellents to areas and plants that have suffered animal damage in the past. Preventative treatments often encourage animals to feed in another location.

Store pesticides in a secure area that is out of the reach of children and pets. Liquids need to be stored out of the light in a frost-free location. Granules need to be kept dry.

DECEMBER

PLANNING

Sit back, relax, and take a look out the window. Get out your gardening journal and record your thoughts on the past growing season. Make a few notes about what you want to do differently and what can stay the same. Now look out the window again. Is your landscape working for you now? Make a list of additions that should be considered in next year's plan. Consider adding some plants for winter interest, attracting wildlife, or feeding your family. See January, February, and September "Helpful Hints" on pages 263, 265, and 279 for specific plant recommendations.

PLANTING

Clean and pack away the tools—another planting season is over. While storing your tools do a quick inventory. Remember the holidays are coming and gardening tools would make a great gift to give—or better yet, to receive! Melinda will take a good pruning saw over a blender any day.

CARE

Check winter protection and make sure it is securely in place—keeping out the animals or protecting the plants from harsh winter weather and deicing salt.

Carefully add holiday lights to the winter landscape. Do not wrap branches with strands of lights. Drape the lights over the branches or loosely secure the lights to the stems. Remove lights in spring. If left in place the ties can damage fast-growing shrubs.

WATERING

No need to water once the ground freezes. Check soil moisture in above-ground planters. Water planters anytime the soil thaws and dries. Drain and store the hose for winter.

FERTILIZING

Store fertilizers for the winter. Keep granular fertilizers in a cool, dry place. Liquids should be stored in a cool (above freezing), dark location.

PRUNING

Continue dormant pruning on summer- and fall-blooming shrubs. Wait until after bloom to prune spring-flowering shrubs. Once the snow falls, limit your pruning to repair damage.

Prune off a few branches of **red twig dogwood**, **juniper**, **winterberry**, **arborvitae**, and **yews**. Add these to your indoor or outdoor holiday decor.

PROBLEMS

Secure fencing and animal barriers. Continue applying repellents to areas and plants frequently browsed by animals. Reapply after harsh weather and as recommended by the label directions.

Store pesticides in a secure location out of the reach of children and pets. Store granules and powders in a cool, dry location. Keep liquids in a cool (above freezing), dark location. Make a note of old products you no longer use. Watch for community clean-sweep programs next spring. These programs collect and dispose of old pesticides. Store the unwanted materials together and plan on disposing of them at the next community clean-sweep event.

CHAPTER TEN

Trees

Trees create the framework of your landscape. They provide longevity and structure for the rest of your plantings. As they grow and mature, they also impact the environment for the surrounding plantings. Mature trees increase shade—and decrease the water available to neighboring plants.

Trees impact your environment. Use them as windbreaks to block the cold winter winds blowing in from the north and west. Plant them on the east or west side of the house to keep your home cooler in summer. Avoid planting shade trees on the south side of the house, or you'll be blocking out the important winter sun that helps warm our homes and reduces heating costs in winter. Use trees to create beauty and function in the landscape. They can help block bad views or frame good vistas. Select trees that produce nectar for butterflies and bees, seeds and fruit for the birds, or shelter for wildlife—and some edibles for you as well.

PLANNING

Growing a tree into a healthy and attractive asset for the landscape starts with a plan.

Select trees that are suited to the growing conditions. They should be able to thrive in the light, winds, and existing soil.

Make sure that the tree will still fit the space available once it reaches its mature size. Those little trees will grow big and often outgrow the small space we have allotted.

Grow the most pest-resistant trees and cultivars available. Healthy trees will live longer with less care and cleanup from you. Plant for the future, not just immediate impact. Fast-growing trees are usually the first to break apart in storms, decline, or die from disease. Use a mix of fast- and slow-growing trees for immediate and long-term enjoyment. The slow growers will take over as the fast-growing trees begin to decline.

As you narrow down your selection, look for trees that provide year-round interest. Summer is short and memories of that beautiful summer landscape fade quickly during the long months of winter. Select trees with:

Colorful bark or interesting growth habits for the winter landscape.

Flowers and fruit for added color and for attracting birds and butterflies to your outdoor living space.

Evergreen leaves or needles to give the garden unity from one season to the next, and give a substantive splash of green in the dark and dreary winter.

PLANTING

Start with a call to a utility locating service in your state—at least three working days before planting. This free service marks the location of all underground utilities. Working with these utility-locating services can prevent costly damage to underground utilities and may save your life. You also risk a very stiff fine if you don't get this info. Adjust planting locations to avoid conflicts with both underground and overhead utilities.

Visit your local nursery, home, or garden center while waiting for the utility service. Decide what type of planting stock best serves your needs. Trees are sold as bare-root, balled-and-burlapped, or container plants.

Trees

Bare-root trees are inexpensive and lightweight, but they have the poorest survival rate. They must be planted as soon as possible after digging. This makes them a less than ideal choice for most homeowners. They are frequently used by municipalities, parks, and other organizations for large-scale plantings. Bare-root plants are only available for you to buy from a few sources.

Balled-and-burlapped trees are dug in early spring before growth begins or fall after leaf drop. The trees are dug with a small portion of the rootball intact. They are more expensive and heavier, but they have a greater rate of survival than bare-root trees.

Container-grown trees are planted and grown in pots for several years. The smaller root system and pots make them easier to manage. They are moderately priced and can be planted spring through fall.

No matter what type of planting stock you select, make sure it is a healthy tree. Look for trees with straight trunks, a strong central leader (main stem), or appropriate growth habit. Avoid trees with damaged trunks, wilted or scorched leaves, or signs of insect and disease damage.

Give your healthy tree a safe ride home. Use a pickup, trailer, or large vehicle to move the plant. Loosely tie the branches to minimize breakage. Cover the canopy with plastic or fabric if the leaves have started to grow. Carefully lay the tree on its side. Wrap the trunk with carpet or fabric anywhere it comes in contact with the vehicle to prevent damage. Tie the tree in place, and do not forget the red flag for trees that extend 3 feet beyond the vehicle. Many nurseries will help.

Sound like a lot of work? You may want to spend a little extra money to have the experts deliver your tree. They have the staff and equipment to handle and move large trees. Many nurseries will even place the tree in a prepared planting hole for you. Consider the delivery charge as an insurance policy on your initial investment. A few nurseries even guarantee the tree—if they plant it. It may be worth the money if is a large tree.

Once your tree is home, follow these planting tips:

Store trees in a cool, shaded location until they can be planted. Cover the roots of bare-root and balled-and-burlapped trees with woodchips. Water all planting stock often enough to keep the roots moist.

Locate the root flare on the tree by gently pulling the soil away from the trunk. The root flare is the area where the roots gradually spread from the trunk. This area is often covered by soil.

Measure the distance from the root flare to the bottom of the rootball. This is equal to the depth of your planting hole.

Dig a hole the same depth as the rootball (wider on the bottom) and at least two to three times wider than the root system.

Make a wide, shallow, saucer-shaped planting hole. Research has shown that the roots will be better able to penetrate the surrounding soil.

For container-grown trees:

1 Roll the pot on its side or push on the container to loosen the roots.

2 Cut away the bottom of the container.

3 Place the tree in the planting hole so that the root flare is at or slightly above the soil surface.

4 Slice and peel away the container. Loosen the roots by hand or with a sharp knife.

For balled-and-burlapped trees:

1 Place the tree in the planting hole so that the root flare is at or slightly above the soil surface.

Trees

2 Remove the twine and cut away the burlap and wire cages. These materials do not decompose in most soils and can interfere with root growth and eventually girdle parts of the tree.

For all trees:

1 Use your shovel to roughen the sides of the planting hole. This prevents glazing (smooth sides) in clay soils, which keeps the roots from growing into the surrounding soil.

2 Fill the planting hole with existing soil. Highly amended soils discourage root development into the surrounding soil. Water or gently tamp to help settle the soil and remove air pockets.

3 Mulch the soil with a 2- to 3-inch layer of woodchips or shredded bark. Keep the chips away from the trunk to avoid disease problems.

4 Water the planting hole and the surrounding soil to encourage root growth after planting. Water frequently enough to keep the top 12 inches of soil moist, but not wet. Most trees are killed with kindness from overwatering.

5 Remove only broken and damaged branches. Wait two to four years before doing major pruning.

FERTILIZING

Start with a soil test. A soil test will tell you how often and what type of fertilizer to apply. Contact your local office of the Cooperative Extension Service for soil test information. Wait a year to fertilize newly planted trees. Use a slow-release fertilizer with the analysis and amount recommended by your soil test report. Most established trees need infrequent fertilization. They get nutrients from decaying mulch or lawn fertilizer.

Increase natural fertilization by leaving grass clippings on the lawn. Shred fall leaves and leave them on the soil to decompose. Both add organic matter and nutrients to the soil without harming the lawn. For more details on fertilization, see April and September "Fertilizing."

WATERING

Proper watering is the key to successful planting and establishment. Excess water is the cause of many tree deaths. Water trees thoroughly, but only when needed.

In clay soils, water the trees until the top 12 inches are moist. Check in a week. Water again when top 6 to 8 inches begin to dry. The soil will feel moist, but crumbly.

Sandy soils need a thorough watering twice a week in hot, dry weather. Water thoroughly until the top 12 inches are moist. Check in four days. Water when the soil begins to dry.

PRUNING

As trees grow and develop, they will need occasional pruning to maintain a strong, healthy, and attractive structure.

Remove only broken and damaged branches on newly planted trees. More branches mean more leaves and more energy produced to help the tree grow new roots.

Prune young trees to establish one trunk with a strong framework of branches.

Prune established trees to repair damage, remove hazards, and strengthen the tree's framework.

See January and February "Helpful Hints" for more details on pruning.

Trees

PESTS

Minimize pest problems by planting the right tree for your location. Trees suited to their environments have fewer pest problems.

Check trees frequently for pest problems. Look for speckled and discolored leaves, holes, spots, and other signs of insects and disease. Early detection can make control easier and more effective. It may also save your tree.

Contact a certified arborist or your county Cooperative Extension Service for help in diagnosing pest problems. Consider hiring a professional for large jobs. They have the equipment and training to do the job safely and right. A list of certified arborists for your area is available at isa-arbor.com.

Did You Know?

Overzealous grass cutters often nick and injure tree trunks with the mower or weed whip, trying to get that last blade of grass. These small wounds create entryways for insects and diseases. Reduce damage to your trees and maintenance chores for you by creating large beds of mulch or groundcovers around your trees.

Mulch the area under trees with woodchips or shredded bark. It improves the growing conditions, keeps mowers and weed whips away from the trunk, and means less work for you.

Don't like mulch? Consider planting perennial groundcovers, such as **vinca**, **pachysandra**, and **deadnettle**, around trees. See August "Helpful Hints" for details on adding flowers and groundcovers without killing the tree.

Trees

Tall Trees

Common Name (Botanical Name)	Hardiness Zones	Maximum Height/ Spread (In Feet)	Comment
Ash, White (*Fraxinus americana*)	3 to 5	50+/50	Prefers moist soil; red to purple fall color; good shade tree.
Fir, White (*Abies concolor*)	4 to 5	70/30	Best fir for our region; good substitute for Blue Spruce; softer texture and fewer pests.
Ginkgo (*Ginkgo biloba*)	4 to 6	80/40 (great variability)	Slow-growing but tough plant with no pests; select male clone (fruit on female stinks).
Hemlock (*Tsuga canadensis*)	3 to 5	75/25	Shade-tolerant evergreen; needs moist soils and a protected location.
Honeylocust (*Gleditsia triacanthos inermis*)	4 to 5	60/variable	Tough tree that is overused; casts only filtered shade so grass can grow beneath; select podless varieties for less mess.
Kentucky Coffeetree (*Gymnocladus dioicus*)	4 to 5	60/40	Possible substitute for Honeylocust; tough tree with bolder texture.
Linden (*Tilia* spp.)	3 to -5	60+/40	Size and hardiness vary with species; Littleleaf, Redmond, and Silver are all suited to tough conditions; American prefers more yard-like setting; yellow fragrant flowers in summer.
Maple, Freeman (*Acer fremannii* 'Autumn Blaze')	3 to 5	50/40	Cross between Red and Silver; good fall color; more tolerant of alkaline soils.
Maple, Norway (*Acer platanoides*)	4 to 5	50/25	Tough tree that is overused and becoming invasive in our woodlands; dense canopy and surface roots.
Maple, Red (*Acer rubrum*)	3 to 5	50/25+	Must have moist, acid soils; smooth gray bark with red fall color.
Maple, Sugar (*Acer saccharum*)	3 to 5	75/50	Needs rich, moist soils; keep away from salt and heat; wonderful fallcolor.
Oak, Bur (*Quercus macrocarpa*)	3 to 5	80/60+	Adaptable; dry to wet soil; bold addition to the landscape.
Oak, Red (*Quercus rubra*)	3 to 5	75/60	Good Oak for urban situations; one of the faster growing Oaks; keep out of oak wilt-infested areas.

Trees

Tall Trees

Common Name (*Botanical Name*)	Hardiness Zones	Maximum Height/ Spread (In Feet)	Comment
Pine, Austrian (*Pinus nigra*)	3b to 7	50/40	Full sun and dry soils; tough but overused tree, suffering from a wide range of insect and disease problems.
Pine, Scots (*Pinus sylvestris*)	3 to 7	50/40	Orange bark and blue-green needles; full sun and well-drained soils.
Pine, White (*Pinus strobus*)	3 to 7	50/40	Picturesque with age; brittle wood, branches snap in severe weather and heavy snow; not an urban tree; full sun and moist soil.
Spruce, Blue (*Picea pungens*)	3 to 7	60/20	Prefers sun; has stiff, formal habit; used extensively; suffers from insect and disease problems.
Spruce, Serbian (*Picea omorika*)	4 to 7	50/20	Full sun; narrower than the Blue Spruce with pendulous branches.
Spruce, White (*Picea glauca*)	2 to 6	50/20	Prefers full sun; 'Black Hills' variety is smaller, denser, and tolerates drier soil.

Medium Trees
(30 to 40 feet)

Common Name (*Botanical Name*)	Hardiness Zones	Maximum Height/ Spread (In Feet)	Comment
Alder (*Alnus glutinosa*)	4 to 7	40/20	Fast grower that tolerates moist to poorly drained soils.
Amur Chokecherry (*Prunus maackii*)	3 to 5	35/35	Fast-growing tree with coppery bark.
Birch, Paper (*Betula papyrifera*) *Betula platyphylla*	2 to 6	40/30	Favored for its white bark; needs cool, moist soils; subject to borer; grow 'Whitespire Senior' for a borer- resistant white bark Birch.
Birch, River (*Betula nigra*)	3 to 9	40/50	Tolerates wet to dry soil; exfoliating brown, cream, and pink bark; borer resistant.
Ohio Buckeye	3 to 7	30/30	Prefers rich, moist soil; fruit can be messy; orange to

(*Aesculus glabra*)   red fall color.

Small Trees

Common Name (*Botanical Name*)	Hardiness Zones	Maximum Height/ Spread (In Feet)	Comment
Arborvitae (*Thuja occidentalis*)	3 to 5	40/10	Prefers moist soil and full sun to part shade; columnar form makes it suitable as a screen.
Callery Pear (*Pyrus calleryana*)	5	30/20	Glossy foliage, white flowers in spring, and red fall color. Grow 'Autumn Blaze' or one of the other hardier varieties.
Crabapple (*Malus* hybrids)	3 to 5	10-30/ variable widths	Select disease-resistant cultivars with small, persistent fruit. Many sizes and shapes are available with white, pink, or red flowers and yellow, orange, or red fruit.
Hawthorn (*Crataegus* spp.)	3 to 5	20-30/25	Hardiness varies with species; white flowers; yellow to red fall color and fruit for wildlife; thorns.
Japanese Tree Lilac (*Syringa reticulata*)	3 to 5	25/15	Prefers sun; large white flowers in mid- to late June; attractive bark.
Magnolia, Star (*Magnolia stellata*)	4b to 5	15/10	Needs moist, rich soil; has fragrant white flowers before the leaves appear; smooth gray bark.
Maple, Amur (*Acer ginnala*)	3 to 5	15/15	Full sun to part shade; orange to red fall color; starting to appear in native areas (invasive).
Pagoda Dogwood (*Cornus alternifolia*)	3 to 5	15/20	Native tree with strong horizontal branching; needs moist soil and prefers part shade.
Redbud (*Cercis canadensis*)	4 to 5	40/12	Beautiful heart-shaped leaves. Early blooming with edible (if tree is not sprayed) pink flowers have pea-like flavor and crunch. Plant in protected site. Select 'Columbus' or Minnesota strains.
Redcedar (*Juniperus virginiana*)	3b to 5	20/15	Full sun; well-drained to dry soils; do not plant with Crabapples and Hawthorns (alternate hosts for rust disease).
Serviceberry (*Amelanchier species*)	3 to 5	25/variable	Four-season tree with white flowers and blueberry-like edible (if tree is not sprayed) fruit; range to red fall color, and smooth gray bark. Prefers full sun to part shade and moist soils.

PLANNING

January is a great time to update an existing landscape or start something new. Start with a tour of your landscape followed by a visit to the library and arboretum. A winter walk is a great way to plan changes and shed a few holiday pounds.

While touring your landscape:

- Look for areas that would benefit from the addition of trees. Trees can provide screening, seasonal interest, shade, and act as windbreaks.

- Select planting areas large enough to accommodate the trees when fully grown.

- Avoid planting too close to buildings, power lines, and other utilities.

While at the library, check out books on landscape design, trees, and plantings for your area. Landscape designs can be modified for our climate by substituting hardy trees for those not suited to our area. Check Cooperative Extension Service publications for help selecting trees best suited for your landscape.

Trips to botanical gardens, arboretums, and parks can help you select the best tree for your landscape.

See which trees grow best in your climate.

Look for trees with colorful bark, persistent fruit, or attractive form for winter interest. Add **Washington hawthorn** and **crabapples** for their decorative fruit and bird attraction. Consider **magnolias** and **serviceberry** for their smooth gray bark that adds interest to the winter landscape.

Evaluate trees based on their mature sizes and shapes.

PLANTING

It is winter, the ground is covered with snow, and the planting season is a mere thought. So sit back, relax, and rest up for spring planting.

A few stretching exercises will help keep your gardening muscles limber. Use a little elbow grease to clean and sharpen your planting tools. A shovel with a sharp edge makes spring planting much easier.

CARE

Monitor and adjust snow removal to minimize winter injury. You can take steps to reduce damage this season and reduce winter injury next year.

Shovel snow before reaching for the deicing salt. Removing the snow by hand will reduce the need for plant-damaging salt.

Check trees for snow and ice damage. Do not try to knock frozen snow and ice off trees. This can cause more damage than the snow and ice.

Make notes on next year's calendar to adjust winter protection and prevent future problems. List all winter protection—such as tying evergreens, shielding plants from salt and wind, and watering in well before the ground freezes—that you want to complete before the snow flies.

WATERING

The ground is usually frozen, and there is no need to water outside. Water above-ground planters anytime the soil is not frozen and dry.

FERTILIZING

Wait until spring to fertilize. Fertilizing frozen soil does not help your trees and pollutes the groundwater.

Shovel snow before reaching for the deicing salt. Removing the snow by hand will reduce the need for plant-damaging salt.

PRUNING

Trees can be pruned during the dormant season. It is much easier to see the overall shape of the tree and what needs to be removed. Prune **oaks** and **honeylocusts** in winter to reduce disease problems. See February "Helpful Hints" for more pruning tips.

Save branches from flowering trees, such as **crabapples**, **magnolias**, and **pussy willows,** for indoor bloom. Recut the stems and place in a bucket of water in a cool (60 degrees Fahrenheit), brightly lit location.

Mist the branches several times a day, if possible, until the stems start to bloom.

Flowering stems can be used in arrangements with other flowers or by themselves.

Prolong the blossoms by storing the blooming stems in a cooler spot (40 degrees Fahrenheit) at night.

PROBLEMS

Walk through the landscape and check for animal damage and overwintering insects. A little prevention now can save lots of headaches and extra work come spring.

Check and repair fencing and other animal barriers. Reapply repellents or alternate scare tactics to prevent and reduce animal damage. Remove egg masses of gypsy and tussock moths.

Helpful Hints

Pruning With a Purpose

Prune with a purpose in mind. Strive to maintain the plant's natural shape. Prune young trees to establish a strong framework. Use proper pruning to maintain a strong structure and healthy growth, as well as to improve flowering and fruiting on established trees.

Wait two to four years after planting to start pruning for structure. The more top growth (branches and leaves), the faster the tree will recover from transplanting.

Remove any branches that are crossed, sprouting from the same area on the trunk, or growing parallel to each other.

Remove any branches that are growing straight up and competing with the main trunk.

Remaining branches should be more horizontal (perpendicular to the trunk) than upright.

Make sure branches are well spaced from top to bottom and around the tree trunk.

Well-trained trees need minimal pruning.

Consider hiring a certified arborist (see November "Planning") for large jobs. They have the training and equipment to do the job safely and properly.

Start by removing dead and damaged branches.

Next, prune out watersprouts (upright shoots on branches) and suckers (upright shoots at the base of the trunk) as close to their bases as possible.

Prune off lower branches only for safety and clearance. The lower limbs are the tree's best defense against disease and old age.

FEBRUARY
Trees

PLANNING

Continue researching and planning additions to your landscapes. Visit area garden and home shows for landscape and planting ideas. Winter hikes through botanical gardens can be inspiring and a great way to beat the winter blues. Once you select the type of tree, you need to consider the size and type of tree to purchase. Larger trees (over 3 inches in diameter) will give you bigger trees immediately, but they stay the same size for several years as they adjust to their new locations. Smaller trees adapt faster to transplanting and often outgrow their larger counterparts.

PLANTING

Patience is a virtue—especially for northern gardeners. Planting season is still at least a month or more away. Start contacting nurseries for information on plant availability and planting stock. Trees can be purchased as bare-root, balled-and-burlapped, or container-grown stock.

Bare-root trees are the cheapest and lightweight, but they have the poorest survival rate. They must be planted as soon as possible after digging. This makes them a less than ideal choice for most gardeners. Bare-root plants are only available for from a few sources.

Balled-and-burlapped trees (often called B-and-B) are dug in early spring before growth begins or in fall after leaf drop. The trees are dug with a small portion of the roots intact. They are more expensive and heavier, yet they have a greater rate of survival than bare-root trees.

Container-grown trees are planted and grown in pots for several years. The smaller root system and pots make them easier to manage. They are moderately priced and can be planted from spring through fall.

CARE

Shovel the snow before applying sand or deicing salt to reduce the need for deicers that can be harmful to trees and other plants. Consider using some of the more plant-friendly deicers, such as calcium chloride, calcium magnesium acetate, or sand (salt-less), which are kinder to the plants and landscape.

Continue monitoring the landscape for animal and winter damage. Make notes of problems in your journal. Record problems with ice loads, snow damage, and poor drainage. Check November "Care" for maintenance strategies to reduce winter injury.

WATERING

The ground is still frozen, so there is no need to water outside. Check soil moisture in tree planters overwintering in the garage or screened-in porch. Water the planters thoroughly whenever the soil is thawed and dry.

FERTILIZING

No need to fertilize. Check your journal and any soil test information to start planning for spring fertilization. Fertilizing frozen soil will not help the trees, and it contributes to groundwater pollution.

PRUNING

Prune trees during the dormant season when it's much easier to see the overall shape of the tree and what needs to be removed. Prune **oaks** and **honeylocusts** in winter to reduce disease problems. See January "Helpful Hints" for more pruning tips.

Remove damaged and hazardous branches as they appear. Consider hiring a certified arborist for large jobs. They have the tools, equipment, and training to do the job safely. See November "Planning" on page 312 for information on hiring an arborist.

Crossing, parallel, or rubbing branches can also be removed. See "Helpful Hints" for more details.

Prune **birches**, **walnuts**, and **maples** can be pruned in late winter. The running sap does not hurt the tree; it just makes the job messy.

Save branches from flowering trees such as **crabapples**, **magnolias**, and **pussy willows** for indoor bloom. See January "Pruning" for details on forcing these to bloom indoors.

PROBLEMS

Continue checking trees for over-wintering insects. Egg masses of tent caterpillars look like small, shiny blobs of mud on stems. Gypsy and tussock moth egg masses are fuzzy masses found on tree trunks. Remove and destroy these whenever found. Squash them or scrape them off the tree into a zippered bag to get rid of them.

Apply a dormant oil spray, such as Volck® and All Seasons®, on warm days when temperatures are 40 degrees Fahrenheit or above for at least 12 hours. Dormant oil sprays are used to control many gall-causing insects (for aesthetic reasons only), some scales, aphids, and mites. Galls cause bumps

Did You Know?

Limb Removal

How you remove a branch is as important as deciding which branch to remove. Improper cuts create perfect entryways for insects and disease.

Make the pruning cut flush with the branch bark collar. See the final cut of the three-step pruning cut illustration. Pruning cuts flush with the trunk are slow to close and make a great entryway for pests and decay. Stubs left behind look unsightly and also increase pest problems.

Remove branches where they join the trunk or other branches. This will help maintain the tree's natural form and encourage balanced growth.

Larger branches (2 inches in diameter or greater) should be double-cut to prevent branch splitting and bark tearing.

Make the first cut on the bottom of the branch about 12 inches from the final cut. Cut about one-fourth of the way through the branch.

Make the second cut on top of the branch within 1 inch of the first cut. Continuing cutting until the branch breaks off.

Do not apply pruning paints or wound dressings to pruning cuts. Recent research shows that these materials actually trap moisture and disease in rather than keeping them out. Oaks pruned during the growing season are the only exception.

on leaves while scale, aphids, and mites cause discolored and brown leaves. Make sure you have a problem before using this or any chemical.

Limb Removal

PLANNING

Finalize your landscape plans. Stop by local nurseries and garden centers, or visit home and garden shows. Ask about additional ideas and plant availability. Some of the newer varieties or unusual plants may be difficult to find. Shop early to find potential sources.

 PLANTING

Late winter and early spring are the best times to transplant trees. Moving trees can be tricky and heavy work. Save large, expensive, and special trees for professionals. They have the experience and equipment to move larger plants successfully. For more details, see September "Planting."

 CARE

As the snow melts, animal damage and winter injury becomes more obvious.

Prune or remove damaged branches. See February and this month's "Helpful Hints."

Check the base of plants for girdling by rabbits and voles. Damage appears as a lighter area on the trunk. You can often see the teeth marks. Vole and rabbit damage interrupts the flow of water and nutrients between the roots and leaves. Severe damage (feeding around most of the trunk) can kill trees. When in doubt, wait and see if the tree will survive.

Remove and replace severely damaged trees. Some gardeners try bridge grafting in a last attempt to save special plants. Take a piece of branch from the damaged tree. Graft one end above and the other end below the damaged portion. You must line up the vascular system of the graft with the trunk of the tree. This difficult process requires lots of skill and a little luck.

Remove tree wraps as temperatures warm. Research has shown wrapping tree trunks is not beneficial and can even be harmful to trees. If you use tree wraps, remove them in spring, and throw them away.

 WATERING

Wait for the ground to thaw, then check the soil moisture before watering. You may need to lend Nature a hand in years with limited snowmelt and dry springs. Thoroughly water trees subjected to deicing salt. This will help wash the chemicals through the soil and away from the tree roots.

Continue to water trees in aboveground planters. Water thoroughly whenever the soil is thawed and dry.

 FERTILIZING

Wait until the ground thaws. Fertilizing on snow and frozen soil will not help the trees and contributes to groundwater pollution. Contact your local county office of the Cooperative Extension Service for soil test information. Take a soil test as soon as the ground thaws so that you will know if you need to fertilize your trees.

 PRUNING

Finish pruning before trees leaf out. Pruning during leaf expansion increases the risk of trunk and branch damage. See January and February "Helpful Hints" for details on proper pruning.

Complete pruning on **oaks** and **honeylocusts**. Dormant-season pruning helps reduce the risk of oak wilt on these trees.

birches, **walnuts**, and **maples** can be pruned in late winter. The running sap does not hurt the tree; it just makes the job messy.

Remove storm-damaged branches as they occur.

PROBLEMS

If needed and desired dormant oil sprays, such as Volck® and All Seasons®, can still be applied tp dormant trees. Make sure the temperature is 40 degrees Fahrenheit or higher when you spray, and for the following 12 hours. Dormant oils are used to control some scale insects, galls (mainly an aesthetic concern), and other overwintering insects. Look for bumps caused by galls and discolored or brown leaves caused by mites, aphids, and scale feeding during the growing season. Only spray if a problem exists that requires this type of treatment.

Continue to monitor and destroy egg masses of Eastern tent caterpillar, gypsy moth, and tussock moth.

Cankerworms are voracious insects that eat the leaves of **oaks**, **elms**, **apples**, **crabapples**, and many other trees. These brown or green wormlike insects can be seen munching on tree leaves. Fortunately, birds and weather usually keep these pests under control. Severe

Helpful Hints

Snow, ice, and winter winds can often damage or destroy the main leader of **spruce** and other evergreen trees. Without the central leader, the tree loses its nice pyramidal shape. As other branches compete for the lead position, the tree tends to flatten out. You can help restore the shape by giving Nature a helping hand.

To create a new central leader:

1 Cut off the damaged leader, leaving a 1½-inch stub.

2 Select one of the shorter side shoots to serve as the new leader.

3 Tie the side shoot to the remaining stub. Over time, this branch will start to grow upright and become the new leader.

4 Remove the tie after one year.

5 Several side shoots may begin to grow upward. Prune out all but the leader trained to be an upright growing stem.

infestations can be controlled. Apply sticky bands around the trunks of trees that were severely defoliated the previous season. Use a band of fabric treated with a sticky material, such as Tanglefoot, to avoid injury to the tree. Put sticky traps in place in mid-March through mid-June and in mid-October through mid-December.

Prune out black knot cankers. The cankers start out as swollen areas on the branches of **ornamental** and **edible plums**, **cherries**, and **flowering almonds**. They eventually release disease-causing spores and turn into black knots on the tree. Removing the cankers now reduces the risk of future infection.

APRIL
Trees

 PLANNING

Plan a special Arbor Day event for your family, friends, neighborhood, or school group. Find out when your community celebrates arbor day and participate.

 PLANTING

Start planting trees as soon as plants are available.

To plant your tree: Dig a wide, shallow hole. Make it at least two, preferably three or more times wider than the rootball. The depth should be equal to the distance from the root flare to the bottom of the rootball. See the "Planting" section in the chapter introduction for details.

 CARE

It is time to start preparing for spring:

Remove screening, cloth strapping, and other winter protection. Hardware cloth fencing can stay in place. Make sure the material is not rubbing or girdling the plant.

Remove winter insulation (bales of straw). Move trees growing in aboveground planters out of winter storage.

Renew mulch around trees in lawn areas and planting beds. A 2- to 3-inch layer of shredded bark or woodchip mulch helps conserve moisture, reduce weeds, and add organic matter. Keep the mulch several inches away from the trunk of the tree.

Keep lawn mowers and weed whips away from tree trunks. Mower blight (tree decline due to equipment damage) is the biggest killer of trees. Mulch, groundcovers, or planting beds reduce the need to hand trim and also protect trees from mowing equipment.

 WATERING

Water trees when the ground thaws and the soil is dry. Established trees will only need watering during dry periods. Thoroughly soak, with 1 to 2 inches of water, the area under the drip line when the top 6 to 10 inches of soil are moist and crumbly. This will be more frequent in sandy soils and during high temperatures.

Thoroughly water trees subjected to deicing salt. This will help wash the deicing chemicals through the soil and away from the tree roots.

Water new plantings often enough to keep the rootball and surrounding soil slightly moist. Provide 1 inch of water when the top 6 to 10 inches are moist and crumbly. This may be several times each week in sandy and gravelly soil, and as little as every two weeks in clay soils.

Continue to water trees in aboveground planters. Water until the excess drains out of the bottom of the pot. Check containers at least twice a week and water as needed.

 FERTILIZING

Spring—before growth begins—is a good time to fertilize established trees. Let the plant and a soil test be your guide. Trees often get nutrients from decomposing mulch, lawn fertilizers, and grass clippings left on the lawn.

Contact your Cooperative Extension Service office for soil test information.

Check trees for signs of nutrient deficiencies. Poor growth and off-color leaves may indicate the need to fertilize.

Wait a year to fertilize new tree plantings. They have been well tended in the nursery, and fertilizer may harm the newly developing roots.

If soil tests are not available, use a slow-release fertilizer containing just nitrogen or three times more nitrogen than phosphorus and potassium. Check the fertilizer analysis on the bag. The three numbers stand for the percentage of available nitrogen, phosphorus, and potassium in the fertilizer, in that order. The first number should be three times larger than the other two.

Apply 2 to 4 pounds of actual nitrogen per 1,000 square feet. This is equal to 20 to 40 pounds of a 10 percent nitrogen fertilizer and 10 to 20 pounds of a 20 percent nitrogen fertilizer.

Sprinkle fertilizer and rake through mulch. Water to move the fertilizer into the soil.

Place fertilizer in the soil for trees growing in lawn areas. Remove small cores of soil 6 inches deep and 2 to 3 feet apart throughout the area around the tree. Holes should start several feet away from the trunk and continue several feet beyond the drip line of the tree. Divide needed fertilizer evenly between the holes. Water until the top 12 inches of soil are moist.

PRUNING

Do not prune after the buds open and the leaves begin to grow. The tree is very susceptible to damage during this phase of growth. Resume pruning once the leaves are fully expanded.

Do not prune **oaks** and **honeylocusts** once growth begins. Wait until the dormant season to avoid disease problems.

PROBLEMS

This is a great time to prevent or reduce pest problems that may develop later in the season.

Insects. Reduce the spread of spruce gall on small trees. They prune out the small swollen sections (they look like miniature cones or pineapples on the stem) while they are green and the insects are still nesting inside.

Start checking **crabapples**, **birches**, and other ornamental trees in late April for signs of Eastern tent caterpillars. These wormlike insects build webbed nests in the crotches of tree branches. Remove or destroy the tent (can be knocked down with a long stick) to control this pest.

Birch leaf miners are insects that feed between the upper and lower surface of the leaves. Their feeding causes the leaves to turn brown. They do not kill the tree but add to the stress, making the white-barked **birches** more susceptible to borers. A soil systemic labeled for use on **birches** to control leaf miner can be applied now to prevent infestations. Do not treat trees that were treated with a soil systemic the previous fall.

Dead branch tips on your **Austrian pine** may mean it has Zimmerman moth. Consult a certified arborist for advice and treatment. Spray applications when the **saucer magnolia** is in the pink bud stage.

Diseases. Apple scab is a common problem on **crabapples** and **apples**. This fungal disease causes black spots and eventual leaf drop. Badly infested trees may be leafless by July. Raking and destroying infected leaves will reduce the source of disease. Fungicides labeled to control apple scab on **crabapples** will help reduce infection on susceptible trees. Make four to five applications of fungicides at ten-day intervals starting at bud break. Consider hiring an arborist with the training and equipment to do the job safely.

Dead branches on **spruce** are often caused by cytospora canker. Remove infected branches and disinfect tools with rubbing alcohol or a solution of one part bleach to nine parts water. Mulch the soil under the tree and water during dry periods.

MAY
Trees

PLANNING

The growing season is finally becoming a reality. Keep your landscape plan and garden journal handy. Record purchases and new additions to the garden. Check the growing conditions and your planting plans before purchasing new plants. All those beautiful plants are hard to resist after a long, cold winter. Make sure you have the space and proper growing conditions before purchasing additional trees.

PLANTING

Keep planting trees in the landscape. See the "Planting" section of the chapter introduction for details. Remove plant tags from the trunk and branches. Left in place, these can eventually girdle the stem.

CARE

Evaluate the size and thickness of mulch rings around trees. Bigger is better in this case. A wide ring of mulch, covering most of the area under the tree canopy, creates a good environment for the tree roots. Shredded bark and woodchips help conserve water, reduce weed growth, and add nutrients to the soil beneath.

Do not use weed barriers under bark, woodchips, and other organic mulches. They are only a temporary solution for weed growth and can create a maintenance headache in the long run. As the mulch on top of the weed barrier decomposes, it creates a perfect place for weeds and grass to grow. A weed barrier also prevents the organic matter from improving the soil beneath the barrier.

Get the most benefits from mulch by:

- Mulching both new and established trees.

- Maintaining a 3-inch layer of mulch around trees.

- Keeping the mulch several inches away from the tree trunk. Piling mulch around the trunk can lead to trunk decay.

WATERING

Spring often means lots of rain, but you may still need to lend a hand in dry years or with new plantings. Keep the rootball and surrounding soil of newly planted trees slightly moist, but not wet. Water the area thoroughly so that the top 10 to 12 inches of soil are wet. Water again once this area begins to dry. New plantings usually need to be watered once every seven to ten days in clay soil and twice a week in sandy soil.

Established trees have a larger root system to retrieve water. Spring rains usually provide ample moisture. Give established trees a thorough watering every two weeks during extended dry periods. **Paper birches** and other moisture-loving trees should be watered regularly during dry weather. Check these plants once a week and water when the top 6 inches of soil start to dry. Water aboveground planters thoroughly so that the excess water drains out the bottom. Check regularly and water as the top 6 inches of soil begin to dry.

FERTILIZING

We often kill plants with kindness. Trees receive many nutrients from grass clippings left on the lawn, decomposing mulch, and lawn fertilizers. Fertilize only when needed. Start with a soil test or consult a tree care professional if your trees do not look healthy.

Fertilize aboveground planters with any complete plant fertilizer, such as 10-10-10 or 12-12-12. Follow label directions for frequency and concentration.

A wide ring of mulch, covering most of the area under the tree canopy, creates a good environment for the tree roots. Shredded bark and woodchips help conserve water, reduce weed growth, and add nutrients to the soil beneath.

PRUNING

Give your saw a temporary break. Limit pruning to disease control and repair. Save major pruning for after the leaves have fully developed. This reduces the risk of damaging the bark.

Do not prune **oaks**. Pruning cuts increase the risk of oak wilt. Save **oak** pruning for the dormant season whenever possible.

PROBLEMS

Insects, like plants, are influenced by the weather. In cool seasons, insect problems develop one to two weeks later. In a warm spring, their populations are already starting to increase. Continue monitoring for the pests described in April "Pests."

Insects. Honeylocust plantbugs and leafhoppers begin feeding soon after buds break. This causes new growth to be distorted and sparse. Once the insects are done feeding, the trees will leaf out and be fine. Patience and proper care is the best control.

Remove tent caterpillar nests from infested trees. Do not burn the nest while it is in the tree. This is more harmful to the plant than the insects.

Watch for signs of gypsy moth larvae. These wormlike insects eventually grow to 2 inches long and have two rows of red and blue warts on their backs. Catch caterpillars as they crawl down the tree trunk looking for shade during the day. Wrap a 12- to 18-inch-wide strip of burlap around the tree trunk at chest height. Tie a string around the burlap 6 inches from the top. Let the top 6 inches of burlap flop over the string. Check under the burlap everyday between 2 and 6 p.m. Use gloves to remove caterpillars; drop them in soapy water to kill the insects or a zippered food storage bag.

European **pine** sawflies are wormlike insects that feed in colonies. They will do a little dance for you when you get too close. Check **mugo pines** and other common landscape **pines** for feeding colonies of this insect. Even in large numbers, they are easy to control. Slide on a leather glove and smash the insects. Or prune out the infested branch and destroy the insects.

Aphids and mites are common landscape pests. They suck out plant juices, causing leaf discoloration and distorted growth. Nature usually keeps them in check with rains and natural predators. In dry seasons, use the garden hose and a strong blast of water to dislodge the insects and reduce the damage. Lady beetles are a great aphid control.

Diseases. Phomopsis blight is a fungal disease that attacks **junipers** and **Russian olives**. It is most prevalent in cool, wet springs. The infected branches turn brown and die. Remove infected branches and disinfect tools between cuts.

Fireblight is a bacterial disease that infects susceptible **crabapples, pears, and European ash.** It causes the leaves to turn black and branch tips to curl. This disease spreads by splashing water, pollinating bees, and infected tools. Avoid pruning **crabapple** trees during wet periods. Prune out infected branches 12 inches below the canker (sunken, discolored area) on the stem. Disinfect tools between cuts with rubbing alcohol or a solution of one part bleach to nine parts water.

PLANNING

Summer storms can leave you with broken branches and uprooted trees. Proper care and preventative pruning can help reduce storm damage to trees. Consider contacting a certified arborist (tree care professional) to evaluate the health and soundness of your trees. Together you can develop a long-term plan to maintain or improve your tree's storm resistance. If damage does occur, you will have a good working relationship with a professional who can help you manage storm damage. See November "Planning" for tips on hiring an arborist.

PLANTING

Nurseries and garden centers still have a good supply of balled-and-burlapped and container-grown trees. Increase planting success by:

- Selecting healthy trees with green leaves free of brown spots, dry edges, or other signs of pest damage and neglect.

- Protecting newly emerged leaves while transporting your tree home. Wrap the canopy with a blanket or plastic tarp. Many nurseries will wrap the tree canopy for you, but it is best to come prepared.

- Storing trees in a shaded location until you are ready for planting.

- Checking the trees daily. Water frequently enough to keep the roots and surrounding soil moist. Cover the rootball of balled-and-burlapped trees and containers with woodchips if the trees will be stored for a long period of time.

See the "Planting" section of the chapter introduction for planting details.

CARE

Continue mulching trees as needed. A 3-inch layer will help improve tree growth and reduce maintenance for you. Keep the mulch several inches away from the trunk to avoid rot.

Consider replacing annual plantings under trees with perennial groundcovers. This means less root disturbance for the tree and less work for you in the long run.

WATERING

Watering frequency is dependent upon the age of the tree, weather conditions, and soil. Most established trees need infrequent watering. Water established trees every two weeks during extended dry periods. Apply enough water to moisten the top 12 inches of soil. Moisture loving trees, such as **paper birch**, may need to be watered once a week during dry weather. Apply enough water to moisten the top 12 inches of soil. Water again when the top 4 to 6 inches begin to dry.

Young trees should be checked once or twice a week and watered thoroughly as needed.

Clay soil holds moisture longer and need less frequent watering. Thoroughly soak the top 10 to 12 inches of soil and wait until the top 6 inches begin to dry before watering again. Check the soil moisture every seven to ten days. Sandy soil dries out faster. Check the soil moisture every four to five days. Water thoroughly and wait until the top 6 inches of soil dry before watering again. Check the soil moisture in aboveground planters every day. Water trees when the top 6 inches of soil begin to dry.

FERTILIZING

Yellow and off-color leaves may indicate a nutrient problem. Take a soil test before adding fertilizer. The soil test will tell you what type and how much of each nutrient you need to add. Adding nutrients your tree does not need can harm the plant and the environment, as well as waste your time and money.

Frequent watering of aboveground planters washes many nutrients out of the soil. Use a complete fertilizer, such as 10-10-10 or 12-12-12, to replace these. Follow label recommendations.

PRUNING

The old saying, "Prune when the saw is sharp" applies to June. Concentrate your efforts on repair rather than shaping. Remove crossing, broken, or diseased branches. Make cuts where branches join other branches or flush to the branch bark collar.

Do not paint pruning cuts. Research shows that the tree will heal better without these products. Disinfect tools between cuts on sick trees with alcohol or a solution of one part bleach to nine parts water. Wait for the dormant season to prune **oaks**. Oaks pruned during the growing season are the only exception.

PROBLEMS

Continue monitoring for pests. Distorted, spotted, and discolored leaves may indicate you have an insect or disease problem.

Insects. See May "Pests" for tips on controlling gypsy moths, Eastern tent caterpillars, mites, and aphids.

Continue proper care of **honeylocusts** as they start to re-leaf and recover from leafhopper and plantbug damage.

Watch for Japanese beetles. The small, metallic green beetles feed on over 300 species of plants. The beetles skeletonize the leaves by eating the leaf tissue and leaving the veins intact. The Japanese beetle population has crossed the Mississippi and outbreaks are appearing throughout the Prairie Lands. Stressed trees or those repeatedly defoliated by Japanese beetles would benefit from treatment. Use an insecticide labeled for use on trees to control this beetle. Consult a tree care professional for treatment of large trees. Consider treating Japanese beetles when they are in the grub stage, munching away under the lawn. A one-time application of milky-spore (a bacteria that will kill only the grubs; not harmful to people or pets). Apply a tablespoon of the powder every three or four feet; your lawn will look like a chessboard from *Alice in Wonderland* before you water it in (can last for 20 years or more in the soil providing that you do not use insecticides, herbicides, or any pesticide on the lawn or areas bordering the turf).

Diseases. Complete scab treatments on **crabapples** (see May "Pests" for details).

Continue branch removal of cytospora-infected **spruce** branches, fireblight-cankered **crabapples**, and phomopsis-infested **junipers** and **Russian olives** (see May "Pests" for more details).

Rake anthracnose-infected leaves as they drop from trees. This fungal disease causes brown spots on lower leaves of **oak**, **maple**, **ash**, **black walnut**, and **sycamore**. Though annoying, the disease is usually not life threatening. **Sycamores** may benefit from future preventative treatments.

JULY
Trees

PLANNING

The heat of the summer is a good time to evaluate your landscape. Make sure your shade trees are working for you. Check tree locations and their impact on your environment. Do you have trees located in areas where you want shade for outdoor leisure and activities? Are there trees on the east and west side of the home to keep your home cooler throughout the summer? Make a note on the landscape plan in your journal if you need some additional plantings.

PLANTING

Keep planting container-grown and spring-dug balled-and-burlapped trees. Check trees for signs of drought stress prior to purchase. Avoid buying trees with brown leaves and bare stems. Drought-stressed trees take longer to adapt to transplanting and have a lower survival rate. Summer-planted trees need extra attention during the hot part of summer. Check plants more often during extremely hot and dry weather.

CARE

Monitor the landscape for opportunities to reduce maintenance and improve plant health.

Create planting beds by joining several isolated trees together into one large garden. Fill the space with shrubs and perennials. Larger beds mean less mowing and eliminate the need for hand trimming around individual trees. Remove weeds and other unwanted plants from the bases of your trees. Renew mulch as needed. A 2- to 3-inch layer of woodchips will help conserve moisture and keep the roots cool throughout the heat of summer.

WATERING

Summer often means hot, dry weather. You may need to lend nature a hand as the temperatures rise and summer rains cease. You may be forced to prioritize water use during extended periods of drought. Trees in planters will need daily attention and frequent watering. New plantings will need the next most frequent watering. Check new plantings in sandy soil twice a week. Water thoroughly when the top few inches start to dry. New trees growing in clay soil should be checked every five to seven days. Water as needed.

Established and mulched trees can go the longest time between waterings. Even large established trees may need supplemental water during extended dry periods. Water thoroughly until the top 8 to 12 inches are moist.

FERTILIZING

Wait until next spring to fertilize newly planted trees. Fertilizing now may damage newly formed roots. Continue fertilizing trees growing in aboveground planters. Follow label directions. Monitor established trees for signs of nutrient deficiencies. Small, pale leaves or stunted growth may indicate your tree needs to be fertilized. Root rot and flooded or droughty soils can also cause these symptoms. Take a soil test to determine the cause of the problem. Wait until fall to add any needed nutrients.

PRUNING

Remove dead and damaged branches as they are found. Save large tree pruning for professionals. They have the equipment and training to do the job safely. It may be cheaper to hire an arborist than to pay the medical bills that could result from a pruning mishap!

PROBLEMS

Monitor all trees for signs of insects and disease. Proper care and sanitation (the removal of infected plant parts) will help minimize damage and reduce future problems.

Insects. Aphid and mite populations can explode during hot, dry weather. These small insects suck out plant juices, causing speckled and discolored leaves. One or two summer thunderstorms or a strong blast of clear water from the garden hose helps contain the problem.

Japanese beetles are out and feeding on a variety of trees, shrubs, and flowers. These small, metallic green beetles eat the foliage into a lacy mass of veins. Isolated populations have been found throughout the state. Healthy plants can tolerate the damage. Treat now with an insecticide or hire a professional to make a fall application of a soil systemic to prevent problems next summer on stressed trees.

Check gypsy-moth-infested trees for pupal cases (cocoons). Look in bark crevices and protected areas of the tree trunk. Destroy any that are found.

Diseases. Bare **crabapples** are a common sight in summers following a cool, wet spring. The cause is probably apple scab. Rake and destroy leaves as they fall. This will reduce the source of disease next season. Consider replacing disease-susceptible **crabapples** with newer scab-resistant cultivars. See April "Pests" for information on chemical control for apple scab.

Anthracnose, a fungal disease, can cause spotting and eventually leaf drop on **oaks**, **maples**, **ashes**, **black walnuts**, and **sycamores**. Healthy trees will survive this damage. Sprays are not effective at this time. Rake and destroy fallen leaves to reduce the source of infection for next season.

Continue to prune out dead and cankered branches. Disinfect tools with rubbing alcohol or a solution of one part bleach to nine parts water.

Helpful Hints

Honeydew

Have you ever parked your car under a large tree and returned to find the windshield spotted with a clear, sticky substance? It is not tree sap, but honeydew. If you could see into the tree canopy, you would find it full of aphids. These small, teardrop-shaped insects can be green, black, white, or peach in color. As these insects suck out plant juices, they secrete the excess as honeydew.

Occasionally a black fungus, sooty mold, grows on the honeydew. The fungus does not infect the plant, but it does block sunlight, causing leaves to yellow and even drop. Lady beetles often move in and eat the aphids before this pest is even discovered. Other years, you may need to step in with a strong blast of water from the garden hose. Insecticidal soap will help control aphids and remove the sooty mold.

AUGUST
Trees

PLANNING

Get out your garden journal, sit under the shade of one of your lovely trees, and make some notes on the growing season. Record the details of your new plantings, the weather, pest problems, and plant care. This information will help you prepare for next season.

PLANTING

Late summer and early fall are excellent times to plant trees. The hot weather will soon pass, and the trees will have the cool temperatures of fall to get established. Many stores have sales on plants at this time of the season. Good nurseries and garden centers have religiously watered and properly maintained their planting stock throughout summer.

Some stores offer trees at reduced prices. Make sure you really are getting a bargain. Drought-stressed and poorly maintained trees are not a deal. They are very slow to establish and may never fully develop into healthy landscape specimens. After several years of struggling, you may end up replacing the tree. Not only have you spent money and time buying and planting two trees, but you have also lost valuable time—tree-growing time.

CARE

A walk through the landscape helps you discover any maintenance practices that may be harming your trees. Pull mulch away from the trunks of the trees. Check new plantings and remove any labels, wires, twine, or other materials that can eventually girdle the trunks. Inspect all trees for trunk damage. Expand planting and mulch beds to protect trees from weed whips and lawn mowers.

Watch for early signs of autumn. Trees that color early are letting you know they are in distress. Construction damage, girdling roots, root rot, and decline can cause all or part of your tree to turn fall color prematurely. Proper watering and care may help a stressed tree. Other problems need to be addressed by a certified arborist.

WATERING

August is often a hot, dry month. You may need to break out the garden hose and give Nature a hand. New plantings remain a high priority. Check soil moisture once or twice a week. Trees growing in sandy soil need a thorough watering every three to five days during drought. Those growing in clay soil should be checked every seven to ten days.

Trees in aboveground planters should be checked daily. Water thoroughly when the top 6 inches begin to dry.

Mulched and established trees need less frequent watering. Soak the top 8 to 12 inches of soil under the tree canopy every ten to fourteen days during extended droughts.

FERTILIZING

Do not fertilize. Late-season fertilization can stimulate late-season growth that is damaged or killed by cold winter temperatures.

Continue monitoring plant health. Stunted and discolored leaves can indicate nutrient deficiency, root rot, drought, or waterlogged soils. Take a soil test if you suspect nutrient problems.

PRUNING

Save major pruning chores for fall. Late-season pruning can stimulate late-season growth that may be damaged in winter. Avoid pruning **honeylocusts** and **oaks** during the growing season. The open wounds increase the risk of disease.

Watch for early signs of autumn. Trees that color early are letting you know they are in distress.

 PROBLEMS

Insects. Watch for aphids and mites that can continue to be a problem during the hot month of August. These small insects suck out plant juices, causing leaves to discolor and eventually turn brown. Let lady beetles and other predacious insects take care of these pests. High populations can be reduced with a strong blast of water from the garden hose.

Inspect the landscape for Japanese beetles that are finishing their aboveground feeding. Heavy infestations may be treated in fall with a soil systemic. This will kill the next year's beetle population as they feed on treated trees. Also see July "problems" for other beetle controls.

Check tree trunks for female gypsy moths. The off-white, flightless moths crawl up the trunk to mate and lay eggs. Remove and destroy the female and egg masses as you find them.

Diseases. Continue to rake and destroy diseased leaves as they fall from the trees. This will reduce the source of infection for next season. Continue to

Helpful Hints

Surface roots are those that grow slightly above the soil and dull your mower blades as you cut the grass or interfere with the grass growing under your trees. Do not get out the axe. Those roots are important to the support and well being of your tree. Consider mulching under the tree canopy. A 2- to 3-inch layer of mulch provides a good environment for the tree and keeps the surface roots under cover.

Do not build a raised bed around your tree. Burying tree roots can kill many species of trees. The roots of those that do not die will soon reach the surface again.

Plant perennial groundcovers under the tree. These plants help insulate the roots, but do not out-compete the trees for water and nutrients. Here's how:

- Do not rototill or add soil to the planting area.
- Kill the grass by covering it with newspaper and mulch.
- Select plants suited to the growing conditions. See the "Vines and Groundcovers" chapter for suggestions.
- Space the plants throughout the areas.
- Dig a hole slightly larger than the root system of the groundcover.
- Amend the small planting holes with peat moss, compost, or other organic matter. Plant, mulch, and water in with transplant solution (follow label instructions) to encourage root growth.
- Weed control is critical for the first few years. Once the groundcovers fill in, your weeding chores will be minimal.

remove cankered and diseased branches as they are found. Prune 9 to 12 inches below the cankered (sunken or discolored) areas of the branch. Disinfect tools with rubbing alcohol or a solution of one part bleach to nine parts water. Continue to give trees proper care to reduce the adverse effects of the disease.

SEPTEMBER
Trees

PLANNING

Continue writing in your garden journal. Make sure planting records are complete. Record plant name, source, and planting location. Evaluate and record pest management strategies. This will help improve next year's success. Record fall color in your landscape. This may be a feature you want to improve in the future.

PLANTING

Fall is for planting. The cooler temperatures mean less watering for you and an easier time for the trees to get established. See October for a list of plants to avoid for fall planting. See the "Planting" section of the chapter introduction for planting details.

This is the second-best time to transplant trees. Wait until the leaves drop and the trees are dormant. Remember, moving trees can be tricky and heavy work. Save large, expensive, and special trees for professionals. They have the experience and equipment to move larger plants successfully. Start transplanting once the trees begin dropping their leaves:

1 Loosely tie lower branches to prevent damage and keep them out of your way.

2 Dig a trench around the tree slightly larger and deeper than the desired rootball. See "Helpful Hints" for recommendations on the size of rootball to make for the tree being moved.

3 Undercut the rootball with your shovel. A sharp spade will make the job easier. Use hand pruners and loppers for larger or tougher roots.

4 Slide a piece of burlap or canvas under the rootball. Have several friends lend a hand. Extra hands and strong backs will make the job easier and reduce the risk of dropping the tree and damaging the rootball.

5 Set the tree in the prepared site. Carefully cut away or slide the tarp away from the tree.

6 Backfill the hole with existing soil, water in and mulch.

CARE

As the beautiful fall leaves start dropping to the ground, the cry for raking help can be heard throughout the neighborhood. Before you start to grumble, consider recycling your leaves. It saves you work and improves the landscape. Shred leaves with the mower and leave them on the lawn. As long as you can see the grass blades through the shredded leaves, the lawn will be fine. In fact, the leaves will quickly break down, adding nutrients and organic matter to the soil.

Rake leaves, shred them with your mower, and dig them into annual vegetable and flower beds. The leaves break down over winter, improving the soil for next year's garden.

Bag leaves and tuck them behind the plantings near your home. The bagged leaves add insulation to the house. In summer, use the leaves as a mulch in flower and vegetable gardens. Shred leaves with the mower and throw them in a heap to decompose and become leaf mold—composted leaves. Composting really is that easy. The more prep work you do, the faster you make compost.

WATERING

Cooler fall temperatures usually mean less watering. Continue to monitor soil moisture and water new plants as the top 6 inches of soil begin to dry.

Evergreens, new plantings, and transplants will survive winter better when they receive sufficient moisture throughout fall.

FERTILIZING

Fall, after the trees go dormant, is a good

time to fertilize established trees. Let the plant and a soil test be your guide. Trees often get sufficient nutrients from decomposing mulch, lawn fertilizers, and grass clippings left on the lawn. Contact your local Cooperative Extension Service office for soil test information.

Check trees for signs of nutrient deficiencies. Poor growth and off-color leaves may indicate the need to fertilize. Wait a year to fertilize new tree plantings. They have been well tended in the nursery and fertilizer may harm the new, developing roots.

If soil tests are not available, use a slow-release fertilizer containing just nitrogen or three times more nitrogen than phosphorus and potassium.

Apply 2 to 4 pounds of actual nitrogen per 1,000 square feet. This is equal to 20 to 40 pounds of a 10 percent nitrogen fertilizer and 10 to 20 pounds of a 20 percent nitrogen fertilizer. Fertilizer can be sprinkled over and raked through mulch. Water to move the fertilizer into the soil. Place fertilizer in the soil for trees growing in lawn areas. Remove small cores of soil 6 inches deep and 2 to 3 feet apart throughout the area around the tree. Holes should start several feet away from the trunk and continue several feet beyond the drip line of the tree. Divide needed fertilizer evenly between the holes. Water until the top 12 inches of soil are moist. Do not fertilize

Helpful Hints

Recommended Rootball Size for Transplanting

Tree Diameter at Chest Height	(Size in Inches) Rootball Diameter	Rootball Depth
1/2	14	11
3/4	16	12
1	18	14
1 1/4	20	14
1 1/2	22	15
1 3/4	24	16
2	28	19

aboveground planters. Fall fertilization stimulates growth and reduces winter survival.

PRUNING

As the leaves drop, it is a good time to start pruning. Bare trees make it easy to see the plant's structure and determine which branches stay and which ones go. See January and February "Helpful Hints" for more pruning details.

Contact a certified arborist for professional help training young trees and pruning large trees. See November "Planning" for hiring tips.

PROBLEMS

Check tree trunks for gypsy moth egg masses. The eggs are covered with a yellow to beige, fuzzy substance. Each cluster can contain over 600 eggs. Remove and destroy any egg masses found.

Fall applications of soil systemic insecticides can be made for spruce galls, birch leaf miners, Japanese beetles, gypsy moths, plantbugs, and several other pests. Be mindful of the improper and excessive use of chemicals when gardening. In time, they percolate down and end up in our aquifers, rivers, and lakes—the sources of our drinking water.

OCTOBER
Trees

PLANNING

As you finish your last few growing chores, it is time to start preparing for winter. Review last year's garden journal. Start making a list of plants that need winter protection from cold, snow, and animals. Start gathering materials now so that you won't need to scramble for materials as the first flakes of snow drop from the sky.

PLANTING

Small trees can be transplanted once the leaves color change and fall. See September "Planting" for details on transplanting trees.

Fall is a great time to plant most trees and shrubs. The soil is warm, air temperatures are cool (good for the plant and the person planting), and trees are in place and ready to start growing as soon as spring arrives.

Purchase healthy balled-and-burlapped and container-grown plants from local nurseries, home centers, and garden centers.

Only buy healthy trees that are free from signs of pests and stress. Scorched (brown edges), tattered, and discolored leaves are clues that the plant is struggling. That bargain tree may not be such a deal if it needs replacing in several years.

Plant evergreens by early October whenever possible. This will give their slow-growing roots time to establish before the ground freezes.

Avoid planting trees that are slow to root. Wait until next spring and summer to plant the following trees:

- *Acer rubrum* **Red Maple**
- *Betula* spp. **Birches**
- *Crataegus* spp. **Hawthorn**
- *Gleditsia triacanthos inermis* **Honeylocust**
- *Liriodendron tulipifera* **Tuliptree**
- *Magnolia* spp. **Magnolia**
- *Malus* spp. **Crabapples** and **Apples**
- *Nyssa sylvatica* **Black Gum**
- *Populus* spp. **Poplar**
- *Prunus* spp. **Ornamental** and **Edible Plums** and **Cherries**
- *Pyrus calleryana* **Callery Pear**
- *Quercus* spp. **Oaks**
- *Salix* spp. **Willows**
- *Tilia* spp. **Lindens**

CARE

Continue recycling leaves. Shred them and leave them on the lawn, or recycle them in the garden or compost pile. See September "Care" for more ideas.

Start gathering winter protection materials—burlap for windscreens and salt barriers, fencing for snow loads, and animal barriers.

WATERING

Water as needed until the ground freezes.

Evergreens and new plantings need special attention. Water these plants thoroughly before the ground freezes. This will help minimize winter damage.

FERTILIZING

Fall, after the trees are dormant, is a good time to fertilize established trees. Fertilize only if the soil test results or plant growth indicates a nutrient deficiency. Most trees get sufficient nutrients from decomposing mulch, lawn fertilizers, and grass clippings left on the lawn.

Wait a year to fertilize new tree plantings. They have been well tended in the nursery and fertilizer may harm the new developing roots.

Do not fertilize trees growing in aboveground containers. Late-season fertilization may reduce winter survival.

See September "Fertilizing" for fertilizer rates and method of application.

Evergreens and new plantings need special attention. Water these plants thoroughly before the ground freezes. This will help minimize winter damage.

PRUNING

Keep pruning as needed. Start by removing crossed, broken, or diseased branches.

Select healthy branches with wide crotch angles (the angle between the trunk and branch) that are evenly spaced around the trunk for the basic structure. Make cuts where a branch joins another branch, above a healthy bud, or flush with the branch bark collar. See January and February "Helpful Hints" for more pruning information.

PROBLEMS

Start installing animal fencing around new plantings, fruit trees, **euonymus**, and other animal favorites. Place a 4-foot tall cylinder of hardware cloth (reinforced wire screen) around these trees. Sink it several inches into the soil to keep voles and rabbits away from tree trunks.

Fall soil applications can still be made by professionals for preventing damage from spruce galls, birch leaf miners, Japanese beetles, gypsy moths, and several other pests. Only treat trees that have suffered problems in the past.

Helpful Hints

Winter, snow, and ice are on the way. Deicing products can be hard on our landscape plants. Salts applied to walks and drives can wash into the soil and damage plants. Road salts can spray on nearby plants causing damage to twigs and needles. Salt damage causes stunted or distorted growth, leaf burn, poor flowering and fruiting, and premature fall color. Repeated exposure to deicing salts can kill plants. Shovel first and then apply only traction materials or melting compounds to walks and drives.

Use sand or some of the newer more environmentally friendly deicing products, such as magnesium chloride or calcium-magnesium acetate. Create physical barriers between the plants and salt spray. Decorative fencing, burlap screens, or salt-tolerant plants can all protect salt-sensitive plants from injury. Thoroughly water salt-laden soils in spring. Thorough and repeated watering helps wash the salt through the soil and away from the tree roots.

A few salt-tolerant (soil and spray) trees:

- **Austrian Pine**
- **Black Alder**
- **Cockspur Hawthorn**
- **Eastern Redcedar**
- **Ginkgo**
- **Green Ash**
- **Greenspire Littleleaf Linden**
- **Hackberry**
- **Hedge Maple**
- **Honeylocust**
- **Kentucky Coffeetree**
- **Norway Maple**
- **White Ash**

Install cankerworm traps if these voracious insects have caused repeated defoliation of **oaks**, **elms**, **apples**, **crabapples**, and many other trees. These small, green or brown, wormlike insects did their damage last spring. Apply sticky bands around the trunk of trees that were severely defoliated the previous season. Use a band of fabric treated with a sticky material, such as Tanglefoot, to avoid injury to the tree. Place sticky traps in place in mid-October and remove in December.

NOVEMBER
Trees

PLANNING

Now is the time to finish your journal entries for this growing season. Once the snow flies and holidays arrive, it will be hard to remember the details of the past summer.

You can do a lot to maintain the health of your trees, but sometimes it may be necessary or better to call in a professional.

Ask friends and relatives for recommendations. Check the Yellow Pages or contact the state Arborist Association for a list of certified arborists. You may also visit www.isa-arbor.com for a list of local arborists. These are tree care professionals who have voluntarily participated in an international program that certifies a standard of tree care knowledge. Quality tree care companies participate in professional organizations, such as the International Society of Arboriculture, and National Arborist Association. They also provide staff with training and educational opportunities.

PLANTING

Finish planting deciduous trees as soon as possible to will give plants a little time to adjust to their new locations. Consider having large tree additions made over winter. Some nurseries dig the rootball (leaving the tree in place) in fall. Once the rootball freezes, they move the tree to a prepared hole in its new location. The success rate has been good. It is expensive, but one way to get an instant tree.

Planning on having a live Christmas tree this holiday season? Dig the hole now before the ground freezes. Cover the hole with a board or fill it with mulch. Cover the soil to prevent freezing, making winter planting easier.

CARE

Keep raking and mulching leaves as long as they keep falling. See September "Care" for tips on managing leaves in the landscape. Install wind, sun, and salt screens. Burlap, weed barrier fabrics, or other barriers can protect new plantings and sensitive plants from winter damage. Wrap **arborvitae** and upright **junipers** with strips of cotton or old nylon stockings. This will prevent the snow load damage that frequently occurs.

Do not use tree wraps for winter protection. Research has shown that they do not protect the plant and can cause damage if left on the tree too long. If you feel you must use tree wraps, apply them now and remove them in the spring. Move containers to an unheated garage for the winter. Water the soil whenever it is dry. Or protect the roots of plants left outdoors by surrounding them with bales of hay.

WATERING

Make sure your new plantings and evergreens are thoroughly watered before the ground freezes. Then, it is time to drain and store the garden hose for winter.

FERTILIZING

There is still time to fertilize. Healthy trees need little if any supplemental fertilization. Consult your soil test results to see if your trees need any additional nutrients.

PRUNING

Continue pruning as needed. Prune trees to repair damage or establish structure. Always prune with a goal in mind. Consider waiting until late winter for major pruning jobs. This way you can remove winter damage at the same time you improve the tree's structure. Winter is a good time to prune **oaks** and **honeylocusts**. Wait one to two years before pruning newly planted trees. Then prune to establish a strong framework. Wait until spring to prune evergreens. Large branches removed in the fall can be used for holiday decorations.

PROBLEMS

Finish installing animal protection. A 4-foot-high cylinder of hardware cloth around the trunk of new and thin-barked trees will reduce the risk of rabbit and vole damage. Sink the bottom few inches of the fencing into the ground before it freezes. This will keep out the voles.

Start applying repellents to plantings that are favored by deer and rabbits. All young trees as well as fruit trees, **ornamental plums**, and **euonymus** are a few of their favorites. Start before feeding begins. This encourages them to go elsewhere for dinner. Reapply after heavy rains or as specified on label directions.

Leave cankerworm sticky traps in place until December.

Look for egg masses of gypsy moths and tent caterpillars. Remove and destroy as soon as you find them. Store chemicals and fertilizers in a cool, dark location. It should be locked and free from light and freezing (for liquids) temperatures.

Helpful Hints

Start looking for a local nursery or Christmas tree farm that sells living Christmas trees.

Find out if it is balled and burlapped or container grown. Balled-and-burlapped trees will need a large container for indoor display.

Dig a hole large enough to accommodate the tree. Roughen the sides of the planting hole with your shovel. Slice or scrape the surface to prevent glazing. Cover with a board or fill it with woodchips. Store soil under a tarp or in a location where it will not freeze.

Purchase a tree that meets both your landscape and holiday needs. Make sure the tree will tolerate the growing conditions and fit in the planting location once it reaches mature size. Store the tree in a cool, protected location outdoors. Water often enough to keep the roots moist.

Move the tree inside to a cool location just prior to your holiday celebration. Place containers on a large saucer and balled-and-burlapped trees in a large tub. Keep the roots moist. Move the tree back outdoors after seven to ten days. Any longer in the warm indoors and the tree may break bud and begin growing. If the tree does start to grow, you will have an indoor evergreen tree to decorate for Valentine's Day, Easter, and May Day.

After the holidays, move the tree to a screened-in porch or garage for several weeks. This allows the tree to gradually adjust to the cold outdoor temperatures.

Plant, water, mulch, and shield from winter wind and sun. And keep your fingers crossed—it never hurts!

DECEMBER
Trees

 ## PLANNING

Look out your windows and take a look at your trees in winter. Do they provide nice scenery as you look outside? Growth habit, bark color, and fruit can all add color and interest to the winter landscape. Note areas that are large enough to accommodate a tree and need a little winter interest.

 ## PLANTING

Live Christmas trees need to be planted as soon after the holidays as possible. Make sure you dig the planting hole before the ground freezes. See November "Helpful Hints" for more information.

 ## CARE

Keep the roots of living Christmas trees moist at all times. Minimize the time inside to maximize your chance of success. If the tree begins to grow, you are stuck with a big houseplant until next spring.

Be careful when hanging holiday lights on outdoor trees and shrubs. Always use lights made for outdoor use.

Loosely attach lights to the tree branches and trunks. Remove lights in spring before growth begins. Tightly wrapped lights can girdle a tree in one season. Use a sturdy ladder and work with a buddy. Or consider hiring a professional. Many landscape companies now install lights and other holiday decor. They have the equipment and training to do the job safely.

 ## WATERING

Watering is usually not needed. Once the ground freezes, it is time to pack away the garden hose.

FERTILIZING

Review your soil tests and make plans for next season. Record time, type, and amount of fertilizer used on trees. This will help keep track of future fertilization needs.

Make sure all liquid chemicals are stored in a cool, not freezing, dark location away from children. Store granular fertilizers in a cool, dry location away from pets and children.

 ## PRUNING

Prune trees in winter to repair damage and improve structure. Wait until spring to do the majority of evergreen pruning. You can remove large branches that block walks and drives. These can be used for holiday decorations.

PROBLEMS

Finish installing animal fencing. Apply repellents throughout the winter to new plantings and those favored by deer and rabbits.

Continue to scout and destroy egg masses of tent caterpillars, tussock moths, and gypsy moths.

CHAPTER ELEVEN
Vines & Ground Covers

Vines and groundcovers are the wall covering and carpet for your outdoor living space. They serve both functional and aesthetic purposes in the landscape.

Use vines and groundcovers to soften hard surfaces and structures, block bad views, and decrease maintenance.

Grow vines on trellises to create privacy, screen a bad view, or cover an ugly fence. Use them in both large areas and narrow spaces where most shrubs outgrow.

Cover an arbor or trellis with vines to create shade. A decorative arbor covered with vines can create quick shade for outdoor patios and decks. Or create your own shade for shade-loving plants, such as **hostas** and **ferns**.

Use groundcovers under trees and shrubs to improve growing conditions. A perennial groundcover helps keep tree and shrub roots cool and moist throughout the growing season. It also keeps harmful mowers and weed whips away from trunks, stems, and surface roots.

Create groundcover beds around trees and shrubs to reduce mowing and hand trimming. It's easier to mow around one large bed of groundcover, trees, and shrubs instead of individual plants. Add texture and seasonal interest to vertical and horizontal spaces. Vines and groundcovers allow you to expand planting options.

PLANNING

Choose the right plant for your growing conditions. Select the plants that prefer the soil and light in the growing location. Matching a plant to the growing conditions reduces pest problems, minimize maintenance, and give you the most attractive plant possible.

Make sure the plant and its flower buds are hardy in your area. **Oriental wisteria** plants will survive our cold climate but the flower buds may not. Select the **Kentucky wisteria** that is both plant- and flower-hardy in northern climates.

Avoid aggressive plants that can take over the landscape. These vines and groundcovers will require a lot of work to keep them inbounds. Several, such as **crown vetch** and **Oriental bittersweet**, have become invasive and should not be planted.

Select vines that are best suited to climb the wall, trellis, or support you have selected. Or select the support structure best suited to the vine you want to grow. Use twining type vines, such as **honeysuckle**, **clematis**, and **five-leaf akebia**, for chain-link fences, trellises, and arbors. Cover walls and stones with wires and netting to train vines over these types of structures. Consider using clinging vines, such as **euonymus** and **climbing hydrangea**, on stone and brick structures. These vines use rootlike structures to hold fast to the surfaces they climb. Do not train clinging vines directly on wooden buildings. Their roots can damage the wood and the excess foliage can trap moisture, causing the wood to deteriorate.

Use groundcovers and vines in mass or mixed with other plants. Select companion plants that are equally aggressive and require the same growing conditions. Mix plants with plain, variegated, or colorful foliage and various flowering times to extend the season-long interest. Mix annual and perennial vines. The annuals will provide quick cover and flowers while the perennial vines are getting established.

Vines & Ground Covers

SOIL PREPARATION

Soil preparation varies with the location, existing conditions, and plants you are growing. Do minimal digging around established trees and shrubs. Extensive, deep tilling can damage roots and kill the very plant that you are trying to enhance. Cathy urges that modifying the planting hole, but not the surrounding area, can limit plant root growth beyond the planting hole. Select the soil preparation method that best fits your growing conditions.

Start with a soil test. This will help you determine what, if any, fertilizer and amendments you will need. Add organic matter to new garden areas. Use organic matter as a mulch to slowly improve soil under established trees and shrubs.

For new beds (avoid the roots of young trees and shrubs):

1 Remove or kill the existing grass and weeds. Use a total vegetation killer, such as Roundup or Finale, to kill existing vegetation. Wait four to fourteen days (check the label for the product you elect) to till up and rake off the dead grass.

2 Add the recommended fertilizer and several inches of organic matter to the top 6 to 12 inches of soil. Follow soil test results, or use 2 to 4 pounds of a low-nitrogen (first of the three numbers on the bag) fertilizer per 100 square feet. Use fertilizers with little or no phosphorus (middle number on the bag) or potassium (last of the three numbers) since our soils tend to have excess amounts of these.

For plantings around established trees or where erosion is a concern:

• Kill the existing weeds and turf. Leave the dead layer intact to serve as mulch. Plant groundcovers through the dead layer. Cover the dead layer with woodchips, shredded bark, or other organic mulch. The double layer of mulch helps suppress weeds, prevent erosion on slopes, and adds organic matter to the soil.

• Or cut the existing grass and weeds very short. Cover with several layers of newspaper and woodchips. Plant the groundcovers through the mulch.

PLANTING

Start planting once the site is prepared.

1 Dig a hole at least two to three times wider but no deeper than the container.

2 Use the trowel or shovel to roughen up the sides of the planting hole. This eliminates a glazed surface that prevents roots from penetrating the surrounding soil.

3 Gently push on the container sides to loosen the roots. Slide the plant out of the pot. Do not pull it out by the stem. Place the plant in the hole so that the rootball is even or slightly higher than the soil surface.

4 Or cut away the pot on delicate, poorly rooted, or potbound plants. Remove the bottom of the container. Place the plant in the hole (with rest of the container still attached) so that the rootball is even or slightly higher than the soil surface. Once in place, slice through the side of the pot and peel it away from the rootball.

5 Use special care when planting **clematis**. Try to protect the plants from breakage. Use the cut-away pot method to minimize stress on the **clematis**.

6 Fill the hole with the existing soil. Water to settle the soil and eliminate air pockets.

7 Mulch the plants with woodchips, shredded bark, or other organic matter.

Vines & Ground Covers

WATER

Check new plantings several times per week. Water whenever the top few inches just begin to dry. After several weeks, water thoroughly but less frequently. Wait until the top 3 inches just start to dry. Then water enough to moisten the top 6 to 8 inches.

Water established plants on an as-needed rather than calendar basis. Thoroughly water, wetting the top 6 inches of soil. Water whenever the top 4 to 6 inches start to dry.

FERTILIZING

Test your soil before adding fertilizer, sulfur, or lime. A soil test will tell you how much, if any, of these amendments you need to add. Contact your local County Cooperative Extension Service for soil testing.

Or use 1 pound of actual nitrogen per 1,000 square feet. This is equal to 3 pounds of ammonium nitrate (33-0-0), 4 pounds of ammonium sulfate (21-0-0), or 16 pounds of Milorganite (6-2-0). One pound of synthetic inorganic fertilizer is equal to 2 cups, while 1 pound of Milorganite™ equals 3 cups.

Select a fertilizer (such as those mentioned) with little or no phosphorus, since our soils tend to be high to excessive in this nutrient. Calculate the amount of fertilizer you need to add to your planting area.

1 Start with the fertilizer rate. Use this formula to convert actual nitrogen to actual pounds of fertilizer you will need.

2 Divide 100 by the percentage of nitrogen in the bag. Then multiply it by the amount of actual nitrogen recommended. This gives you the pounds of fertilizer needed per 1,000 square feet.

3 Now calculate the square footage of your garden. Multiply the length by the width of the planting space. Divide this by 1,000 since the fertilizer rate is usually given per 1,000 square feet.

4 Lastly, multiply the amount of fertilizer needed per 1,000 square feet by our area factor calculated above.

For example: If your planting bed is 6 feet wide and 24 feet long. Use ammonium sulfate (21-0-0) for our fertilizer.

Calculate the fertilize rate: 100/21 (percentage of nitrogen in the fertilizer) ÷ 21 (the amount of actual nitrogen needed per 1,000 square feet) = 4.8 pounds of 21-0-0 fertilizer per 1000 square feet.

Calculate the area: 6 x 24 = 144 square feet. Then divide by 1,000 = 0.144.

Now multiply 4.8 pounds of fertilizer per 1,000 square feet 0.144 = 0.7 (a little less than $^3/_4$) pound of fertilizer for the planting area.

PRUNING

Prune vines and groundcovers with a purpose in mind. Cut back rampant growers to control their size, remove diseased or insect infested stems to reduce pest problems, and cut out wayward branches to direct growth.

Remove diseased and damaged branches as soon as they appear. Disinfect tools between cuts with a solution of one part bleach to nine parts water.

Time other pruning based on plant growth and flowering. Prune spring-flowering plants such as **five-leaf akebia** and **barrenwort** after they bloom. Trim summer and fall bloomers such as **sweet autumn clematis** and **honeysuckle** anytime during the dormant season. Late winter allows you to combine winter repair with routine pruning.

Prune **juniper** groundcovers in early spring (April) before growth begins or in mid-July when they are semi-dormant. Avoid fall pruning that opens up the plants to winter wind and sun damage.

See April "Pruning" for pruning guidelines for selected groundcovers and vines.

Match the pruning technique to the desired results.

Renewal prune established plants to encourage new basal growth. Remove one-third of the older stems to ground level.

Control vigorous growing vines and groundcovers with rejuvenation pruning. Cut the entire plant back to 2, 4, or 6 inches above ground level.

Use heading cuts to shape and control wayward growth. Cut the stems back to side branches or just above a healthy bud.

PROBLEMS

Avoid problems by placing the right plant in the most suitable location. Always select the most pest-resistant vines and groundcovers available. Check plants throughout the growing season. Remove spotted leaves and small insect populations as soon as they appear. This is usually sufficient for controlling most insects and disease.

Properly identify any problem before reaching for a chemical control. It is important for the health of your plant, the safety of the environment, and the effectiveness of the control that you use the right product at the proper time and rate.

Some vines and groundcovers can be invasive and become a "pest" in the landscape.

Vines & Ground Covers

Annual Vines

Common Name (Botanical Name)	Light	Height	Flower Color	Attachment	Comments
Black-Eyed Susan Vine (*Thunbergia alata*)	Full sun to light shade	up to 6 feet	cream, yellow, or gold with dark center	twining stems	Nice in hanging baskets or as a vertical accent in a container.
Canary Vine (*Tropaeolum peregrinum*)	Sun to part shade	up to 8 feet	yellow	twining stems	Avoid excess nitrogen that can prevent bloom.
Cardinal Climber (*Ipomoea × multifida*)	Full to part sun	up to 10 feet	crimson	twining stems	Unusual, deeply lobed leaves. Attracts hummingbirds.
Cypress Vine (*Ipomoea quamoclit*)	Sun to part shade	up to 8 feet	red	twining stems	Light and airy foliage makes a nice backdrop for red flowers.
Hyacinth Bean (*Lablab pupureus*)	Sun	up to 12 feet	lilac, pink to purple, or white	twining stems	Provides fragrant edible flowers and attractive purple beans throughout the season.
Firecracker Vine (*Ipomoea lobata*)	Sun to ligth shade	up to 10 feet	reddish-orange with a tinge of yellow and white	twining stems	Blooms as it grows throughout the season.
Mandevilla (*Madevillia* species)	Sun to light shade	up to 6 feet	pink	twining stems	Overwinter indoors or purchase large plants to obtain bigger sizes.
Morning Glory (*Ipomoea* species)	Sun to light shade	10 feet	blue, pink, lavender, or white	twining stems	Avoid excess water and fertilizer that can prevent flowering; reseeds readily.
Sweet Pea (*Lathyrus odoratus*)	Sun to part shade	4 to 6 feet	assorted	clinging tendrils	Prefers cool temperatures, so plant directly outdoors in early summer for fall display.

Perennial Vines

Common Name (Botanical Name)	Hardiness Zone	Light	Attachment	Comments
American Bittersweet (*Celastrus scandins*)	3 to 7	Sun to shade	twining	Rampant grower that tolerates drought; plant male and female for fruit.
Arctic Beauty Kiwi Vine (*Actinidia kolomikta* 'Arctic Beauty')	4 to 6	Sun	twining	Attractive foliage; green with pink and white blotch. Plant male and female for edible fruit.

Perennial Vines

Common Name (Botanical Name)	Hardiness Zone	Light	Attachment	Comments
Boston Ivy (*Parthenocissus tricuspidata*)	4 to 7	Sun to shade	holdfasts	Fast growing with blue fruit and red fall color. Try 'Veitchii' for finer texture and a less aggressive plant.
Clematis (*Clematis* species and cultivars)	3 to 8	Sun	twining petioles	Mulch roots; see March "Helpful Hints" for pruning tips.
Climbing Hydrangea (*Hydrangea petiolaris*)	4 to 7	Shade	aerial rootlets	Large flowers in mid-June, with peeling orange bark.
Dutchman's Pipe (*Aristolochia macrophylla*)	4 to 8	Sun to shade	twining	Large leaves and unusual pipe-shaped flowers Tolerates a wide variety of soil.
English Ivy (*Hedera helix*)	5 to 8	Sun or shade	holdfasts	Plant in a protected area. Subject to browning and winter dieback. Use the hardier 'Thorndale' ('Sub-Zero') for more reliable results.
Five-leaf Akebia (*Akebia quinata*)	4 to 8	Shade	twining	Suffers some tip dieback in winter; rosy red flowers in early spring followed by purple fruit.
Grapes (*Vitis*)	3 to 7	Sun	twining tendrils	See "Fruits" chapter for recommended cultivars.
Hops (*Humulus lupulus*)	4 to 7	Sun	twining	Fragrant flowers; used for making beer and grown for ornamental value.
Porcelain Berry Vine (*Ampelopsis brevipedunculata*)	4 to 8	Sun to part shade	clinging tendrils	Can be rampant grower or dies out over winter. Variegated foliage often reverts to green. Porcelain-blue fruit develops in late season.
Trumpet Vine (*Campsis radicans*)	4 to 7	Sun	aerial rootlets	Large orange or yellow flowers attract hummingbirds. Be patient and avoid over-fertilization to ensure flowers.
Virginia Creeper (*Parthenocissus quinquefolia*)	3 to 7	Sun to shade	holdfasts and tendrils	Rampant grower with blue fruit and red fall color; attracts birds.
Wintercreeper (*Euonymus fortunei* cultivars)	4 to 8	Shade	aerial rootlets	Plant in protected location; protect from winter wind and sun.
Wisteria, Kentucky (*Wisteria macrostachya*)	4 to 7	Sun	twining	Large flowers bloom with leaves. Flower buds are hardy (unlike the oriental types).

Vines & Ground Covers

Common Name (Botanical Name)	Hardiness Zone	Light	Comments
Ajuga (Bugleweed) (*Ajuga reptans*)	4 to 8	Sun to shade	Prefers moist soil. Evergreen foliage with spikes of red, white, or purple flowers.
Deadnettle (*Lamium maculatum*)	3 to 8	Shade	Tolerates dry shade. Variegated foliage with pink or white flowers; often used in containers and hanging baskets.
English Ivy (*Hedera helix*)	4 to 8	Sun to shade	Plant in sheltered location and protect from winter wind and sun.
Epimedium (Barrenwort) (*Epimedium* species)	3 to 8	Shade	Prefers moist, organic soil; evergreen with red or yellow flowers.
Ferns (Various species)	2 to 8	Shade	Several species of Ferns make excellent groundcovers in moist shade. Some are evergreen.
Ginger, Canadian (*Asarum canadense*)	3 to 8	Shade	Prefers rich soils; shade tolerant.
Ginger, European (*Asarum europaeum*)	4 to 7	Shade	Evergreen; provide winter protection. Prefers rich soils; slow to spread; part shade
Hosta (*Hosta*)	3 to 8	Shade	Various sizes, leaf shapes, and foliage colors available.
Juniper (*Juniperus* species)	3 to 9	Sun	Select low-growing type and allow plenty of room for mature size.
Moneywort (Creeping Jenny) (*Lysmachia nummularia*)	3 to 8	Sun to shade	Rampant grower that weeds out easily; green leaves with yellow flowers. Do not use near natural wetlands.
Pachysandra (*Pachysandra termialis*)	4 to 9	Shade	Evergreen that needs protection in zone 4 and winter shade; white flowers in early spring.
Periwinkle (Myrtle) (*Vinca minor*)	4 to 8	Shade	Evergreen foliage that needs winter shade; blue and white flowers with solid green or variegated foliage.
Russian Cypress (*Microbiota decussata*)	3 to 8	Sun to part shade	The look of an Arborvitae with the growth habit of Juniper; avoid waterlogged soils.
Variegated Yellow Archangel (*Lamiastrum galeobdolon* 'Variegatum')	4 to 9	Part sun	Aggressive; variegated foliage with yellow flowers. Tolerant of dry shade. Good in shrub beds and containers.
Wintercreeper (*Euonymus fortunei* 'Coloratus')	4 to 8	Shade	Evergreen with leaves that turn purple in winter. Plant in a protected area; shelter from winter wind and sun.

PLANNING

Take advantage of cabin fever and start planning new additions. Gather garden catalogs, last year's journal, and your most current landscape plan. Review any videotape and pictures of last season's garden.

Look for areas that need a little vertical interest. Will a vine-covered arbor, trellis, or obelisk brighten up, shade, or screen problem areas in your landscape?

Identify areas where groundcovers can be used to unify a planting bed, mask surface roots of large trees, or fill a bare area where grass will not grow.

Visit lawn and garden shows for ideas on how to incorporate these plants into the landscape. Many landscape companies build elaborate displays featuring vine-covered structures and beds filled with groundcovers.

PLANTING

It is winter in the Prairie Lands, and it is way too early to plant. Use this time to look for solutions to difficult planting situations. Consider a few of these and include some of your own creative solutions:

Minimize root disturbance when planting annuals under established trees. Sink old nursery pots in the soil so that the upper lip is even with the soil surface. Each year, set a smaller container filled with colorful annuals inside the buried pot. Replace them each season without disturbing the tree roots.

Set aboveground containers among groundcovers. They add height, structure, and color without damaging the tree roots.

Use annual vines in place of spiky plants (**dracaena**) for vertical interest in container gardens. Check out your favorite garden center for the smaller trellises and obelisks that fit inside containers.

Grow berry vines such as **clematis**, **porcelain vine**, and **climbing hydrangea** in containers to add vertical interest to patios and decks. Overwinter tropical vines, such as **mandevilla**, indoors like houseplants. Hardy vines can be wintered outdoors. Sink the pot in the ground to insulate the roots from cold winter temperatures. Or store the planters in an unheated garage, placed in a protected corner away from the door. Use packing peanuts or other material to help insulate the roots. As a last resort, try protecting the container outdoors in a protected location near your home. Insulate the roots by surrounding the pot

with bales of straw or hay. Water whenever the soil is frost-free and dry.

CARE

Take a walk through your property and see how the vines and groundcovers are surviving winter. Note plants that are subject to snow loads and salt. Evaluate these plants in spring. You may need to move sensitive plants or change snow management practices in the future.

Evaluate winter sun and winds. Both can be drying to evergreen groundcovers and vines. Use your old Christmas tree to create a windbreak and shade for **pachysandra** and **english ivy** other sensitive plants. Make a note to move, shelter, or create a more permanent solution.

Check vines, trellises, and arbors to make sure they are securely mounted. Secure them against strong winter winds that could dislodge the structure and damage the vines or nearby plantings.

WATERING

No need to water outdoors. Monitor the landscape for ice buildup and flooding. Consider amending the area or moving the plants in spring to reduce winter damage caused by these conditions.

Water tender vines that were moved indoors for winter. Water thoroughly until the excess runs out the bottom. Pour out the water that collects in the saver. Wait until the top few inches dry before watering again. Check planters stored in the garage. Water the soil whenever the ground is thawed and dry. Apply enough water so that the excess runs out the bottom.

 ## FERTILIZING

Monitor the health and growth of tender vines growing indoors. Use little to no fertilizer on these plants. The low light and low humidity is hard on these plants. Adding fertilizer can add to the stress. Only fertilize actively growing plants with pale or stunted growth. Use a diluted solution of any flowering houseplant fertilizer.

 ## PRUNING

Remove broken and damaged branches as they are discovered. Wait until the weather improves and snow clears to do routine pruning.

Helpful Hints

Tired of a garden full of green? Select groundcovers that add seasonal interest to the landscape. Use groundcovers with variegated foliage to brighten shady locations, while flowering types can be used to add color throughout the season. Add some that have colorful leaves in fall or evergreen foliage and attractive seedheads for winter.

Ajuga: Select one of the bronze or variegated cultivars for added color.

Creeping phlox: Covered with white, rose, or purple flowers in spring. The evergreen foliage provides year-round cover.

Hostas: Many cultivars of various sizes with green, chartreuse, or blue-green foliage are available. Some have white, cream, or yellow variegation. White and purple flowers in summer or fall are an added benefit by gardeners. Some have fragrant flowers.

Deadnettle: Green leaves with various amounts of silvery white variegation. Mauve or white flowers in summer stand above the foliage.

Moneywort: Bright yellow flowers cover the green leaves in summer. Use the less assertive, yellow-leafed variety for a colorful change.

Orange stonecrop: Covered with yellow-orange flowers in summer; the foliage turns yellowish orange in fall.

Pachysandra: White flowers in spring with glossy green evergreen foliage.

Variegated Yellow Archangel (*Lamium galeobdolon,* 'Variegatum'): Variegated green and silver foliage with yellow flowers in summer; aggressive plant tolerates dry shade.

Wintercreeper: Low-growing evergreen groundcover; variegated foliage on some varieties.

 ## PROBLEMS

Check outdoor plants for animal damage. Look for tracks, droppings, and other signs of animal damage. **Wintercreeper, junipers**, and other groundcovers make great winter housing and food for rabbits and voles. Apply commercial or home-made repellents to high-risk plantings. Repeat as recommended following label instructions..

FEBRUARY
Vines & Ground Covers

 PLANNING

Attend garden lectures and workshops for ideas on landscaping with vines and groundcovers. Visit the library and check out landscape books and magazines for ideas and pictures of how to incorporate these plants. Consider letting a few vines run wild. Use them as groundcovers or let them crawl over stones, onto shrubs, and up tree trunks. Use non-aggressive plants that will not suffocate their neighbors or strangle the stems and trunks. **Climbing hydrangea** and **euonymus** can be allowed to climb tree trunks for added interest. Do not use twining vines, such as **bittersweet**, that can girdle the tree and potentially kill it.

 PLANTING

Buy or build the support structure for new or existing vertical plantings. Whenever possible, install these structures prior to planting to avoid damaging tender roots and young stems. Select a structure that can adequately support the weight of the vine and provide a surface for the plant to cling around or attach to. See this month's "Helpful Hints" for one type of functional trellis.

 CARE

Monitor the health of tender vines overwintering indoors. Increase the light and humidity around failing plants. Move them in front of an unobstructed south-facing window. Add artificial light if needed. Hang fluorescent lights above or aim spotlight-type fluorescent lights up into the foliage.

Increase the humidity around the plant by grouping it with other plants. As one plant loses moisture (transpires), those around it will benefit. Or place pebbles in the saucer. Place the pot on the pebbles. Keep water in the tray below the pot. As the water evaporates, it increases the humidity around the plant where it is needed.

 WATERING

Keep watering vines growing indoors for the winter. Water thoroughly so that the excess water runs out the drainage hole. Allow the water to collect in the gravel tray, increasing the humidity around the plant.

Check container plants overwintering outdoors and in the garage. Water whenever the soil is frost-free and dry. Apply enough water so that the excess runs out the bottom.

 FERTILIZING

Fertilize nutrient-deficient vines growing indoors for winter. Look for pale leaves and stunted growth. Use a diluted solution of any flowering houseplant fertilizer.

Do not fertilize plants that are showing signs of stress from low light and humidity. Stressed plants lose leaves and have little if any new growth. Correct the problem before fertilizing. Adding nutrients to stressed plants can injure the plants.

 PRUNING

Trim dead and damaged branches on outdoor plants. Wait until late March or April to do routine pruning.

Check vines growing indoors. Remove and discard dead leaves. Prune off wayward and dead branches. Cut them back above a healthy leaf or where it joins another branch.

PROBLEMS

Check indoor plants for signs of whiteflies, aphids, and mites. All these insects suck out plant juices, causing leaves to yellow and brown.

Use yellow sticky traps to trap whiteflies. They will not eliminate the problem, but usually reduce the populations to a tolerable level. Purchase traps from a garden center or make your own. Cover yellow cardboard with Tanglefoot or other sticky substance. Mount on a stick and stand in the soil or hang from a branch in the plant.

Spray aphid- and mite-infested plants with insecticidal soap. Be sure to cover the upper and lower leaf surfaces. Repeat once a week until these pests are under control.

Helpful Hints

Try adding a few trellises alongside your home. Vine-covered structures can brighten the outside of your house, soften the feel, and anchor your home in the landscape. Unfortunately, they also get in the way of house painting and other routine chores.

Try constructing a hinged trellis to provide you with all the benefits of a vine covering, while still allowing easy access to your siding.

1 Select lattice or other attractive material suited for climbing vines. Cut it to the size needed for the plant and shape you prefer.

2 Cut 18 - to 24-inch-long legs of pressure treated 2-x-2s, 2-x-4s, or 4-x-4s, depending on the size of the trellis and mature size and weight of the vine. Mount the legs directly to the trellis using hinges. Or mount the legs to a pressure-treated 2-by-4 that is the same size as the bottom of the trellis. Attach this to the trellis using hinges. Melinda has seen this constructed from PVC pipe as well.

3 Sink the legs into the soil so that the hinged portion is just above the soil surface. Attach eyebolts to the building and hooks to the trellis. Secure the trellis to the building using the hooks and eyebolts.

4 Grow your perennial vines next to the trellis. Tie the vines to the trellis until they attach by their own means.

5 Unhook and carefully bend the vine-laden trellis away from the wall whenever you need to paint, repair, or access that part of your home.

Continue to check outdoor plantings for animal damage. Reapply repellents as needed throughout winter. Try noisemakers and other scare tactics in an attempt to keep pests away. Make note of additional fencing or animal barriers that need to be installed prior to next winter.

MARCH
Vines & Ground Covers

PLANNING

Finalize your plans and start your planting list. Take advantage of nice days and stake out new planting beds and measure existing gardens where groundcovers will be added. Calculate the square footage of your new and existing groundcover beds. Multiply the length times the width to get the square footage of the planting beds. This information will be used to calculate needed plants and fertilizer.

Use the "Spacing Chart" to calculate the number of plants needed. Divide the square footage of the garden by the spacing factor. The answer is the number of plants you will need. For example, let's say your garden is 10 by 12 feet, and you want to grow **moneywort** that needs to be spaced 15 inches apart. Multiply 10 feet times 12 feet to get 120 square feet. Looking at the spacing factor for 15-inch spacing; it is 1.56. Divide 120 (square feet of planting space) by 1.56 (spacing factor), which equals 77 plants.

Let's walk through the math:

1 Calculate the square footage of the garden by multiplying the length times the width of the planting bed.

2 Now look at the spacing requirements of the groundcovers you plan to use. Multiply the spacing needed by the same number to get the square inches needed per plant. Divide this by 144 to convert it to square feet, as the area of the garden.

3 Divide the square footage of the garden by the square footage of the groundcover you are trying to grow. The answer equals the number of plants needed to fill the planting bed.

Using the example above, your planting bed is 10 x 12 feet. You want to grow **moneywort** that needs to be planted 15 inches apart.

Find the square footage of the garden: 10 x 12 = 120 square feet

Calculate the square footage needed per plant: (15 x 15) / 144 = 1.56

Estimate the number of plants you need: 120 / 1.56 = 77 plants

Spacing (Inches)	Spacing Factor
4	0.11
6	0.25
8	0.44
10	0.70
12	1.00
15	1.56
18	2.25
24	4.00
30	6.25
36	9.00
48	16.00
60	26.00

PLANTING

Begin soil preparation as soon as the snow melts and the soil thaws and it is dry enough to work.

1 Start by removing or killing (with a total vegetation killer) the existing weeds and grass. Leave the dead grass intact under established trees or on hillsides where erosion is a concern.

2 Add the needed fertilizer and amendments to new planting areas. Wait for the soil to dry slightly before tilling. Grab a handful of soil and gently squeeze. Lightly tap the soil with your finger. If it breaks into smaller pieces, it is ready to work.

3 Work the needed fertilizer and 2 to 4 inches of organic matter into the top 6 to 12 inches of soil. See this month's "Fertilizing" in the chapter introduction for help on calculating needed fertilizer. Rake the bed smooth and wait for the soil to settle. Do not till deeply under established trees and shrubs.

CARE

Start spring-cleaning in your planting beds. Remove debris and leaves that have collected in groundcover beds and under vine plantings. Remove winter-damaged leaves and stems. Check shallow-rooted groundcovers for frost heaving. These plants are often pushed out of the soil after a winter of freezing and thawing. Gently press them back into the soil and water in place.

Edge planting beds with a sharp spade or edging tool. This will help keep the groundcovers in and the surrounding grass out of the planting beds.

WATERING

Water indoor vines when the top few inches of soil are dry. Apply enough water so that the excess runs out the bottom of the pot. Allow it to collect in the pebbles in the saucer.

FERTILIZING

Take a soil test of new planting beds. Consider testing established plantings that are lacking vigor or have not been tested for several years. The soil test report will help you determine what type and how much fertilizer you need to add.

Helpful Hints

Prune **clematis** to control growth, encourage branching near the base of the plant, and improve flowering. The type of **clematis** you are growing will determine the time and type of pruning it requires. Spring-blooming **clematis** bloom on old wood.

Repeat-blooming **clematis**, such as 'Nellie Moser', 'Henry', 'The President', and 'Bees Jubilee' bloom on old and new growth. Prune dead and weak stems back to a healthy stem or ground level in late winter or early spring before growth begins. Prune the remaining stems back to a pair of strong buds.

The last group of **clematis** blooms on new growth. Prune these in late winter or early spring before growth begins. Remove dead stems back to ground level. Cut the remaining stems back to 6 to 12 inches.

Fertilize before growth begins. Use the type and amount of fertilizer recommended by the soil test report. Or apply 1 pound of actual nitrogen per 1,000 square feet. This is equal to 3 pounds of ammonium nitrate (33-0-0), 4 pounds of ammonium sulfate (21-0-0), or 16 pounds of Milorganite™ (6-2-0). One pound of synthetic inorganic fertilizer is equal to 2 cups, while 1 pound of Milorganite™ equals 3 cups. For more details, see "Fertilizing" in the chapter introduction.

PRUNING

Time to start pruning vines and groundcovers. Remove dead and damaged stems and branches. See specific directions for some common vines in this month's "Helpful Hints" and in April "Pruning."

PROBLEMS

Check **Wintercreeper** for scale. Mark your calendar so that you will remember to treat the scale when the **Japanese tree lilac** is in bloom (mid- to late June).

Continue monitoring animal damage. Apply repellents as long as animals are present and food supply is limited.

APRIL

 PLANNING

The planting season is underway. Record the name, variety, and source for all the vines and groundcovers you add to your landscape. Note pruning and trimming done on new and established plants.

 PLANTING

Prepare soil for planting. See March "Planting" for details on preparing the site.

Plant bare-root plants as soon as they arrive. If you can't plant right away, pack the roots in moist peat, and keep the plants in a cool, frost-free location until planted. Plant so that the crown (the point where stem joins the roots) is even with the soil.

Plant container-grown vines and groundcovers as described in the "Planting" section of the chapter introduction. Keep them slightly moist until they can be planted.

Start annual vines from seeds indoors. Starting them indoors results in earlier flowering for a longer bloom period. See January and February "Planting" in the "Annuals" chapter for tips.

 CARE

Remove damaged leaves on groundcovers. To make spring flowers more visible, cut off old leaves on **barrenwort** (*Epimedium*) before growth begins.

 WATERING

Continue to water as described in March and May "Watering." Keep the soil moist around new plants.

 FERTILIZING

Incorporate fertilizer into the soil prior to planting. Fertilize existing plants in spring before growth begins. See "Fertilizing" in the chapter introduction for additional information.

 PRUNING

Remove damaged leaves and stems. Prune following these guidelines:

English ivy (groundcover): Prune in early spring. For established plants, use a mower or hedge shears to control growth; though winter often does this chore for us. In this case, cut off dead tips.

Wintercreeper (groundcover): Prune in early spring. Cut established plants back to 4 to 8 inches to encourage vigorous, dense growth. Use a hedge clipper or mower (on its highest setting) for large plantings.

Junipers: Prune in early spring or early to mid-July. Remove dead branches and shape in spring. See July "Pruning" for details.

Bittersweet: Prune in winter or early spring. After planting, prune to train young stems to climb the plant support. For established plants, trim to control size. Cut overly long shoots back to three to four buds from the main stem. Prune back large shoots to 12 to 16 inches above ground level. Do not over-prune. This stimulates excess growth that will require additional pruning.

Boston ivy and **Virginia creeper**: Prune during the dormant season. After planting, train young stems to their support. For established plants, prune to control growth and keep them within bounds. Remove or shorten any stems that are growing away from their support. Renovate overgrown plants by pruning them back to 3 feet of the base. Wear a leather glove to rub the remaining dried pads off the support.

English ivy (vines): Prune in late winter or early spring. After planting, pinch back weak stems to encourage new growth. For established plants, remove dead tips and stems killed over winter. This is usually the only pruning that is needed. Cut back any wayward growth back to a healthy bud. Prune back within the plant to hide the cut.

Wintercreeper (vines): Prune in mid- to late spring. For young plants, tip prune to encourage fuller growth. For established plants, remove old and dead wood. Train new growth to cover the support.

Five-leaf akebia: Prune after flowering. Follow the pruning guidelines for **hardy kiwi**.

Grapes: Prune in late March or early April. See March "Helpful Hints" in the "Fruits" chapter for pruning information.

Hardy kiwi: Prune in late winter or early spring. After planting, cut back to strong buds about 12 to 16 inches above the ground. Train five to seven strong shoots on the support. Next spring, prune stout side shoots (laterals) by one-third and weak laterals back to one or two buds. For established plants, shorten growth by one-third to one-half to control its size. Occasionally remove an old stem to ground level. This stimulates new growth at the base of the plant.

Honeysuckle: Prune in early spring. After planting, cut back young plants by two-thirds. This encourages strong shoots to develop at the base of the plant. Next year, select strong shoots to form a framework. Remove other shoots. For established plants, prune out the tips of shoots that have reached the desired height. Cut off overly long shoots to healthy buds. Renovate overgrown plants by pruning stems back to 2 feet above the ground. Thin the new growth as needed.

Porcelain berry: Prune in late winter. After planting, train young shoots to cover support. For established plants, prune as you would grapes to control growth. See March "Helpful Hints" in the "Fruits" chapter.

Trumpet vine: Prune in late winter or early spring. After planting, prune all stems back to 6 inches above ground level. Remove all but two or three of the strongest shoots. Train these stems to the support. Allow the framework to develop over the next two to three years, or until the plant fills the support. For established plants, prune yearly to control growth. Remove weak and damaged stems to the main framework. Cut the side shoots back to two or three buds from the main stems forming the framework. Prune out dead main branches to

the base. Train the strongest shoot to replace it. Renovate by cutting all growth back to 12 inches off the ground.

Wisteria: At planting, cut back the main stem (leader) to a strong bud about 30 to 36 inches above ground level. Train two strong side shoots (laterals) over the fence, trellis, or arbor. Next spring, prune the leader back to 30 inches above the topmost lateral branch. Shorten the laterals by one-third of their total lengths. Select another pair of laterals to grow and help cover the trellis. Next winter, cut the leader back to 30 inches above the uppermost lateral. Then prune all the laterals back by one-third. Repeat each winter until the plant reaches full size. Prune established plants in early summer right after flowering. Cut offshoots (small branches) back to within five or six buds of a main branch.

 PROBLEMS

Pull weeds as soon as they appear.

MAY

Vines & Ground Covers

PLANNING

Use one of the rainy spring days to catch up on your garden record. Update landscape plans to include new additions. Record the name, variety, source, and planting information for each added plant.

PLANTING

Kill or remove the grass and prepare the site for planting. Leave dead grass as mulch to control erosion on slopes and to minimize root disturbance under trees. Prepare the soil prior to planting according to the directions in March "Planting." Harden off annual vines started indoors or in a greenhouse. Stop fertilizing and allow the soil to dry slightly before watering again. Place outdoors in a shaded location. Move into the sun for 1 or 2 hours the first day. Increase the amount of sun the plants receive each day. Move indoors or cover on cool nights. The plants will be ready to plant in two weeks.

CARE

Move tender vines outdoors at the end of May or in early June, once the danger of frost has passed. Gradually introduce them to the outdoors.

Dig and divide overcrowded, declining, and poorly flowering groundcovers. Use a shovel to lift plants. Remove dead centers and declining plants. Cut the remaining clump into several smaller pieces. Add organic matter and needed fertilizer to the top 6 to 12 inches of the soil. Plant the divisions at the recommended spacing for that species.

WATERING

Check new plantings often. Keep the soil slightly moist. Water when the top 2 inches begin to dry. Water thoroughly enough to wet the rootball and surrounding soil. Water established plantings during dry weather. Soak the top 6 to 8 inches whenever the top 4 to 6 inches are dry. Apply needed water once every seven to ten days in clay soils and half the needed water twice a week in sandy and rocky soils. Water potted plants thoroughly as needed.

FERTILIZING

Fertilize existing plantings if needed and it has not yet been done. Follow soil test results or apply 1 pound of actual nitrogen per 1000 square feet. For more details, see the "Fertilizing" in the chapter introduction.

PRUNING

Cut back **creeping phlox** after the flowers fade. Prune plants back halfway to encourage fresh, new growth.

PROBLEMS

Monitor **wintercreeper** vines for euonymus caterpillar. These wormlike insects spin a webbed nest in the plants. Remove and destroy. Or treat with *Bacillus thuringiensis.* Spray the webbed nests and surrounding foliage. This bacterial insecticide will kill the caterpillars, but it will not harm people, pets, wildlife, or other types of insects.

Check **junipers** for phomopsis blight. This fungal disease causes individual stems to turn brown and die. Prune dead branches back to a healthy stem or the main trunk. Disinfect tools between cuts with rubbing alcohol or a solution of one part bleach to nine parts water.

Helpful Hints

Start new vines from existing plants. This is a great way to share special plants and family heirlooms with relatives and friends. Propagate groundcovers and vines by division, cuttings, and layering.

Dig and divide groundcovers whenever they are overcrowded, fail to bloom, the center dies, or you want to start new plants. Use a shovel or garden fork to dig a large plant. Use a sharp knife or two shovels to divide the clump into smaller pieces. Add organic matter to the original planting site and return one division to this space. Use the others to start new plants or share with friends.

Experiment a little with cuttings of vines and groundcovers. Herbaceous plants (with soft stems) are easier to propagate this way than those with woody stems. Some root best from new growth in spring, while others root better from cuttings taken in winter.

1 Take short cuttings 3, 4, to 6 inches long from new growth. Dip the cut end in a rooting hormone and place in a container filled with moist vermiculite.

2 Keep the vermiculite moist and the plant in warm, bright (no direct sun) location. Wait several weeks for the plant to root.

3 Plant the rooted cutting in a container filled with well-drained potting mix. Plant it in its permanent location outdoors once the plant roots have filled the small pot and weather allows.

Layering is the most successful method of rooting woody vines.

1 Bend one of the long, flexible stems to the ground. Remove the leaves from the portion of the stem located between 6 and 12 inches from the tip. Cut halfway through the stem. Treat the cut with a rooting hormone.

2 Dig a shallow trench and bury this portion of the stem in moist soil. Leave the growing tip, with leaves attached, above the ground.

3 Keep the soil slightly moist throughout the season while the buried stem forms roots. It will continue to get water and nutrients from the parent plant through the attached stem.

4 Next spring, cut the long, flexible cane where it enters the soil. Dig and transplant the newly rooted vine.

JUNE

 PLANNING

Take a break from planting to evaluate your progress. Melinda often finds her paper plans do not always fit the space, look, or reality of her garden space. Adjust your plans as needed. Note any changes you made on your landscape plan. Continue to record the name, variety, and sources of the plants you add. Write their locations on the landscape plan and in your journal.

Monitor for pest problems. Make a record of problems encountered throughout the season. List the plant affected, the pest problem, and the control methods used. Evaluate and record the results. This will help you avoid and control future problems.

 PLANTING

Keep planting. Container-grown vines and groundcovers can be planted throughout the growing season.

Finish hardening off and transplanting annual vines into the garden. Anchor the trellis in place before or right after the planting. Gently tie vines to the trellis to get them started climbing on their new support.

 CARE

Apply a 2- to 3-inch layer of mulch around groundcovers and vines. Use this to conserve moisture, reduce weeds, and improve the soil.

Do not bury the crowns of the groundcovers or the base of the vines. This can lead to rot and decline.

Use shredded leaves, evergreen needles, cocoa bean shells, woodchips, or twice-shredded bark. Renovate overgrown and weedy groundcovers. Dig out the healthy plants and remove them from the garden. Remove and compost or use a total vegetation killer to kill all the weeds and unwanted plants. Amend and fertilize the soil. Divide the healthy plants into smaller pieces. Plant the divisions at the proper spacing, water thoroughly, and mulch.

 WATERING

Check container plantings every day. Water whenever the top 2 inches begin to dry. Add enough water so that the excess runs out the bottom.

Water new plantings often enough to keep the soil around the roots slightly moist. Soak the top 6 to 8 inches of soil each time your water. Gradually decrease watering frequency. Water well-rooted plants when the top 2 to 3 inches of soil start to dry. Check plants growing in clay soils once a week and those in sandy or rocky soils twice a week.

Established and mulched plants need less frequent watering. Check during extended dry periods. Water when the top 3 or 4 inches are dry. Add enough water to wet the top 6 to 8 inches of soil.

 FERTILIZING

Do not overfertilize your plants. Avoid the temptation to give them just a little extra. Too much fertilizer can result in excess leaf growth, poor flowering, disease problems, and root damage. Follow soil test recommendations or limit fertilization to once a season.

Fertilize vines growing in containers. Use a diluted solution of any flowering plant fertilizer according to label directions. Or incorporate a slow-release fertilizer that will provide needed nutrients all season long.

Do not bury the crowns of the groundcovers or the base of the vines. This can lead to rot and decline.

 # PRUNING

Clip back or lightly mow **bugleweed** after flowering. This improves the appearance and prevents unwanted seedlings from taking over the garden.

Cut back **creeping phlox** if this was not done earlier. Prune foliage back halfway. This encourages new, healthy, more attractive growth. You may even be rewarded with a few more flowers later in the season.

Prune **climbing hydrangea** after it flowers in June. For young plants, limit pruning to broken and damaged branches. These slow-growing plants do not need formative training. For established plants, prune overly long shoots and outward facing stems. Very little pruning is needed.

 # PROBLEMS

Insects. Treat euonymus scale found on **wintercreeper.** These hard-shelled insects can be found on the stems and leaves. Spray the plants with insecticidal soap or ultrafine oil when the **Japanese tree lilacs** are in bloom. This is about mid- to late June. Repeat at 10- to 12-day intervals for a total of three applications. Check plants for mites and aphids. High populations will cause leaves to look speckled, yellow, and often become distorted. Spray plants with a strong blast of water. Follow up with insecticidal soap if necessary. Repeated applications may be needed.

Diseases. Remove spotted leaves and stems on **lily-of-the-valley** and **pachysandra**. These fungal leaf spot and blight diseases can usually be controlled with sanitation. Remove infected leaves and stems as soon as they appear. In fall, rake fallen leaves off the plantings to reduce the conditions that increase the risk of this disease.

Check **clematis** for wilt. Leaves wilt, and both the leaves and areas of the stem turn black. Prune infected stems back to healthy tissue or ground level. Disinfect tools between cuts. Use a solution of rubbing alcohol or one part bleach to nine parts water.

Remove brown branches, possibly phomopsis blight, on **junipers**. Cut brown stems back to a healthy side shoot or main stem. Disinfect tools between cuts.

Monitor **bugleweed** (*Ajuga*) for crown rot. Look for patches of dead and dying plants. Remove and discard sick plants. Improve soil drainage and avoid overhead watering to reduce future problems. You may want to treat the infected area with a fungicide before replanting with bugleweed or other susceptible plants.

PLANNING

Visit botanical gardens and arboretums. See how they use vines and groundcovers in their gardens. Take a few pictures, sketch some ideas, and start making a list of additions and changes you want to make.

Participate in your area's garden tours. Most are sponsored by beautification committees, master gardeners, and other not-for-profit groups. Support their efforts while gaining some insight from landscape designers, expert gardeners, and plant lovers like you.

 ## PLANTING

Dig and divide overgrown and declining plants. Midsummer transplants need extra attention to help them through the summer heat. Mulch and water whenever the soil around the roots begins to dry. Reduce watering as the plants become established. Keep planting. Always prepare the soil before adding groundcovers and vines. The goal is to grow a healthy plant in this location for many years to come. See "Planting" in the chapter introduction for guidelines.

 ## CARE

Mulch groundcovers and vines. Add a thin layer of woodchips, pine needles, or shredded leaves to the soil surface. Do not bury the crown of the plants or the base of the stems.

 ## WATERING

Water container plantings every day during hot, dry weather. Apply enough water so that the excess runs out the bottom of the pot.

Check new plantings lightly several times a week. Keep the roots moist for the first several weeks after planting. Reduce frequency as the root system develops. Water when the top 2 to 3 inches start to dry. Add enough water to wet the top 6 to 8 inches of soil.

Water established plants during extended dry weather. Moisten the top 6 to 8 inches whenever it starts to dry. Check plants growing in sandy and gravelly soil twice a week and those in clay soil once a week.

 ## FERTILIZING

Only fertilize plants showing signs of nutrient deficiency. Look for stunted growth, poor flowering, and lack of vigor. Consider having a soil test before adding any fertilizer. Otherwise, supplement the spring fertilization with a small amount (3 to 4 pounds per 1,000 square feet) of a low-nitrogen fertilizer. Apply the fertilizer beside the plants on the soil surface.

Fertilize vines growing in containers. Use a diluted solution of any flowering plant fertilizer. Read and follow label directions for the proper rate.

 ## PRUNING

Mow **goutweed**, also known as **snow-on-the-mountain** and **bishop's weed**, back to 6 inches several times during the growing season. This will prevent flowers, reduce reseeding, and keep the foliage fresh. Or prune back once when foliage declines or scorches (turns brown on its edges). Cut the plants back to 6 inches and wait for new and improved growth.

Cut off wayward and overgrown stems on groundcovers and vines. Prune back to a healthy bud or side shoot. Make the cut within the outline of the plant to mask the pruning job.

Prune **junipers** in mid-July. Remove dead and damaged branches back to a healthy stem deep in the plant to hide cuts. Disinfect tools with a solution of one part bleach to nine parts water. Remove overly long branches back to shorter side shoots to control size.

Deadhead the summer-blooming **sedum.** It improves the appearance and can encourage repeat bloom.

PROBLEMS

Pull weeds as soon as they appear. This is a big task when establishing a groundcover. Invest time now to eliminate the need to renovate a weed-infested planting. See this month's "Helpful Hints" for more ideas on controlling weeds.

Watch for scorch on groundcovers and vines growing in hot, sunny locations. Mulch the roots to reduce drought stress and scorch. Move plants that continually suffer from scorch to a shadier location.

Helpful Hints

Consider groundcovers as an alternative to grass. They add interesting texture, colorful foliage, and often flowers to the landscape. They do not require frequent mowing, but they do require weed control. And it is a little more time consuming, especially during establishment, than lawns.

Try these tips for weed control:

• Pull weeds as soon as you see them. Remove them before they set seed and create more weeds—and work for you—in the future.

• Mulch new and established plants with cocoa bean shells, twice-shredded bark, shredded leaves, or other organic material. This reduces weeds while conserving moisture and improving the soil.

• Use a pre-emergent weedkiller to prevent annual weed seeds from germinating. Apply these early in the season and repeat as recommended on the label.

• Spot treat quackgrass and other perennial weeds with a total vegetation killer, such as Roundup® or Finale™. Be careful not to get any on the groundcover. These herbicides kill anything green they touch. Use a sponge-type brush and paint the weed leaves with the herbicide. Do not let the wet leaves or herbicide touch the groundcover. Cut the top and bottom out of a plastic milk jug. Cover the weeds with the milk jug and spray the weed inside the container. Once the herbicide dries, move the jug to the next weed and repeat.

Monitor plants for Japanese beetles. These insects have made it to the Prairie Lands and are causing damage in several areas. These metallic, green-brown beetles eat the leaves of hundreds of different plants. Pick beetles off the plants and drop in a bucket of soapy water.

Continue watching for mites and aphids. Look for speckled, yellow, and distorted leaves caused by their feeding. Spray infected plants with a strong blast of water. If that does not work, try several applications of insecticidal soap.

AUGUST

PLANNING

Are there areas where you should consider adding more vines and groundcovers? Annual and perennial vines can provide quick shade, decorative windbreaks, and screening in the landscape. Consider them as an option for narrow spaces too small for trees and shrubs. Use groundcovers under trees where the surface roots make it hard to mow or the shade makes it impossible to grow grass. This will save work for you and create a better environment for the trees.

PLANTING

Keep planting groundcovers and vines. There is still time for the plants to establish roots before winter sets in.

Minimize the impact on established trees when planting groundcovers beneath their canopy.

1 Do not cover the roots heavily with soil or till deeply. Cultivation damages the fine feeder roots located in the top 12 inches of soil.

2 Use an edger or sharp shovel to edge the new planting bed. Remove or kill the grass with a total vegetation killer, such as Roundup® or Finale™.

3 Leave the dead grass (if killed with an herbicide) intact to serve as your first layer of mulch. You will cover it with a decorative mulch after planting.

4 Dig a hole twice the width but the same depth as the groundcover. Remove the container and set the groundcover in the hole at the same depth as it was growing in the pot.

5 Fill with soil. Water with transplant solution to help remove air pockets and settle the soil.

6 Mulch the area with woodchips, evergreen needles, or shredded leaves.

CARE

Mulch new and existing groundcovers. See July "Care" for more information. Watch for brown leaf edges that can indicate scorch. Pay special attention to **hostas** and other shade lovers grown in sun. Water is not always the solution. Often the plants are unable to take the water up fast enough to replace what they lose during extreme heat. Mulch the soil, water properly by moistening the top 6 inches whenever the top 3 to 4 inches start to dry, and consider moving plants to a more suitable location in the future.

WATERING

Check container-grown vines daily. Water whenever the top 2 to 3 inches of soil begin to dry. Apply enough water so that the excess runs out the bottom.

Keep the soil moist around the roots of new plantings. Reduce watering frequency as plants become more established in a few weeks. Water whenever the top 3 to 4 inches of soil start to dry. Apply enough water to wet the top 6 to 8 inches of soil.

Water established plantings during extended dry periods. Wet the top 6 to 8 inches when they become dry.

FERTILIZING

Do not fertilize in-ground plantings. Late-season fertilization can stimulate late-season growth that will not have time to harden off over winter.

Annual and perennial vines can provide quick shade, decorative windbreaks, and screening in the landscape.

Continue fertilizing annual and tropical vines grown in containers. Use a diluted solution of any flowering fertilizer according to label directions. Stop fertilizing any perennial vines in containers that spend their winter outdoors.

PROBLEMS

Check **honeysuckle** vines for aphids. A soil systemic insecticide applied to the soil may be easier to use than trying to cover the large plant with a spray.

Capture and destroy slugs eating holes in the leaves of **hostas** and other shade lovers. Set out shallow tins, sunk into the ground, filled with beer. The slugs crawl inside and drown. Or place beer in an empty soda or beer bottle and lay on its side. This gives you a built-in cover to prevent the beer from being diluted by the rain. Tuck bottles under the plants for a tidier look.

Watch **honeysuckle** and other plants for powdery mildew. This fungus causes a white film on the leaves. Severe infestations block the sunlight, causing leaves to yellow. Increase sunlight and air circulation to reduce this problem. Try some of the new soap- and neem-based fungicides to reduce further infection.

Helpful Hints

Renovate overgrown and weed-infested groundcover plantings. Starting over can be easier than trying to fix the existing planting.

1 Dig out the healthy plants. Heel in or place in pots for temporary storage. Dig a trench and set the groundcovers in an unplanted area of the landscape. Water often enough to keep the roots moist.

2 Edge the bed with a shovel or edger. Spray the area with a total vegetation killer, such as Roundup or Finale. Avoid contacting trees, shrubs, and other desirable plants.

3 Add 2 to 4 inches of organic matter. Include fertilizer if renovation is done early in the season. Otherwise wait until next spring to add needed nutrients. Apply 1 pound of actual nitrogen per 1000 square feet. This is equal to 3 pounds of ammonium nitrate (33-0-0), 4 pounds of ammonium sulfate (21-0-0), or 16 pounds of Milorganite-tm (6-2-0).

4 Till or spade the organic matter and fertilizer into the top 6 to 12 inches of soil. Rake smooth and allow to the soil to settle.

5 Divide healthy groundcover plants that were potted up or heeled in. Discard dead and less vigorous portions of the plant. Set plants at proper spacing with the crowns (the point where the stem joins the roots) even with the soil surface.

6 Water thoroughly with transplant solution, wetting the top 6 inches of soil. Mulch the soil with woodchips, shredded leaves, or other organic matter. Keep the roots lightly moist for the first few weeks. Then water when the top 2 to 3 inches of soil start to dry.

PRUNING

Remove badly scorched leaves.

Prune unsightly **bishop's weed** (**goutweed**) back to 6 inches. This removes spent flowers and scorched leaves. Watch for better looking growth in a few weeks.

September
Vines & Ground Covers

PLANNING

Time to start preparing for winter. Locate a sunny location or space under lights for tender vines that will soon move indoors. Decide how to manage perennial vines that need some winter protection. These can be planted in ground, stored in an unheated garage, or given extra protection for winter.

Keep evaluating the landscape. Take pictures, draw sketches, and update your landscape plans. This will help you when trying to make changes over winter.

PLANTING

Keep planting. Fall is a great time to add new plants to the landscape. The soil is warm and the air is cool. These are perfect conditions for establishing new plants.

1 Start planting once the site is prepared. Dig a hole at least two to three times wider, but no deeper, than the container.

2 Gently push on the container sides to loosen the roots. Slide the plant out of the pot. Do not pull it out by the stem. Place the plant in the hole so that the rootball is even with the soil surface.

3 Fill the hole with the existing soil. Water to settle the soil and eliminate air pockets. See "Planting" in the chapter introduction for more details.

Plant **autumn crocus** in groundcover beds. These bulbs sprout leaves in spring. The leaves fade, and you will be surprised with pink or white leafless flowers in the fall.

CARE

Move tender vines indoors for winter as the temperatures cool, but before the first killing frost.

Prune tropical vines back just enough to make them manageable for their indoor home.

Isolate these plants from your other houseplants for several weeks. Monitor for insects, such as mites, aphids, and whiteflies. These insects cause the leaves to appear speckled, yellow, and often distorted.

Spray infested plants with insecticidal soap to treat mites and aphids. Repeat weekly until the pests are under control. Use yellow sticky traps to reduce whitefly populations. Purchase them at a garden center or make your own. Apply Tanglefoot™ or other sticky material to a piece of yellow cardboard. Place near the plants.

WATERING

Continue watering container plants thoroughly, until excess water runs out the bottom. Check outdoor container gardens daily. Water whenever the top 2 to 3 inches of soil begin to dry.

Water new plantings as needed. Keep soil moist around recently planted vines and groundcovers. Allow the top 3 to 4 inches of soil to start to dry before watering plants that have been in the ground for several weeks.

Check established plants during extended dry periods. Water when the top 4 inches of soil are dry.

FERTILIZING

Keep fertilizing tenderl and annual vines in containers. Use a diluted solution of a flowering fertilizer according to label directions.

Do not fertilize other vines and groundcovers. Late-season fertilization can stimulate late-season growth that is subject to winterkill.

Keep planting. Fall is a great time to add new plants to the landscape. The soil is warm and the air is cool.

PRUNING

Remove damaged and diseased leaves and stems. Wait until late winter or early spring for routine pruning.

PROBLEMS

Continue monitoring for insects and disease. Remove and discard spotted and discolored leaves as soon as they are discovered. This will reduce the source of disease next season. Only treat when there is a problem; overuse of pesticide can lead to other pest problems.

Watch for insects. They should be less of a problem as the weather cools. Note scale insects that can be treated by professionals in the fall with a soil-applied insecticide. Or mark your calendar so that you remember to control them in winter with a dormant spray or next season with an insecticide.

Helpful Hints

Select vines and groundcovers for fall interest. Many provide fruit, flowers, and colorful foliage as a grand finale to the growing season.

Smell the fragrance of **sweet autumn clematis** as it climbs over an arbor or trellis. The delicate white flowers brighten the landscape, while the fragrance fills the air. Melinda's grows on a fence between her house and my neighbor's house. The vigorous vine often climbs onto the **Boston ivy** on her home. We both enjoy the fragrance and attractive combination of white flowers and dark green leaves.

Watch for fall color in the landscape. **Hostas** turn a brilliant yellow in fall. This echoes the yellow of **ginkgo** and other trees and shrubs in the landscape.

Boston ivy and **Virginia creeper** are some of the first plants to show their fall color. They turn a beautiful red color that stands out against your home, trellis, or arbor providing support. Enjoy the blue fruit uncovered by falling leaves. But just look, do not eat!

Check out *Sedum kamtschaticum* as the leaves turn a lovely bronze to gold in fall. This can add a little fall surprise at ground level in the landscape.

Enjoy the fruit on **bittersweet**. The orange and yellow fruit adds interest to the fall and winter landscape. Or harvest some to use in dried arrangements and wreaths. You may need to add a male pollinator or female fruit producer if your mature plants fail to bear fruit. Check the flowers next spring to find which one is missing. The female will have a swollen base, while the male has nothing but pinlike structures. Add the missing male or female plant for pollination and fruit formation.

OCTOBER

 PLANNING

Enjoy the change of season. Watch and evaluate the changing color of your landscape. Take pictures and videotape the colorful vines and groundcovers.

Take a few minutes to record the highlights and challenges of this growing season. Use this information, pictures, and garden reviews to plan future improvements and reduce pest problems.

 PLANTING

Finish planting early in the month. This gives the plants time to start rooting into surrounding soil before the ground freezes. Wait until next spring to plant tender and borderline hardy plants. Give them as much time as possible to become established before winter.

Plant bulbs throughout groundcover beds. Use them to spark up plantings and add another season of color. See this month's "Helpful Hints" for suggestions.

Store unplanted groundcovers and vines for winter. Find a vacant garden space in a protected area. Sink the pots into the ground. This insulates the roots from below-freezing temperatures. Do the same for hardy vines growing in

containers. Mulch after the ground lightly freezes.

Or move the potted vines into an unheated garage for winter. Place in a corner as far from the door as possible. Pack the pots with Styrofoam peanuts or other insulating material. Water whenever the soil thaws and is dry.

Or move the planters to a sheltered location. Pack bales of straw around the pot for added root insulation.

 CARE

Blow or rake fallen leaves off plants. Large leaves trap moisture, block sunlight, and lead to crown rot and other disease problems on groundcovers.

Or try this technique. Cover plantings with netting to catch the falling leaves. Remove the leaf-covered netting. Drag it off or roll it up to keep the leaves on the netting until you clear the groundcover planting. Replace the netting and keep removing leaves until all of them have fallen to the ground.

Try overwintering tubers of 'Blackie', 'Marguerite', and 'Pink Frost' **sweet potato vines.** Dig plants after a light frost has killed the leaves. Discard any damaged or diseased tubers. Remove foliage

and allow the tubers to dry overnight. Pack tubers in peat moss and store in a cool, dark location.

 WATERING

Water tender vines growing indoors whenever the top few inches of soil begin to dry. Water thoroughly so that the excess runs out the bottom. Place a saucer filled with pebbles under the pot. Allow excess water to collect in the pebbles while the pot sits above the water. This increases the humidity around the plant, while eliminating the need to pour excess water out of saucer.

Check potted vines wintering outdoors. Water anytime the soil is thawed and dry. Water thoroughly so that the excess runs out the bottom.

Cooler temperatures mean less watering. Wait until the top 3 to 4 inches begin to dry before watering again. Apply enough water to moisten the top 6 inches of soil.

Water new and established plantings thoroughly before the ground freezes.

Do not fertilize. Late-season fertilization can lead to late-season growth that can be winterkilled.

Take a soil test if this has not been done in the past. Start with new plantings or those showing signs of stress. Stunted plants with off-colored leaves may indicate a nutrient deficiency.

Take several 4- to 6-inch-long plugs of soil from scattered sites throughout the planting bed. Combine the plugs, mix together, and measure out 1 cup of soil for testing.

The soil test report will help you determine what type and how much fertilizer you need to add. Follow soil test recommendations to improve plant health and eliminate over-fertilization. Stop fertilizing container plantings. Properly managed annual plants have plenty of nutrients to finish out the growing season. Perennial vines need to harden off for winter, and tropical vines need to adjust to the low light of the indoors.

Helpful Hints

Plant a little extra color in your groundcover beds. Add hardy bulbs to **vinca**, **wintercreeper**, **deadnettle**, and other groundcovers.

Select bulbs with flowers and foliage that complement, not compete with, the groundcover. Make sure the groundcover masks the fading bulb foliage rather than the bulb foliage detracting from the developing groundcover.

Pick bulbs that flower with the groundcover for a nice combination. Or use bulbs with groundcovers that bloom in different seasons. This helps extend your flower display.

Wait until October to start planting hardy bulbs. The cooler temperatures reduce the risk of early sprouting. Use a narrow trowel to dig a small hole for the bulb. This will minimize root disturbance. Plant the bulb at a depth that is two to three times its height. Cover with soil and water. Mix **autumn crocus** with **vinca**. The **crocus** leaves grow and die back in spring before the **vinca** grows and flowers. Watch for the pink or white flowers that make a surprise appearance in fall.

Use **Siberian squill** and **glory-of-the-snow** with **deadnettle** or **sweet woodruff**. The bulbs' pretty blue flowers make a nice prelude to the groundcovers' decorative foliage and flowers.

Mix **daffodils** with **Virginia bluebells** and **hostas**. As the **daffodils** and **bluebells** fade, the **hosta** leaves begin to emerge to hide their fading foliage.

 PRUNING

Prune out diseased stems and leaves. Disinfect tools between cuts with rubbing alcohol or a solution of one part bleach to nine parts water.

 PROBLEMS

Continue weeding. Fall is the time many weeds set seed for next season's crop. Removing them now will greatly reduce your weeding chores next season.

Rake and destroy fallen leaves. Remove diseased and dead leaves from groundcovers. These can harbor pests and serve as a source of disease in next year's garden.

NOVEMBER
Vines & Ground Covers

 PLANNING

Start planning for next season. Survey the landscape and look for alternatives to traditional planting techniques. Consider adding a few vines to crawl through the perennial garden or up the trunk of a tree. Avoid fast-growing, twining vines that can strangle other plants. **Climbing hydrangea** and **wintercreeper** climb trees without girdling the trunk. Use twining vines, such as **clematis**, **hardy kiwi**, and **akebia**, to disguise down-spouts and mailboxes.

Mix two different **clematis** vines or an annual such as **morning glory** with a **trumpet vine** for added bloom and inter-esting foliage effect.

Try the same with groundcovers. Mix several **sedum** for color and texture vari-ation. Use solid and variegated cultivars together. The lighter foliage contrasts nicely again the solid green leaves.

Always select partners that are suited to the growing conditions and are equally aggressive. Otherwise, you will end up with only one—the stronger of the two—plant in the end.

 PLANTING

It is too late to plant vines and ground-covers. Store unplanted vines and groundcovers for winter. Sink the pots of these plants in the ground in a vacant garden space. This insulates the soil from cold winter temperatures. Mulch once the ground freezes.

Keep adding bulbs to groundcover plant-ings. Look for creative ways to brighten up your garden beds. See October "Helpful Hints" for a few ideas.

 CARE

Remove the last of the fall leaves. **Maple**, **oak**, and other large leaves trap moisture and block sunlight from reaching groundcovers. This leads to crown rot and other fungal diseases. Gently rake or blow leaves off groundcover plantings.

Shred and compost or recycle the fallen leaves. Shredded leaves can be placed on the soil surface and used as a winter mulch. They help insulate the roots, con-serve moisture, reduce weeds, and add nutrients to the soil as they decompose.

 WATERING

Water all outdoor plants thoroughly before the ground freezes. Moisten the top 6 to 8 inches of soil.

Drain and store the garden hose for win-ter. It will last longer if properly stored in an area that doesn't reach freezing tem-peratures.

Water container plants whenever the top 2 to 3 inches of soil begin to dry. Apply enough water so that the excess runs out the bottom. Water pots stored outdoors and in the garage whenever the soil is thawed and dry.

Check indoor plants several times a week. Water only when the top 2 to 3 inches begin to dry. Place the pot on a gravel-filled saucer. Allow the excess water to collect in the gravel. As the water evaporates, it increases the humidity around the plants. This also eliminates the need to empty the excess water from the saucer each time you water.

Shred and compost or recycle fallen leaves. Shredded leaves can be placed on the soil surface and used as a winter mulch. They help insulate the roots, conserve moisture, reduce weeds, and add nutrients to the soil as they decompose.

FERTILIZING

Review plant growth and note areas that need soil tests. Use this as your first step in correcting problems. The soil test results will indicate if a lack of nutrients or incorrect fertilization is causing the problem.

Give tender vines time to adjust to their indoor home. Yellow and falling leaves are due to low light and poor growing conditions. Once new growth begins, you can start fertilizing. Use a diluted solution of any flowering houseplant fertilizer. Apply to indoor vines with stunted growth.

PRUNING

Remove dead and damaged branches whenever they are found. Disinfect tools between cuts on diseased plants. Use rubbing alcohol or a solution of one part bleach to nine parts water.

Helpful Hints

Tired of watching grass die in the shade of your house or **Norway maple**? Consider one of the shade-tolerant groundcovers for these areas. They provide an attractive solution to this problem. Consider plants with variegated leaves. They brighten up the shade and provide color all season long. **Deadnettle** (Lamium) grows well in the dry shade found under many large shade trees. Use one or more of the many colorful **hostas** to brighten up the shade.

Try **Canadian ginger** under **spruce** and **pine** trees. They tolerate the heavy shade and grow right through the evergreen needle mulch. The attractive leaves provide texture throughout the season.

Do not forget the flowers. **Vinca (periwinkle)**, **moneywort**, **deadnettle**, and **epimedium** will flower even in the shade.

This seasonal flash of color is something your **bluegrass** could not provide.

Quit fighting the shade and give in to nature. Use woodchips or shredded mulch around trees where it is too shady for even these groundcovers grow. Or strategically place flagstone steppers in heavily shaded areas. Allow the moss to grow and call it a moss garden.

PROBLEMS

Gather liquid fertilizers and pesticides from sheds and unheated garages. Inventory and store these and other pesticides in a secure location away from pets and children. Keep liquids out of direct sun and in a frost-free location. Move granules to a secure, dry space for storage. Protect plantings from voles and rabbits. Place a cylinder of hardware cloth around **euonymus** vines and other susceptible vines. Sink it several inches into the soil. Make sure it is at least 4 feet tall to discourage rabbits. Or spray susceptible vines and groundcovers, such as **cranberry cotoneaster**, with a homemade or commercial repellent. Repeat throughout the season.

DECEMBER
Vines & Ground Covers

PLANNING

Winter has arrived, and it is time to relax, enjoy the holidays, and finish taking notes on the past growing season. Gather photos, plant tags, landscape plans, and your journal.

PLANTING

It is too late to plant outside and too early to plant inside. Look at the catalogs and landscape plans, and start a planting list.

CARE

Check on vines stored in the garage or protected area for winter. Adjust location or winter mulch if needed. Use evergreen boughs to protect **European ginger** and other tender plants from winter injury. Use your discarded holiday tree to create shade and windbreaks for tender vines. Evergreen vines, such as **wintercreeper**, often suffer leaf burn from winter winds.

WATERING

Water tropical vines growing indoors for the winter. Water thoroughly whenever the top 2 to 3 inches begin to dry. Apply enough water so that the excess runs out the bottom of the container.

Check potted vines stored in the garage and sheltered locations outdoors. Water whenever the soil thaws and the top 2 to 3 inches are dry. Add enough water to moisten all the soil. Stop watering when the excess begins to run out the bottom of the pot.

FERTILIZING

Do not fertilize outdoor plants. Fertilizing frozen soil can lead to groundwater pollution.

Helpful Hints

Another season ends and once again your **trumpet vine** did not bloom. All the books say "easy to grow, free flowering," but this is not the case for you and many others.

Be patient. **Trumpet vines** need to reach maturity to flower. Keep rampant growers under control. Prune them back to several buds beyond the main framework.

Check the growing conditions. Make sure the plant is growing in full sun.

Avoid high-nitrogen fertilizers that encourage leaf growth and discourage flowers. Keep fertilizers away from this luxury feeder. **Trumpet vine** will seek out and use all the nutrients it can find, leading to a large plant with few flowers.

Root prune as a last resort. Use a sharp shovel and slice through a few roots. Do this in one or two locations several feet from the trunk. Do not cut the roots all the way around the plant. This can injure the plant.

PRUNING

Remove dead and damaged stems as they appear.

PROBLEMS

Take a walk outside before the snow gets too deep. Note any existing and potential problems to watch for in the future.

Glossary

AARS: (All-America Rose Selections) Since 1938, winners of 2 year trials in more than 20 test gardens across America. A great honor to be bestowed on a rose.

AAS: (All-America Selections) A network of industry-based trial gardens throughout the country that test new introductions of flowers and vegetables and flowers. Winners are top-notch plants that are sure to be around for a long time.

Acid soil: soil with a pH less than 7.0. This is often found in regions with high rainfall. Most garden plants thrive in a slightly acidic soil with a pH between 6.0 and 7.0.

Alkaline soil: soil with a pH greater than 7.0. Sometimes called sweet soil. Limestone (or concrete leaching from a house foundation) can contribute to alkalinity. Much of the Prairie Lands has alkaline soil.

All-purpose fertilizer: powdered, liquid, or granular fertilizer with a balanced proportion of the three key nutrients—nitrogen (N), phosphorus (P), and potassium (K). It is suitable for maintenance nutrition for most plants. 10-10-10 is an all-purpose, balanced fertilizer.

Amend: the addition of organic matter (compost, peat moss, manure, etc.), minerals, or other matter, such as builder's sand, to improve the soil.

Annual: a plant that lives its entire life in one season. It is genetically determined to germinate, grow, flower, set seed, and die the same year. In our region, there are numerous plants that are perennial in warmer climates that we grow as annuals. Rightfully these should be called "tender perennials."

***Bacillus thuringiensis* (Bt):** a biological insecticide that can kill good and bad insects when sprayed at the right stage of an insect's growth. It can control caterpillars, cabbage-worms, and mosquito larvae. Another species (*B. papillae*), more commonly known as milky spore disease, is used to treat Japanese beetles and other grubs.

Backfill: the soil that is put back into a planting hole after the plant has been positioned. This soil may be native (as is) or amended.

Balled and burlapped: a tree or shrub grown in the field whose rootball was wrapped with protective burlap (cloth or plastic) and twine when the plant was dug up to be sold or transplanted.

Bare root: a dormant plant that has been packaged without any soil around its roots. (Often young shrubs, trees, roses, and sometimes perennials purchased through the mail arrive with their exposed roots covered with moist peat or sphagnum moss, sawdust, or similar material, and wrapped in plastic.)

Beneficial insects: insects or their larvae that prey on pest organisms and/or their eggs. They may be flying insects, such as ladybugs, parasitic wasps, praying mantis, and soldier bugs, or soil dwellers such as predatory nematodes, earthworms, spiders, and ants.

Bicolor: a flower or leaf which is comprised of two colors; in leaves this is often called variegation.

Biennial: a plant that takes two years to complete its life cycle; sprouting and leafing out the first year, flowering, setting seed and dying the second. Many, such as foxglove and hollyhock, reseed and seem perennial.

Blackspot: a fungal disease of roses that manifests itself as small black spots on the leaves. Leaves eventually turn yellow and fall off. May also infect the canes or branches.

Bog: a waterlogged area of land, which is usually acidic. In water gardens, the area around the pond where excess water spills is usually a bog.

Bones: the hardscape of a garden; the background that provides the structure; all non-plant material in the garden.

Bract: a modified leaf structure on a plant stem near its flower that resembles a petal. Often it is more colorful and visible than the actual flower, as in dogwood and pointsettia.

Glossary

Bt: see Bacillus thuringiensis.

Bud: a small swelling or nub on a plant that will develop into a flower, leaf, or stem.

Bud union: the place where the top (tender) variety of a plant (usually a rose) was grafted to the hardier rootstock; on roses this is seen as a rounded area near the bottom of the stem. With roses In the Prairie Lands states, plant the bud union at least two inches below soil level.

Cane: a long pliable stem, such as a grape or raspberry; most commonly one of the main stems of a rose.

Canopy: the overhead branching area of a tree, usually referring to its extent including foliage.

Catkin: a dense spike of small flowers without petals, such as on a willow or birch tree.

Climber: a plant with the ability to wend its way upward, whether by tendrils, rootlets, adhesive pads, or twining stems; needs to be planted near a support.

Cold hardiness: the ability of a plant to survive the winter cold in a particular area.

Compost: decomposed organic material used as a fertilizer and soil amendment. Every gardener should be making his or her own compost, no matter how small the garden

Compost tea: liquid fertilizer made by steeping compost in water for several days; for general watering or foliar feeding.

Composite: 1. a flower that is actually composed of many tiny flowers. Typically, there are flat clusters of tiny, tight florets (disk), surrounded by wider-petaled florets (ray), such as sunflower, black-eyed Susan. Composite flowers are highly attractive to bees and beneficial insects. 2. A daisy-like flower.

Compost: organic matter that has undergone progressive decomposition by microbial and macrobial activity until it is reduced to a spongy, fluffy texture. Added to soil of any type, it aerates the soil and improves drainage and fertility.

Conifer: a tree or shrub with needlelike leaves that forms a cone that holds the seeds. Most (hemlocks, pines, cedars) are evergreen, but a few (larch, dawn redwood, bald cypress) are deciduous.

Container-grown: a plant that has been grown from seed or cutting in a container, usually at a nursery. As opposed to a plant that is dug up from the ground and put into a container with soil.

Corm: the swollen energy-storing structure, analogous to a bulb, under the soil at the base of the stem of plants such as crocus and gladiolus.

Corymb: a cluster of flowers or florets that starts blooming on the outer edges and works its way in.

Crotch: the place where a major stem or branch of a shrub or tree joins the trunk.

Crown: the base of a plant at, or just beneath, the surface of the soil where the roots meet the stems.

Cultivar: a hybrid plant variety (CULTIvated VARiety) that is only reproduced vegetatively (from cuttings) or inbred seed. It was selected for particular desirable qualities. In a plant name, the cultivar name is always denoted within single quotes, such as a specific lilac—*Syringa vulgaris* 'Scentsation'.

Cutting: 1. a method of propagation where a portion of the stem is cut from the plant and induced to produce roots, eventually growing into a plant on its own.   2. The part of a plant cut off from the parent plant that is treated so it produces roots and becomes a plant itself.

Cyme: a branched cluster of flowers or florets; flowers start opening from the center outward.

Dappled shade: the pattern of light cast by trees with branches open enough to let light pass through their leaves, branches, or needles.

Glossary

Deadhead: to remove faded flowerheads from plants to improve their appearance, prevent seed production, and stimulate further flowering. May be done manually or by pruning. Deadheading, however, will remove seeds that some birds and other animals use as a food source.

Deciduous plants: trees and shrubs that drop their leaves in the fall and send out new leaves in the spring. Plants may also drop their leaves in order to survive a prolonged drought.

Desiccation: drying out of foliage tissues, usually due to drought or wind.

Dibble: a small, pointed, wooden hand tool used to make small holes in soil for seeding or transplanting small seedlings. Also known as dibber.

Dieback: a stem that has died, beginning at its tip and continuing inward, most often caused by cold temperatures; may also be a result of insufficient water, insect attack, nutrient deficiency, or injury.

Dioecious: male or female flowers are on separate plants (holly, etc.). A plant of each sex is necessary for fruiting.

Disk flower: the center of a composite flower, composed of tightly packed florets. This is the center of a daisy, black-eyed Susan, purple coneflower and others.

Division: the practice of splitting apart perennial plants to create several smaller-rooted segments. The practice is useful for controlling the plant's size and for acquiring more plants; it is also essential to the health and continued flowering of certain perennials.

Dormant: the state in which a plant, although alive, is not actively growing. For many plants, especially deciduous ones, this is the winter. A survival method for cold or drought. Spring-blooming bulbs are dormant from summer through winter.

Double-flowered: a flower that has more than the usual number of petals, usually arranged in extra rows.

Drip line: the area underneath the farthest-reaching branches of a tree that receives water from rain dripping down from the leaves and branches.

Dwarf: a naturally occurring smaller version of a plant, such as a dwarf conifer. The dwarf is small in relation to the original plant, but is not necessarily diminutive in stature.

Established: the point at which a newly planted tree, shrub, or flower begins to produce new growth—either leaves, flowers, or stems. This indicates that transplantation was successful and the roots have begun to grow and spread.

Evergreen: perennial plants (woody or herbaceous) that do not lose their foliage every year with the onset of winter. Needled or broadleaf foliage will persist and continues to function on a plant through one or more winters, aging and dropping unobtrusively in cycles of three or four years or more.

Fertilizer: a substance that is used to feed a plant—may be liquid, granular, or solid form.

Firm: to gently press the soil down around a plant with your hands—never feet—after planting in order to eliminate air pockets.

Floret: a small individual flower, usually part of a cluster that comprise the larger flower

Foliar: of or about leaves.

Foliar feeding: spraying the leaves with liquid fertilizer (often kelp or fish emulsion, but may be a other liquid fertilizer diluted according to package directions); leaf tissues absorb liquid directly for fast results, and the soil is not affected.

Floret: a tiny flower, usually one of many forming a cluster, that comprises a single blossom (lilacs, alliums, hydrangeas).

Genus : (plural genera) a group of species which have certain traits in common. When written, the genus is capitalized, and both genus and species are italicized (*Rosa rugosa*).

Glossary

Germinate: to sprout. Germination is a fertile seed's first stage of development.

Graft : the area on a woody plant where a plant with hardy roots was joined with the stem of another plant. Roses are commonly grafted. Some plants, such as members of the apple family may be grafted onto a different plant such as an apricot onto a peach. This technique is often used to produce dwarf plants.

Hardscape: the permanent, structural, non-plant part of a landscape, such as walls, the house, sheds, pools, patios, arbors, and walkways.

Herbaceous: plants having fleshy or soft stems that die back with frost; the opposite of woody.

Hybrid: a plant that is the result of intentional or natural cross-pollination between two or more plants of the same species, variety, or genus.

Leaflet: the leaflike parts that make up a compound leaf, as a rose, for example.

Low water demand: describes plants that tolerate dry soil for varying periods of time. Typically, they have succulent, hairy, or silvery-gray foliage and tuberous roots or taproots.

Mulch: a layer of material put over bare soil to protect it from erosion, slow the evaporation of water, modulate soil temperature, prevent the soil from heaving due to thawing and freezing in the winter, and to discourage weeds. It may be inorganic (gravel, fabric) or organic (wood chips, bark, pine needles, chopped leaves). Mulch is usually put around and between plants.

Naturalize: 1. to plant seeds, bulbs, or plants in a random, informal pattern as they would appear in their natural habitat; 2. to adapt to and spread throughout adopted habitats (a tendency of some nonnative plants).

Nectar: the sweet fluid produced by glands on flowers that attract pollinators such as hummingbirds and honeybees for whom it is a source of energy.

Neutral soil: soil with a pH of 7.0. It is neither acid nor alkaline.

Organic material, organic matter: any material or debris that is derived from plants. It is carbon-based material capable of undergoing decomposition and decay.

Peat moss: organic matter from peat sedges (United States) or sphagnum mosses (Canada), often used to improve soil texture. The acidity of sphagnum peat moss makes it ideal for boosting or maintaining soil acidity while also improving its drainage. It also helps hold moisture.

Perennial: a flowering plant that lives over two or more seasons. Many die back with frost, but the roots survive winter and generate new shoots in the spring.

pH: a measurement of the relative acidity (low pH) or alkalinity (high pH) of soil or water based on a scale of 1 to 14, 7 being neutral. Individual plants require soil to be within a certain range so that nutrients can dissolve in moisture and be available to them.

Pinch: to remove tender stems and/or leaves by pressing them between thumb and forefinger. This pruning technique encourages branching, compactness, and flowering in plants, or it removes aphids clustered at growing tips.

Pollen: the yellow, powdery grains in the center of a flower. A plant's male sex cells that are transferred to the female plant parts by means of wind, insect, or animal pollinators to fertilize them and create seeds.

Raceme: an arrangement of single stalked flowers along an elongated, unbranched axis.

Ray flower: a flat petal-like floret in a composite or daisylike flower. The ray flowers surround the central disk flower.

Glossary

Rhizome: a swollen energy-storing stem structure, similar to a bulb, that lies horizontally in the soil, with roots emerging from its lower surface and growth shoots from a growing point at or near its tip, as in bearded iris.

Rootbound (or potbound): the condition of a plant that has been confined in a container too long, its roots having been forced to wrap around themselves and even swell out of the container. Successful transplanting or repotting requires untangling and trimming away of some of the matted roots and repotting into a larger container.

Root flare: the transition at the base of a tree trunk where the bark tissue begins to differentiate and roots begin to form just before entering the soil. This area should not be covered with soil when planting a tree.

Self-seeding: the tendency of some plants to drop their seeds, or have the wind scatter them freely around the yard. These plant, often annuals and biennials, will come back year after year, as in cosmos, hollyhocks, and cleome.

Self-sowing: another term for self-seeding.

Semievergreen: a plant that remains evergreen in a mild climate but loses some or all of its leaves in a colder one.

Shearing: the pruning technique whereby plant stems and branches are cut uniformly with long-bladed pruning shears (hedge shears) or powered hedge trimmers. It is used when creating and maintaining hedges and topiary; also used to cut back the spent flowers and some of the foliage from some annuals and perennials such as dianthus and sea thrift.

Slow-acting fertilizer: fertilizer that is water insoluble and therefore releases its nutrients gradually as a function of soil temperature, moisture, and related microbial activity. Typically granular, it may be organic or synthetic.

Succulent growth: the sometimes undesirable production of fleshy, water-storing leaves or stems that results from overfertilization.

Tamp: when sowing a seed or putting a plant in the ground, the act of gently pressing on the soil with the palms of your hands to make contact of seed and soil, and to help eliminate air pockets.

Tender perennial: a plant that is perennial in warm climates (usually hardiness zones 8 to 10) that cannot survive below-freezing temperatures of winter. These plants are grown as annuals in cold-weather regions.

Sucker: a new growing shoot. Underground plant roots produce suckers to form new stems and spread by means of these suckering roots to form large plantings, or colonies. Some plants produce root suckers or branch suckers as a result of pruning or wounding.

Tuber: a type of underground storage structure in a plant stem, analogous to a bulb. It generates roots below and stems above ground (example: dahlia).

Variegated: having various colors or color patterns. The term usually refers to plant foliage that is streaked, edged, blotched, or mottled with a contrasting color, often green with yellow, cream, or white. Usually two different colors, less commonly three or more.

Wings: 1. the corky tissue that forms edges along the twigs of some woody plants such as winged euonymus. 2. the flat, dried extension of tissue on some seeds, such as maple, that catch the wind and help them disseminate.

Mail-Order Nurseries

Andre Viette Farm & Nursery
608 Longmeadow
Fishersville, VA 22939
540-943-2315
www.viette.com

Arnold's Greenhouse
1430 Highway 57 SE
Leroy, KS 66857
620-964-2463

B & D Lilies
PO Box 2007
Port Townsend WA 98368
360-765-4341
www.bdlilies.com

Bluestone Perennial
7211 Middle Ridge Road
Madison, OH 44057-3096
800-852-5243
www.bluestoneperennials.com

Brady's Nursery
11200 West Kellogg
Wichita KS 67209
316-722-7516

Brent & Becky's Bulbs
7463 Heath Trail
Gloucester, VA 23601
804-693-3966
www.brentandbeckysbulbs.com

Chaplin Nursery
27814 27th Drive
Arkansas City, KS 670015

Forest Farm
990 Tetherow Road
Williams OR 97544-9599
541-846-7269
www.forestfarm.com

Gurneys Seed & Nursery
110 Capital St.,
Yankton, SD 57079
605-665-1930
www.gurneys.com

Henry Field Seed & Nursery Co
415 N Burnett St
Shenandoah, IA
www.henryfields.com

Heronswood Nursery
7530 E 288th Street
Kingston, WA 98346
360-297-4172
www.heronswood.com

Hillside Nursery
2200 S. Hillside
Witchita, KS 67211
316-686-6414
http://www.360wichita.com/tours/land
scaping/hillside.html

Lilypons Water Gardens®
6800 Lilypons Road
Post Office Box 10
Buckeystown, Maryland 21717-0010
1-800-999-5459
info@lilypons.com

Oakcrest Gardens
22871 Kane Ave.,
Glenwood, IA 51534
712-527-4974
www.oakcrestgardens.com

Nichols Garden Nursery
1190 Old Salem Road NE
Albany OR 97321
541-928-9280
www.nicholsgardennursery.com

Oakcrest Gardens
22871 Kane Ave.,
Glenwood, IA 51534
712-527-4974

Prairie Nursery
PO Box 306
Westfield, WI 53964
800-496-9453
www.prairienursey.com

Ridge Road Nursery,
3195 Saint Catherine Rd.
Bellevue, IA 52031
563-583-1381

Roslyn Nursery
211 Burrs Lane
Dix Hills, NY 11746
631-643-9347
www.roslynnursery.com

Seed Savers Exchange
3076 North Winn Road
Decorah, IA 52101
563-382-5990
www.seedsavers.org

Song Sparrow Perennial Farm
13101 East Rye Road
Avalon, WI 53505
802-553-3715
www.songsparrow.com

The New Peony Farm
St. Paul, MN
Phone: 651-457-8994
General Information:
kent@newpeonyfarm.com

Willowglen Nursery
512 Lost Mile Rd.
Decorah, IA 52101-7746.
319-735-5570

Gardens to Visit

Iowa

Arie den Boer Arboretum
Water Works Park
408 Fleur Drive
Des Moines, IA 50321
515-283-8700
www.ilovegardens.com/Iowa˙Gardens/iowa˙gardens.htm

Bellevue Butterfly Garden
Bellevue State Park, Hwy. 52 South
Bellevue, IA
563-872-4019
www.traveliowa.com/thingstodo/attractions/east/bellevue/34/

Bentonsport Gardens
Hawk Drive
Bentonsport, IA 52565
www.netins.net/showcase/rosegarden/

Better Homes and Gardens Test Garden
(Call for open hours)
1716 Locust Street
Des Moines, IA 50309-3023
515-284-3994
http://www.bhg.com/bhg/story.jhtml?storyid=/
templatedata/bhg/story/data/10706.xml&catref=C77

Bickelhaupt Arboretum
340 S. 14th Street
Clinton, IA 52732-5432
563-242-4771
www.bickarb.org

Brenton Arboretum
2629 Palo Circle
Dallas Center, IA 50063
515-992-4211
www.brentonarboretum.com

Brucemore
2160 Linden Drive SE
Cedar Rapids, IA 52403-1748
319-362-7375
www.brucemore.org/

Cedar Valley Arboretum and Botanic Gardens
1927 East Orange Road
Waterloo, IA 50701
319-226-4966
www.cedarnet.org/gardens

Crapo and Dankwardt Parks
Great River Road
Burlington, IA 52601
319-753-8117
www.visit.burlington.ia.us/parks.html

Des Moines Botanical Center
909 East River Drive
Des Moines, IA 50316
515-323-8900
www.botanicalcenter.com

Dubuque Arboretum and Botanical Gardens
3800 Arboretum Drive
Dubuque, IA 52001
563-556-2100
www.dubuquearboretum.com

Earl May Nursery and Garden Center, Trial Gardens
Highway 59 S
Shenandoah, IA 51601
712-246-2780
www.earlmay.com

Iowa Arboretum
1875 Peach Avenue
Madrid, IA 50156
515-795-3216
www.iowaarboretum.com

Municipal Rose Garden
2204 Grant Street
Bettendorf, IA 52722
319-359-1651
www.ilovegardens.com/Iowa˙Gardens/iowa˙gardens.htm

Gardens to Visit

JANUARY · FEBRUARY · MARCH · APRIL · MAY · JUNE · JULY · AUGUST · SEPTEMBER · OCTOBER · NOVEMBER · DECEMBER

Noelridge Park
4900 Council Street NE
Cedar Rapids, IA 52403
319-398-0247
www.cedar-rapids.com/parks·recreation·camping.html

Prairie Pedlar
1677 270th Street
Odebolt, IA 51458-7555
712-668-4840
www.showcase.netins.net/web/ppgarden/

Reiman Gardens
Iowa State University
1407 Elwood Drive
Ames, IA 50011
515-294-2710
www.reimangardens.iastate.edu

State Center Rose Garden
300 Third Street SE
State Center, IA 50247
515-482-2559.

Vander Veer Botanical Park
214 West Central Park
Davenport Iowa 24803
563-326-7318
www.davenportmon.homestead.com/VanderVeerPark.html

Kansas

Botanica, The Wichita Gardens
701 Amidon,
Wichita, KS 67203
316-264-0448
www.botanica.org

City Park Rose Garden
Poyntz Avenue & 11th Streets
1101 Poyntz Avenue
Manhattan, KS 66502
785-587-2489

Dyck Arboretum of the Plains
Hesston College
177 West Hickory Street
Hesston, KS 67062
620-327-8127
www.dyckarboretum.org

International Forest of Friendship Trail
Rt. 59, Warnock Lake
Atchison, KS 66002
913-367-2427
www.ninety-nines.org/fof3.html

Johnson County Community College
12345 College Blvd.
Overland Park, KS 66210
913-469-8500 x 4536
www.web.jccc.net/academic/science/greenhouse/greenhs.htmcontact

Kansas State University Gardens
2021 Throckmorton Plant Sciences Center
Manhattan, KS 66506
785-532-6170
www.ksu.edu/gardens/

Konza Prairie Research Natural Area
McDowell Creek Road, 232 Ackert Hall
Manhattan, KS 66506-0112
785-587-0441
www.ksu.edu/biology/bio/major/konza.html

Municipal Rose Garden
Huron Park, between 6th & 7th
Parks & Recreation, 3488 W. Drive
Kansas City, KS 96109
913-596-7077

Overland Park Arboretum & Botanical Gardens
179th & Antioch
8500 Santa Fe Drive
Overland Park, KS 66212
913-685-3604
www.opprf.org/arboretum.htm

Gardens to Visit

Parsons Arboretum
2100 Wilson
Parsons, KS 67357
316-421-5677
www.parsonsks.com/arbor.htm

Riggs Arboretum
10 mi. E of Kingman
Waterloo, KS
785-227-3858
www.home.earthlink.net/~bragan78/StJohnTreeBoard/
riggs1.html

Smith Municipal Rose Garden
Loose Park, 51st & Wornall
5200 Pennsylvania
Kansas City, KS 64112
913-784-5300

Nebraska

Alice Abel Arboretum, Nebraska Wesleyan University
5000 St. Paul Avenue
Lincoln, NE 68504
402-465-2374
www.arboretum.unl.edu/poppages/affiliates.html

All America Selection Garden at Fort Omaha
30th & Fort
Omaha, NE 68104
402-556-7028
www.arboretum.unl.edu/poppages/affiliates.html

Arboretum at University of Nebraska, Kearney
905 W. 25th Street
Kearney, NE 68847-4238
308-865-8883
www.arboretum.unl.edu/affiliate.html

Bellevue College Arboretum
Galvin Road
Bellevue, NE 68005
402-291-8100

Blair Community Arboretum
1129 Still Meadow Circle
Blair, NE 68008
402-426-4644
www.arboretum.unl.edu/poppages/affiliates.html

Chautauqua Park Arboretum
205 N. 4th Street
Beatrice, NE 69310
402-228-5248
www.arboretum.unl.edu/affiliate.html

Doane College Arboretum
1014 Boswell Avenue
Crete, NE 68333-2497
402-826-2161
www.arboretum.unl.edu/affiliate.html

Fontenelle Forest Nature Center
1111 Bellevue Blvd. North
Bellevue, NE 68005-4000
402-731-3140
www.fontenelleforest.org/come.html

Governor Furnas Arboretum
3419 S. 42nd Street
Brownville, NE 68321
402-825-6637
www.visitnemahacounty.org/nature/furnas.html

J. Norman Walburn Memorial Arboretum
Cambridge City Park
Cambridge, NE 69022
308-697-3317
www.arboretum.unl.edu/poppages/affiliates.html

John G. Neihardt State Historic Site
Elm & Washington Streets
Bancroft, NE 68004-0344
402-648-3388
www.nebraskahistory.org/sites/neihardt/

Gardens to Visit

Joshua Turner Arboretum, Union College
3800 S. 48th Street
Lincoln, NE 68506-4300
402-488-2331
www.ilovegardens.com/Nebraska Gardens/nebraska
gardens.html

Lauritzen Gardens, Omaha's Botanical Center
100 Bancroft St.
Omaha, NE   68108
402-346-4002
www.omahabotanicalgardens.org

Metropolitan Community College Arboretum
30th & Fort Streets
Omaha, NE 68111
402-449-8400
www.arboretum.unl.edu/affiliate.html

Midland Lutheran College Heritage Arboretum
900 N Clarkson
Fremont, NE 68025
402-941-6328
www.mlc.edu/studentlife/arboretum/

Nebraska College of Technical Agriculture Arboretum
404 E 7th Street
Curtis, NE 69025
308-367-4124
www.arboretum.unl.edu/affiliate.html

Nebraska State Fair Park Arboretum
1800 State Fair Park Drive
Lincoln, NE   68508
402-474-5371
www.statefair.org

Nebraska Statewide Arboretum
University of Nebraska
206 Biochemistry Hall
Lincoln, NE 68583-0715
402-472-2971
www.arboretum.unl.edu

Nine-Mile Prairie
West Fletcher Avenue, Air Park North
Lincoln, NE
402-472-2715
www.snrs.unl.edu/wedin/nefieldsites/NineMile/ninemile
prairie.htm

Pheasant Point Arboretum
Lower Republican NRD
PO Box 618
Alma, NE 68920
308-928-2182
www.arboretum.unl.edu/poppages/affiliates.htm

Prairie Pines Arboretum
112th & Adams Street
Forestry, Fisheries & Wildlife, UNL-101 Plant Indu
Lincoln, NE 68583-0814
402-466-2491

Sallows Arboretum and Conservatory
324 Laramie Avenue,
Alliance, NE 69301
308-762-7422
www.westnebraska.com/SallowsSunkenGard.htm

**University of Nebraska-Lincoln Botanical Garden
and Arboretum**
38th & Holdrege
P.O. Box 880609
Lincoln, NE 68508-0609
402-472-2679
www.unl.edu/unlbga

Wayne State College Arboretum
Wayne State College
1111 Main St.
Wayne, NE 68787
402-375-7384
www.arboretum.unl.edu/popPages/affiliates.html

Gardens to Visit

West Pawnee Park Arboretum
2122 14th Street
Columbus, NE 68601
402-564-0914

North Dakota

Berthold Public School Arboretum
Berthold, ND 58718
701-453-3484
www.ilovegardens.com/NorthDakotaGardens/northdakota-gardens.html

Capitol Grounds Arboretum Trail
600 East Boulevard Avenue
Bismarck, ND 58505-0130
701-328-2471
www.state.nd.us/fac/historyinfo/grounds/arboretumtrail.html

Dickinson Research Extension Center
1133 State Avenue
 Dickinson, ND 58601
701-483-2348
www.ag.ndsu.nodak.edu/dickinso

Fort Stevenson State Park Arboretum
41st Ave. NW
Garrison, ND
701-337-5576
www.ndparks.com/Parks/stevenson/nature.htm

Gunlogson Arboretum Nature Preserve
Icelandic State Park, Star Route 1, Box 64A
Cavalier, ND 58220
701-265-4561
www.npwrc.usgs.gov/resource/othrdata/natareas/gunlogso.htm

International Peace Garden
RR 1 Box 116 (at U.S./Canadian border)
Dunseith, ND 58329-9761
701-263-4390
www.peacegarden.com

Myra Arboretum
on the south branch of the Turtle River
Larimore, ND 58251
http://www.ilovegardens.com/NorthDakotaGardens/northdakotagardens.htm

Red River Zoo
4220 21st Ave. S.
Fargo, ND 58104-8603
701-277-9240
www.redriverzoo.org

South Dakota

Journey Museum
222 New York Street
Rapid City, SD   57701
605-394-6923
www.journeymuseum.org

Kuhnert Arboretum
E. Melgaard Road
Aberdeen, SD 57401
605-626-7015
www.aberdeencvb.com/rec.html

McCrory Gardens
6th St. & 22nd Ave.
SD State Univ. Horticulture Dept.
Brookings, SD 57007
605-688-5137
martin˙maca@sdstate.edu

McKennon Park
600 E. 7th St.
Dept. of Parks & Recreation, City of Sioux Falls
Sioux Falls, SD 57102-0406
605-367-7060

Sioux Prairie
Talbot Road
Wentworth, SD
712.258.0838
www.avalon.net/~yiams/scprairie.html

Bibliography

Bailey, L. H. *How Plants Get Their Names*. New York, New York: Dover Publications, Inc., 1963.

Bailey, Liberty Hyde Hortorium. *Hortus Third*. New York, New York: Macmillan Publishing Company, 1976.

Ball, Liz. *Step-by-Step Garden Basics*. Des Moines, Iowa: Better Homes and GardensR Books, 2000.

Ball, Liz. *Step-by-Step Yard Care*. Des Moines, Iowa: Better Homes and GardensR Books, 2000.

Barash, Cathy Wilkinson. *Choosing Plant Combinations*. Des Moines, Iowa: Better Homes and Gardens Books, 1999.

Barash, Cathy Wilkinson. *Edible Flowers from Garden to Palate*. Golden, Colorado: Fulcrum Publishing, 1993.

Barash, Cathy Wilkinson. *Evening Gardens*. Shelburne, Vermont: Chapters Publishing Ltd., 1993

Barash, Cathy Wilkinson. *The Climbing Garden*. New York, New York: Friedman Fairfax Publishers, 2000.

Barash, Cathy Wilkinson. *Prairie Lands Gardening Guide*. Nashville, Tennessee; Cool Springs Press, 2003.

Barash, Cathy Wilkinson and Wilson, Jim. *The Cultivated Gardener*. New York, New York: Simon & Schuster, 1996.

Beales, Peter. *Roses*. New York, New York: Henry Holt and Company, 1992.

Beaubaire, Nancy, editor, *Native Perennials*. Brooklyn, New York: the Brooklyn Botanic Garden, Inc., 1996.

Bennett, Jennifer, editor. . *Groundcovers*. Camden East, Ontario, Canada: Camden House, 1987.

Binetti, Marianne. *Tips for Carefree Landscapes*. Pownal, Vermont: Storey Communications, Inc., 1990.

Brickell, Christopher and Zuk, Judith D, editors-in-chief. *The American Horticultural*

Society A-Z Encyclopedia of Garden Plants. New York, New York: DK Publishing, 1996.

Burrell, C. Colston. *Perennials for Today's Gardens*. Des Moines, Iowa: Better Homes and GardensR Books, 2000.

Cutler, Karan Davis, editor. *Flowering Vines*. . Brooklyn, New York: the Brooklyn Botanic Garden, Inc., 1999.

Cutler, Karan Davis, editor. *Starting from Seed*. Brooklyn, New York: the Brooklyn Botanic Garden, Inc., 1998

Coughlin, Roberta M., *The Gardener's Companion—a Book of Lists and Lore*. New York, New York: HarperPerennial, 1991.

Dirr, Michael. *Manual of Woody Landscape Plants - Their Identification, Ornamental Characteristics, Culture, Propagation and Use*. Champaign, Illinois: Stipes Publishing Company, 1990.

DiSabato-Aust, Tracy. *The Well-Tended Perennial Garden*. Portland, Oregon: Timber Press, 1998.

Druse, Ken with Roach Margaret. *The Natural Habitat Garden*. New York, New York: Clarkson Potter Publishers, 1994.

Dunn, Dawn. *Growing Herbs*. London, England: Cassell Publishers Limited, 1997.

Editors of Sunset books and Sunset Magazine. *Herbs, An Illustrated Guide*. Menlo Park, California, Sunset Publishing Corporation, 1993.

Ellefson, Connie, Stephens, Tom, and Welsh, Doug. *Xeriscape Gardening—Water Conservation for the American Landscape*. New York, New York: Macmillan Publishers, 1992.

Frieze, Charlotte M. *The Zone Garden 3 – 4 – 5*. New York, New York. Fireside, Simon & Schuster, 1997.

Gershuny, Grace. *Start with the Soil*. Emmaus, Pennsylvania: Rodale Press, 1993.

Griffiths, Mark. *Index of Garden Plants*. Portland, Oregon: Timber Press, 1994.

Bibliography

JANUARY · FEBRUARY · MARCH · APRIL · MAY · JUNE · JULY · AUGUST · SEPTEMBER · OCTOBER · NOVEMBER · DECEMBER

Halpin, Anne. *Horticulture Gardener's Desk Reference*. New York, New York: Macmillan, 1996.

Halpin, Anne Moyer and the editors of Rodale Press. *Foolproof Planting*. Emmaus, Pennsylvania: Rodale Press, 1990/

Heger, Mike & Whitman, John. *Growing Perennials in Cold Climates*. Lincolnwood (Chicago), Illinois: Contemporary Books, 1998

Hogan, Sean. *Flora, A Gardener's Encyclopedia*. Portland, Oregon: Timber Press, 2003

Hyland, Bob, editor. *Shrubs, The New Glamour Plants*. Brooklyn, New York: the Brooklyn Botanic Garden, Inc., 1994,

Lanza, Patricia. *Lasagna Gardening*. Emmaus, Pennsylvania: Rodale Press, 1998.

Loewer, Peter. *Tough Plants for Tough Places*. Emmaus, Pennsylvania: Rodale Press, 1992.

Jason, Dan. *Greening the Garden – A Guide to Sustainable Growing*. Philadelphia, Pennsylvania: New Society Publishers, 1991

Jefferson-Brown, Michael. *The Patio Garden Month by Month*. Devon, England: David & Charles, 1997.

Marinelli, Janet, editor. *Going Native*. Brooklyn, New York: the Brooklyn Botanic Garden, Inc., 1994,

Neal, Bill. *Gardener's Latin*. Chapel Hill, North Carolina: Algonquin books of Chapel Hill, 1992.

Ottesen, Carole. *The Native Plant Primer*. New York, New York: Harmony Books, 1995.

Philbrick, Helen and John. *The Bug Book—Harmless Insect Control*. Pownal, Vermont: Storey Communications, Inc., 1986.

Phillips, Ellen & Burrell, C. Colston. *Rodale's Illustrated Encyclopedia of Perennials*. Emmaus, Pennsylvania: Rodale Press, 1993

Proctor, Rob. Annuals, *A Gardener's Guide*. Brooklyn, New York: the Brooklyn Botanic Garden, Inc., 1992,

Ruggiero, Michael. *Perennial Gardening*. New York, New York: Pantheon Books, 1994.

Rushing, Felder. *Tough Plants for Northern Gardens*. Nashville, Tennessee; Cool Springs Press, 2003.

Scanniello, Stephen, editor. *Easy-Care Roses*. Brooklyn, New York: the Brooklyn Botanic Garden, Inc., 1995.

Schultz, Warren, editor. *Natural Insect Control*. Brooklyn, New York: the Brooklyn Botanic Garden, Inc., 1994.

Sternberg, Guy and Wilson, Jim. *Landscaping with Native Trees*. Shelburne,

Vermont: Chapters Publishing, Ltd., 1995.

Wallheim, Lance. *The Natural Rose Gardener*. Tucson, Arizona: Ironwood Press, 1994

Weiner, Michael A. *Earth Medicine Earth Food*. New York, New York: Fawcett Columbine, 1972

Wolfe, Pamela. *Midwest Gardens*. Chicago, Illinois: Chicago Review Press, Incorporated, 1991.

Index

Index

Index

Index

Index

Index

Index

Meet the Authors

Cathy Wilkinson Barash

Cathy Wilkinson Barash is a life-long organic gardener. She has been active in the Garden Writers Association (a group of over 1,800 profession garden communicators) since 1988. She is currently President of the Garden Writers Association.

From childhood, Cathy has held a firm belief in economy of space and time in the garden by planting beautiful and tasty edibles among ornamentals. A garden designer whose designs have been published nationally, Cathy specializes in low-maintenance and edible landscapes. Anne Raver of the The New York Times was the first to give her the appellation "gourmet horticulturalist."

Cathy is author of eleven books, and is a successful photographer, nationally acclaimed speaker, and avid cat lover. She is best known as the author of Edible Flowers from Garden to Palate. The book, published in 1993 and celebrating its 10th year in distribution, was nominated for a Julia Child Cookbook Award and garnered an Award of Excellence from the Garden Writers Association of America.

Her other books include *The Prairie Lands Gardener's Guide, The Climbing Garden, Choosing Plant Combinations, Taylor's Weekend Guide: Kitchen Gardens, Edible Flowers: Desserts & Drinks, Vines & Climbers, Evening Gardens, Roses,* and *The Cultivated Gardener*, co-authored by Jim Wilson. Her writing and photographs have appeared in hundreds of books, calendars, magazines, and newspapers including the New York Times, Christian Science Monitor, Horticulture, Woman's Day, and Home.

A life-long New Yorker (Long Islander), she moved to Des Moines in 1997. She transformed her front lawn into a showplace garden in four months. Her garden combines edible landscaping with container plantings, and innumerable Prairie Lands plants. Of her gardening experience in Des Moines, she says, "It was like learning to garden all over again."

Melinda Myers

Melinda Myers, best known for her gardener-friendly and practical approach to gardening, has more than 25 years of horticulture experience in both hands-on and instructional settings. She has a master's degree in horticulture, is a certified arborist, started the Master Gardener program in Milwaukee, and is a horticulture instructor at Milwaukee Area Technical College.

Outside the classroom, Melinda shares her expertise through a variety of media outlets. Her most recent books include *Jackson and Perkins' Beautiful Roses Made Easy: Midwestern Edition, Jackson & Perkins' Selecting, Growing and Combining Outstanding Perennials: Midwestern Edition* and the *Birds and Blooms Ultimate Garden Guide*. She hosts "Great Lakes Gardener," seen on PBS stations throughout the United States, the "Plant Doctor" show on WTMJ radio in Milwaukee, and appears regularly on WTMJ-TV, Milwaukee's NBC affiliate. She also writes the twice monthly "Gardeners' Questions" column for The Milwaukee Journal Sentinel and is a contributing editor and columnist for Birds and Blooms and Backyard Living magazines.

Meet the Authors

JANUARY · FEBRUARY · MARCH · APRIL · MAY · JUNE · JULY · AUGUST · SEPTEMBER · OCTOBER · NOVEMBER · DECEMBER

Melinda has written several other books, including *The Garden Book for Wisconsin, My Wisconsin Garden: A Gardener's Journal, Month-by-Month Gardening in Wisconsin, Minnesota Gardener's Guide, The Minnesota Horticultural Society's Month-by-Month Gardening in Minnesota*, and *The Perfect Lawn Midwest Series*.

Her 13 years of experience at the University of Wisconsin Extension allowed Melinda to work with backyard, community, and master gardeners throughout Wisconsin. In addition, she began the Master Gardener Program in Milwaukee County. As Milwaukee's Assistant City Forester, Melinda helped manage the city's street trees, boulevards, and green spaces. She worked with the Young Adult Conservation Corps supervising crews that maintain University of Wisconsin Extension urban test gardens and provide trail repair and other conservation work. She serves as a horticulture consultant to numerous community and beautification groups.

For her work and media presence, Melinda has received recognition and numerous awards, including the 2003 Garden Globe Award for radio talent and the 1998 Quill and Trowel award, both from the Garden Writers Association, and the 1998 Garden Communicator's Award from the American Nursery and Landscape Association.

366